W9-CAL-411

Lloyd:
What Happened

Lloyd:
What Happened

A Novel
of Business

Stanley Bing

CROWN PUBLISHERS, INC.
New York

Copyright © 1998 by Gil Schwartz

All rights reserved. No part of this book may be reproduced or transmitted in
any form or by any means, electronic or mechanical, including photocopying,
recording, or by any information storage and retrieval system, without
permission in writing from the publisher.

Published by Crown Publishers, Inc., 201 East 50th Street, New York, New York
10022. Member of the Crown Publishing Group.

Random House, Inc. New York, Toronto, London, Sydney, Auckland
www.randomhouse.com

CROWN and colophon are trademarks of Crown Publishers, Inc.

Printed in the United States of America

Library of Congress Cataloging-in-Publication Data
Bing, Stanley.
Lloyd, what happened : a novel of business / Stanley
Bing. — 1st ed.
I. Title.
PS3552.I48L57   1998
813'.54—dc21 97-36286
CIP
ISBN 0-517-70349-1

10   9   8   7   6   5   4   3   2   1

First Edition

Lloyd's
corporation did
a lot of good for
a lot of people.

D e d i c a t i o n

To Roger and Chuck and Jane and Burt and Bill and Peter and Jack, for being the very best bosses they could be.

To Dworkin and Lazenby and Finster and Rafferty and Morgenstern and Kline, and many more whose names I cannot now remember, for being such good friends in the cold world of business.

To all the guys I rolled over to get here. Thanks.

And to Sue and Nina and Willy, for making everything not only possible but fun, too.

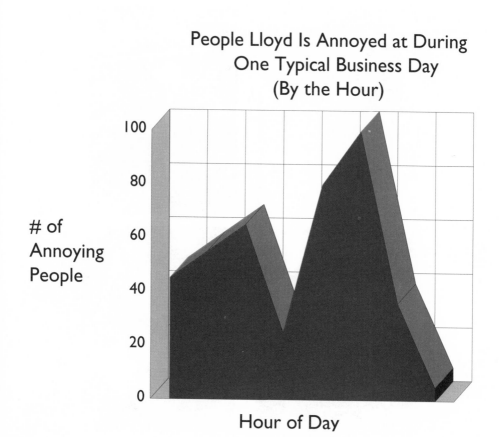

People Lloyd Is Annoyed at During One Typical Business Day (By the Hour)

of Annoying People

100
80
60
40
20
0

Hour of Day

C o n t e n t s

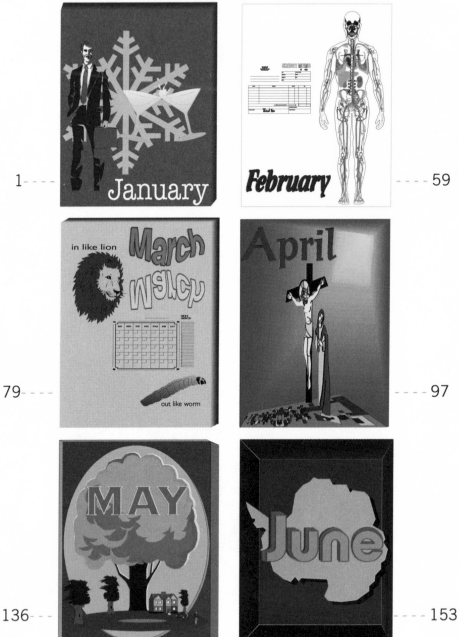

With Presentation Graphics by the Author

Scanned Objects

Manipulated Clip Art

Charts and Graphs

- Money
- Stock
- Laptop
- Car
- Posh Hotels
- Drinking
- Eating Well

Executive Compensation 1990 – 2000

Introduction

This is a story about a guy in business. It takes place over the course of one year, from January to the following New Year's Day.

Like any business information, the story of Lloyd is supported by graphics that clarify and illuminate complicated situations and concepts, rendering them into visuals that even a person with an MBA can understand.

During this twelve-month period, Lloyd's karma, which has always been somewhat charmed, turns a hard right and heads into the land where the game is played for keeps. Having heretofore floated on a cloud of privilege and indolence, Lloyd finds himself suddenly and consistently punished for the excesses he has committed in his savage, repulsively indulgent existence. As an executive, his life is a disgusting monument to greed and the insensitivity of postindustrial capital. He's not a bad guy, though. Maybe that will see him through.

■ % of Lloyd's mind thinking about revenue streams

■ % of Lloyd's mind indulging in fruitless guilt

■ % of Lloyd's mind concentrating on Mona's foot

Slide Show One

Once upon a time,
there was a meeting.

Slide 1

This is the saga of Lloyd, a man as large and full of boisterous, yeasty life as the times in which he lives. Which is to say, not that much.

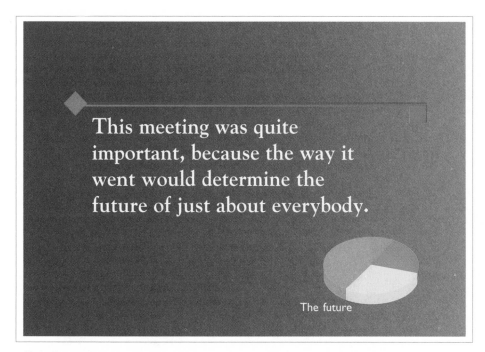

This meeting was quite important, because the way it went would determine the future of just about everybody.

The future

Slide 2

Lloyd has these kinds of meetings a lot, and they scare the hell out of him. After some time in the workplace, he has come to the conclusion that people in suits are just as crazy as people out of them. In fact, the pressure of stuffing a jumbo-sized personality into all those constricting clothes may force the more dramatic personalities to pop out even more insistently, like steam from the collar of an angry toon.

3-D columns

Lloyd, nervous

Lloyd was understandably nervous about it.

Slide 3

Lloyd, worrying

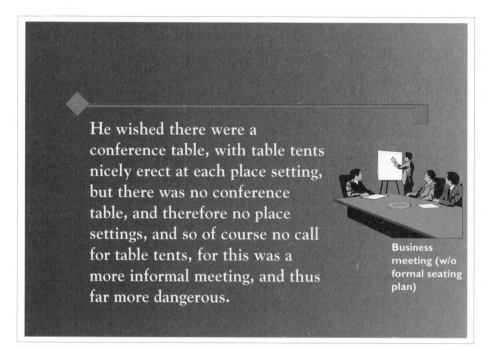

He wished there were a conference table, with table tents nicely erect at each place setting, but there was no conference table, and therefore no place settings, and so of course no call for table tents, for this was a more informal meeting, and thus far more dangerous.

Business meeting (w/o formal seating plan)

Slide 4

The story of Lloyd is told both in words and in pictures. All business information is presented in this fashion, because businesspeople get bored very easily, and it helps to give them something to look at.

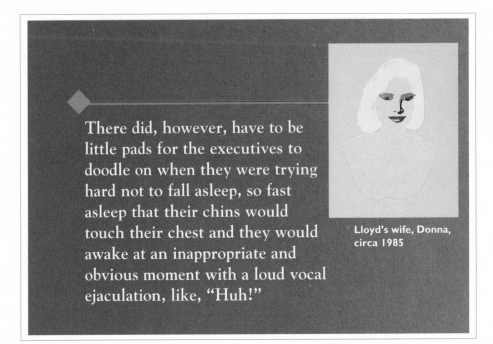

Slide 5

There did, however, have to be little pads for the executives to doodle on when they were trying hard not to fall asleep, so fast asleep that their chins would touch their chest and they would awake at an inappropriate and obvious moment with a loud vocal ejaculation, like, "Huh!"

Lloyd's wife, Donna, circa 1985

Slide shows like this one will accompany the text at periodic intervals, acquainting us with developments in Lloyd's finances, diet, sexual encounters, and even a brief trip to . . .

GERMANY!

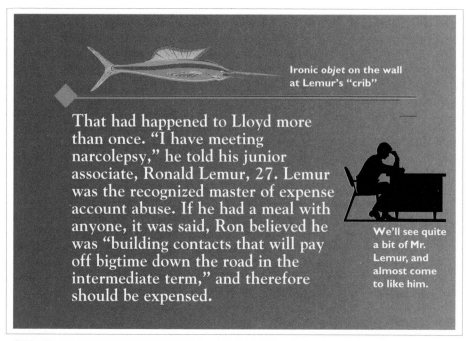

Ironic *objet* on the wall at Lemur's "crib"

That had happened to Lloyd more than once. "I have meeting narcolepsy," he told his junior associate, Ronald Lemur, 27. Lemur was the recognized master of expense account abuse. If he had a meal with anyone, it was said, Ron believed he was "building contacts that will pay off bigtime down the road in the intermediate term," and therefore should be expensed.

We'll see quite a bit of Mr. Lemur, and almost come to like him.

Slide 6

There are many characters we will come to meet, characters of enormous intellect and personal power, for the pursuit of business is, at bottom, a serious enterprise in which dedicated people strive to achieve something lasting they can leave behind for the next generation of men and women who come to live within the bosom of the corporation, something they can take home with them when their life's day is done. For this, they must employ every ounce of wit, zeal, and, above all, pure reason. For the businessperson, the brain, and the brain alone, is the most important organ in the body.

Slide 7

Yeah, right.

The first month of Lloyd's year begins on an auspicious note, with plenty of drinking, eating, and meeting at a corporate retreat in Pittsburgh. We meet Walt, Lloyd's boss, his associate and subordinate, Ronald Lemur, as well as the rest of the haute VPs that make up Lloyd's peer group.

Unfortunately, the final meeting of the three-day professional bender is one of those historic Roman senatorial sessions that leave half the participants bleeding on the sofas, one in which confrontation between manly men is the thing most excellent above all others. "Well, Jack," smooth strategic planners leer across an open table at a heretofore cordial associate, "as far as I can see, the general failure of the project was just the result of sheer bad management on your watch. Or maybe I'm wrong. Help me out here." And the other men hang back and watch how the targeted executive will handle the situation with his guts falling out all over his hands.

The word is reengineering, and it's just one of the really big themes, with surprising staying power. We get a pretty good peek at this particular reengineering session, where the decruitment of many, many people is discussed and a new organizational paradigm is implemented. Just as the newly focused, far more disciplined, and productive cadre of key executives is ready to leave the dead behind and march off into the future, humming, a new and menacing presence enters their midst. There is a power, it seems, above the one we know. And it comes from corporate headquarters in Chicago.

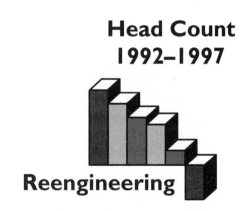

Head Count 1992–1997

Reengineering

This chart reports the salient facts about the two chiefs of Lloyd's tepee. As president, and Lloyd's boss, Walt is the supreme temporal power, master of all reporting structures, owner of fierce loyalty from a very large crew, ring-giver, dread Lord of the material world. Doug, however, is God—unknowable, distant, often absent when needed most, tender to his creations whenever he possibly can be, and essentially malevolent. When he calls, one cannot choose but serve. Or can one? The sensible thing would be for these two enormously talented, driven, passionate, charismatic men to work together for the good of the enterprise. Which, of course, they do!

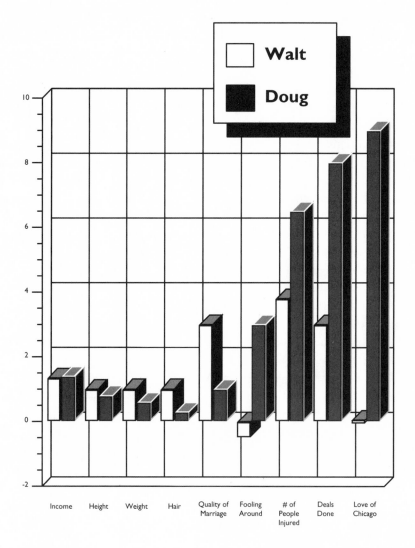

Lloyd Wakes Up

Lloyd opened one eye and looked at the digital clock. It was beeping. The television was on, as well. Wow, thought Lloyd. What time is it?

He sat up in one great lurch and peered into the darkened space before him. He could tell that outside the massive drapes it was bright morning. If he parted them just a bit, the ribbon of the Monongahela River would wink back at him. He could smell his own breath without putting his hand in front of his face.

"It's cold out there," said a very fat weatherman on the local morning news show. "You betcha," said the anchor. Then they both cracked up, as if some absolutely hilarious bon mot had passed between them. But nothing looked funny to Lloyd.

Lloyd was in Pittsburgh for a corporate retreat. It was hard to hurt yourself in a town like Pittsburgh. Although the drinks they served were tremendous—eight ounces of scotch in a twelve-ounce broad-bottom tumbler was common—they stopped serving them very early. Lots of guys bailed out at 10:30 with a pack of yawning excuses. But Lloyd and Lemur had decided to hang tough. At midnight, Lloyd had given up on beer and moved over to martinis without any vermouth in them.

The pounding in his head was incessant. There was a tight, acid churning in the pit of his stomach. The slightest motion of his head produced a chasm not only beneath his feet but on both sides of him. He went into the bathroom and attempted to hurl, succeeding only in drawing 85 percent of his blood into his face and neck, which, in his condition, produced such exquisite pain, he gave up hanging over the bowl and sank to the floor, pressing his face against the cool tiles. He slept, awakening ten minutes later with a loud exclamation. "Buh!" Then he yawed to his feet and ran the shower as hot and hard as it would go. "I'm up!" he yelled to nobody in particular.

He remembered something about ladies dancing in a bar. A girl had sat down next to him. "Hi," she said. She smelled like powder. He remembered that the woman kissed him. "What was I thinking?" he said. He was aware in the shower that there was no blood at all in his face now, and that he was about to faint in a minute. He sat down in the shower. Maybe I'm having a heart attack, he thought. There was no aspirin.

"Ach," Lloyd said. He was on his hands and knees like an elephant, swaying into the main room now. All he wanted to do was make it to the bed

and lie there until his head cleared. He brought the little tin wastepaper basket with him to put in the space between the two queen-sized beds. On the
basket was an American eagle in a furled silver banner. It looked fierce.
"Never," Lloyd said to himself. "Never, never." He lay down flat on his back
on the bed and wrapped himself in the stiff quilt. The telephone rang. "This
is your wake-up call," said the voice. "It's twenty-eight degrees in downtown
Pittsburgh. Good morning!" Lloyd hung up.

"Christ on his cross," said Lloyd.

The telephone rang. "I just called in to see what condition your condition
was in," said Lemur's voice.

"I hurt myself, Ron," said Lloyd. "I hurt myself bad. I don't think I can
be doing that anymore. I'm too old and it's not good for my credibility as an
executive. Who's going to take a guy seriously at nine in the morning who you
saw barking like a dog six hours before at a fried-chicken restaurant?"

"You were magnificent," said Lemur.

He hung up. The clock suddenly erupted in furious beeping again. Lloyd
jumped at least three inches off the bed. "Fat people who want to commit
suicide! Today on *Geraldo!*" said the television set. Lloyd sat up. His head
felt as if it were not connected to his body. His face felt very, very cold and
his teeth were chattering. "I'm poisoned," he said. Hands shaking, he closed
on a sock with an almost-imperceptible grip and began to dress. His meeting was in an hour and fifteen minutes. If he could dress, stand up without
falling to his knees, walk without throwing up, exit the hotel without attracting notice, make his way to a convenience store to purchase aspirin and
grapefruit juice, walk in the fresh, cold air for a couple of minutes, make his
way to Walt's hotel, go to Walt's room without collapsing in the elevator,
enter Walt's room, seat himself, and deliver a complete briefing to Walt on
the sixteen or twenty industry issues that might come up in his morning
panel discussion with fellow executive vice presidents, he could come back
to his room and perhaps grab a couple of z's before the 8:30 mandatory
informal breakfast that preceded the three-hour financial review of all business units.

"I want to die," said Lloyd.

Lloyd Gets Out

It was a very fine day, notwithstanding. Clouds sprayed a bit of spume now
and then, but the rest of the time it was quite pleasant; sunny, even, between
the more extended periods of what would have to be called . . . murk.

Lloyd felt terrible. There were no other people on the streets. Except, now
he noticed, a man moving very slowly down the wide main thoroughfare,

talking in a guttural snarl to himself about matters in which Lloyd was sure he had no interest.

The PPG building reared above his head, an ugly spire of glass and steel that was meant to look modern and grand, Lloyd supposed. The psychotic had noticed him across the open square and was sort of heaving sideways toward him with a menacing, determined expression. Lloyd sped up as best he could, but he by no means could summon the fortitude necessary to pick up his tempo beyond that of a common street whack.

Before he was halfway to his destination—a corner deli that seemed to recede as he hove closer to it—the beggar descended on him, murmuring something that could have been "Help me out help me out," except it had no consonants in it. "Here," said Lloyd, thrusting a handful of coins in the bum's open mitt.

"Hey!" The guy smelled like a wet dog. "This is a quarter, man!" The bum was working himself up, spinning and weaving.

"Get out of my face, man!" Lloyd screamed at the top of his lungs. He was clenching his teeth so tightly, his larynx hurt.

The bum hurtled backward. "Big time," he said. "No problem. God bless you, man, getting right, and Jesus talks to strangers," or some damn thing that Lloyd found not only incomprehensible but very annoying. "Here, man, I'm sorry, take a dollar," he said, holding out a piece of paper to the guy, who now appeared more like a classic harmless village idiot than a dangerous madman.

"Wow, man, yeah," said the bum. He took the paper and left.

Lloyd was freezing-cold and sweating profusely at the same time. He went into the deli.

In the Deli

The soft-drink refrigerator area was nearly as long as a football field. In the case, there was Coke, Pepsi, diet Coke, diet Pepsi, twenty-four different kinds of Snapple (some appalling), Orange Slice, Fresca (light and regular), Yoo-Hoo, a rainbow of cranberry derivatives, root beer, eight or nine different kinds of water—orange, prune, apple, grape—and, finally, grapefruit juice. Lloyd reached into the depths of the storage space and found that the beverage he wanted was just a hair farther than the last molecule on the end of his longest finger. "God," he said, and leaned farther in. For a moment, his fingers stuck on the metal of the freezing rack inside, then, at last, closed on an eight-ounce container. He reeled it back in, tore open the paper top on the side that said "Open other side," and drank until he had to pause to catch his breath. "Better. Ah. Ah," said Lloyd. A piercing stab of bright yellow pain had riveted the soft brain tissue behind his left eye.

He was thinking about how the loss of limited partnership deductions had put a massive, killing dent in the value of their commercial real estate portfolio. It was frightening. Why, if the entire load was for one reason or another called in, the exposure to the corporation could top out at $11 billion. Lloyd figured that at least two-thirds of it was bad. That, of course, would never come out. Rather, for that fact to be known, or, indeed, to make a difference, everything would have to conspire against the company in so many different ways, it didn't pay to think about it. It would be the end of everything.

Lloyd made his way to the front of the store. At the counter, he asked the Indian guy for some Advil. Lloyd ripped open the miniature bottle, thrust the cotton batting onto the countertop, poured three tidy little brown pellets into his palm, threw them down his gullet, and washed them down with an enormous bolt of grapefruit juice. "That's better," he said.

His face suddenly tightened, as if a sardine key had been placed behind his right ear and twisted, hard. He had once stood behind Frank Sinatra on line at a dry cleaners in Van Nuys, California. Behind each of Sinatra's ears was a hard-boiled egg of meaty tissue left over from the excess face he didn't need after the most recent of his face-lifts. Lloyd had at the time imagined those knobs being tightened to refresh Frank's looks. But nobody was tightening his ears. He knew that.

Lloyd's knees, never the greatest, had begun to wobble.

"Buddy, you okay?" said the clerk. "You look sick."

"I'm fine," said Lloyd, and lost all control of his legs. He would have slumped down like a large boneless sardine, but he had the presence of mind to grab the countertop.

"Come sit," said the clerk. He took Lloyd by the arm and led him behind the counter. Tucked in one tiny corner of the space was a comfortable armchair, blue once, maybe, now a torn, ratty thing that looked more like a pile of hay. Lloyd sat down in it and felt the coarse retro fabric of it under his forearms.

"Thanks," said Lloyd.

"Just don't rob me, man. My insurance doesn't say liable if I bring you in here."

Lloyd sat in the convenience store and thought about things. He didn't want to go to the meeting. It wasn't the first time he had been asked to do something he didn't want to do and had complied because it was easier to do so than to resist. Still, on some level, he was always resisting. That was his punishment for being a hypocrite, for wanting to be comfortable all the time. He was never all that comfortable, either.

At the age of eight, Lloyd had joined Little League. One of his clearest remembrances from childhood was the feeling that swept over him when, on a Saturday morning, the sun had sequestered itself behind a cascade of clouds and rain, thick, relentless walls of rain, came pounding down with no promise of surcease, black greasy rain that eradicated all hopes of an outdoor day. The sensation of running toward an infinitely distant first base as the softball he had socked almost to the parking lot of the Sunset Supermarket was retrieved by the deep center fielder, thrown to the kid playing short center, from thence to the second baseman, and then over to first, where Lloyd was either caught straining to force his foot to reach the bag in time or, having misjudged the whereabouts of the ball, had rounded first and was thundering toward second, only to be nabbed in a rundown . . . Lloyd was slow.

"I've got to get up now and walk over to the Royalton," Lloyd said to the proprietor.

"The Royalton?"

"The hotel. Where is it?"

"You sure you don't mean the Windsor Court?"

Lloyd wasn't sure at all. What was the name of the hotel? He plunged deep into his pockets and hauled out quite a few minuscule scraps of paper with notes to himself on them. There was a parking stub, lint, a ball of aluminum gum wrapping, eight pennies, and a tiny ad for a 678-megabyte hard drive. No information about the hotel. "What do I owe you?" Lloyd said.

"Make it five bucks and we can call it even, dude." This seemed low to Lloyd for the amount of grapefruit juice and Pepto-Bismol he had drunk, and the gum he was chewing.

"Thanks, man," said Lloyd. "I feel better. You have no idea where this hotel I am looking for is?"

"No, man. What was its name again?"

Lloyd went out into the street and took a huge lungful of some of the crispest air he had ever hauled into his lungs. Around the corner, Lloyd found a huge hotel with a circular driveway and a gang of odd-shaped guys, mostly with big guts, in brown livery who were there to park cars or usher guests inside. They had gold buttons on their uniforms and looked basically pretty unfriendly.

Lloyd went straight to the reception desk and inquired if Walt was, in fact, there. He was. "Man," Lloyd said as he sat down in one of the comfy lobby chairs. He was hurting still, yes, but a fine crust of equilibrium had spread like rivulets of ice on a slowly freezing pond. If not jostled, it might serve.

In the Hotel at Last

The elevator was by Westinghouse. He liked that. He trusted the Westinghouse name because it evoked the days when household appliances were magical objects, really big toys grown-ups got to play with: washing machines, dryers. Why did grown-ups get so excited about them on game shows when they won them? They were useful, sure. But why jump up and down and scream about it?

Lloyd realized that he knew the guy across from him in the elevator.

"Do I know you?" Lloyd said to the guy.

"I'm Dick Van Patten." Lloyd immediately realized that it was, in fact, Dick Van Patten, and that he didn't know Dick Van Patten, not really. All he knew was Dick Van Patten's face from countless sixties sitcoms and game shows.

"I love your work" was all Lloyd could come up with, and not before a couple of floors had gone past.

"Thank you," said Dick Van Patten. He looked pleased. Lloyd got off on the fifty-second floor. The carpet felt ankle-deep. The corridor stretched off into the distance without end. Lloyd peered at the five-digit numbers that signified the direction he should go if he wanted to reach room 52876, the Matador Suite. Across from the elevator bank was a glassed-in room. THE SKYTOWER CLUB said gold lettering on the glass door. EXTENDED AS A COMPLIMENT TO THE MOST EXCLUSIVE BUSINESS TRAVELER. Lloyd looked at his watch, which read 7:56.

"I have four minutes," said Lloyd, pushing open the heavy glass door.

The place was jammed and there was fruit everywhere—bananas and pears and bruised red cherries, apples in red and green. On a sideboard that in the evening must have served as a bar was a splendid assortment of breadstuffs. There were croissants the size of footballs, so oily that the paper beneath them was a soft green, iridescent. There were some very strange bagels, quite plump, but also unexpectedly tiny, bagels that were never intended to receive anything but one bite-sized dollop of cream cheese, not lox or smoked salmon or gravlax with capers, bagels that were produced by people who had never had a real one, who viewed the object as an oddity that must be served to certain exotic guests from the East. There were enormous bran muffins with raisins so plump, Lloyd was suspicious of them, and baskets lined with cloth towels containing respectably hot toast, English muffins, and salt sticks. Behind the bar in a kitchenette, a large and somewhat haughty black man of about twenty-four years of age stood in a tall white toque, serving from steam trays of eggs, sausages, bacon, oatmeal, and what looked like grits and gravy. The smell of the hot food seated on those sweating metal trays began to hoist Lloyd's stomach from its seat in his midsection up through his esophagus to a point just south of his uvula. I can't hurl here, he thought to himself, not here. He sat down in a ridiculously roomy leather chair with brutal grommets that subtly impressed themselves upon his buttocks. His face had once again turned to the consistency and texture of Silly Putty. He even tasted Silly Putty. He found himself thinking about Silly Putty.

"All right?" It was a semielderly executive in a cream-colored business shirt, suspenders, and a bloodred tie. He was holding a *Wall Street Journal* folded vertically, a pair of angular reading glasses perched on the tip of his nose. Although it seemed impossible, Lloyd could swear the guy was laughing at him, not a big chuckle or anything, just a sort of gentle sneer of amusement.

"Yes," Lloyd said, looking up into those warm, gentle eyes. "Just popped in. Bite to eat. Sit and think. Nice room."

"Well, then," said the man, drifting across the room. He put down his coffee cup and paper and picked up a suit jacket so supple and dark, it was not a physical presence at all, just a spatial area that absorbed all light that came near. "See you later."

Lloyd wanted to be him, to be past the excess and sickness, past the riot of spirit, past all caring and wanting and fearing and full of nothing but the ease of it, fully in command of the fact that it was all just a game, like tennis, or golf, or poker. Lloyd knew that if the man he had just seen was terminated without cause this very morning, he would still be set for at least the next three years to do nothing but relax and think about what he wanted to do next. His heart ached. He pounded his chest for a while, trying to burp. Eventually, he did.

On the table in front of him were neat rows of newspapers and magazines, all the reading matter a learned businessperson would need to achieve the mythic state of perfect informedness mandatory for any who wished to achieve the true higher levels of omniscience necessary to conduct even a moderately successful business career. Lloyd picked up *USA Today* but couldn't really look at it. It was more of a prop. Just to sit there without appearing busy doing something was a clear tip-off that here was a dysfunctional individual of some sort who did not belong in these exclusive surroundings.

He was now five minutes late.

Outside, about a mile below, the Monongahela River met the Allegheny and the Ohio, forming the confluence of waters upon which stood Pittsburgh. Three Rivers Stadium yawned, empty and frozen in the early-morning mist. Traffic moved with stately calm to and from the tunnel that fed into the downtown area on one end, off to the ancient green hills of Pennsylvania on the other. I wish I could open a window, he thought. Of course, that was impossible. Once you get to a certain level of success in American business, no windows open.

"I gotta get out of here," said Lloyd.

And yet he did not go.

At 8:09 A.M.: An Almost-Tragic Mix-up

Lloyd knocked and waited in the hall for Walt to come to the door. Down the hallway, he saw the remains of several disgusting breakfast trays that had been shoved out of their rooms by people who had begun their day at an even

9

more ungodly hour. Right next door, there was the detritus of a meal that had clearly consisted of steak, fries, and a bottle of red wine. Lloyd stared at the stuff. Next to a large piece of fat, there was a napkin crunched up and stuffed under a plate. It was encrusted with blood. Fascinated, Lloyd wandered over to the tray and bent down to verify his perception, which he was perfectly willing to classify as compromised. Kneeling down, he gingerly picked up a fork from the tray and poked the fabric of the napkin. It could be ketchup, he thought. But even at this close range, Lloyd had to admit that it could also be blood. If that was the case, it was certainly a lot of blood, covering fully a third of the napkin. It was a dark brown, no longer red, and caked into a hard crust. Lloyd's legs turned flaccid again, so he sat down in front of the tray, hoping the seizure would pass, or, rather, that he would regain motor function before Walt opened the door. Meanwhile, Walt was not opening the door. In an effort to pull himself back from the abyss, Lloyd put his hands out to steady himself and leaned up against the wall. Underneath his right hand, he felt the smooth plastic bag holding the complimentary *Pittsburgh Post Gazette*. He removed the paper from its bag and perused the front page. There was an update about some skin condition that had been brought to the attention of the American public by Michael Jackson, who apparently suffered from it on his penis.

"Gotta get up," he said to nobody in particular.

"Yo, sir." Lloyd looked up. There was a young black man with a shaved head and a nose ring looking down at him with concern. "Get you anything?" he said.

"No, thanks," said Lloyd. "Just stopped by for a second to, like, you know . . . read the paper. . . ." Lloyd felt lame. The guy has seen enough paralyzed bums in his life to recognize one, Lloyd thought.

"You know what room you lookin' for?" said the guy.

"Yes, I do," said Lloyd.

He hauled a small slip of paper out of his pocket and read off the room number aloud, ending with an unexpected hesitancy in his voice.

"You on the wrong floor, man," he said with a tinge of sadness. "You in the wrong wing."

"Wing?" said Lloyd. A tsunami of despair washed over him.

"Come on, pal, I'll take you there." Lloyd toyed with the idea of leaping onto the large platform cart the bellman was pushing, but did not.

"Big hotel," he said. His guide was moving swiftly down the hallway. Lloyd had to move along at what felt to him like the speed of light just to keep up. He saw now that he had been wrong about the guy's hair. He wasn't completely denuded of frondage. On the side of his head were the initials BZP in raised hair. Carving them must have been a labor of love for someone. The guy couldn't have done it for himself. He wanted to comment on the look, but didn't.

They came to the end of the corridor and turned left, walked for another couple of minutes, and found themselves back at the elevator banks just opposite the Sky Club. "Fucking elevators," said Lloyd.

"I hear you," said the bellman.

They descended back down to the lobby. It was 8:19 now and Lloyd was getting nervous. He had punctured the window of acceptable lateness two minutes ago. They went across the lobby, down into a conversation pit, past several stores and down a corridor lined with shops, and into another lobby just as big and pretentious as its sister. At some point, his guide had left his cart behind and was simply striding along, looking back every now and then to see if Lloyd was keeping up. "You go out clubbin'?" he said to the air in front of him.

"Oh yeah," said Lloyd, and tried to laugh.

"Ought to have signs or something," said the guy. Lloyd thought that perhaps he should ask the fellow his name, then thought better of it. Pretty soon, they would part, never to see each other again.

"Name is Bob," said the guy, giving Lloyd a serious start. Were his thoughts that transparent? They had climbed in the elevator to the same floor as in the other tower, and Bob turned to say good-bye. "This is it," he said.

"Thanks, man," said Lloyd. He pushed a ten into the guy's hand. "Thanks a lot."

"Call the desk anytime, man. Ask for Robert. If you, like, y'know, need help or something."

"I do, Bob. I do need help."

Walt

Lloyd knocked on the door and prayed to God that the human being who answered would be familiar to him. So little was. When one traveled, the world presented an alien face. T-shirts from New Orleans had greeted him in the Pittsburgh airport shop, for instance. He had been walking along at the W. H. Smith's, looking for a book that was not by John Grisham. John Grisham annoyed him because his books were set up in a large display that featured a life-sized picture of the author sporting a three-day growth of beard. With a three-day growth of beard, Lloyd knew, he would look about as fit for a marketing display unit as Koko the talking gorilla. And here was John Grisham with three separate books displayed, including his new hardcover, looking so tasty that Lloyd would not have found it surprising to have seen a stewardess humping that display. Bah. Right next to the Grisham thing was an entire shelf given over to stuff about New Orleans. Cajun pepper, shirts, skirts, little dolls with white Gallic faces, mugs, even jewelry, and banners that read I PARTIED IN THE BIG EASY, or some such thing. If there was any town in the United States of America that was less like New Orleans than Pittsburgh, Lloyd didn't know what it was. What was this stuff doing here?

"Lloyd," said Walt. He had opened the door and was standing in the portal with his customary uninflected expression, save for a slight turn of his lip. "We thought that perhaps you had died. Glad you didn't. Come on in."

Walt preceded him down the corridor that led into the foyer that opened into the sitting room that lay outside the bed chamber that took up two large rooms on the top floor. In the middle of the sitting room was a low glass table loaded with food. On the sideboard were coffee, juice, hot water. Walt had moved over to this dispensary and was carefully filling a cup with scalding-hot black coffee, probably the third on a day that would eventually contain no fewer than twelve such cupfuls, taken very hot, very black, usually while standing. "Have something," said Walt.

Walt looked terrific to Lloyd. He was fifty, not tall, really, but up there in the top part of the atmosphere, two inches above the heads of mortal men. Trim. Flat tummy. Like all gifted executives, he was capable of maintaining a shirt so white, you could almost see your face in it, crisp and cheerful and polished and substantial. Lloyd had tried many times to acquire shirts that made him look like this, but he had never succeeded.

"What are you looking at, white man?' said Walt affably. His eyes were plumbing the depths of Lloyd's physical presence, not simply taking him in but diving down beneath the surface of what appeared to be Lloyd into the inky black depths that lie beneath material existence. Lloyd knew Walt wasn't really looking at him, but into himself. Walt's personality was so huge, his body could not contain it. It filled the air around him, invaded the curtains, wafted out of the doorway and into the bathroom, where it took on a heavier scent of soap and aftershave. Right now, Walt's personality was seeping in long, delicate tendrils of green and light blue and wrapping itself around Lloyd, pulling him into a gentle, not unpleasurable hypnotic state of hyper-awareness.

"I thought I was late," said Lloyd.

"Late?" said Walt. He took out a piece of Dentyne and mashed it up between his fingers thoughtfully, then popped it into his mouth. "I gotta hit the head," he said, stalking off into the next room like a man who had just been given his orders setting out on an important mission. Lloyd sat down on one of the comfy chairs and looked at the food.

Lloyd Almost Gags

There comes a time in the affairs of men and women when disaster is averted so narrowly that one is forced to wonder what track life might have followed if the worst had, in fact, transpired. In the months that followed that first and most terrible meeting, Lloyd often wondered if it might have been better if he had not been able to overcome the powerful feeling that had seized him at 8:27 A.M., twenty seconds after he had stupidly tucked the piece of Danish into his face. So much suffering might have been averted, Lloyd often thought, if he had killed his career and saved his life.

What happened was this: Lloyd, at the edge of digestive and neurological equilibrium for the first time in fourteen hours, submitted to a twinge of what in normal circumstances would have been physically interpreted as hunger but in this case was nothing more than a momentary hiatus in the systemic collapse that had been threatening since he poisoned himself with alcohol and fat (in the form of bar nuts) the night before. He saw on the table, surrounded by other effluvia that did not appeal to him, the precise sort of sweet roll that, under better conditions, always had made his mouth water and his stomach declare its intention to run for election: a light, puffy Danish, glazed with egg and burnished to a dull shine, with apricot filling. Under the apricot was a small dollop of very lightly whipped cream cheese.

"You will be surprised—or your money back!" a garrulous voice with a touch of hostility said. Walt had turned on the small black-and-white television that was suspended by a metal flange from the wall of the bathroom.

Lloyd bit into the Danish. The minute it hit his tongue, he knew he was in trouble.

The television in the other room went off.

Lloyd had a choice. The Danish in his mouth was not moist. It was bone-dry and not delicious. He could spit it out into a saucer. But he was uncertain. It was possible that if he sent anything in the wrong direction, much might come rushing after. But he could no more swallow the quickly hardening object now being transformed into an indigestible ball in the back of his throat than he could eat a donkey. He chewed. Walt was standing in the door of his room.

"How ya doin', Omar?" Walt sometimes called Lloyd Omar. At other times, he favored "the Lloydmeister."

Lloyd swallowed the wad of starch. It immediately began to claw its way back up his throat. With every bit of willpower that he could summon, Lloyd tightened his esophagus and drove the alien object down his gullet and into his stomach much as a python would force a pig through its system by concentric waves of muscular activity. When he was done, there were tears in his eyes and Walt had discreetly moved over in his slightly herky-jerky style of locomotion to the window. After a time, he lit a cigarette, took two long drags, dropped it into a cold cup of coffee that was sitting on the courtesy table, and waved the air in front of him with some repugnance.

"We should go over a couple of things before the other guys get here," Walt said. He was staring with calm intensity out the window, being careful not to look anywhere in Lloyd's direction.

Lloyd wanted to answer, but he was forcing a roiling pool of hot bile back down, where it had already eaten a hole into his gallbladder, probably. The lower part of his bowel was also threatening to misbehave. A tremendous knot of pain formed in his midsection and walked about in his guts for a while.

"Last year I went to a Patriots game up in Boston with a couple of friends of mine who are in brand management with P&G," said Walt. "We had a box up top. I had about six very cold Absoluts in an hour or so. Then I found I couldn't walk as well as I usually like to. A good fellow took me back to the hotel, but I don't remember who. Been drinking white wine since then, except for, you know, at home, at night, before dinner with my wife, that kind of thing."

"No kidding," said Lloyd. The spasm had eased somewhat. "Thanks, Walt," he said.

"Listen," said Walt. He pounced down into the armchair opposite Lloyd and honed in on Lloyd's face, sucking it into his own with the magnetic pull of his desire. "We have five minutes and I want you to know the lay of the land. Things are not what they seem."

"Things don't really seem like anything, Walt," said Lloyd. "I have no idea what the agenda is."

"Shut up for a minute and listen, will ya!" screamed Walt. His face had gone from white to red to purple in less than three seconds.

The doorbell rang.

"Well, fuck it," said Walt. He rose and looked down at Lloyd. It hurt Lloyd's neck to tip it upward, so he leaned back on the couch and kind of peered upward into the corona of Walt's power. "Just listen to what's going on and don't say more than is absolutely necessary. If you need to get angry so that I don't have to, do it." He turned to go to the door.

"What's going on?" said Lloyd. "I thought this was a rehearsal for the strategic plan presentation."

"This is no rehearsal," said Walt. "This is the real thing."

Lemur in the Doorway

It was Lemur in the doorway. Walt looked displeased, and Walt looking displeased was a very ugly thing, not in terms of aesthetics or anything, ugly in terms of the effect his displeasure had on anyone viewing it. He assumed an air of intense calm that, had one not been looking closely, might have fooled the onlooker into believing that Walt was having a marvelous time and wished you were here. Upon closer inspection, the fact was that his face was very slowly shifting like a lava lamp from pink to red to blue to orange.

This frightened Lloyd.

"I believe you know this person," said Walt to Lloyd. Then he turned abruptly and marched into the bedroom, where he immediately began indulging in a classic Waltean session of annoyed nose blowing. Out came the hankie, appearing as a flash of white only long enough to be tossed ever so slightly into the air and seized with an entire angry fist, balled up, and rammed into an eye/ear/nose and throat subsystem fully engaged in a violent episode of some sort. Lloyd did not need to see this to know it was happening.

"What are you doing here, Ron?" Lloyd said, pulling Lemur into the hall. This gathering in Walt's suite was intended to be a delicate mélange of key players, a mind meld of only the cream corporate thinkers, drifting into the same nimbus long enough to reach conclusions, determine courses of action, then disappearing back into the mists, each to his own fiefdom, his own vassals, crops, and dragons. It was one of those interfaces that came but three or four times a year, and they represented the hard and flinty nugget at the heart of business, whether people were dressed as animated mannequins, as usual, or as informal wild Hawaiian touristas, or as lockjawed boating enthusiasts. The appearance of Lemur was most retrograde to Lloyd's desire. It was uncool.

"You left the Project Apollo stuff in the 'To Do' folder. I thought you'd want it," said Lemur.

Lemur was at his most corporate today, resplendent in a dark blue pinstripe three-piece that had to have set him back eight or nine hundred dollars. Totally out-of-decade yellow-pink-and-green dog-barf tie. Had to talk to Lemur about the tie. And how typical of the boy to overdress for an out-of-town day. As always, Ron was working too hard. Wanted into the room, too. Lloyd didn't know where he could find the strength to fend off Lemur this morning. He reached deep and got set to weather the upcoming storm of need, petulance, and self-promotion.

At the age of twenty-seven, Ron Lemur already felt like it was just about time to kill any Boomer standing in his way. Unable to accomplish that, he spent a lot of time wishing a fair number of Boomers would die soon, not painfully, just decisively enough to clear his path. A lot of people found him charming. Lloyd liked him well enough, and he felt somewhat proprietorial about him.

"So . . . I . . . got the stuff," said Lemur.

"Good," said Lloyd. "I might even use it."

"Let me come in, Lloyd. Really. I wanna come in. Please."

"Get out of here, Ron. I can barely stand up. I feel like I'm going to huark for sure."

"Yeah." Lemur put an avuncular hand on Lloyd's shoulder. "Great night. You were a behemoth. I cringe in your shadow. Those last three plum wines on top of all that Chinese food will stand as an enormous obelisk of achievement in an otherwise-barren landscape of sobriety and wellness."

"I'll call you when it's over and we'll deconstruct the whole situation."

"Okay," said Lemur. "I'll be in my little warren." Actually, Lemur's room was a respectable, if not overly capacious, enclave in a lesser hotel on the other side of Gateway Center. It wasn't a power space. But it was a prepower space. For a guy under thirty, it was a statement of respect. Lemur was very dissatisfied with it, and he had actually complained to Lloyd about the dis to his standing he felt his quarters at this meeting represented.

"About your room, Ron," Lloyd said, placing his hand on Lemur's elbow.

"My room. Yes," said Lemur, his ears moving forward and rolling outward a tiny bit.

"Go back to it. And Ron?"

"Yes, Lloyd."

"Remember that Spectravision is not a legitimate expense."

"Hey. It's not me who's got my face surgically attached to the nipple of the corporation," said Lemur. He then turned abruptly on his heel and strode manfully down the hall, turning with a flourish into the elevator bank and disappearing from view. Lloyd went back into the suite.

"He's a good guy," he said to Walt, tossing the file in a pile of documentary debris on the sideboard. Walt was busy removing invisible lint from the fabric of his slacks with a piece of Scotch tape torn from a roll he carried in his pocket for breaks in the action exactly like this one. He stared up at Lloyd and his eyes betrayed no recognition whatsoever. He was deep in Waltspace.

"I can't wait to get this thing over with," said Walt. "The . . . human aspect of these things is always a variable you can't forecast reliably. And . . . I like these guys."

The doorbell rang.

Walt Starts the Meeting, Sort Of

The theme of the ongoing discussions was supposedly productivity, a concept that Lloyd had always hated. *Productivity* was a screen term, a word meant to dignify the process of getting fewer people to do more for less. Lloyd had always hated doing more for less. Like most executives, he believed in doing ever-increasing amounts of less, for more. The unfortunate turn of their conversation arose from a critical error that had occurred on day two of their retreat. Instead of simply reporting on what was new and good to one another, instead of chatting about potential mergers, visions, and strategies, Walt had led them down the road to a serious exchange of views about such arcane and brain-damaged notions as reengineering—doing more for less in brand-new ways!—and also something called "achieving operating synergies through technical innovation, organizational creativity, and willingness to act upon our strategic assumptions." What could that mean? Pain. It meant pain.

At the sound of the doorbell, Walt slammed down his coffee cup, gave his mouth a blast of Binaca, and handed Lloyd a piece of paper. "Read this, Bud." He strode to the door and flung it open, exposing Darling and Fitz in faux casuals. "Gentlemen!" he boomed, as they stood there projecting an aura of pleasant befuddlement.

Meetings like the ones scheduled for this morning were unusual. They stank of substance. They were not scripted beforehand, at least not into a shape that anyone, with the possible exception of Walt, could recognize. It was therefore incumbent on both men at the door to appear open and excited and ready to produce massive insights.

"Come in, men," said Walt. They came, muttering those curt, affable jabbers that businesspeople use to fill up the emptiness of insincere discourse.

"Dudes," said Lloyd by way of greeting. The guys liked this. It made them feel like surfers.

Lloyd read the note. It was an E-mail from Chicago. "Walt," it said. "The first-quarter numbers are not what we had hoped. I know this is not due to any shortfall in your operating group, but companywide, the issue of both margin and IBT must be addressed. Let's use the offsite in Pittsburgh to wrestle with some of this. Don't go to any additional trouble, but be prepared to set aside your existing presentation to meet and master more immediate issues. Doug."

There were CCs to a variety of people. It was a scary note. There was no salutation, no fond adieu. The term was *all-business,* and nobody not in business knew how truly chilling that could be.

"Ugly," said Lloyd to himself. He handed the note back to Walt, who was carefully stuffing a small hunk of Danish into his mouth.

"Ugly?" said Walt. He looked annoyed. "What's ugly about it? It's a corporate directive. It's our opportunity to be heroes. I don't need any negative crap from any of you on this, Omar." He stalked away to the opposite end of the room and lit a cigarette, blowing a long cloud of smoke down the air-conditioning vent. This wasn't the first time Lloyd had felt that Walt hated him royally, at least for brief, intense moments. The good news was that Walt would feel bad about it very soon, and then make it up to him in some substantial way, a plum assignment that showed that, rather than being thought of as a stone nitwit without the least shred of credibility, Lloyd was, in fact, a serious player with access to the inner ear of power. Once a year, Walt made sure Lloyd got a generous raise. He had also bought Lloyd a car, and he never questioned his expense account. For this, Lloyd loved Walt. He didn't dream about him or anything, and he wasn't blind to Walt's faults, but the quality of the annoyance, the anger, the loyalty, the desire to please, the fear and friendship was not, in its heart, businesslike. It was personal, and fraught with psychic danger, destined for grief, disappointment, and a lifetime of hurt. It was family.

The door barked again and Lloyd felt his stomach turn over and contract in on itself, adhering to his spine where its back met his. The meeting sort of . . . faded. Then the room began to fade. "You all right, Lloyd?" said Fitz, the senior vice president of Human Resources. He did not look as if he meant it altogether kindly. He was beaming wickedly and obnoxiously, as if he was happy, in some way, that it was Lloyd, and not he, who was this time suffering a humiliating lack of equilibrium.

"Excuse me, man," said Lloyd. He went into the bathroom.

In the Bathroom

Lloyd looked in the mirror. There was an infinitesimal rivulet of dried mucus ringing the interface between his nostril and his upper lip. He chipped it away. How could Walt have permitted him to appear like this at such an important meeting?

Lloyd was suddenly knocked back by a tremendous wave of rage, rage so huge, it reared up and blotted out all light. He sat down on the closed toilet and prepared to wait it out.

This had happened to him before.

The year was 1984. Lloyd was a director of something relatively unspecific at the time. His boss, Jane, a thunderbolt of a woman, moved on to a better job elsewhere, and Lloyd found himself up against another director for control of the department. Lloyd thought he would automatically get the job because he did all the work and he deserved what was coming to him. The other person got the job, however, because for the past several years, Lloyd's department had been the only one in the building that was headed by a woman, a status that itself was an embarrassment to the corporation, which wanted to eradicate the glass ceiling. In short, Barbra got the job because she was a woman. And perhaps that's as it should be. Under other circumstances, it's quite possible Lloyd would have seen that. In this particular instance, he did not.

It was proof of how far gone into la-la land Lloyd had been that not until the moment that Fitz had called to give him the bad news did he ever once consider that eventuality, so ridiculous did it seem to him. The afternoon they told him was the first day of Lloyd's summer vacation. He took the news very badly. True, Fitz had secured his ongoing employment. This was no surprise to Lloyd, and he was not completely grateful. They kept him on because Barbra had no technical skills, per se. One morning, for instance, she called him on the intercom. "Chet wants to know the ten top priorities for the department this year," she told Lloyd.

"Yes?" said Lloyd.

"Yes," said Barbra. "So . . . what do you think the top priorities of the department are for the coming year?"

"You're the department head, Barbra," said Lloyd. "You figure it out."

Ten minutes later, Barbra called back. "I think our files are in deplorable shape," she said. "I think putting them in order would be a top priority."

"Definitely," said Lloyd. "You put that down."

In the end, Lloyd ended up doing the list anyway. But that first day, he hadn't made any spiritual accommodation at all. He got in his car and proceeded to wend his solitary, tedious, creeping way to East Hampton, a four-and-a-half-hour trip from Manhattan. He sat in the car, and he wept, wept because he could not walk away. He worked for Barbra for two years. She never made vice president and left to get married. Now she lived in Topeka, Kansas, and there was no department. There was only Lloyd, and Alice, his secretary. Lloyd was head of them. Still, he would never forgive the individuals who were responsible. Some of them were still around. Bob Darling, for instance, who he knew had advised Chet, then the chairman, to be "sensitive to the appearance of EEO compliance." He had read the memo, much later, after Barbra had gone and Chet was in an expansive, paternal mood.

But what was infuriating him now? Not something that had already happened, surely. No, it was something that was about to happen. He ran a sinkful of very cold water and plunged his face into it, drinking some of it as he did so. He dried his face, straightened his tie, and opened the door to the bedroom. If there was going to be blood, he thought, he might as well have some fun, and come out of the whole thing alive.

Yes, Darling

Bob Darling was standing in the bedroom that lay off the main living room of the suite. He was pacing and talking on the telephone that sat on the minidesk beside the bed. The receiver was jammed between his ear and shoulder. In one hand was a full glass of tomato juice with a small wafer of lemon in it. The other was balled up into a fist. He was yelling, but there was no volume behind it. To be able to shout at a very low volume was a talent picked up by only the highest corporate executives, who worked in close proximity with others more powerful than they, on matters they often didn't want people to know about, under considerable pressure, often with people who needed sticks as well as carrots to get the job done.

"Well, that's just fucking great," he rumbled into the phone. Lloyd was glad he wasn't on the receiving end. Darling was known throughout the corporation as one of those guys capable of tormenting small, defenseless lifeforms, and he had, in fact, fired a technician once who, ignorant of the fact that Darling himself wore one, made fun of somebody who sported a very bad toupee. "You think guys who wear a rug are funny, Blatt?" he told the former employee that day. "See how funny you find the fact that your job was just discontinued from lack of use." There was no turning him aside from that, either, once he had made up his mind, no matter how hard Fitz, the great humanist, had pressured him to reconsider.

"No, Sean," said Darling. He was looking at the carpet now, changing the direction of the pile back and forth, back and forth with the toe of his wing tip. "Lower the unit price," he said. "No, honestly, I don't give a shit how that sets you up down the road. I need you to get there this quarter, without fail. It's my butt here, and if it's my butt, it's your butt. Get there." He hung up, turned, and gaped slack-jawed at Lloyd for a rude amount of time, at a loss.

"Whassa matta, Bob?" said Lloyd.

"Lloyd!" said Darling, his face exploding with the force of his sudden grin.

"Howya doon," said Lloyd. He was suddenly feeling very belligerent. Darling, who loved to wear other people's "guts for garters"; Darling, who had made his fame by nuking so many jobs and the people in them that workers around the nation began referring to him as a neutron bomb who took all living things with him but left the buildings standing; Darling, who never picked up a check, leaked sensitive information to any reporter who could gain his trust by doing one very special thing: calling him up on the telephone; Darling, who spoke without surcease about productivity, and never missed an opportunity to go someplace, do something, be somebody for free. Beyond that, Lloyd could take him pretty well most of the time.

"Doin' fine, Lloyd, buddy," said Darling, although he did not look fine, not fine at all. He looked how Lloyd felt.

"Good first-quarter numbers?" asked Lloyd.

"Given market conditions, tolerable," said Darling. What a bullshitter.

"Of course, you're trying to stand up to some awesome projections, aren't you, Bob?" It was true. Darling had been the star of last quarter's executive management cabal, when he rolled out a set of promised revenue and operating profit achievements for the coming year that would have made Leibniz blush.

"Yeah," said Darling, narrowing his eyes, which were squinty, tiny, and bulbous all at the same time. "We don't make that number, we just might have to figure out how to save some expense at the corporate level, huh, bub?" This was a deliberate threat to Lloyd. Lloyd generated no income whatsoever. Field operating guys like Darling could question the wisdom of a headquarters department that ate up more than a million dollars a year in costs. The vogue at this time was to listen hard to whatever opinions the field operations put out, no matter how destructive, self-serving or nonsensical those ideas might be. This willingness to fawn and abase the company's central brain-stem function to please the organizational extremities fell under the general concept of *decentralization,* which itself was deemed a priori, a superb thing.

"I agree with you, Bob," said Lloyd, smiling broadly, sashaying across the room and placing a brotherly arm around Darling's huge misshapen shoulders. "I've been trying to tell the big dudes for years: Save the money. Buy me out. Put me on the beach. That's all I want: five or six million dollars. A small office on thirty-four. You think you could put in a good word for the concept?"

"I could try," growled Darling.

"Do," said Lloyd. "Give it a shot. You look great, by the way. You seemed to be getting kind of strung out there for a while. I like what those ten extra pounds does for ya."

Darling was uncertain how to take this last observation. Like all formerly thin, now beefy men, he harbored suspicions that he looked a lot better than he really did in the cold light of a normal mirror. It was quite possible, he thought, that he had mysteriously acquired a good look at some point in the last several weeks as he continued to build body fat and drink himself into an early grave.

"Thanks, man," he finally said.

"Don't mention it," said Lloyd.

The Pregame Show

Lloyd entered the central area of the suite.

The circular conversation area in which they sat had only one cushioned chair, and several deeply serious couches in a range of sumptous but appropriate fabrics, each different from but compatible with the others, as well as a couple of hard straight-backed chairs for those not requiring a high level of physical ease.

They were all assembled, attempting to appear nonchalant in immaculate casuals—the off-duty uniform. Lloyd had never been able to get it right. One time, he forgot the colorful socks that were supposed to go with the scrupulously pressed khakis and was forced to wear black hose that looked ridiculous with his Reeboks. Another time, he forgot a cloth belt and had to make do with a leather one that clearly wouldn't pass muster on any golf course outside of Bulgaria. He hated the way he looked in casual clothing, as if he was appearing in public naked, without the concealing, impersonal comfort of his dress pinstripes.

As they all waited for the festivities to start in earnest, Lloyd was forced to hear, without really listening, an asphyxiating torrent of golf talk. Golf was rock and roll to these men, and drugs, too. It was the perfect interface between business, life, friendship, and art. Each was capable of long, highly detailed recollections of holes gone by, traps avoided or, disastrously, not, water hazards hazarded, balls lost, seagulls beaned, carts upended, beers guzzled, hooks and slices mended, glimpses of brilliance displayed, hopes dashed, money won and lost. They could, and did, speak of these things for hours, growing ever cuddly toward one another as they did so. Had any departed into talk of hard drives, chips, interfaces, and clock speeds, Lloyd could have joined them, but as it was, he was an albatross at an ever-replenished wedding feast. He had given up resenting it, though. What was the point? At least when they were on the mental golf course, no one would be hurt.

The nineteenth green, of course, was another matter.

As the air ran out of the juicy tales of fucked-up eighteenth holes, and greens so fast that you could roll a ball of spit down the middle of 'em, and bars on the back of a rolling golf cart that follows you to hell and back, and so many lost balls that you hadda go all the way back to the pro shop to get more, they sat and shuffled papers and waited, clearing their throats, appearing as busy as people who have no idea what is going on can.

At heart, no one was amused. A fear was there, hanging, plump and rotten, in their midst: that somebody here would lose his reporting structure, his upward path, his sense of forward direction, at a time in his career when he didn't have the jism for another big push. None of them wanted that for any of his brothers, unless it could forestall it happening to himself. Lloyd knew it would not be he, for one simple reason: Last night at 5:30 P.M., before they had gone out to dinner and alcohol immersion, Walt had called Lloyd. He answered it in the shower.

"Yes?" he said. A dollop of house shampoo weaseled its way down his cheek and into his mouth. A bit found its way into his eye. It hurt.

"Lloyd? Walt. Got your book handy?"

"No, Walt," said Lloyd.

"Monday morning. Seven A.M. My office. Bring coffee. A roll or something. Tell Fitz, him too. See ya," barked Walt, and hung up.

So Lloyd thought it was pretty safe to assume that nothing had changed since just yesterday, and that he was not targeted for extermination just yet. Lloyd hoped that when the bullet came speeding at him one day, he would still be sharp enough to see it coming, not to step out of the way—no, few are that adroit—but at least to see it. That was something.

Walt was stalling, for some reason. He was pretending to talk to Ed Sweet, the former megaconsultant who had mutated into the new, unassailable *über* vice president of Sales. Walt was still playing the karmic bubble of the room, that was it, waiting for the point at which the cohesion of the group would break apart and fly into a thousand pieces if he did not speak. Lloyd could feel his eyeballs begin to roll in their sockets, like a horse awakening to fire.

"Walt," he said at last. "Let's roll, huh?"

"Indeed," said Walt. "You guys want anything? You comfortable?"

"We're comfortable, Walt," said Lloyd.

"Good," said Walt. "Good, good, good. It's about the numbers, guys. But I'm sure you know that."

The Numbers

The numbers were off; that was the reason for everything that had happened, that was happening, that would happen, for while the six men were powerful, they were not the ultimate power in the corporation. First, there was the real world of business as Lloyd could perceive it from his tiny cornice in its infrastructure, the real world that contracted and expanded in seismic waves that drove all of them up and thrust them down basically without relation to their efforts. For control freaks, this was a difficult reality to comprehend, let alone accept. Second, and perhaps more to the point, there was an executive structure in Chicago that did little but manage managers, attending an incessant procession of technical presentations that determined the future of thousands, including key players. Some of these friendly and constructive inquisitions were held at immense mansions, hollow and empty of life except for the distant murmur of conferring voices. Others took place in palatial retreats, with pine forests abutting the golf course, and the wind in their hair, and sunshine, and pelicans. Sometimes the big meetings took place on the fiftieth floor of division headquarters on Sixth Avenue in New York City, because no one could have any fun up there. It was gray, and removed from the sun, a huge mahogany boardroom, with chairs that made you feel small and comfy. Times like now, you found yourself here. Here was a hotel. Hotel food. Hotel space. Hotel beverage profusion. Hotel bar nuts. Hotel smell. Hotel smile. Hotel.

Walt was not comfortable sitting. He stood.

Walt Gets Fidgety

Walt strolled around the suite, deep in thought, for a long time. Nobody spoke. He was working his lower lip between his right index finger and thumb, folding it into a little envelope of plump skin and muscle. It was unwise to disturb Walt when he was at his lower lip, as more than one junior financial type had found out, to his regret.

"Not that they're outstandingly bad, the numbers, mind you," said Walt. An enormous inaudible shiver of collective relief swept through the group like a reflexive yawn. The black hole of cogitation was past. Walt was speaking!

That's Walt's genius, Lloyd thought. By the time he's ready to talk, we have been to the valley of the shadow of negation. The antimeeting. Whatever he has to say, it's got to be better than . . . Nothing. In fact, we can't wait to hear Walt talk, no matter how terrible it may be for us personally. That's management. "We still lead all operating units in a wide range of measures, as I'm sure you know is true," he said. Lloyd did know this to be true. Operating profit was up 8 percent over last year, which had been up more than 18 percent over the year before that. Good, but not great. Greatness was called for. But how? Customer demand was strong, but not as ridiculously hefty as it should be. Prices were high already, and might even be pushed downward, for God's sake. There was only one answer: costs.

Sadly, cost control always meant one thing: getting rid of people who made a small amount of money. And even sometimes, once in a very great while, one or two who made a lot. Where would I be without this gig? thought Lloyd. He remembered the first three or four years of his marriage, when he and Donna used to stroll up Columbus Avenue in New York City, reading the menus at the real restaurants before heading over to the Four Brothers. Poverty wasn't bad. They had been happy then. Of course, they were happy now, too. Nothing about money in itself actually prevented happiness. It was not just the money, either. It was meetings like this one, too. Where would he be if he couldn't go to those? Home in his jammies.

"We've got to ratchet down the cost line and ramp up some serious containment efforts," Walt continued. "We've talked about it for quite a while. Now we've got to start firing with live ammo." Lloyd stuck a finger in his ear and scratched his eardrum thoughtfully. That Walt was getting into the military parlance this early in the morning was a real bad sign. Now Walt looked at his watch. "We'd better hump this mother," he said. "We don't have a whole helluva lotta time."

"Why, Walt?" said Lloyd from his perch at the window. "What's going on for the rest of the day that we don't know about?"

"Big doin's," said Walt. He didn't look happy about it.

Darling was wrestling with something he had jammed into the breast pocket of his jacket, giving a pretty fair impression of a man attempting to haul out his own innards. "Goddamned tiny pockets good for nuthin', motherbugger," said Darling. He finally got the sheaf of papers out and handed one page of the stack to each person. "That's it," he said. "I don't know if I need to remind you how much of our premium pricing is supported by image and positioning, and how deeply our weekly turnover is related to local spot advertising. Line sixteen," he said. He then, to everyone's utter disquiet, plunged into a line-by-line justification of his operation. This is a nightmare, thought Lloyd. But nobody can stop Bob. Once he starts down this road, no one, not even Walt, can afford to look unengaged, for is not business about solid, intractable things—numbers, proofs, hard-eyed analysis? Careening willy-nilly to a chaotic, unforeseen outcome powered by emotion—that's not business. That's life.

"Dollar per customer for unit sales is tracked on line one oh seven, way back in the indexed material," Bob was saying. Was that a glint of sadistic pleasure in his eye? Lloyd pinched the nail of his thumb into an open palm. Do not fall asleep, he said to himself.

And suddenly, he was not there.

Mona

It was at the first Christmas party of the first year of Lloyd's ascension to relatively high senior middle management, a position from which he could address the entire corporation with impunity and speak with Walt pretty much whenever he wished. The feeling of having *arrived* was unique, and arousing.

Mona was at the party, which took place on the rooftop atrium of a midtown hotel. Mona was new to the company at that point, having recently arrived from Pepsi. She was younger than he had thought at first. Younger, and . . . different. He ate a celery stick for a long while, surreptitiously watching her work the room. Then he forgot about her.

He was standing in the corner with Ganzak, discussing the relationship between chaos theory and the art of lying in budget reviews, when he became aware of a pricking in the back of his neck and the sensation that someone was looking at him intently from behind. He cautiously turned, to find that she was assessing him frankly . . . boldly, if you had to characterize it honestly. She was laughing, too. Looking right at him and . . . laughing. Lloyd looked back and tried to appear inscrutable, never one of his main assets.

She had medium-length thick reddish-gold hair and an open face that spoke of crisp winds and tweaked cheeks. Her eyes were bright and focused on him, no one but him. She found him interesting? Lloyd was amazed, and he stared into her eyes at the distance of the hors d'oeuvres table. They were green, her eyes—no, blue—no, gray—no, he saw now, green flecked with black. He felt a small but unmistakable stirring in his groin.

Jesus, he thought, and went over to make chitchat with her. It was the only thing to do, after all. To simply stare at each other at a distance for much longer would border on the uncouth.

They spoke for a while. Idle work-related hubbub transmogrifying into movies seen, articles read, and other bourgeois background noise. He realized that in spite of the fact that what they were talking about was gibberish, he was strangely comfortable. A warm glow suffused his being.

He found himself staring at her teeth, her somewhat swollen lower lip, wondering what it would be like to take it gently between his own lips and envelop her mouth in a gentle, guilty kiss. "Once a week, they have a piece in the Science *Times* about subatomic particles," he said, apropos of nothing. "Why do you think that is?"

"It makes middlebrows feel intellectual," said Mona. It was clearly something she had thought about before, incredibly. "I can't read that speculative pseudoscientific stuff, you know," she said with some passion. "Hawking, stuff like that. I think it's a form of theological writing, not meant to be understood without a leap of faith." Lloyd thought this was a highly intelligent thing to say. Her teeth were quite irregular, he saw. One lower bicuspid was askew entirely, sort of sunk inside her gumline, almost hidden in the deep shadow within that concealed her tongue, the deep cavern of her mouth. Mouth, he thought.

"I'm surprised you care about this stuff at all," he said. "It doesn't exactly go with an MBA in macroeconomics from Harvard." Which, in fact, was what Mona possessed. Lloyd found this fact to be an antiaphrodisiac, as was any mention at all of Harvard. For some reason, many people who went to Harvard found it necessary to acquaint you of that fact immediately after the onset of any conversation. For a while, during the eighties, Lloyd had found this amusing. By 1991, it had quietly mutated into annoying. Mona had not brought it up at all. The status of her higher education had rocketed through the corporate culture immediately after her hiring into the executive stratosphere. Now it was Lloyd who brought it up.

Lloyd works a party badly.

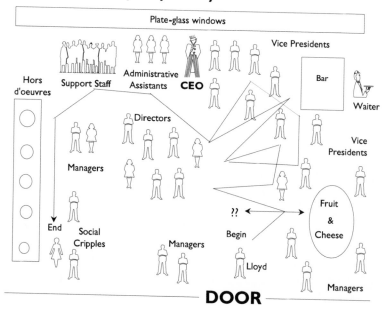

Lloyd works a party well.

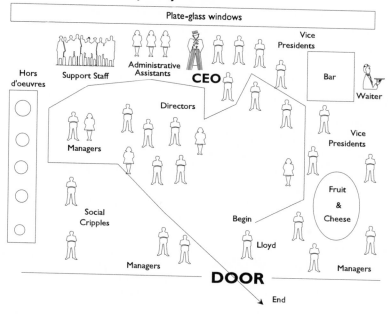

"I went out for four years with a guy from MIT," Mona was saying, completely ignoring the reference to her alma mater. "I came to view discussion of scientific theory as a relaxing break from economics." They laughed.

Lloyd then stupidly launched into further brainless nattering about quarks and gluons, hoping that his mounting level of physical excitation was not showing in some embarrassing way. In the meantime, she was gazing at him as a child would assess the man in the moon.

This woman is barely thirty-five years old, Lloyd thought. And she is interested in me. She thinks I am funny. And smart and cute. She doesn't want to drift away to some other equally banal conversation. She wants to stay in this one. God, let me hold on to her.

So Lloyd kept on talking about high-velocity molecular interactions, which had been the subject of the *Times* article of the week. But he was quietly contemplating her purple dress. Black pumps. No stockings! He put his hands in his pockets and puffed out the front of his pants, better to conceal the tiny tent that was being pitched there. Had she noticed? Beneath the simple purple shell, there would be a firm, highly torqued assembly of muscle and bone structure that, together, sang in the moonlight. Lloyd blinked, and the vision of her naked form evaporated.

"I agree with you," Lloyd said. "At the bottom of the universe, if we believe what they're telling us, and possibly even if we don't, there are entities that are essentially nothing more than poetic conceits. There's no proof any of them exist, but we need them to exist, in order for the march of understanding to carry on. So we posit their existence, and pretty soon we forget the provisional quality of this actuality." What the hell was he talking about? "They're metaphors for symbolic concepts that may be intuitively grasped but not actually observed."

"Like love," said Mona.

"Hm?"

"Like love," she repeated with the utmost seriousness, not a trace of the coy or seductive about it whatsoever. "Just because you've never seen it, never observed it firsthand, never directly felt the effects of it, that doesn't mean it doesn't exist, isn't, in fact, working on every aspect of your being at all times, making everything larger and more ostensibly important, that without it there, as a building block of nature, sort of, nothing at all would exist in any real sense of the word, or at least be important enough to notice. If love didn't exist, in other words, we would have to posit its existence to continue on as human beings."

"Would you like a beer or something?" Lloyd said. When she had said the word *love*, he had suffered an almost-inescapable desire to touch her in some way.

"Oh, no," she said. "Unless, like, there's some right here, nearby."

"Come on," said Lloyd. "Let me get you something."

"Really," she said, as if she had said too much already. "I'm fine."

He got her a beer, but by the time he came back, she was in concourse with Fitz on the issue of consolidation in joint-venture situations. He joined them, handing her the Beck's she had requested. She took it and placed a hand on his arm in thanks. His head now clear, Lloyd went to the coat check, got his coat, and got out of there without saying good-bye to anybody.

Since then, there seemed to be something special between them. They liked each other. Beyond that, of course, there was the natural chemical reaction that takes place between healthy men and women in the workplace, nothing more inappropriate than that. Nor was it likely to be, if they both kept their wits about them. And why shouldn't they? Didn't they each have a lot to lose if they did not? Well? Didn't he?

What the heck was he thinking about?

Back to Bob

Lloyd was slammed back into his body. Walt was screaming at Bob. Not loudly. Softly. But it was screaming nonetheless, and it took each man's entire powerbank to keep from putting his hands over his amazed and terrified ears.

"I think you'll agree," Walt quietly observed, "that we need some solutions that are impactful and effective in the near term, Bob, and we're not talking cuts, goddamn it. I certainly hope you see that, Bob. We're talking about improved process, improved methodology, working smarter, better, faster, with a greater attention to the customer than ever before, Bob, and I have to be honest with you, Bob, those who are not creative about this issue are pretty much not engaged on the kind of one hundred percent level that the future calls for. Do you read me, Bob?"

"I read you, Walt," said Darling.

"Now, Bob, you've started out really badly, really badly, Bob, so what I'm going to do is go into the next room and blow my fucking nose for a while and collect my composure a little so that when you do start to talk I don't rip the top of your scalp from the skull that's nearly poking out from under your stupid toupee!"

Walt left the room.

"Wow," said Lloyd. "That was harsh."

"Good going, Bob," said Fitz, who seemed to be having a marvelous time.

Walt, after some additional honking and tooting just beyond their view, had come back and was standing, straight and tall, in the doorway. He was staring with a glare of utter hatred at Darling, who appeared to be too big for his corner of the couch. "Yes," Bob said, pulling discreetly at the seat of his pants and glaring at the document on his lap. There was a silence. "Okay, we can close regional marketing offices in Atlanta, Cleveland, and maybe San Francisco, which can be handled, I guess, out of L.A. That will bring our operating expenses down, like, what, eleven percent? A couple million bucks, anyhow. That's a start, huh?"

"It's all about people, gentlemen," said Walt, and Lloyd saw little dewdrops in the corners of his eyes. Nobody is mistier about the entire subject of human suffering, Lloyd believed, than a corporate executive about to kill a couple of thousand or so. Lloyd had once seen a tape of Ross Perot, the American populist, speaking of his employees at EDS. Perot was practically crying when he talked about how wonderful, dedicated, talented his people were. A few months later, he sold the company and all those people were screwed quite badly.

"People are . . . *important*," Walt was saying. "But not people as a, like, general idea or anything. Not all people is what I'm saying. The right people is what I mean. The right people make all the difference. If you have the right people, you have everything."

"I thought if you have your health, you have everything," said Lloyd, to absolutely no response at all.

Sweet walked to the window and looked out at the apex of Western civilization glimmering far below. His voice was dusky. "I know we're talking about people," he nearly whispered. "But tough. What are we going to do, kill ourselves? Destroy the company we all rely on?" This "we" annoyed Lloyd, but it was unavoidable. Former consultants always used the second-person plural, making up for the years when a laptop and voice mail were their only friends. Sweet continued. "Survive for a time, just to limp along. Finally to be bought by some multinational conglomerate?"

"We are a multinational conglomerate," said Darling.

"Yes, yes," said Sweet. "I meant a big multinational conglomerate."

"We are pretty big," murmured Darling.

"Screw you, Bob," said Sweet.

"Cursing each other out won't do any good," said Walt. "Let's—how do the kids put it?—keep ourselves together."

"I think the last kid who said that turned forty-three last week," said Lloyd.

"Let's chill, then," said Walt. "That okay with you, Lloydmeister?"

Lloyd hated it when Walt called him Lloydmeister in front of the team. It made him look like a pet or something. Lloyd didn't like the feeling that Walt could, without much of a stretch, treat him as if he, Walt, were the father.

What kind of a father could terminate you without cause? Still, in doing so, Walt was cutting to the heart of what the corporate bond really was all about: love, hate, desire, hope. Big feelings that had nothing to do with money. All but one of them. Greed—that had to do with money. But there was no place for greed in this sort of meeting.

"Besides," said Walt. "I want to remind you guys that if we don't make the crazy operating profit number dictated by Chicago, we're not going to max out our bonus situation, which, in the case of some of you guys, could amount to a personal loss of more than a couple hundred grand? Options are also being issued at two points below market price and the number we each get will be determined by financial performance, and right now we're on track to do okay, but nothing to write home about. And I don't know about you guys, but I want to write home. I can take about six, seven more years of this shit; then I want to be someplace on a beach."

There was an enormous bolt of bright blue laughter and then everybody stood, grunted, and began to mill around the room.

"Let's take five," said Walt.

During the So-Called Break

Darling strolled over to the coffee table, selected a lemon, and, after a moment of consideration, plunged it into his mouth, sucking it fiercely. "What are your estimates of disemployment companywide, Ed?" he said to Sweet.

"I don't know . . . twenty percent over eighteen months, going to about a third by year five?" said Sweet.

"Don't you think the wheels will fall off?" said Lloyd, who felt so queasy during these sort of discussions that he could barely put up a fight against them.

"Lloyd," said Walt. "Are you with this process or against it? Just asking."

"Oh, for it, absolutely," said Lloyd. If there was one thing Walt hated, it was guys who didn't get with the program but went ahead and took the money, the car, the plastic, then suffered personal angst over the status of their souls. Walt wanted those people dead, and often he had other people kill them for him.

"Good," said Walt. He was pouring coffee. "I'd like to reveal to you guys that the twenty percent level was my original game plan. So, naturally, I agree with myself, and I'm glad you do, too."

A rattling, mucus-filled laugh filled the room. "Screw you, too, Ed," said Darling, slamming Sweet in the back. A spasm of hysteria seized them. As they all settled down again, Walt pulled Lloyd aside. "Going well, I think," he said.

"Couldn't be better," said Lloyd.

"I want Bob out of here. Tomorrow would be nice, but March would be all right. Give Ron Lemur the job. He wants it. He's aggressive. And he doesn't have balls of fat, either. Do it."

"I don't think so, Walt," said Lloyd.

"Fucking pantywaist makes me fucking sick," said Walt.

"Getting on toward lunch and everybody's a little cranky," said Lloyd. "We'll eat after a while and you'll feel better about the whole thing."

"Maybe," said Walt. He stared at Lloyd, hard. "Yeah," he said finally, putting a gentle hand on Lloyd's shoulder and drawing him a bit too close. "I could eat a free-range horse!" he barked. Then he shoved Lloyd hard, with his shoulder, using all his weight, a semi-football move that Walt was fond of. Surprised and somewhat annoyed at himself for not seeing it coming, Lloyd pitched forward and landed basically on Fitz's lap.

"Walt is getting violent," he said to Fitz.

"Let's get this over with," said Fitz, his long legs extended well beyond the couch. As always, his face was a little too ruddy and a curiously malevolent twinkle glimmered from the corners of his eyes. He was nearly fifty, looked forty, drank like a high school linebacker.

"There's already been one casualty," said Lloyd.

"Ugly when it happens, ain't it?" Fitz was smiling.

Lloyd smiled back. Fitz was an okay guy. He hoped nothing was about to happen to him.

Short and Violent

I'll match Bob's numbers," Fitz said laconically.

Darling, a doughnut hole between his teeth, had emitted a gagging, throaty sound. It was unclear whether this was due to the dryness of the food or his assessment of Fitz's estimated head-count reduction.

"Let's keep this meeting on a verbal level," said Walt. "Although I will say, Ted . . ." The room had frozen in distressed silence. "I will say that this kind of parity thinking from the standard-bearer in HR is not what I was looking for."

"Level of functionality" was all that emerged from Fitz.

"You got so many people, even *you* couldn't count them, Ted," said Darling, not unkindly. This happened to be true. Nearly one-third of all Omnivore employees were in some way related to Fitz's administrative function.

32

Slide Show Two

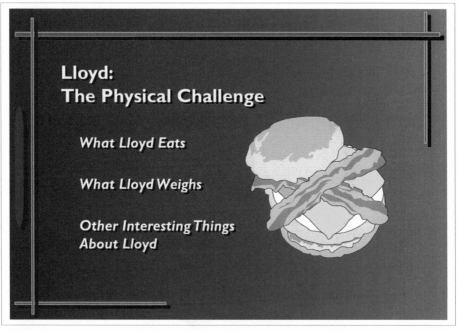

Slide 1

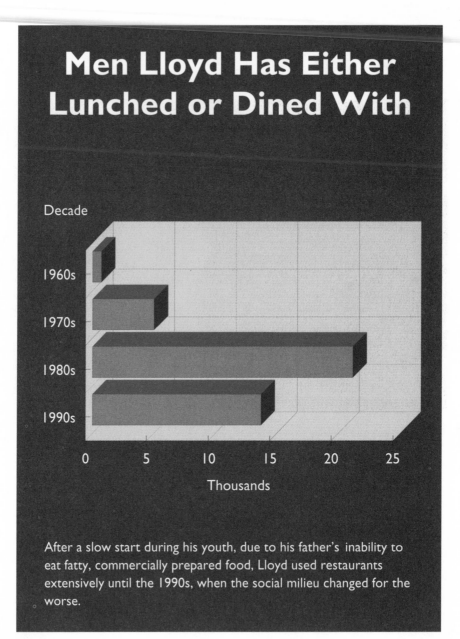

Men Lloyd Has Either Lunched or Dined With

Decade

Thousands

After a slow start during his youth, due to his father's inability to eat fatty, commercially prepared food, Lloyd used restaurants extensively until the 1990s, when the social milieu changed for the worse.

Backup chart 1

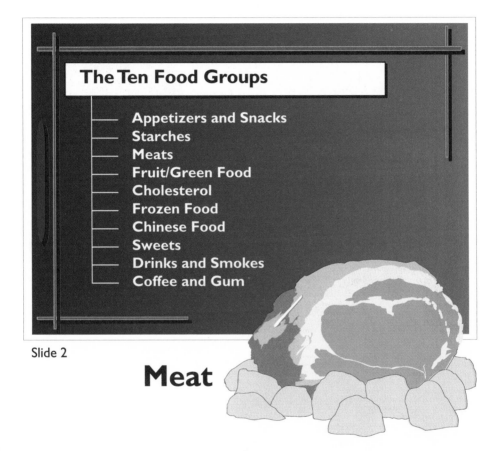

Slide 2

Meat

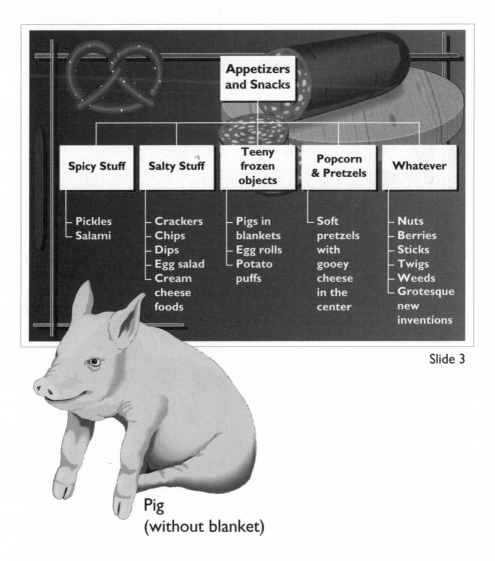

Slide 3

Pig
(without blanket)

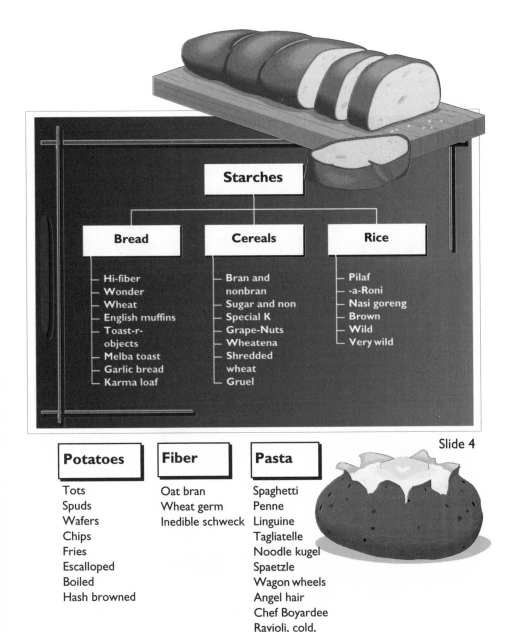

Starches

Bread
— Hi-fiber
— Wonder
— Wheat
— English muffins
— Toast-r-
  objects
— Melba toast
— Garlic bread
— Karma loaf

Cereals
— Bran and
  nonbran
— Sugar and non
— Special K
— Grape-Nuts
— Wheatena
— Shredded
  wheat
— Gruel

Rice
— Pilaf
— -a-Roni
— Nasi goreng
— Brown
— Wild
— Very wild

Slide 4

Potatoes
Tots
Spuds
Wafers
Chips
Fries
Escalloped
Boiled
Hash browned

Fiber
Oat bran
Wheat germ
Inedible schweck

Pasta
Spaghetti
Penne
Linguine
Tagliatelle
Noodle kugel
Spaetzle
Wagon wheels
Angel hair
Chef Boyardee
Ravioli, cold,
from the can

37

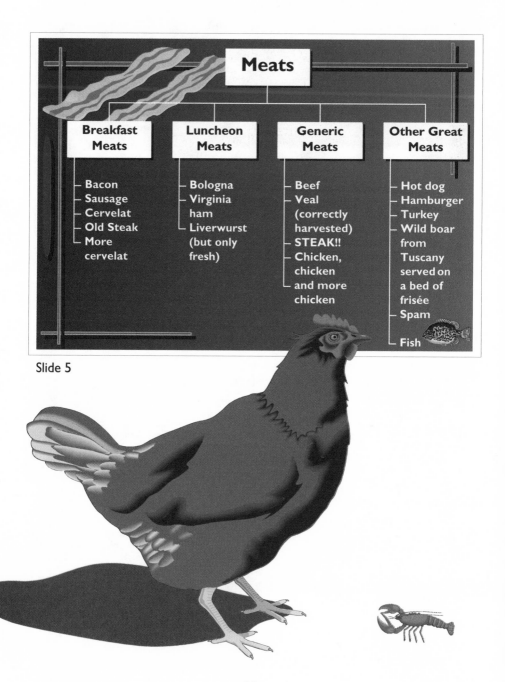

Slide 5

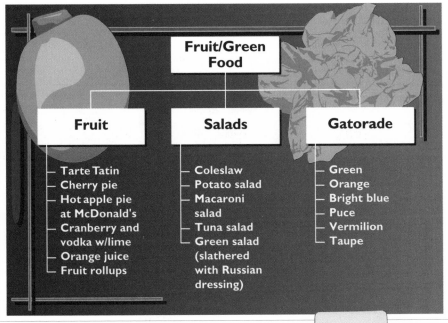

Fruit/Green Food

Fruit	Salads	Gatorade
— Tarte Tatin — Cherry pie — Hot apple pie at McDonald's — Cranberry and vodka w/lime — Orange juice — Fruit rollups	— Coleslaw — Potato salad — Macaroni salad — Tuna salad — Green salad (slathered with Russian dressing)	— Green — Orange — Bright blue — Puce — Vermilion — Taupe

Slide 6

OJ (without vodka)

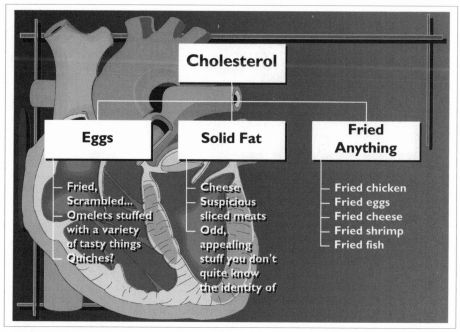

Slide 7

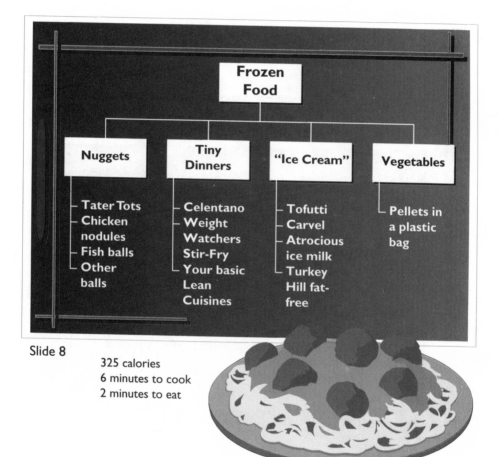

Slide 8

325 calories
6 minutes to cook
2 minutes to eat

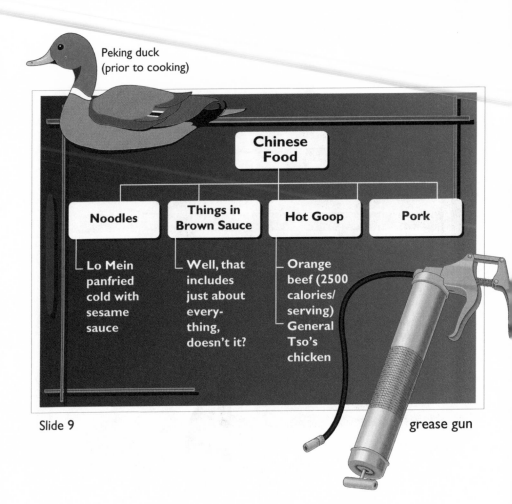

Peking duck
(prior to cooking)

Chinese Food

Noodles	Things in Brown Sauce	Hot Goop	Pork
Lo Mein panfried cold with sesame sauce	Well, that includes just about everything, doesn't it?	Orange beef (2500 calories/serving) General Tso's chicken	

Slide 9

grease gun

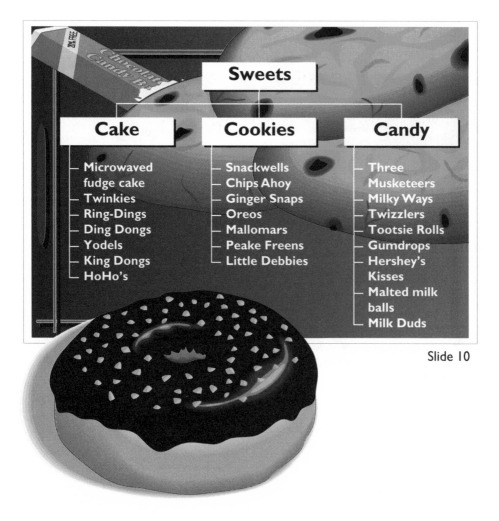

Slide 10

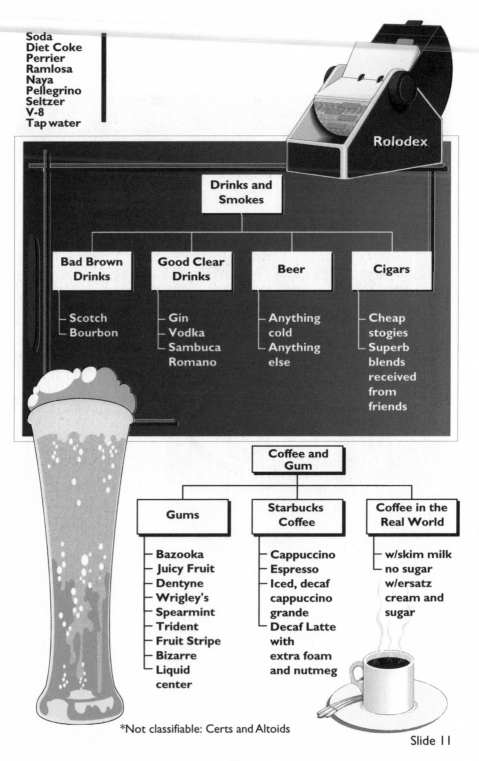

Soda
Diet Coke
Perrier
Ramlosa
Naya
Pellegrino
Seltzer
V-8
Tap water

Rolodex

Drinks and Smokes

Bad Brown Drinks
- Scotch
- Bourbon

Good Clear Drinks
- Gin
- Vodka
- Sambuca Romano

Beer
- Anything cold
- Anything else

Cigars
- Cheap stogies
- Superb blends received from friends

Coffee and Gum

Gums
- Bazooka
- Juicy Fruit
- Dentyne
- Wrigley's
- Spearmint
- Trident
- Fruit Stripe
- Bizarre
- Liquid center

Starbucks Coffee
- Cappuccino
- Espresso
- Iced, decaf cappuccino grande
- Decaf Latte with extra foam and nutmeg

Coffee in the Real World
- w/skim milk
- no sugar w/ersatz cream and sugar

*Not classifiable: Certs and Altoids

Slide 11

44

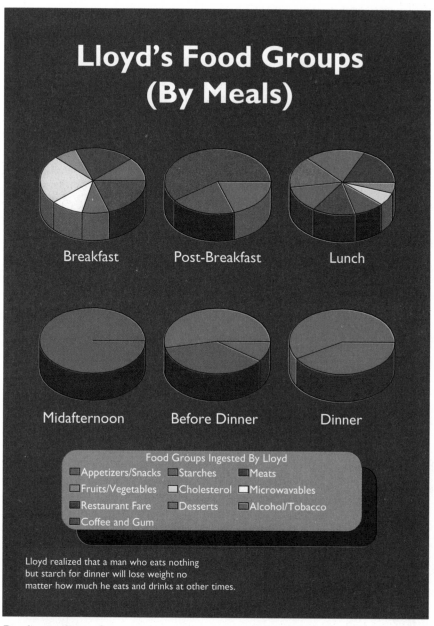

Lloyd realized that a man who eats nothing
but starch for dinner will lose weight no
matter how much he eats and drinks at other times.

Backup chart 2

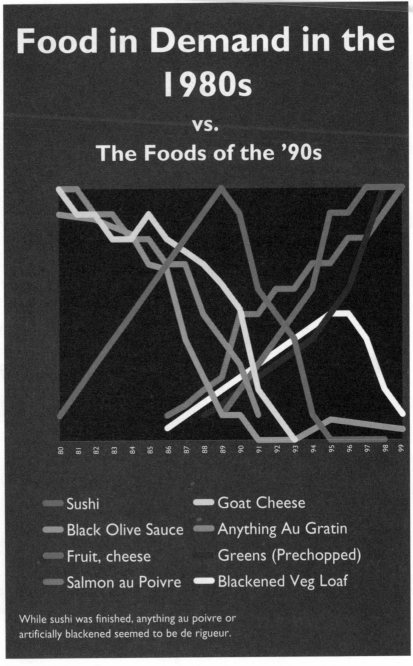

Food in Demand in the 1980s
vs.
The Foods of the '90s

- Sushi
- Black Olive Sauce
- Fruit, cheese
- Salmon au Poivre
- Goat Cheese
- Anything Au Gratin
- Greens (Prechopped)
- Blackened Veg Loaf

While sushi was finished, anything au poivre or artificially blackened seemed to be de rigueur.

Backup chart 3

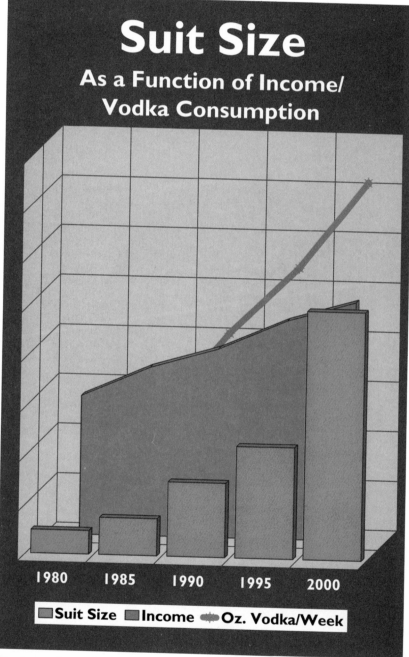

Backup chart 4

Home sweet home

"Yeah. Okay. I see the handwriting on the wall here," said Fitz. He sat upright, as if he had just remembered something. "Why can't we have any real food in here, instead of this swill?" he said.

"Swill?" said Walt. He looked hurt. "I selected this food myself from the room-service menu. And this is one of my favorite hotels." Lloyd knew it was more than that. It was the location where Walt had first met and romanced his wife, whose name was Lisa but whom everyone, for some inexplicable reason, called "Skeeter."

"Oh," said Fitz. "Excuse me, Walt." But it didn't sound like a heartfelt apology. For reasons that were murky to Lloyd, Fitz got away with a towering level of general rudeness that would not only have rendered others unviable but would have made them unlikable, which Fitz wasn't.

"We'll think about it in a couple of minutes," said Walt.

Fitz sat lower in his seat and grumbled under his breath like a four-year-old. The only thing Lloyd caught was the phrase "a couple of rashers or something."

"No bacon, Ted," Lloyd whispered to Fitz. "I beg you. I don't think I could stand to smell it, let alone eat it."

"I recognize that one out of six employees of this corporation is related to my function, but we're talking about quality management here—that's the bottom line—so let's keep control over our operations, guys, or give up any illusions we may have about the effectiveness of our management."

"We must never give up the illusion of effective management," Walt said solemnly. Once again, there was a resonant chuckle and an audible snap in the level of tension.

"Well, I'm not gonna commit to anything until we resolve this food issue," said Fitz. He was chomping on a very large apricot Danish, a bit of which had flaked off and was, oddly, perching on his forehead.

"You have a piece of Danish on your forehead, Ted," said Lloyd.

"The hell I do," said Fitz. He left it there.

"Bob," said Lloyd. "Does or does not Ted have a piece of Danish the size of a marble on his stupid forehead."

"No," said Darling.

Fitz probed both of them for a moment, then brushed the fleck off his face.

"Thank you, Lloyd," he said.

"Spartan meetings are part of our culture, Ted," said Walt. "I'm sure as keeper of the people side of our business you don't want to change some of the more established facets of our culture, particularly one pertaining to individual restraint."

"First comes eating. Then comes culture," said Fitz. He folded his arms over his chest.

Walt scratched his nose. "I think if we do break with custom in this case and order up a mess of victuals—"

"Victuals!" said Lloyd.

"We should settle on one choice of food. That's as far as I'm willing to go. I can't see coming to any agreement with a man who's munching on a sticky sparerib while I'm toying with a medallion of veal."

"Medallions of veal would be fine!" said Fitz.

"Medallions of veal all around?" There was a lusty huzzah. "Good," Walt said, pressing a button on the phone. "Room service? We're ready for that order now. Make sure the beverages are properly chilled, wouldja?" He hung up and addressed the astonished men. "You see, gentlemen, I anticipate your needs, as always. You may kiss my ring." Again, there was laughter, but laughter of a different color, maroon, perhaps, without mirth, full of phlegm and bile.

"We have food coming," said Darling with a deep sense of grandeur and awe, a potent sense that all would be light where before there was only darkness. "Now all we'd need would be a couple of beers."

"Let's get a little more done first, Bob," said Walt. "Hey, the way things are going, we could be out on the range by one-seventeen, just like I planned!"

There was a general murmur of approbation. The range Walt was referring to was an indoor maze not far from the hotel, in the outskirts of the city. There, grown men strapped on plastic suits and special guns, wove around the enclosure, trying to cover one another with paint from exploding nodules. They had done it as a group a couple of times and liked it all right. Walt believed it built cohesion, and Lloyd wasn't altogether sure he was wrong.

"We can't take the kind of cuts that Sweet's talking about," said Fitz. "I'll give you my org chart. You show me how to do it and I'll do it."

"You could retire everyone over fifty-six—that's one thing," said Darling.

"Those are my senior managers! The heart of my culture!" stormed Fitz.

With the look of a man who had just made a decision, Walt strolled behind Fitz and placed his hands on Fitz's shoulders, massaging them with fatherly warmth. Fitz froze to the couch like a gargoyle, terrified. "What's this about culture, Ted? Tell me about it."

"It sounds like bullshit," said Fitz, "but it's not. It's the idea that what we have here is a family where everyone cares and believes in everyone else. Maybe we don't all get along—hell, who does in a family? But we all respect the other guy's right to his job, his friends, his hobbies, his vices. Without a culture, you've got chaos—every man for himself. I don't know about you, but that's not the kind of place I want to live." Under his tarpaulin of emotional reserve, Fitz was flushed with passion. "And our culture is a lot better than most. We do a nice job for our customers and we're fun to work for.

We're not above playing a little hardball on your face, but we'd rather shake your hand. The only people we're really tough on is ourselves, because we demand quality, service, and profits, and we're just not going to settle for anything less. We're good folks, that's all, just plain good folks, every single last one of us. And when we have to cast a few good sheep from the fold, damn it, we'd better make sure as shooting we've got a solid business reason for it. And there is no business reason to cut HR. Shit. We're as lean as a goat already. You cut out our guts big-time last summer. We provide service to the only people who really count—our people. We stay."

"I'd like to know what makes you so special," said Darling. "Don't you think we feel the same way about our Marketing people? No one's shedding a tear for them; no one's comparing them to sheep. Their lives are just as important. They've busted their humps just as much as HR desk jocks. I demand cuts across the board! If there are no cuts at HR, I won't take any in Marketing!"

"Yes you will," said Walt.

"Of course I will," said Darling. "I just don't think it's fair."

"Of course it isn't," said Walt, "but I hope I can count on you to be a team player, Bob."

"Of course you can," said Darling. "I'm sorry. I'm upset."

"Of course you are," said Walt. "We all are. But there will be no cuts in HR over and above the twenty percent I would have suggested even in the best of times. Can you live with that, Bob?"

"Do I have any choice?" Darling slumped down into the depths of the couch, comically morose, hands drooping between his knees, eyes gazing deeply into an infinite pond of green despair.

"You see the solidity of Fitz's argument, don't you, Bob?" Walt pressed, apparently concerned.

"I do," said Darling. Rising and going to the window, he made a number of suspicious choking noises and blew his nose with quiet ceremony.

"Gee, Walt," said Fitz. "Er . . . did I just hear you say that you want me to find twenty percent of my head count?"

"What about it?" said Walt.

"No problem, Walt," said Fitz. "I just wanted to know if I heard you correctly."

"We now proceed to you, Ed," said Walt, his face clear as a baby's butt again. He turned to Sweet, who was lying on the couch, staring up at the ceiling.

"Pardon me," said Sweet, "but I thought we went over this. Cost centers must cut. We all know that. Sales, on the other hand, is the pump that drives our lifeblood—revenues—through the system. So I think I'm very much in tune with the drill when I suggest that my contribution to this effort of spiritual regeneration will be to resist my impulse to deliver easy solutions and cut people. Instead, I'm going to suggest an addition of about . . . oh . . . eighty new sales associates nationwide, at a cost of approximately sixteen million to overall operating expenses during the calendar year. For that increase, I will promise a revenue gain of fifteen points and an impact on operating profit by year end of eight points, or one hundred and twenty million dollars."

There was a silence. Very large, very deep.

"Yeah, well," said Walt, "okay. Don't let the door hit your ass on the way out if you fail to make that number, though, Ed. You know I'm serious."

"No sweat, boss," said Sweet. Lloyd could see he meant it, and he knew why. One: The decision to add a bulk of sales weasels was certainly not made right there and then. Walt and Ed had wired this particular part of the proceedings beforehand. This portion of the pageant was being played just for show. This did not surprise Lloyd. When he had been a consultant, Ed had spent untold hours strategizing with Walt. Much of today's events were, in fact, his scenario of reengineering put into action. Sweet never went into a meeting not knowing how it was going to turn out. Two: Along those lines, he figured Sweet had already found a good part of the promised $120 million lying around in another slush fund that all operating VPs kept squirreled away for the dark days when revenues did not live up to expectations. In other words, Ed had already made his number. The rest was show.

"Well, that's it!" said Lloyd. "Can we eat yet?"

"As a matter of fact, Lloyd, that brings us to you."

Lloyd, who had a feeling that was the case, got up and went to the mirror over the indeterminate piece of furniture by the wall. "Do you think I'm losing it up here in front?" he said, leaning over and peering at his hairline, which he felt moved forward and back, up and down, each and every day, depending on how he was feeling.

"I'd like you guys to know that I've made a decision about our wacky friend over here," said Walt.

"Put me on the beach, Walt," said Lloyd.

"No, Lloyd, I'm not going to fire you," Walt said, and for a moment Lloyd feared he was going to ruffle his hair. "I'm going to make your life a lot more miserable than that."

Lloyd sat on a chair and waited for it to happen. He should have known it was going to happen, but for some reason, he hadn't.

Lloyd Gets the Word

"A major initiative like this—the retooling of an entire culture, its people, its processes, its strategies, all that can't be done without central honchoing by some poor slob who doesn't have any other real defined function. That leaves only one of you in this room, and I believe you know who that is. In addition, the process needs someone thoughtful, decent, human, with a good way with the troops. You can't have a Nazi like Bob over here in charge. You need a good guy. Congratulations, Lloyd. You're it."

"I don't want to do it, Walt," said Lloyd.

"Of course you don't. That's why you're doing it," said Walt.

"Can we talk about this in private?" Lloyd felt as if he was suffocating.

"About tactics, sure," said Walt. "About the substance of my decision, no, Lloyd. And don't worry. I know that the tradition here is for the guy who does the reengineering to be the last one out the door when the job is done. I'm telling you right up front, in public view of your friends and associates, that there are no such plans for you. We have other plans for you, Lloyd, and they're all good. Right, guys?"

Fitz was the first on his feet, but the rest were quick to join him. They surrounded Lloyd and laid hands on him in one way or another, patting him, poking him, and, in one case (which Lloyd believed was Fitz), kneeing him firmly in the butt.

"I'm going to need superauthority over all these guys and quite a few others, to make them do stuff when they don't wanna," said Lloyd. He could feel himself getting into it, the power, the prospect of busy days and nights to come.

"No question, but first, Lloyd, there's the little matter of something closer to home."

"Home?" said Lloyd. Suddenly, desperately, he missed his wife, Donna, his children, Nora and Bob. He wanted to be with them, watching Saturday-morning cartoons in his boxer shorts and T-shirt.

"I think we're fat as a house around here, and by here, I mean headquarters," Walt said. There was a profound, ominous silence.

"What do you think needs to be done?" asked Lloyd, only it wasn't a question.

"What's the current headquarters head count?"

"Five hundred and fifty," said Lloyd.

"Oh, I don't know," Walt murmured. "Let's think about it."

"Most of the staff have been with the company for a significant amount of time," said Fitz. "In addition, they've been promised a certain modicum of job security. I'm not saying this is a major stumbling block, but there is a certain good-faith issue to address."

"I agree," said Walt. "How do we address that issue?"

"With money," said Fitz.

The group emitted a rolling, bubbling chuckle.

"Fact is," said Ed Sweet, really warming to the subject, "I've looked at this issue and I truly believe that we have a seventy-five percent redundancy in a variety of home-office functions. Accounting is now managed by computer and database. What do we need with the people here? Management Information is handled by an independent contractor out of Dubuque. Public Relations we can farm out to a consultant, but that would, I think, be considerably more expensive. We can get the same out of a reamed-out staff right here, or simply disregard the function, like a lot of corporations do these days. Then there's the whole Marketing and Sales area, which is Bob's turf. Correct me if I'm wrong, Bob, but a lot of the stuff can be trimmed here and replaced by decentralized local management under regional supervision."

Lloyd felt himself sinking into the center of his chair, which now seemed very, very soft, until he was just a tiny blip on the top of the upholstery. "Let's get this over with," he said.

"I think we ought to cut New York by fifty percent, Lloyd," said Walt. "Our culture is rooted in the regions. Sure, we have to have people in New York to make sure contracts are fulfilled, essential services provided, and that no larceny is taking place on a local, district, or regional level. But really, what do we need troops there for? Nothing. If the business doesn't work on a local level, we're sunk anyway. I think we should all target about fifty of our best hands and terminate the rest. We'll take up the slack in the boonies. What do you say?"

Lloyd tried on several excellent replies before concluding that there was, in fact, nothing to say, except, perhaps, "I'm leaving now," which he was not going to say. At this point, with salary and bonus taken together, Lloyd made in excess of $200,000 a year. The previous year, he and his wife and kids had managed to save approximately six thousand dollars of that sum. No, Lloyd was going nowhere.

"So we're in agreement, then," said Walt. There was a knock on the door. Nobody moved. After looking them over, Walt clearly perceived that nobody had the strength to carry on except for him. This pleased him. "Let's eat," he said, marching over to the door and swinging it open.

All Over but the Shouting

Walt seemed to be in one of the best-possible moods, and his playful esprit quickly filled the room and crowded out all other sentiments. The men raised their heads and looked at one another and found that, yes, they were all still there. None of them had grown sharp incisors. None had sprouted horns or shaggy pelts. They were still themselves. Things would be all right.

The veal was served with tiny potatoes that were braised in a distant kitchen over very high heat. By the time the nuggets reached them, they were virtually impervious to the fork, and the men were forced to pick them up with their fingers and chew them with deliberation, if not zeal. The veal, however, was a different story. Soft and tender, redolent of lemon and dry vermouth, the medallions yielded to the fork as parchment to summer rain. They ate, and felt better.

Immediately after their entrée, as if by common consent, they fell into an orgy of phoning. There were four phones in the suite, each of which was used, and most of them had cellular babies they could employ if they leaned very far out the window and extended their antennas, necks, and arms as far as they would go. The yattering was intense, and when it wound down, all were ready to leave the ugly events of the morning behind them and party hearty. Lloyd found himself imagining how it would feel to shoot Walt in the face with a full portion of red paint, and he smiled.

Business was like a trip to the moon, really. An adventure unlike any other, in beautiful and strange surroundings, absolutely impossible to describe to those who had not been there.

"Now," said Walt, as they settled down to coffee and butter cookies, "I think we're where we want to be."

"Almost," said a poised voice in the corner.

It was the man in the dark blue suit whom Lloyd had seen in the executive lounge. Amazing I didn't notice him in here before, Lloyd thought to himself. He must have been in the room for quite a while, entering when they were taking their brief phone break.

"Doug," said Walt.

"Walt," said Doug.

Doug

"I suppose I should introduce you to Doug here," said Walt with maximum breeze, "who will be an integral part of our effort—in fact, he will in some way be, you know, leading it, in a sense, seeing that Chicago has placed such importance in our ongoing piece of the corporate pie. It's perceived, at any rate, that day-to-day strategic guidance must be there for us to draw on, and that's what Doug here is all about. Strategy, not execution. Right, Doug?"

"Right, Walt," said Doug. He had not moved, not one single molecule, but he did not look stiff.

"Doug is an enormous executive vice president for the home office in Chicago," Walt continued, as if he were introducing a valued guest contestant who had already won a considerable amount of money on the show. "His title is still being worked out, but the word *chairman* has been mentioned, and nothing would please us more. Say hi to Doug."

Still, Doug did not stand, and he made no move toward them. He was the only man in the room whose jacket was still comfortably draped around his upper body. His shirt collar was buttoned. The suit remained a marvel to Lloyd, who gazed at it rather than meet Doug's eye right at that moment. The suit was not a perfect blue, Lloyd noticed. There was a pinstripe hiding in there, the way three-dimensional constructs hid behind the surface in those Magic Eye books, visible only with the kind of practice that helped one alienate the movements of one eye from the other. Lloyd thought about the fact that he had nearly barfed in front of the new *magister ludi*.

"Thanks, Walt," said Doug. He had, as Lloyd had noticed, a very pleasant, even, contained, moderate baritone that evoked not only the impression of calm and intellect at work but also a slight twist of knowing, sardonic humor that seemed to speak of relative size of human problems in the vast scheme of the universe. Perspective, that was it. Doug carried it, gently, like his fabulous suit.

"I think Chicago would like to know how this division got to this point in time," he said. "There are massive strengths, yes. But the strategic issues, guys. We're looking at a future in which we're an intermediate-size force in a consolidated, global marketplace. In my view, that's a position that's got some serious challenges attached to it, especially with the international arena gravitating toward first-tier players pretty much all the way down the line. Has anybody but me noticed this here? Aside from the operating issues, I mean."

There was a silence as deep as one of those points in the galaxy that are accretions of mass impenetrable to light, matter, or energy. There seemed to be little inducement to breaking it up into its constituent parts.

"We were on a positive growth curve until the second quarter '98," Walt observed somewhat too nonchalantly, "and it wasn't until fourth quarter last year that we knew some alternative scenarios had to be investigated. When it was clear the strategic plan was inoperative, we moved. We are moving now."

"But I think we can all agree this was a management screwup that included all of us, since we're the stewards of this business," said Doug.

"Get to the heart of it, Doug," said Walt. It was anger, Lloyd knew, not fear, that produced that tone.

"You've given yeoman service to the corporate family, Walt," said Doug, staring benignly at Walt. "But Chicago feels that a more substantial oversight and control function needs to be implemented. So one thing you told your excellent cohorts here is slightly off center. My title has been determined. I'm the chairman."

"Well . . . Great!" said Walt. He rose and took the three or four large steps required to cross to the foot of Doug's chair. "Looking forward to working with you," he said, and stuck out his hand.

Doug rose and took it. They shook hands. Everyone else rose.

"Gentlemen, sit," said Doug. They did. All but Walt, who walked with great, delicate dignity to the window and looked out at the street way down below.

"You understand now, men," said Doug, smoothing his perfect hair. "In some regards, you will not even know that I am here. You will continue to report to Walt, who has earned your loyalty, your trust. You and I will enjoy nothing more than a matrix relationship."

A matrix relationship? thought Lloyd. That sounded . . . icky. "Come into my matrix," said the spider to the fly. Nonsense. Good guy, Doug. All of them, good guys. Or else . . . then what?

"It's a little strange, I grant you," Doug was saying. "But this is a gesture that has to be made, both internally and externally. It speaks well for you that the correct steps have been taken this morning without my prompture, steps that I believe will be effective. We need your kind of management on tap if we're going to meet the challenge offered by the Japanese and German ingenuity that's giving us such a pain in the keister and will, we think, continue to do so in the near, intermediate, and outer term. That's why we're bringing you boys closer to dad here. It's a new arrangement, with greater oversight than you're used to. But I think it's going to work. Do you? Be honest."

Lloyd had never felt less desire to be honest in his life. His heart ached for Walt. He wanted to go to him and seize him by the shoulders. Embrace him like a Roman.

"Of course it will," said Walt.

"And you, Walt. Are you prepared to lead, Walt? Under these altered circumstances, are you prepared to exercise your genius for leadership?"

"Nice of you to put it that way, Doug," said Walt, and Lloyd could see he was moved in spite of himself. His face was a roasted maroon hue now, a mix of pleasure, shame, and regret. "Yes, I am" was all he could get out.

Doug, too, was displaying the first suspicion of human emotion. He was subtly glowing, his ears a splendid, almost Victorian purple hue. Lloyd found himself looking at Doug's teeth, which appeared to be extremely tiny and evenly spaced.

"Which one of you is Lloyd?" said Doug.

"Me!" said Lloyd, much too loudly. He stood, then sat.

"I hear you spin things, Lloyd," said Doug, regarding him with slightly sinister amusement. "What's our positioning on this entire reorg? How should we make this thing work for both an internal and external audience? It's a really tough plan. It won't be easy to establish the requisite positive message and avoid any impression of radical change and disharmony."

"It's been a long sixteen months. We've had to make some tough choices and we've made them. Twenty percent of our workforce will be reduced by this time next year. We'll try to do most of it by attrition and one of the best retirement packages in industry history. When we're done, we'll have come back lean, down to fighting weight, with new strategic direction and some new faces you just might come to like. One of those is you, Doug. We'll tell a little bit about you. We'll picture you, too, but always with Walt at your side. Shirtsleeves, I think. Poised over a blueprint or something. You're comfortable together. Two big assets instead of one."

"Sing it, Lloyd," said Fitz, and they all laughed. A good laugh. Strong. Manly.

"Get one thing straight, though. This is not turmoil. This is change. Change for strength, for direction. For the past is behind. The future lies ahead. We're proud to be back on the hunt for double-digit growth, and we're here to stay." Lloyd was really hot now. The spirit of the deep was upon him and he could feel it. "Not that the time for tough choices and decisions is past," he went on as the group regarded him with amazement, as if he were a creature from beneath some undiscovered sea, "because that time is never really past, nor should it be. Change is tough and the road to it is, too. But some things . . . some things never change, have never changed, will never change, not in the one hundred–plus years we've been in business or the hundreds of years we have to go. This company is a family, and we don't give a damn about those who seek to destroy us. We will go on, and we will never, ever, give in. Beyond that? Watch our smoke."

"You can sell that crap?" said Doug, and now there was an ocean of laughter, laughter of relief, of joy. Doug said "crap"! He's an okay guy!

"Good, Lloyd," said Walt. "Let's run with it."

In less than two minutes, the entire group had vacated, gone to their rooms to prepare for the bogus paint battle that would take up their afternoon, before the next sumptuous meal.

All but Walt and Lloyd—Walt because it was his room, Lloyd because he wanted to talk to Walt. And Doug, who was scheduled to take the next plane back to Chicago. "We'll talk," he said quietly to Lloyd as he picked up his overnight bag from the corner. Walt was in the other room, on the phone to his wife.

We will? thought Lloyd to himself. About what?

"Oh, about a lot of things. Mostly opportunities," said Doug, giving Lloyd a nasty start.

If they had just acquired an ultrasenior officer who could read minds . . . man, it was going to be a long and scary year.

February

Lloyd's friend Schoendeinst, a finance guy two floors down, a young man in his forties, suffers a heart attack. Lloyd goes to the hospital and sees Schoendeinst in his pajamas. Lloyd is shaken, and begins to think about issues pertaining to his mortality. We learn more about what Lloyd eats and how, in general, he lives his life from day to day.

Lloyd's visit to his friend rocks him back on his heels. What's life all about, anyway? And how long has he, Lloyd, got—huh? He eats horribly. He drinks as if he is always thirsty. His work consumes him with a variety of passions. And yet . . . life is good. Yes! Filled with lust and beer and the laughter of little children! Money and cars and birdies in the spring!

How Lloyd Spends His Time

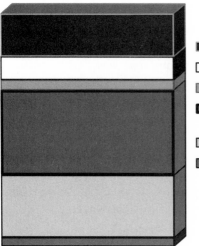

- ■ Daydreaming
- ☐ Kids
- ■ Marriage
- ■ Necessary Functions
- ☐ Drinking
- ■ Eating

4:32 A.M., February 1

The telephone was ringing. Lloyd was having a dream of some sort. Marnie Landauer played some symbolic role. Marnie was a peer of Lloyd's who basically replicated his function elsewhere in the corporation. Chicago, specifically. When she came to visit, they traded information on a friendly basis for a couple of days. Marnie was not one of the bad people. In this dream, however, she kept appearing at the door to Lloyd's office and saying, "Things didn't work out well on the Rand McNally offering." Lloyd's company had no business with Rand McNally. They made maps, and maps were documents that helped you find out where you were going, or perhaps where you had been, or were now situated. These properties were clearly wanting in Lloyd's current cosmos. Hence, he thought, the value of the mapping in his dream mind. This dream, like so many he had experienced lately, had the quality of a nightmare, even though its content seemed relatively benign. In his nocturnal ramblings, Lloyd would be sitting or standing in some remote location, all by himself, feeling relatively calm, when some intruding presence would be felt in his vicinity, an ostensible friend, perhaps, or a minor character in his daily life—the soup man at the corner; his shoe salesman. Out of the blue, this individual would say something that would, for no apparent reason, fill Lloyd with dread and make him awaken with a horrendous start. Sometimes it was nothing more than "Should you be here?" spoken by a crepuscular voice from an unclear location. Other times, it was something more precise, like "Lloyd, come in here. I need you," that sent him reeling in his bed at 5:00 A.M.

This time, Marnie was about to deliver some bad news to him. Lloyd knew it subliminally, even though she wasn't speaking at all, but was merely standing in his doorway, looking at him in silence. In the dream, his phone kept ringing, even though he answered it. Finally, hugely frustrated, Lloyd realized in his dream that he would have to wake himself up in order to stop the ringing. "I have to wake up now, Marnie," he told her while she shook her head, annoyed by his lack of attention to the matter at hand. Lloyd could tell she was worried about his future with the corporation. Why? Lloyd thought he was doing fine. Maybe he wasn't. Maybe that was it.

Lloyd sat up, still asleep, and answered the real phone.

"Hello," he said. He was aware that at this hour, a telephone call signified nothing but death. Nobody received the information they had won the lottery at four o'clock in the morning.

"Yes?" said Lloyd. The connection was very bad. It was a cellular phone call, made from the bowels of some steel-and-iron-encrusted building that barely allowed the escape of telephonics. The line cracked and whistled. Who has died? Lloyd thought. Would he have to hang up and wait to find out?

"Lloyd?" said a tiny voice at the other end of the line. "This is Edie Schoendienst. Hello? Lloyd?"

"Edie?" said Lloyd. He was rubbing his face, hoping that the friction would help to assemble it.

"Uh, Lloyd? Can you can hear me?" There were tears and loneliness and frustration behind the voice. He felt a fist of pure terror tighten behind the scar tissue in his stomach.

"I can hear you, Edie. What's the matter?" said Lloyd.

"It's Rickie," said Edie. Lloyd had known it would be something like that. Rickie Schoendienst, widely known as "the Rickster" throughout the upper tier of senior management, was a highly regarded senior vice president and one of Lloyd's golfing and drinking buddies at the corporation. Edie and Rickie lived not thirty minutes up the road in Connecticut, and Lloyd and Donna had often explored the wide variety of mediocre restaurants in the vicinity with them. It's not that they were friends, really. But corporate friends, yes. In business, the level of true intimacy necessary to establish the special nature of a relationship was very low. Any amount of genuine human feeling was so extraordinary as to be precious beyond measure.

"What is it, Edie?" said Lloyd. "I mean . . . what—"

"We're at Mount Sinai, in Manhattan. Rickie had some kind of a coronary incident is what they're telling me, and they had to put some kind of balloon in his carotid artery, and tomorrow I think he's got to have some kind of bypass. Can you come down here, Lloyd?"

"Yeah, sure, Edie," said Lloyd, "I'll be there in half an hour," and he hung up. As he did so, he realized that he had forgotten to offer a raft of insincere reassurances. Perhaps he would get a chance to do so later.

Lloyd got out of bed and stood there in the darkness, weaving. On the other side of the bed, Donna moved in the darkness.

Donna

Lloyd knew he really should be going. He looked at his wife in the darkened bedroom. After more than fifteen years of marriage, he still enjoyed watching her while she slept, talked on the phone, sorted laundry, worked at her computer, a pencil in her teeth, so intent, she was lost to the yelling children, blaring TV, barking dog at her feet. "Whatchu lookin' at?" she would say when she saw him.

A corkscrew of blond hair had arranged itself perfectly on her cheek while she slept. Except she wasn't sleeping, not really. Nothing escaped Donna's notice, even when she was ostensibly unconscious. Lloyd knew that. Somewhere inside that somnolent form was the totally sentient intelligence of his wife, waiting to speak, capable of immediate action.

"Turn out the light, Leaf. It's time for bed now," she said in a groggy, imperative tone. Perhaps she was not as wakeful as Lloyd had thought.

"I will, hon," said Lloyd. She was sleeping on her side, her hands underneath her cheek and her knees slightly drawn up to her tummy. The sheet had wound itself between her legs and draped itself over one hip quite demurely, but her breasts rose and fell with the regular rhythm of sleep, perfectly formed, white in the streetlamp light from outside the window. Donna slept naked, hating the constraint of anything around her when she was asleep. She was very lean and fit for a woman of any age—Lloyd had seen adolescent girls on the beach besotted with their own narcissistically thonged bodies who couldn't hold a candle to Donna in her tasteful one-piece suit—but the fact that she looked as she now did after nearly forty years of life and two children was a remarkable testament to the power of her will and the efficacy of aerobic and step technology. There was not an ounce of cellulite or flab on the woman, but she wasn't hard, either; she had plenty of body fat. Her muscles were defined but didn't pounce all over you. She was soft but hard. Her breasts were just a little too big for her body. Lloyd regarded the light down of fuzz that rose from between her legs and across her thighs. He felt the blood, suddenly, pounding in his groin. Not insistently, but provisionally. Why was he feeling this way, with his friend in the hospital for Christ's sake? He ought to be up and moving! What kind of person was he?

"Come here, Leaf. I'm cold," said Donna.

"I've got to go, Donkey. Rickie had a heart attack and I've got to get into the city and, you know, help out," Lloyd said. He felt in a frenzy suddenly. Why was he standing here with his dick hanging out when his friends needed him?

"Just for a minute," said Donna. She stretched out her arms toward him in the shadows.

Lloyd got into bed with his wife. In the darkness, she climbed on top of him and he slipped inside of her. She sat up and ran her fingers through her hair, then rode him for a while. He closed his eyes.

"Jesus," said Donna in the darkness. "He's only a couple of years older than you are." She was moving quietly. He could feel her above him.

"Yes, dear," said Lloyd, pulling her down to him and kissing her with all the power he had.

In the Hospital

Lloyd wasn't that late. It was still before 7:30 when he got to the doors of the hospital. It was the wrong door, of course. Instead of ending up at the posh entry pavilion on the west side of the building, Lloyd found himself at the Emergency Room door off the industrial parking lot. A woman jittered by with the uncertain gait of the neurologically impaired. Half her face was immobilized by a stroke, just as his father's had been for the several years between his first incident and his death at the early age of sixty-five. Lloyd thought about his father. Thinking about his father was something that Lloyd found almost impossible, because his father was dead and would never come back. Still, after almost thirteen years, the silence from the corner of Lloyd's being that used to be fully occupied by the massive presence of his father was just as profound and unbridgeable as it had been on that first day, when his mother had called him and told him the . . . news—no, *news* was not the right word. His father's stroke was not news. The drought last summer, that was news. This business of never having his father anymore was a change in Lloyd's plane of existence. There was no moment, no hour or day, in which Lloyd ceased missing his father, and the loss was even worse than it appeared, because the sadness and confusion were so fundamental to his person, they prevented him from ever recollecting the things he needed to remember about his father to move beyond his grief.

A man was sitting in a wheelchair when Lloyd came through the door, dignified, thoughtful. "I've been waiting for three hours," he said to Lloyd in a voice that came from somewhere in the Midwest, Minneapolis, perhaps, someplace broad and flat and cordial, where people did not visit discomfort on one another if they could help it.

"What's the matter with you?" said Lloyd. "You look fine."

"I am fine," said the man, whose head was bald except for a beautifully trimmed frond around his ears and the back of his neck. "I'm being discharged."

"Isn't someone here to meet you?"

"No," said the man sadly. "My daughter works and my son is in Boston."

"Then why are you sitting here? Why don't you take a walk or something? It's . . ." Lloyd looked at his watch. "It's seven-thirty in the morning. If your daughter gets off work at five, you'll be picked up in about ten hours."

"Insurance," said the man, as if that explained something. "While I don't wish to incur a day's additional hospitalization charge, we run the risk of losing coverage, I am told, if I am not safely accepted by a family member and signed for. I had a lung removed."

Lloyd felt intensely queasy all of a sudden. What was in the man's chest? A huge . . . hole? What did they put inside you when they removed something as big as a lung? What would happen to this very nice man if they had to remove a second lung? Could they transplant a third? Lloyd was staring at the man.

"I'm all right," the man said. He was smiling. This man who was condemned to sit all day by himself in a wheelchair, without food, without entertainment except for the little TV that was bolted to the ceiling in the corner and had only one channel, with only one lung and with large brown eyes, Lloyd now saw, big eyes with long, pretty lashes and a quiet melancholy behind them, and wit, too—this man was smiling at him.

"I'm okay. Go on," said the man.

"I will. Thanks. Take care," said Lloyd quite stupidly. He went down the corridor to the elevators.

In the Elevator

A tall, thin, elderly fellow with a buzzard nose and a three-day growth of white stubble stood next to Lloyd with an IV drip on a pole by his right arm.

The elevator finally arrived and the doors slowly slid open. The man with the walking IV had eased in front of Lloyd and was now attempting to get off the elevator. The wheels of his little dolly were stuck in the crack between the elevator and floor beyond. Lloyd picked up the unit and placed it in the hall.

"Thanks," said the man in a weird croak that seemed to bypass his voice box and emerge from his stomach. An inadvertent shiver passed across Lloyd's frame.

"You're welcome," he said, and went into a bathroom at the end of the hallway to wash his hands.

There was a man standing by the window of the bathroom, just past the row of urinals. He was crying. Not big, wrenching sobs, but there were tears running down his face and he was staring into the parking lot below. Lloyd carefully took a leak all the way at the other end of the room, then washed his hands for an implausible amount of time at the farthest sink and left.

Down the hall from the bathroom was a double door. On the door was a red sign posting visiting hours. Weekend visiting hours began at—what was that? Ten o'clock?

"Are you a member of the family?" said a voice behind him. It was a short, wide, businesslike nurse person. She had a clipboard. Lloyd had always

64

been terrified of people with clipboards. If she had had a whistle as well, he might have turned and run. As it was, he felt as if he had just been stopped for speeding, or been caught taking a leak in a public place.

"No," he said. "But I was called by the wife of Richard Schoendienst. He's here. He had a cardiac incident or something." Why did he feel so god-damned lame?

"I'm aware of Mr. Schoendienst's condition," she said briskly. "Mrs. Schoendienst has gone down to Cardiology to speak to Dr. Huffmeister. I believe she was planning on going home at some point to attend to certain personal matters."

"Matters?" The Schoendiensts had two children, one thirteen, a girl. The other nine, a boy. They would be awakening now, to find some kind of care-taker there and their parents gone. While they probably knew what was going on, given the lather that must have been generated by their father's exit in the middle of the night, they still would want their mommy. Lloyd didn't blame Edie for rushing home to make sure they were all right. But he still found him-self a little annoyed that she had forgotten about him. Was that appropriate? To be angry with a woman whose husband had just had a heart attack for being preoccupied, forgetful, even insensitive? "I guess she has a lot on her mind," he said.

"Yes, well, my point is that without her to vouch for you, you'll have to come back during normal visiting hours," she said.

"But I came here . . ." Lloyd was seething. His anger sucked the blood from every part of his body and into his face.

"But . . ." he said again.

"I'm sorry." She turned and made for the nurses' station at the other end of the hall. Lloyd thought of making a dash through the double doors, into the wing where his friend was probably munching on a hot, tasty breakfast. Visions of being escorted out of the hospital by fat, elderly security guards did not appeal to him. "Breakfast," he said to himself.

He went to a phone, dialed the twenty-six-digit code that gave him access to a free connection, and waited. The machine answered on the third ring. "Hi," said Lloyd. "It turns out that visiting hours don't start until ten and Edie must not have known that and went home, and now I can't get in. So I guess I'll . . ." He paused, trying to think about what he actually should do. Grab a meal in the hospital cafeteria, surrounded by doctors and technicians and cleaning staff, people who had been up to their elbows in blood that very morning, who had cleaned up germs and stuff, touched a wide variety of ill-nesses and been touched by them, breathed in billions and billions of microbes, not all of them bad, true, but some they could definitely have lived without, chow down cheek by jowl with sick people suffering from all kinds of unmentionable ailments, and bad food besides? Go across the street and get some eggs, coffee, bacon, sit there for . . . what, two hours? "I guess I'll come home," he said into the phone.

Donna picked up. "Lloyd?" Her voice was groggy. "What time is it?"

"About a quarter to eight."

"Pick up some Sumatran ground for automatic drip, will ya?"

Breakfast at Home

It was twenty minutes or so from the door of the hospital to Lloyd's driveway in his little suburb just north of New York City.

Edie had called as he walked through the door.

"I'm sorry, Lloyd," she said. "Caroline thought she could handle Edward for the morning, but he was kind of hysterical, so I just came home after talking with that horrible heart doctor. Oh, Lloyd." She was crying. Lloyd found it difficult to be angry with her.

"What can I do now, Edie? Tell me what I can do."

"I don't know. I don't think I can get back there until around two, after I leave the kids with my mother-in-law in Queens. Could you be with Rickie for a while between then and now? He's got to be pretty freaked out. It was a mild heart attack, but you know. He's only forty-four." She began to sob now like a little child, without self-consciousness or dramatics, gave herself over to it.

"I'll be there around noon or so, okay, Edie?"

"Yeah, Lloyd. Thanks."

"Okay, then. You going to be okay?"

"Oh yeah," said Edie. "I'll be fine."

Donna had met him at the door, taken his small package of incredibly expensive ground beans, and disappeared into the kitchen. A fine smell of coffee coalescing into a pot emerged from the other end of the house. This quality-coffee thing was pretty much brand-new in his town. A year ago, a place called Alpine Coffee opened in a small shopping strip not far from Lloyd. It featured the usual variety of coffees, a range of strange biscotti, and tiny marble tables with the requisite lumpy sugar cubes. Lloyd hated the place. No matter how few people were in there, it was always crowded, because the three serving people had decided, as a strategy, to lavish all their attention on the first person in line, no matter how inconsequential their order might be. One person ordering one cup of coffee found himself being fawned over by the entire staff, who prepared his napkin, filled his cup, rang up his bill, all while an increasingly impatient line of truly needy people waited, tapping their feet, whistling, grumbling. A coffee bar was supposed to be the apotheosis of mellow. This place was not mellow. Several weeks ago, the astonishing news that a genuine Starbucks was coming to their town had rocketed through the neighborhood. Nothing had galvanized civic pride to this extent since the village had been selected as the site of a new Blockbuster Video. A Starbucks! Pretty soon, people would be comparing them to Seattle!

Lloyd took off his coat and threw it on the living room couch. He was desperately hungry now and wanted food, lots of it. His son, Bob, was lying there, reading a novel by R. L. Stine, their black cocker spaniel, Steve, curled at his feet. Steve's stubby tail wiggled back and forth as quickly as a hummingbird's wings. On the cover of Bob's book, a monster with a kid's body chuckled and leered, a worm growing out of his cheek.

"Hi, Dad," said Bob. Very understated. He had reached the age when a hello kiss was no longer a mandatory exchange, as it used to be, although the boy still liked all the trimmings when he settled down for the night, including the compulsory kiss on the nose for his stuffed polar bear, Pete.

" 'Lo, bagman," said Lloyd, and went through into the kitchen. He could be as cool as a nine-year-old. In fact, it was probably desperately important that he be just that if his future credibility as a functioning parent was not to be permanently damaged. "Eat breakfast?" he said on his way out, as if it were not very important at all, just a thought, you know, no pressure.

"Waiting for you," said Bob. He bent over a page and got up, taking a moment to fall on the dog and crush it under all his weight before hopping again to his feet and thundering into the kitchen.

Lloyd sat down at the kitchen table. His daughter, Nora, was there, doing homework and talking on the phone. She mouthed an extravagant hello to him and kept on talking. Fire could sweep the city. Cats and pepperoni could rain from heaven. Nothing would stop Nora from talking on the phone. It was her art. One day, hopefully, she would be able to get a job doing so, and, like Babe Ruth, she would wonder why someone would pay her money to do the thing she loved. Lloyd wished that for her, since he had sort of given up wishing it for himself. For him, money would have to be enough, and, quite pathetically, it was.

Donna was putting plates of toast and jam and cream cheese and boxes of cereal on the table. Lloyd didn't feel much like cereal. "Anybody want an omelette?" he asked.

"Lots of cheese," said Bob.

"Yeah," said Nora. "Don't forget the cheese." Then she went back to talking to her friend on the phone, something about Mrs. Palsqualuchi, their English teacher, who was feared as farmers fear locusts. Nora's speech, like that of all young people, had an intonation and cadence utterly unlike traditional English. All sentences were canted upward at the end, lilting toward the interrogatory and away from anything definitive. It gave the speech a vaguely Scandinavian sound. This form of discourse required constant interjections by the listener—meaningless grunts and nods—to verify that the minuscule portion of the message had been received, acknowledged, and thoroughly processed and that the speaker could now safely move on to the next six words.

"Nora," he said. "The uptalking is completely out of control."

"Sorry," said Nora. "And Jason?" she said into the phone. "Sorry," she said to Lloyd. "I'm trying." Then she spoke into the phone again, carefully. "And Jason . . . he went parading around the room with the poster folded into a hat?"

"Nora," said Lloyd.

"Oh leave her alone, why don't you," said Donna from her place at the counter near the sink, where she was cutting up a tomato. "They all talk that way."

"I guess so," said Lloyd.

"Yeah, Dad!" said Bob, who was looking at comics. "We all talk this way?"

Lloyd got the eggs out of the refrigerator and took them to the counter. A small tickle was starting in the back of his throat, and he felt a little fleebish. Not anything, probably. Just a woolly insufficiency in his upper brain . . . and a loose gangliness in his kneecaps. Hospitals. Hospitals full of sick people. People coughing up fluids. Bags of soiled green outfits used by doctors in dangerous situations. Food that tasted like stainless steel. Schoendienst there. Poor son of a bitch. Arteries to his heart clogged with fat. Forty-four years old and has to worry every time he tries to climb a flight of stairs, bend down to feed the cat, climb on top of a ladder . . . or his wife . . .

"I hope you're not planning to have one of those eggs," said Donna. "You had one last year and you're not scheduled to have another until April."

"No, I'm not," said Lloyd. Once upon a time, Lloyd had loved eggs. Loved them fried in a basket of white bread, in an omelette with a couple of pounds of bacon on the side, poached with soft slabs of toast dipped in, soft-boiled in little cups that could also be used for eyewash, scrambled with ham and onions, hard-boiled and deviled. So many different ways to die. He took the low-fat American cheese out of the fridge and broke it up into the bowl with the eggs, three of them for the two kids. He ran a little warm water into the mix to augment the amount, then poured it into a pan he had greased with no-fat margarine and then wiped out. The no-fat stuff didn't melt, really; it popped and chuckled and lost solidity, eventually jumping out of the pan vertically like corn kernels when placed under intense heat. But it did the job and tasted like nothing. He let the omelettes grow brown and crusty, the way the kids liked them, then divided them with exaggerated evenness over two plates. He took them to the table and presented them to both children.

"Equal?" he inquired.

"This one has more," said Bob. Lloyd took a fork from the table and removed eight molecules of egg and cheese from the offending plate, then moved it to its companion. "Now the other one has more," said Bob.

"Here," said Lloyd, and showed Nora. "Choose one." Nora took the one that ostensibly had less. Bob took the other quickly, as if he had just put a small but important point up on some running tote board.

It being Sunday, Lloyd ate too much at breakfast. He was not looking forward to going back to the hospital, so perhaps he prolonged the experience even more than usual. It was his belief that since cereal had no cholesterol, it was all right to eat in whatever amounts seemed plausible at the time. His friend Hirsh had the same thought about bagels. At some point in his culinary investigations, Hirsh had discovered that bagels had no fat. At that point, he was suffering under a low-fat diet, the philosophy of which he was constantly refining, expanding. He proceeded, after assimilating this data, to eat no fewer than four bagels on a given morning, and sometimes as many as six. Lloyd felt that since breakfast cereal was high in fiber and low in fat, it was inherently good. He therefore mixed Kix, Fruit & Fibre, Wheaties, cornflakes, Rice Chex, raisin bran, and a small fistful of granola into one gigantic bowl, poured a pint of skimmed milk over the concoction, and plowed his way through it, munching at the same time on a slice of diet white bread lath-

Things Eaten by Donna

Except on the Rarest Occasions

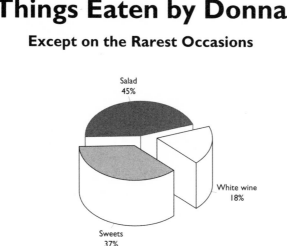

Salad
45%

White wine
18%

Sweets
37%

ered with no-fat cream cheese. By the end of such a meal, he was invariably stuffed as full as a Christmas goose, and not pleasantly, either. This didn't stop him from trying out a similar mix the following weekend. How much more sensible two poached eggs would have been.

Nora had hung up and begun to pick at her scrambled egg. "This is good, Dad," she said. And yet she did not eat, not fully. She would slice a small wedge of egg and cheese off the main body of her serving, fork it, then lift it up to eye level, inspect it closely as if for imperfections in manufacture, then nibble at it until it was gone. Lloyd had given up complaining about this. Compared to the depredations other preadolescents visited on their parents, this seemed tame indeed. At least Nora wasn't like Jennifer Kasoriak, who, according to Nora, "Frenched on the first date." Bad manners were nothing compared to bad values. Donna had joined them at the table with her usual breakfast: a half a bagel with raspberry jam. This was not Donna's favorite breakfast; it was her only breakfast. She had eaten it since 1982, when it had replaced half a bagel with melted Muenster cheese. Lloyd had given up offering her better breakfasts, or more interesting ones, or even teasing her about the tremendous boredom of her continual choice. He just accepted this about her as something that would not change.

Lloyd was beginning to feel fluish. At the start of such illnesses, it was impossible to tell whether it was a malady of the soul or of the physical ecosystem. At this point, he didn't care. He just ate. Every now and then, Donna read him an item from the paper. Invariably, it was something that made him aggravated. After a while, he tuned out. Nora was doing math homework. Bob read him Calvin and Hobbes. Lloyd ate. There was something he wanted to say about how much he suddenly felt they all took for granted and how they should try to talk more.

"Here, Dad," said Bob, shoving a small plastic container across the table to him. "Lookit this."

It was one of those bubbles you get for a quarter at a supermarket vending machine. It was full of small colorful rocks. Bob had removed whatever had come in the container, probably a gushy rubber object, and replaced it with precious stones.

"They're pretty," said Lloyd.

"They're part of my rock collection."

"You know?" said Lloyd. "I don't feel very well."

"We've got nothing to do tonight," said Donna. "How about I rent something and we can just hang out and go to bed early."

"I'm not going to bed early." That was Bob. "I'm not tired." He was never tired.

"Rent me something, too," said Nora. She would never watch it. She would be up until a half an hour past bedtime, doing homework, talking on the phone, engaging her mother in lengthy conversations about hair and the perfect shape of eyebrows. They talked about that kind of thing more and more. Lloyd mourned that he could not participate.

Donna poured herself another cup of coffee, leaned against the sink, and watched Lloyd eat in amused silence.

"You don't eat like a sick person," she said in a rather unkind voice.

"Feed a cold. Starve a fever," said Lloyd. Donna always seemed insufficiently empathetic about Lloyd's discomforts. "Maybe it's because you always feel sorry enough for yourself for both of us," she told him once. "I don't know what you mean," Lloyd had said.

Lloyd was having a little trouble breathing. His stomach felt woozy. The top of his head felt light and removable. What a drag it was being sick! That didn't mean you couldn't have fun. He fantasized about his wife waiting on him hand and foot, worried about his condition, serving him little tidbits, mopping his fevered brow, rubbing his body down with scented oils. "I think I'll go to bed for a while," he said.

"I'll wake you at about eleven o'clock so you can get to the hospital by lunchtime," said Donna.

"Thanks."

"Take the dog out first," she added.

Steve went nuts when he saw the leash. Outside, he dug up two leaf piles and barked viciously at two small girls and a nun who walked by, while studiously ignoring two vaguely threatening high school students who collectively outweighed Lloyd by 120 pounds. Once inside, he got a biscuit, then followed Lloyd upstairs. Lloyd lay down and in a moment was fast asleep.

Schoendienst

Rick was bending over the edge of his hospital bed, attempting to put on a pair of old leather slippers. The back of the slippers were broken down after years of use, the leather cracked, cardboard peeping through. Rick didn't see Lloyd standing in the doorway to the room. But Lloyd saw Rick as he had never seen him before, saw him with the corporate veil down, the man beneath the suit and the pinstripe, beneath the Lacoste shirt and khakis on the weekends, and he felt the weight of his friend's mortality strike him like a hammer on his heart.

Rick was enormous. Not fat, per se. About six feet, 250 evenly distributed pounds. Although he was in his middle forties, Rick had kept all his hair, which he wore close-cropped and parted neatly on the left. Lloyd noticed for the first time that there were flecks of gray and white above Rick's ears. His face, usually taut and rotund and ruddy, sagged a little and came off slightly pale. Perhaps it was the strain of folding his body almost in half in order to put on the slippers. Lloyd coughed to make his presence known. Schoendienst kept at his task, apparently unawares. Wrapped up in himself, maybe. Being sick was like that. The illness sucked out your adult self and replaced it with a narcissistic child, pure and simple in its perception of itself as the center of the world.

In the next bed, there was a tall, thin man of about thirty-five or so, with black hair and a weeklong growth of stubble. He was lying flat on his back, eyes open, stretched out as if in death, his hands neatly folded in a slightly spastic way in the center of his chest. He was drooling, but he didn't seem to mind.

"The Rickster," said Lloyd with no particular expression in his voice. There was a thing in his corporate culture about very specific formulaic greetings. For instance, whenever Stein, his good friend and general manager from Topeka, called on the phone, he always prefaced his remarks with a doleful, repetitive chant of "Lloyd, Lloyd, Lloyd," three Lloyds, not four, six, or two, offered as if Lloyd himself had committed some dreadful act for which there was no possible redress. "Roberto," Lloyd would answer. *"Qué pasarino?"* This exchange was played out year after year, in good seasons and bad, and formed one of many small continuities that made corporate life bearable.

"Lloyd!" said Schoendienst, straightening up. His whole face exploded from the inside out into a charming, warm, boyish smile. Nobody could smile like a sales guy. The key was that they really were happy to see you.

"Thought I would come by and see how you were doing, bud," said Lloyd.

"Really feel terrible, Lloyd. Truly terrible," said Rick. Schoendienst grabbed an enormous Pendleton bathrobe and was busy wrapping it around himself, but not before Lloyd had gotten a full peek at the Rickster's pajamas, which is what really made him feel like crying. No serious grown-up wore pajamas. Pajamas were for kids, or for jerks who wore smoking jackets. Real guys wore sweatpants and a baggy T-shirt. Or boxers. Or even a pajama bottom with no top. But a full suit? With big white buttons and a drawstring for a belt? Little boys wore those. Little boys who were dressed by their mommies. Little boys who were ascared of the dark, and of movies with monsters in them, and things in their closets that munched up little children who weren't careful to close the door well enough. Lloyd looked at the Rickster, whose division grossed more than $100 million dollars a year, and saw little Rickie Schoendienst in his pajamas, Rickie who paid extortion money to the big sixth graders, who never ate as much as he could because he didn't want to get fat, who loved Carmen Barbarini in silence all through the seventh grade and never told her, who wet the bed the first time he went to sleep-away camp, who wore his great, loud, beaming self out where everybody could see and poke at it, because he just hadn't learned any better. Lloyd saw all that when he looked at his friend in those bright, ridiculous red-purple-yellow-and-green pajamas. Then Rick put on his bathrobe and looked like a man again.

"Nice bathrobe," Lloyd said.

"Thanks," Rick said. "Jessie gave it to me for Father's Day." Jessie was Rick's twelve-year-old daughter. "I never thought I would really use the damn thing," said Schoendienst. "But now I'm getting a lot of use out of it. In fact, if I didn't have one, I'd have had to buy one, and I'd probably have bought one that was a lot less comfortable, you know?"

"Yeah, definitely," said Lloyd. There was a small silence, but long enough for both men to realize they didn't want to experience another.

"'Sit you down, father, rest you,'" said Rick. This was not a quotation from *King Lear,* but an oblique reference to the last six-second fade-out of "I Am the Walrus," in which the voice of John Lennon intones that line as if from a great distance. Rick was a big Beatles fan and was constantly quoting little snippets, not to be recognized by the listener, but for his own amusement.

"Sure," said Lloyd, and sat.

What Happened to Lerner

"Have you met Bob Lerner?" said Schoendienst.

"Lerner?" Lloyd looked around him. He saw no Bob Lerner in the room.

"Lerner? Say hello to Lloyd. Lloyd? Lerner." Schoendienst politely swung his arm by way of introduction between Lloyd and the comatose patient in the adjacent bed.

"Nice to meet you," said Lloyd.

"He can't hear you. He's had some kind of brain aneurysm. This is basically what he does. The resident told me he could be doing this exact thing fifty years from now. He has his eyes open for about twelve hours a day and closed for the other twelve. Sometimes his eyes tear for a long time. I guess he's brain-dead. It's funny. All the time at the office, I used to call people brain-dead. 'This guy's brain-dead,' I would say. Or 'That idea is brain-dead.' Lerner here . . . Lerner here is really brain-dead. It's not pretty, is it, Lerner?" Schoendienst changed his voice to a kind of robotized, strobed-out drone. "No, it's not, Rickie. It's a bummer," he said.

Lerner was lying on his back. He did not move. The only sound he made was a very soft gurgle as his mouth and throat attempted to deal with the arduous chore of breathing through all that spit. Lloyd shook his head, as if a fly was bothering his ears. Ook, he thought.

"Three kids and a very nice wife. I hear they came to visit him for a while but now not that often."

"Fitz says we're going to max out," said Lloyd.

"What kind of numbers are we talking about?" Rick was very excited. His face had moved from white to a nice deep rose.

"Two-x," said Lloyd. This meant their bonuses would be twice as big as last year's, because their division had made almost 20 percent more. In the case of the ultratopmost, that could mean six hundred grand or more this time around. The average enormous cahuna would gross three hundred fifty on the thoughtful gift. Good fellows like Lloyd could see, maybe, one twenty-five, which in Lloyd's greedy fantasies quickly became two.

"I've been very sick, Lloyd," said Schoendienst. "Tell Fitz he shouldn't aggravate me with the bonus. Tell him he should err on the side of generosity."

"Just don't tell me what you get," said Lloyd. Schoendienst was very well paid, as he should have been. His bonus could easily be twice Lloyd's. That kind of knowledge is an extremely unpleasant weight on a business relationship. No one ever spoke of it. Their common hunger for lucre, however, was an open and proudly shared heritage, one of the chief unifying forces that kept the executive team together in bad times as well as good.

There was a clatter outside the door of the room and a steamy, starchy smell—gravy? buttered corn?—wafted into the room. "It's lunchtime," Schoendienst said with beamish enthusiasm.

A nurse carrying a tray had entered the room with brusque determination and was arranging Lerner's meal on a rolling tabletop beside the bed. It smelled like fish. A lot.

Schoendienst had eagerly hopped back into bed and covered himself up to his waist, neatly. "I wish I could offer you some, Lloyd, but it's so horrible, I want to eat the whole thing," he said.

"Don't worry about it," said Lloyd. "I'll just catch a bite at the Palm. I'm thinking of having liver and bacon with a lot of onions. Maybe a nice frosty martini. Cup of coffee afterward."

Like all true men in his corporation, Lloyd was a big coffee drinker. So far, nobody had bothered him about it. Rick was another story. The Excess Police, worried about his health, had already made its presence known in a variety of areas, coffee being only one of them. So every now and then, Schoendienst tried to cut down on the stuff and replace it with bottled water. Always, he failed. Same for cigars. Rickie had a lot of bad habits that helped to define him as an admirable and lovable human being. What would he become when stripped of his most unique ways of seeking the kind of pleasure that was harmful not to others but to himself? What would I be without my vices? thought Lloyd. I wouldn't know who I was.

The nurse was in a big hurry. "Mr. Lerner!" she said, and Lerner did, it seemed, summon 1 or 2 percent of the human capacity to focus attention and vaguely offer his mouth for filling. "That's good, Mr. Lerner," said the nurse as she began shoveling a steamed white lump of very white fish, bite by rather large bite, into Lerner, who did not appear to be as much chewing as inhaling.

"What is that?" Lloyd said to the nurse. "Some kind of fish?"

"Yeah," said the nurse. "Fish." She fed on.

Gee, thought Lloyd. I wonder how he can chew that fast.

"Let's have a little vegetables now," said the nurse.

"Where is mine?" said Schoendienst under his breath.

"I'm sure it's coming, Rick. Although I hope you didn't order the stuff they're feeding Lerner here."

"I most certainly did not!" exclaimed Schoendienst brightly. This was one of his most attractive qualities, the ability to shift moods entirely within the space of a nanosecond. This, too, seemed to be almost exclusively the province of salespeople, who needed to trust their emotions and summon up a convincing face at a moment's notice. "You get to circle whatever you want off a specific menu tailored for your affliction," Schoendienst went on. "So I, you know, can't eat everything for a while—like bacon would be out of the question, or ham, or shrimp, or even a T-bone with lots of fat on the edge, or macaroni and cheese smothered with Parmesan, or even peanut butter, I guess. . . ." Here he paused for a minute and stared into the air around his bed. "I used to live to eat; now I eat to live," he said. "I ordered a triple chicken breast, which they serve without any skin—that's okay—and two baked potatoes with fake sour cream and three salads and four rolls and a quadruple fat-free yogurt for dessert."

"Sounds delicious," said Lloyd. "Or at least plentiful."

"Yeah. Plentiful. That's me."

"Here we are!" said a nurse the size of a defensive lineman, who had entered carrying a tray. She had a helmet of blond hair cut very short and a ruddy, jolly face. She was fat, yes, but very solid, with nothing jiggling at all, everything stuffed tight as a liverwurst in the white shiny sateen of the uniform.

"How's my big boy?" she said, fussing with the tray on Rickie's tabletop.

"Big boy hungie," said Schoendienst, giving Lloyd a wink.

"Got a lunch here, there are villages in Ireland haven't seen this much food since 1916," said the nurse. "And it's all good stuff for you, too, Rick. Nothing's gonna kill you here."

"Thank you, Kathy," said Rickie. "This is my friend Lloyd."

"Lloyd, in honor of your visit, I believe we'll let the Big Bopper here feed his fine self." Lloyd, who was scheduled to meet a public relations consultant in thirty minutes at a very fine restaurant, got a stab of hunger and shifted in his chair. His wife was busy, having descended into a vat of boring chores that would inevitably end in a brief trip to Lord & Taylor, not to buy anything, but to return it. Donna bought tons of stuff. Kept a fraction of it. Kids were in karate. Why not run up a legitimate expense? This was even the chairman's productivity consultant. What could be more assiduous than that?

"Looks good, don't it?" said Schoendienst.

"Yeah," said Lloyd.

The nurse, Kathy, had arranged the tray on its movable table, tucked a large cloth napkin under Schoendienst's chubby chin, and retired to the door.

"Perkins," she said to the other nurse, who was at that moment wiping off Lerner's chin, which was covered with fish, potato, applesauce, and cherry pie. "Finish up there and then help me in three nineteen, 'kay?"

The second nurse said nothing, just kept working with a grim, slightly hostile resolve. Attitude there? thought Lloyd. The way she fed the poor brain-addled slob. The failure to respond to her superior. The lack of greeting to the two other people who occupied the room with her at this time. Don't want to be sick and in her care, thought Lloyd. Don't want to be around that kind of woman at all, ever. After several minutes more of this, she left.

"Yum," said Schoendienst. "Want something?"

"No, man," said Lloyd. "You dig in."

It was like watching a kid eat, but Lloyd didn't mind. It was Rickie who had held his head just last year in New Orleans at the national sales meeting, when Lloyd had enjoyed one stinger too many and ended up lurching into Bourbon Street to toss his cookies in the gutter. Rickie had cradled his forehead, being real careful not to get vomit on his blue nautical blazer and khaki pants, but never once had he mentioned the incident, not to Lloyd, not to any of their compatriots, not to anyone.

"Come here and sit down, Lloyd. Tell me about things," he said.

"Fuck the office," said Lloyd.

"There you go," said Schoendienst.

Behind him, there was a sound of a person choking on a piece of fish.

Lerner was emitting a tiny liquid gurgle in the back of his throat, which was accompanied by a very faint wheezing. By the time Lloyd had turned to look at him, the wheezing had grown more desperate. The most horrible thing was the discrepancy between the unconsciousness of Lerner's mind and the profound and immediate comprehension by his body that his life was about to be terminated if some assistance did not arrive immediately. He began hacking spasmodically, attempting to eject the offending bone lodged in his throat. A little alarm buzzer of some kind went off by Lerner's bedside. It sounded like a heart monitor to Lloyd, who had watched a lot of medical television shows throughout his life, starting with *Ben Casey,* where the action was mostly emotional, to *ER,* where people had their chests cut open and probed on camera every week. This one sounded like the kind of alert that is issued when somebody's heart goes into arrhythmia. Fortunately, not fifteen seconds later, about six medical personnel tore into the room with an emergency cart loaded with all kinds of gear. They clustered around Lerner's bed and began pounding and socking and probing him intensively, while at the same time carrying on a blasé and quite sociable conversation among themselves. If Lloyd could hear them properly—which was difficult, since they spoke not only softly but in the shorthand of people who are together sometimes twelve or fourteen hours a day—it was about one of them, the most attractive woman of the group, who did not have a date for Saturday night. She was taking some ribbing about it. By this time, Lerner's entire respiratory system was in some kind of arrest. The team had torn off his gown and was working on him, but it was difficult, due to Lerner's agitation.

"Jesus," said one after a time. "What is this? Fish?"

"Let's get him out of here," said another one. They rolled a stretcher alongside the bed and quickly moved Lerner onto it by swift and capable manipulation of his bedsheet, flipping him like a pancake onto the awaiting surface and strapping him down, disconnecting tubes and wires, and always pounding on him, excavating his oral cavity, puffing in his mouth, shooting him up with liquids to jump-start his system. They started rolling him out. The entire emergency procedure had consumed less than two minutes.

Somewhere inside Lerner, Lloyd thought, there was a towering gray wall of despair and fear and grief and terror that transcended the bubble of rotten tissue that made his brain inoperable. His eyes were rolling in his head as he trundled by on the stretcher. Then he was gone. The room was very quiet. Lloyd looked at Schoendienst, who had, of course, stopped eating and was sitting looking at Lloyd, at the bed where Lerner had been, at his lunch, at the doorway through which Lerner had just gone. Lloyd wanted to say something but didn't know what. Schoendienst seemed as though he wanted either to cry or to laugh. Lloyd couldn't tell which. All he knew was that this silence that existed now between him and Schoendienst was intolerable. It filled Lloyd up with terror that it would never end.

"I think he's got a pretty good case for a lawsuit," said Lloyd.

"Yeah," said Schoendienst. "Man. Killed by a piece of fish. What a way to go."

"That nurse was just shoving that fish in there like she was stuffing a piñata or something," said Lloyd.

"Yeah," said Schoendienst. "But . . . it's not like he was living a quality existence or anything."

"Yeah," said Lloyd.

"Besides . . ." Schoendienst looked down at his plate and noticed there was a buttered roll there. He focused on it thoughtfully. "He could be okay. Once they get him up to ICU, I'm sure they'll straighten things out. He'll probably come waltzing in here later with a brand-new johnny on, tanned, rested, and ready for freddy."

"No question," said Lloyd.

"Man." Schoendienst picked up the roll, regarded it as Hamlet might have regarded the skull of poor Yorick, and bit into it. "No family. No pals around. Just scared and alone. So alone, man. I can't stand to think about dying that alone."

Lloyd thought about all the people who had died on him. His dogs; his friend Jutkowitz, who jumped off the roof of a Howard Johnson's Motor Lodge in Boston at the age of twenty-four. Lloyd had to identify the body afterward. Jutkowitz looked good except for a little yellow bruise on the side of his chin. Lloyd thought about his father, about his father's death; then he didn't think about that anymore.

"Everybody dies alone," said Lloyd.

"Thanks for coming in to cheer me up," said Schoendienst.

"I make house calls, too," said Lloyd.

Afterward, on the way to a $125 lunch, Lloyd stopped off at Nobody Beats the Wiz. It had started out as the Wiz and adopted the longer name after a particularly successful ad campaign featuring that phrase as the slogan. The thing was, a lot of places beat the Wiz. Sometimes Lloyd thought that just about everybody was capable of beating the Wiz. For a while, by way of protest, Lloyd resisted using the entire legal name of the store. It made him feel stupid. But after several years, he gave in and began saying "I'm going down to Nobody Beats the Wiz" when he was going there. He always attempted to sound very ironic when he said it, but for the most part, he was pretty sure he failed and just came out sounding greedy and enthusiastic about the cameras, computers, Discman models, and other gizmos he could buy there.

That day, Lloyd bought himself a $450 boom box for his office, one he'd had his eye on for at least a week. It represented a significant upgrade from the one he now had, which was a little tinny in the lower registers, particularly on the hip-hop funkadelic stuff he liked.

Fifteen minutes after he got home, Lloyd spiked a fever of 102. He did not get out of bed again until the following Thursday. When he arrived at the office, he found Doug and Walt in conference in the boardroom. Walt was leaning forward with tremendous intensity, pouring ideas into Doug's face. Doug was looking at him.

March

Ron, about ten years ago

By the end of the first quarter, things are going very well for Ron Lemur, our whining, social-climbing, intensely ambitious young MBA with a heart as big as all indoors and the moral barometer of a hyena. No life to speak of, but that's not necessarily a bad thing. It makes him the complete business animal. He works all the time and is always ready to work more. He believes in business, in the concept of business as a dignified occupation, like the Law, or Medicine. Trained at Wharton, where it's all about manipulation of assets and balance sheets, then at a small subsidiary of General Electric. "I was built for the eighties and forced to live here," he says, almost as often as he says to other people, in a completely insincere way, "Thanks for making a difference." Then he winks. Many people don't like Ron. But Lloyd does. He finds Ron's superficiality and false jollity refreshing, and Ron's obsession with minutiae is a convenient asset for Lloyd as a manager, making up for his own inability to concentrate on more than one thing at a time.

A word about the name Lemur. In French, *Le Mur* means The Wall. This fact has no relevance, except that it does explain why no one in the Lemur family has ever considered changing it, in spite of the fact that the name makes people think of an animal, and not a very dignified animal at that.

Ron today

79

March 12: Ron at the Office

It was one of the great ones, the apotheosis of the kind of day that marks a man as a player. Or so Ron thought as he sat in his office way after closing time, his big burnished door shut to keep the world away, four juicy, sparkling lines of cocaine laid out on the shiny desktop below his nose.

"Snork!" said Ron. He drew the smallest of portions into his left nasal receptacle, then he put one finger on the side of his right nostril, compressed it, and drew a huge honking lugee up the tube and into his brainpan.

"Ootch!" said Ron.

There was a knock on his door. His heart leapt into his mouth and fluttered there for a long second or two.

"Who is it?" he demanded in his best executive baritone.

"Is cleaning!" said the Croatian maintenance woman, Rosa, who liked to engage Lemur in conversation whenever she could. With her rudimentary command of English, Rosa believed Ron to be a very nice man who was uncommonly interested in everything she had to say. She did not pick up on the giant tectonic plate of irony that underlay Lemur's false, bright manner.

"Is my cousin to stay now with us from Belgrade!" Rosa would exclaim in that effervescent burble that characterizes pidgin communication, particularly in subordinate situations.

"Not to be kidding!" Lemur would reply, his face lighting up with pleasure and sincere interest. "Having room to comfort so many?"

"Is family," Rosa would say, and both would nod at each other as if the limits of words had been reached and nothing but unspoken communication would now suffice.

"Not now, Rosa!" said Lemur this time. His head was buzzing quite nicely, and he had three more towers of the crystalline drug to put where it might do the most good. Rushing the process, or losing a fleck of the precious matter, was most retrograde to his desire. Getting busted by the cleaning woman, on the other hand, was also not the anticipated end to a successful day.

"Okay! I clean later, then!" said Rosa, and waddled off down the hall, pushing her movable trash basket and cleaning tools ahead of her on the dollied platform.

"Njork!" said Lemur, sucking up approximately an eighth of a gram into his right nostril this time. "What it be!" he exclaimed to the empty room.

He cheerfully considered the television set in his office, which was always set on CNBC. He watched the closing stock prices at the bottom of the screen for a while and felt his head take off from the rest of his body and circle like a crazed banshee around the office. "What it is, what it is, what it is, what it is and la da da da dum de dem," he muttered under his breath. The phrase, at least in part, was the central lyric in a song by Alanis Morissette. Ron had seen Alanis Morissette on the MTV music awards and found her sense of injured entitlement foxy. He also liked her hair, which she whipped back and forth while running gracelessly around the stage like a cow tormented by picadors.

Ron leaned back in his fifteen-hundred-dollar Herman Miller executive recliner (inherited from a recently decruited staff vice president) and reflected on the triumph of the day: twelve meetings of one form or another, four excellent meals, including two separate breakfasts—one downstairs at a restaurant he favored, the other standing up, grazing from the muffin array provided for someone else's early-morning gathering—about three hundred phone calls, several unfragrant social interactions in various corridors, hallways, and elevators, then, at 6:30 P.M., a little nose candy in preparation for the night to come. . . . Life was swell in American business. Anyone who said otherwise didn't have a corporate job.

"Whew doggies," he said, and rubbed his gums with his index finger energetically. There were still two lines awaiting his exit from the office, but there would be time for those. Didn't want to peak too soon. Didn't want to top out and be grinding his teeth by ten or eleven, just when the clubs were getting going and there were people to make and do. He was meeting Emily Beatrice-Nardozzi at nine for dinner and did not want to be too fucked up. An editor at a Condé Nast magazine by day, a stoned exhibitionist lunatic by night, Emily was a massive woman of tremendous abilities and complexities.

He once more drew the contents of his nose into his head, but more gently this time, more thoughtfully. He turned in his swivel chair to the credenza behind him and slid a drawer open. The drawer was empty except for a bottle of vodka that lay on its side at the bottom. Ron twisted the top open and took a contemplative blast of the clear, warm beverage.

"Ka-ching!" he said. He was really looking forward to his date with Emily. She was tall, at least five eight, slender, with fine blond hair that she generally wore in a long braid down her back or, at times, in a Carvel twist at the top of her head. Ratio of muscle to body fat was quite good. A jaunty little nose and a spray of freckles across her cheeks and brow. In short, a babe. If this callow judgment of what others might consider a substantial, ambitious, intelligent, and sophisticated woman of the late twentieth century seems somewhat jejune, it must be mentioned that, for one who was good-looking, relatively affluent for one of his generation, and always on the prowl, Ron had virtually no life outside of business. One could say he was unlucky in love, or simply bad at it, but the truth was, he liked things that way. Beneath his eleven-hundred-dollar suit and fabulous demeanor, Ron generally experienced significant problems with humanity of either gender. Lately, he had begun to tell people, "I have trouble thinking through problems and working out possible solutions." This turned out to be a description that he had seen in the *Wall Street Journal* one morning about a dog who was benefiting from daily doses of Prozac. Ron read it several times and thought it described himself perfectly. He clipped it, put it on the wall behind his desk—his museum of personal effluvia—and used the concept in conversation liberally, he liked it so much.

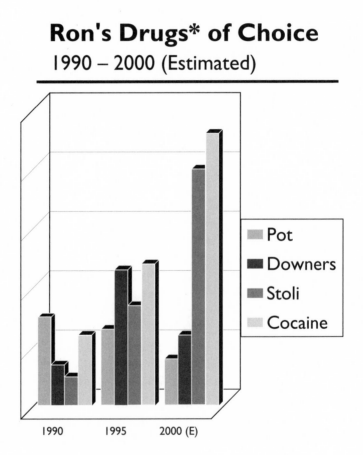

Ron's Drugs* of Choice
1990 – 2000 (Estimated)

* Subject to availability

Speaking about Prozac, Ron wasn't above taking a little bit of it all the time. Also scotch, beer, red wine, white wine, vodka, gin, Campari with lime, Rémy, and, sometimes, very cold champagne, in that order, pretty much. Oh, and pot. Not a lot of pot. Just a joint now and then, like no more than three or four times a week. And Ecstasy, when it was around, of course.

"I was built for the eighties," he told friends often, "but I'm gonna die in the nineties." And it was quite possible that he would, too, and happily.

A warm glow was creeping through Ron's body now, liquefying his nerves, which were quite jittery, for some reason. Smooth and sharp. Raw and mellow. Jangling like an alarm bell and humming like a well-oiled turbine. Ron stared out the window and felt everything very deeply. His heart and mind were bubbling over. There wasn't a thing in his head. He had attained a state of perfect Zen fullness, which, of course, was emptiness. *Trés* awesome, thought Lemur. *Beaucoup.*

Some of today's meetings had been long, like the one with Madeline Marmoset, if that was indeed her name, in which several vision statements had been worked out that would never see the light of day. It was Ron's belief, borne out through long experience, that most meetings were 100 percent bullshit. The crucial thing was simply being there, a very existential concept that was not lost on his otherwise quite literal mind. The meeting with the vision meisters had taken more than three hours, two hours and fifty-seven minutes of which were completely fucking intolerable. They parsed words. They kicked around concepts. They bandied core issues. The whole thing was a huge hot-air vehicle waiting for the nearest pin, as far as Ron was concerned, but you couldn't tell it by the way he had acted. Man, he was engaged, even though, he had to admit it now, he had exited the room more than eight times during the session to "check on his messages" and otherwise give the appearance of a junior senior executive in high play. While out of the room, he scheduled four separate free meals that would pay off for him in the near and intermediate term.

"Come to mama," he told the third line of cocaine.

Schleck! said his nose.

As long and intolerable as was the central meeting of the day, there were three or four impromptu meetings he scored during his breaks. At 11:32, for instance, he met Fitz, the Human Resources nabob, on the way to grab a complimentary soda in the corporate amenities bar.

"Where you been?" said Lemur, snaring a decaf diet Coke.

"Houston," said Fitz, who, truth be told, thought Lemur was an inconsequential nerd with a mean streak, but, as he told Lloyd one night at the Palm, with four pounds of rare meat between them, he "recognized the cold, brutish excellence with which Ron managed his function."

"Bad?" Ron had inquired, drawing content out of the bleak expression on Fitz's face. For all he knew, it could have been the Pay-Per-View event on the hotel TV that had left the guy cramped and embittered. But he took a shot on the possibility that it was the business meeting out there that had put Fitz off his food.

"Nah," Fitz said. "A little concerned out there about Verblin."

"Yeah?"

"Guy wants to fire everybody who works for him," said Fitz, gazing with an odd intensity at Lemur.

Was this some kind of a test? "Not a good sign," said Ron. "Easier to fire his ass than destabilize the entire organization."

"Good, Ron," said Fitz. He gave a sly grin and drew himself a cup of the incredibly strong decaf that Lloyd had brewed some six hours previously. "See ya," Fitz said, and winked.

Ron knew that he had passed. A small test, granted. But in some larger sense, there were no small tests. Not in the current operating environment, in which the entire situation was deeply in flux, all the time. Two points on his tote board was not something to be sneezed at.

"Sneeze this!" Ron chortled, and suddenly he could not catch his breath. He settled for another noseful of Peruvian marching powder. "Yum!" he practically yelled. Got to chill, he thought. His brain was jamming in his skull like a bee in the petals of a buttercup, trapped, but free to engage in a wide variety of excited motion.

Ron ran his fingers through his hair. It was still thick. But he knew something nobody else knew. He knew that every morning his comb came away with sixteen or more strands of curly, thick, beautiful frondage. He would be bald, one day, or at least sport one of those noxious widow's peaks that graced the heads of the pompous, overpaid fortysomethings who were his bosses. Then he would hang himself with his suspenders.

In the afternoon, Ron had several crucial interchanges that he now savored mightily while tenderly sampling his postnasal drip. Like all totally necessary and satisfactory meetings, these were not characterized by length. In one case, it lasted fourteen seconds.

"You doing okay on that Lewinger thing?" said Walt to Lemur as he passed him in the hallway at 3:15 P.M.

"Right as rain!" said Lemur, who had no idea what he was talking about. That situation was in Lloyd's camp, and Lloyd had seen fit not to burden him with either knowledge or duty in pursuit of it.

"Good show, Don," said Walt, moving majesterially past.

A good exchange, no question. True, Walt had shown insufficient cognizance of Ron's name, but that could be easily dealt with. He hadn't gotten it wrong, per se. He had rendered it into one syllable, which was correct, and had the vowel and second consonant right. If one wanted to take a positive spin on it, Walt had got Ron's name 66 percent correct. That was passing in any school Lemur had ever attended. Yet another brief meeting was taken standing in the coffee enclave, with Darling, of whom Ron was very frightened. It was well known, however, that Darling liked jokes, the dirtier and less politically correct, the better. And on this day, Ron had one.

"Mr. Darling!" said Ron. This puffed-up tone was often taken among senior types who didn't feel honorific toward one another but had to seem that way. In assuming it, Ron was craftily promoting himself to their ranks.

"Mr. Lemur," said Darling. Darling was rooting around in the refrigerator, looking for something to eat or drink. He eventually came out with a diet Fresca, popped it open, and took a prodigious pull.

"So listen to this," said Lemur, leaning against the counter and assuming his man-of-the-world demeanor. Darling looked at his watch, and, in truth, Ron had to be back to his meeting in the next few minutes or would be counted absent without leave. "This Chinese guy and his new wife are on their honeymoon and they're having a great time, really going at it, and the wife says to the husband, 'I do whatever you want. Whatever you want, I do.'" For the wife, Ron assumed a slightly higher and somewhat-accented tone of an Asian woman, but not grotesque; a believable voice, one not likely to offend or tip off the punch line. "And the husband says, 'Okay, honey, how 'bout a little sixty-nine?' And the wife says, 'What? You want shrimp with broccoli?'"

Darling did a tiny spit take then, although no Fresca escaped his mouth, and Ron knew that the portly and essentially humorless marketing guy would shortly tell the joke to his staff, who would laugh politely but less enthusiastically than they might have if the teller had not been their superior.

"Good one, Ron," said Darling on the way out.

"Yessss!" Ron gave himself a mental high five when Darling had departed. Then he went back to his regularly scheduled meeting, which was taking place in the boardroom and concerned the use of personal credit cards for company expenses, a common form of financial abuse.

Ron's favorite interface of all, however, had taken place in the men's room. "We have the future of the corporation in our hands," Ron had said to Burbage, whom Ron viewed as an enormously senior financial guy who could truly shape his existence.

"There you go," Burbage had said. This particular reply had been tearing like wildfire through workplace America in the middle of the decade. It was indulged in mostly by people from the middle of the continent who were older than thirty, and it implied several things: first, that the listener acknowledged that that speaker intended to entertain someone, primarily himself, and was on some level succeeding, although not very well, and, second, that the effort at amusement was not unexpected, since he or she could reasonably be expected to "go" on in exactly this way if given the chance all day and night unless promptly discouraged.

The lights were on all over the city now, and Ron opened the side drawer of his desk and extracted a small but very fine pair of Nikon binoculars.

Across the Avenue

Ron looked at the honeycomb of lit-up offices opposite his own. There were some he looked at in particular, having researched the building in question during the sixteen weeks since he had been promoted last and given this A-class office. The binoculars were very good, and if he turned out his lights, leaving on perhaps just the little tungsten bulb that lit only his blotter, he could peer at figures at satisfactory size and clarity as they went about their business. In one area down the block and across a large plaza, office workers bent to chores over their desks, drawing boards, copiers, sorting, stamping things, gathering together in some conference room locations. In another, he liked to watch a dentist, fat and very bald, with tiny legs and petit dancer's feet, as he dug into the gums of a succession of miserable patients. Ron could see him yakking away at them as he drilled and reamed and packed and drained. He rubbed his gums absently. It had been a while since he had gone to the dentist. Sometimes they were not as pink and hearty as they should be. Chet, his former boss, had endured gum surgery several years ago. He had come in looking really weird, his mouth packed with some kind of plastic material, and he had suffered intensely, like someone who had been shot and had to recover his stamina over a considerable period of time.

Glorp! went Ron's ears, nose, and throat. He swallowed a fair-sized hair-ball of sputum and felt the cocaine tickle the back of his epiglottis. Humming, he picked up the binoculars again.

The cubicle that Ron was looking at now, the one he'd been intending to spend his time with all along, was on the fortieth floor of the office tower adjacent to his, no more than a hundred or so yards across the ether. It was the office of an extremely crazy young office worker of middle-management rank who rated good space, not great space, but with excellent appointments. She looked to be about thirty-five or forty, dressed very well, tending to short skirts that rode up on her butt when she leaned manfully against the front edge of her desk to tackle some serious financial issue with another key player. She had medium-length rather wispy brown hair that she wore poking up at various angles quite fetchingly, held aloft usually by one long, capacious barrette or colorful elastic circlet she wore, when not in use, around her wrist. Ron took to watching her work one evening, then found the following day he was looking forward to doing the same again. Each night, he spent longer at it. She worked very late a lot of the time, entranced by the spreadsheet material that lay before her on her work space. She drank a lot of diet Pepsi. Ron watched her drink can after can, and after seven o'clock, when all the lights were out except hers in her row of jewel boxes, she occasionally smoked a cigarette. She didn't wolf it down or anything; she just smoked it, all the way down to its filter, then sat the filter up vertically until it was good and dead, then threw it carefully away in an empty soda can. Ron found that after twenty minutes or so of this, one of two things would have happened. Most of the time, he had grown pleasantly bored and, refreshed as hell, was ready to hit the street with a whole new, positive attitude, as if he had just seen a good pal in a bar and had exactly the right length conversation for that particular friendship. But sometimes, when the woman was in a ruminative mood, drinking or smoking or just lazing away in dreamland a little, Ron found himself getting a small but distinctive hard-on. Like now.

This night, incredibly, something very strange and wonderful was going on. Ron could feel it. It was a special moment for this woman and he was experiencing it with her! He felt graced. She went to the light switch and turned off her fluorescents, leaving nothing but a small desk lamp to illuminate her movements. She then moved to a boom box she kept on her credenza, fished around in several CDs that lay scattered on the surface of the furniture, and put one on. It looked to be something very up-tempo, because she started to dance immediately. She threw herself, thrashing her hair around and hopping in a discombobulated way, hitching and weaving, at one point launching herself horizontally through the air and landing facedown on the couch. Then she flipped over on her back and stared up at the ceiling. Ron wiped away several droplets of spittle that had escaped his mouth and made their way down his chin. The woman abruptly rose in one sinuous motion and went to the boom box and took off the CD. She walked to the window and looked across the chasm directly into Ron's magnified gaze. Ron found himself looking full into her face. She was average-looking. Attractive, certainly. Nice eyes, big and brown and . . . a little soft? Something dreamy there. Pronounced nose, nothing fixed about that one, but not a beak, either, just an honest nose that said, Take me for what I am. Ron liked her nose. He wanted to lick it. High cheekbones, slightly Asian cast to the eyes.

It was hard to believe this woman didn't know that Ron was looking at her. He felt an enormous lump collecting in his throat and gagged it down.

"Hurk," he said. A little acid secreted into the back of his mouth.

He didn't want to break eye contact. Was there a glint from his field glasses? Did she know he was out there? Did she care? He pulled the magnification back a little, so he could see her whole upper torso, which was quite well defined. She worked out, definitely. Now that he could see her closely, he revised her estimated age downward radically. He had imagined her a dedicated campaigner, somewhat war-weary, long practiced in the corporate arts. Now it was clear she was a gifted newcomer, not a month over thirty, possibly as young as twenty-six or -seven. Just about his age.

The woman seemed to be scrutinizing him. His was probably the only dim light on within three floors of his office tower, since most of his corporation had called it quits at least an hour before, particularly the two floors below him, which were filled with accountants and staff lawyers and such. A crafty look had invaded her contemplative features, a tilt to the side of her mouth, a conspiratorial glint in her eyes. She stood facing Ron across the divide, legs planted dynamically apart, her long, tendril fingers playing with the bottom hem of her blouse.

Suddenly, in one fluid motion, with no preamble whatever, she did two things at once. First, she stuck out her tongue like a third grader, and, at the same time, she lifted her blouse with lightning swiftness and exposed her bare tummy and marvelous chest. Her breasts were small but exceedingly round, and around them, pushing them up and together, was one of those Wonderbras, which can do so much for women who have anything at all to work with, and nothing for those who don't. She had the blouse up for no more than two seconds, one of which Ron spent looking at her face. His jaw dropped so far open, he felt the hinge pop.

The woman then turned on her heel, grabbed her navy blue sport jacket, tossed her Hermés scarf around her shoulders, stuffed a laptop into a thin leather briefcase, checked her jacket pocket for keys, and exited her office without turning out the light.

Ron Freaks Out

Ron leapt to his feet. He had no time to lose.

He polished off the remainder of the cocaine and vigorously wiped off his entire nasal region, face, ears, shirtfront, tie, and pants. He ran his fingers through his hair, to make sure it achieved that just-mussed look. Ron parted his hair in the center and allowed his longish tresses to flop nonchalantly to either side, keeping it a bit short in the back. This achieved a conservative modification of the style then in vogue with teenage skateboarders. All he lacked was, perhaps, a tiny stud in the center of one earlobe, but even Ron knew that no serious corporate culture, no matter how informal, had moved to the point where pierced body parts were permissible on anyone but females, and then single perforation of earlobes only.

Moving as quickly as he could—and, given the powers of the Aztec medication he was under, that was quickly indeed—he rummaged through his papers and diskettes to see whether a briefcase was going to be necessary. The sole document that might need some looking at was a lengthy memo on corporate repositioning that he had been preparing for Lloyd's review. It was due yesterday morning. Lloyd had yet to mention it, which led Ron to believe that if it never appeared, Lloyd would not wonder about it or miss it. Still, such documents were the heart and soul of Ron's charter. Skip one, a second might not be deemed necessary. He took the diskette that contained the guts of his presentation and popped it in the breast pocket of his suit jacket. He turned out the lights, leapt across his office, and boldly pulled his door open, mentally preparing to launch himself into the next phase of the evening, an unplanned interception of the crazy, adorable young professional who had just exposed herself to him.

Doug

Doug was standing in the hallway outside his office. He wasn't expecting Ron to be there, but he wasn't surprised, either. He had been deep in thought, occupying a section of the carpeting between his newly assigned corner office and the boardroom. Ron, barreling toward the elevators, screeched into his aura like a bug hitting a windshield.

"Doug!" he exclaimed.

"Yes," said Doug. "Ron, isn't it?"

"Ron! Yes!"

Doug looked at him far too perceptively for Ron's taste. "You're the strategic-planning fellow around here, aren't you?" asked Doug. He seemed to be amused by something, although as far as Ron was concerned, there was nothing funny at all. In fact, the whole situation was sufficiently weird to give Ron the willies. Doug was dressed, as he had been each time Ron had seen him, in a two-piece blue pinstriped suit. It was butter-soft and fit him perfectly. The white of his shirt was the cool, iridescent white of sun-bleached bones. Although it was well after seven in the evening now, Doug's cheek was as smooth as the tender skin inside a baby's elbow. He smelled very faintly of some delicate cologne that did not overpower but glimmered out through the wall of Doug's perfection.

"Yes," said Ron. He could not think of a single thing to say. In fact, a queer lassitude had crept over him. He was looking into Doug's eyes. This was something he did not normally do, gaze frankly into the depths of another human being. Who needed that?

"Tough to make a strategic plan for the future when the present is so garbled, eh, Ron?" This appeared to be a serious question in need of answer, so Ron thought about one.

"Part of the task is to make sure the current situation analysis is responsive to reality," he said. What kind of language was that? Doug had to know he was bullshitting. He tried to regroup. He had to convince Doug he was dealing with someone of ineffable intelligence and potential. But how?

"True. What is your situation analysis, then?"

"The industry is fine, growing at GNP, plus two or three points. We've got a fixed-cost business, so all that growth could flow to the bottom line if we contained costs better. We're just not doing that. When we do, we can move to leverage cash-flow growth into superior buying power and consolidate with smaller players until we are one of the top five companies in our segment. Unless we achieve that goal, we'll be acquisition bait by the end of the decade. Before that happens we have to act decisively."

"Eat, rather than be eaten, then?"

Ron wished Doug would look away, stop that creepy staring. "Yes, ha-ha," said Ron.

"Good, Ron," said Doug. "I wonder if you could do something for me."

Ron wanted to say something, but his heart had leapt into his throat and would not recede to its proper location. Doug, asking him to perform a duty! This was wildly, inexpressibly far beyond the most optimistic hopes his imagination could produce. Mostly, he dreamed that Walt would stop by and ask him to accompany him for a shoeshine. Bigger than that, things could not get. He had seen Lloyd striding out of the building one day with Walt and had watched them go into Manelli's, the premier shine emporium in their section of the city. He had stood on the corner then, obscured by a cart that sold chickpea sandwiches, and waited. Ten minutes later, Walt and Lloyd had reemerged, sauntering down the block, their shoes freshly buffed. Lloyd had passed a stick of gum to Walt, and Ron's entire being had been suffused with an onslaught of self-pity, envy, and hatred. He had run ahead then, and he had beaten them to the elevators by ten or fifteen seconds, and when they had arrived, he had held the door for the two men and asked, in a voice he hoped betrayed no irony, "Ride up with you gentlemen?" To which Lloyd had replied, "If you must, Ron." Walt had sniggered. Most pathetically, Ron realized that he had actually appreciated that snigger more than the anonymity that had preceded it.

"Whazzat" was what came out of Ron's mouth, although in truth, Doug probably heard it as its legitimate English equivalent.

"I wonder if you could do a little strategic review of this corporate center, Ron," said Doug.

"This one?" said Ron stupidly. He felt stupid. Dense. Dense but kind of speedy.

"Yes, this one," said Doug. "An overview of its function, in relation to the field. A look at its charter vis-à-vis risk and opportunity planning. A look at its budget, its capital requirements, head count, organizational model, all that kinda stuff. A strategic assessment, possibly with some recommendations. Nothing fancy. Do you think you could do that?"

"Yes," said Ron. "It would be a pleasure, sir, particularly in light of the trend toward decentralization of line functions now being applied in corporate settings elsewhere, although I'm a big believer in maintaining certain central brain-stem operations no matter how muscular and independent the extremities of the corporate body are encouraged to be." What was he talking about? He was raving like a crazed junkie! This would teach him to get stoned at the office! How eighties of him! He kicked himself, and told himself to shut up, and yet he could not. "If you know what I mean," he said in closing. There was a silence.

"I do, Ron," said Doug, incredibly. "I began in a strategic-planning role myself, you know."

"No, sir, I didn't."

"Yeah," said Doug. "With Lehman Brothers, when it was something very special. And I realize that the whole function is something very close to the corporate poet, in a way, the person who feels his way blindly, like the Greek poets did, tapping along in the dark, drawing inspiration from the trees and wind, feeling the moisture in the air to see if rain was on the way, speaking the truth to those who dared not hear it. It's a good job, a thankless job, but ultimately a very important one."

"Yes, sir. I like to think it is." Ron's spirit had left his body and was floating somewhere far above his head, basking in the pure white light of Doug's attention.

"Call me Doug, Ron."

"Okay, Doug."

"Don't you have a date or something?"

"Nothing that can hold a candle to this, Doug," said Ron. He saw Doug's face flush just a tiny bit with pleasure. Nobody, no matter how large or insightful or powerful or thoughtful, was immune to the right kind of sucking up. The trick was to ascertain just exactly which kind was called for. In the case of Doug, Ron thought, nothing less than true love would do. Nothing false. Nothing tawdry. Just simple, truthful intellectual and spiritual devotion, offered without hope of recompense.

"Be that as it may," said Doug. "I'm keeping you."

"Not at all, not at all."

There was an uncomfortable silence.

"What I mean to say, Ron," said Doug, "is get the fuck out of here."

"Thanks, Doug," said Ron. "Now you're speaking a language I can truly understand."

Ron went down the darkened hallway, suppressing the urge to burst into song. He turned at the door just before he inserted his card key in the slot.

Doug was still standing there, regarding him, regarding nothing, regarding the dark space in the hallway around him.

"Doug?" said Ron.

"Yes, Ron."

"When do you want this document? I mean, it's something that will take just about as much thought as I can put into it. It could take a month. It could take three. It could take a year, if we're not particularly serious about it."

"Give it to me Monday," said Doug.

"Monday." That was five days hence. "No problem," said Ron.

"I didn't think there would be." And just like that, Doug was gone.

Mona

There was but one elevator working at that time of night, and it took its time getting there. It was possible that a group of Japanese executives on some floor between thirty-five and forty was holding the lone conveyance for its boss, who was taking his sweet time extricating himself at what was, for them, a ridiculously early hour. Japanese guys were expected to work round the clock. Ron saw them on the subways at all hours, dressed in matching tan belted topcoats, staring at the vacant air in front of themselves. One time he was on his way home from a particularly late night, all by himself on the number 6 train uptown, and he found himself staring directly into the face of a Japanese man his own age. The guy's face was totally devoid of expression, but in his eyes was a level of fatigue Ron could only vaguely remember, a tiredness he used to experience in his sophomore year at Brown, when he took everything very seriously. He had eaten a bunch of speed that year in the hopes it would make his studying go better. It did not. He hit the books non-stop for several long days and nights, and when it was over, he had reviewed everything and yet remembered nothing. He had to do the whole thing over again, this time straight, except that his eyes would not stay open, and he had to walk upright, pacing the floor and mumbling to himself like an observant Jew, an open book in his hand, his eyes red and bleary and his legs trembling beneath him. Lloyd had told Ron that there was no exhaustion that equaled that achieved by parents during the first three months of a colicky baby's life. But that was just Lloyd, thinking he had invented new levels of physical discomfort unknown before he came on the scene. That was Lloyd all over.

Lemur dipped his card key one more time in the elevator's call box. This was the new system to get an elevator after hours. Like many improvements that had appeared on the scene recently, from cellular faxes to voice mail to personal electronic messaging, the increase in technological capability had not produced a resulting improvement in the quality of human life. It had just changed things in such a way as to make them unrecognizable.

No amount of cursing and stabbing the card key into the slot was going to make the thing come faster. So Ron danced with himself for a while. It was late, and nobody was looking. He ran through a complicated tap routine he had learned some years ago in a class he took one summer. Shuffle heel, shuffle step, flap, flap. His tasseled loafers clicked nicely on the hard marble floor. Why had he taken tap at all? He had seen a movie with Gene Kelly and really loved the way it made him feel. And Kelly made it seem so easy.

So, around the elevator plaza Ron went, tapping and twirling a little and rising above the boredom as best he could. "Tea . . . for two . . . and you . . . and me," he sang, vaguely aware he was getting it wrong.

"That's wrong," said Mona, who had quietly exited the business suite and joined Ron at the elevators.

"Ha! Christ!" said Lemur.

"Chill your jets, Ron," said Mona.

"Mona! Wow. Was my face red."

"It's okay," said Mona. She was toting a thin briefcase made of black leather that had her initials on it, and looked wiped out. As always, she was wearing one of those killer miniskirts that were not completely outrageous only because, first, they were amazingly expensive. If something cost a week's executive wages, could it be in bad taste? And second, no pair of legs that perfect could ever be inappropriate, not as long as there was a feminist rationale for the practice. Mona's legs were famous from corporate headquarters in New York to the smallest field operation outside Tacoma, Washington. They were thin but muscular, but not too muscular, and not too thin, either. Her calves were well defined but not aggressive, and the hem of her skirts stopped well above her knee, just as her thighs blossomed, full, round, soft, rising up beneath what little cloth there was into Mona's impudent rear, which moved nicely as she walked, due in large part to the effects that high heels have on the locomotion of the female hip. Ron found himself regarding Mona's mop of fiery red hair. She didn't seem to mind. The elevator came. They got on.

"Long day," he said after a time.

"If I don't get a drink under my belt, I'm going to go postal," she said. She had lifted one of her feet to rest on the wall of the elevator behind her. Her knee popped up at Ron's waist level, bright and plump and juicy. It was all he could do to refrain from gawking at it. If Mona was aware of this, she didn't let it show. "One very cold vodka martini, straight up, extra olives and dirty," she added thoughtfully.

"Ouch. Hurt me," said Ron with an excess of admiration, the kind that would have been expended marveling at a particularly bodacious batch of shrooms in grad school. He wondered if this was an invitation to the dance. Mona outranked him by eight or nine grade levels. It seemed unlikely. Did she have someone to go home to? Why was she working so late? Had she, too, seen Doug? Did she have any idea of the effect she had on people who also happened to be men? The elevator dinged.

"Well," said Mona. "See you in about thirteen hours."

"Have a good one," said Ron.

The doors opened and they each went in an opposite direction. Ron began to run.

At the Building

As he approached his fantasy colleague's office tower, Ron thought he should stop and take the opportunity to have a full-blown heart attack. Cocaine's effect on the heart was well known by the mid-nineties. It was not the benign mood enhancer party animals had believed in the decade just prior, when it was widely viewed as a safe, expensive way to ratchet up the energy level of an evening or two. Large athletes with perfectly robust physiques had keeled over, one by one, until society at large—and the drug-abuse community in particular—came to see the substance, given the number of alternatives available, including fine liquor, as barely worth the risk. That didn't mean Ron didn't leap at the chance every time it came around. It just meant that when he popped a cold sweat and his heart began to pound in his chest like a character in a Ren & Stimpy cartoon, it gave him pause. This was one of those moments.

There was a large sculpture outside the building. It looked like several sections of large intestine, chopped into links and mounted on an elevated platform. At periodic intervals, the segments would rotate to a new posture. Ron liked the sculpture because he found it stupid but interesting, like television. He sat down on its plinth now and allowed his chest to return to normal.

"Are you all right?"

It was she.

"You don't look very well." Up close, Ron could see that her jacket was very well made. The buttons were large, black and gold and hammered flat. She was wearing a small chain around her neck with one tiny teardrop pearl on it. The pearl fell in the crevasse between her breasts, which rose like thunder before Ron's eyes as she bent over slightly to peer at him. Her blouse was open two buttons' worth. He tore his eyes away from the pearl and hauled them up to take in her eyes. They were green, inquisitive but not genuinely concerned. There was something else. He almost got it as she breathed over

him and he stared up at her. Perfume? No, although she was exuding something sweet and slightly woodsy, redolent of a forest after a spring rain, but
not cloying; a forest with animals in it, maybe. Something else, though. A
feeling of thereness. Nothing on her mind but here. Focus, that was it. She
was not off somewhere. She was done being directed for the day. This was
othertime.

"I'm fine," said Ron. "I was waiting here for you."

"Do I know you?" she said.

"No, no," said Ron. He realized he had started off on the wrong foot,
injected a funky note, vaguely threatening, overly personal. "Sorry," he said.
"Somebody like you is what I mean. I'm not usually this inarticulate. I've had
a hard day. A good day. But they don't get any easier, do they?" He was certainly not going to tell her that he was the guy across the tower of air between
their work spaces. His lights had been off, for the most part. He had not been
wearing his suit jacket, and his face had been obscured by the binoculars. Perhaps she was nearsighted, too. She had shown herself in an act of defiance to
some jerk who was peering into her existence. He intended to toss off a quip
when he saw her, like "Those Wonderbras are remarkable," and watch her
face turn and morph and settle, maybe make her blush a little. Now it didn't
seem right. He stood up.

"Whatever," she said. "Well, see ya."

She was turning to go, but not quickly. Ron realized with the kind of certitude that he rarely experienced that he didn't want her to go. It was a real
feeling, not one based on ambition, or greed, or even need, very much. He just
didn't want her to go. He wanted to see how things would work out if she
didn't go.

"Don't go," is what he said.

"Hm?" She had turned around at the foot of the shallow steps that led
down from the plaza that surrounded her building.

"My name is Ron," he said. "We can get to last names later. I work in the
building right over there. I'm vice president of strategic planning for a gigantic multinational corporation that's exploring the limits of synergy in a consolidating business environment." She laughed. "I make in the extremely low
six figures right now, but my bonus is not to be sneezed at, and last year I
joined the pool where I'm eligible for options. I'm single, straight, and I don't
drink or do drugs unless I have any. The reason I'm telling you this is because
when you were about to walk away from me right now, I didn't want you to,
and I thought if I kept on talking, you might be induced to stay and, ultimately, like, have a drink with me."

"My," she said. "You can talk."

"Oh, yes. It's one of my good points."

"Alix," she said.

"Alix."

"Alix with a *i*. It's not short for Alexis, or Alexandra, or anything. It's just the name my parents gave me."

"I like it. It's a nice name."

"Were you the guy with the binoculars?"

A fist closed on Lemur's sternum. He nearly swallowed his tongue. How should he play it? Was her action an isolated incident, or was she a risk taker? He realized that he had not answered for an inappropriate amount of time, and that she had begun to smile at him in a very odd way. A thought bubbled up. How many times had she observed him, late at night, when he thought he was alone in his tower? What had she seen of him that he thought had been private? Truths unknown even to his conscious self? Was now a time for lies, when all between them thus far had been stripped of artifice and social context?

"Yes," he said.

"I like the Monkey Bar. Do you?"

Lloyd pays his taxes. His finances look great.

Since it's the weekend, we have more than enough opportunity to take a gander at Lloyd's pastoral family existence.

Here's Donna. She just came back from a ski trip with the kids while Lloyd was on some fabulous junket out of town. On the trip, she sat at the bottom of the mountain and read a book by Primo Levi about the Holocaust. Then she drove the kids (who were with a couple of friends) back home, where she treated them to dinner at a cafe they liked. She had a piece of salmon cooked completely without butter or oil.

Donna has never made Lloyd anything less than happy, except when she makes him pick up his shoes, turn off the lights when he leaves a room, things like that. And Donna believes Lloyd to be happy, which he is, no question about it. Lloyd is a happy man. Perhaps that's the problem. Do people really want to be happy?

Lloyd loves his children, Nora and Bob. He is even willing to live in suburbia for them and experience intense family weekends that are scheduled pretty much for their benefit and their benefit alone. During such weekends, a variety of activities are pursued, including but not limited to pancakes, cartoons, a touch-and-feel museum jammed with interactive multimedia that obviates the need for imagination, bike riding, baseball, bowling, basketball, shopping, eating every two hours, continual drinking (never liquor) and search for venues at which such fluids can be cleanly and safely eliminated, motion pictures with no worse than a PG-13 rating (meaning there are no

complete decapitations on-screen and no frontal male nudity), barbecueing, having the Mertzes in, and a lot of other stuff that comes up without warning. One such day is more than enough, so that's what we look at.

At the end of the weekend, on Sunday night of that pastoral day, there is an important phone call from . . . Doug. This is strange, even somewhat inappropriate, since Lloyd reports to Walt. Or does he?

Donna, circa 1984

Moby Deal

It's all about The Deal, which is so huge and elusive it would take a miracle to pull it off. Here's what the high concept looks like:

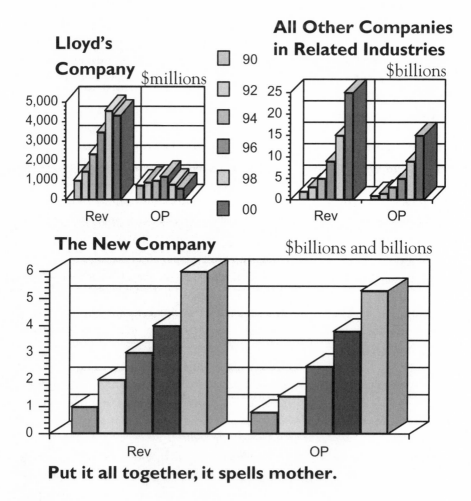

Put it all together, it spells mother.

Positives: Builds revenue growth, rationalizes expenses, leads to world domination and personal wealth (for Lloyd).

Negatives: Really scary partners, destruction of American jobs, possible elimination of middle management (i.e., Lloyd).

The Noneventful Bourgeois Life

There is nothing in this world that is quite so difficult as putting a tight soccer shoe on over a moist oversized sports sock. Lloyd was trying very hard, and Bob wasn't helping much. He was playing with Steve, the cocker spaniel. Steve's job was mostly the creation of fluids from a variety of orifices. Drool was his most copious production, much of which was now absorbed into Bob's sock after Steve had chewed on it.

Lloyd would have exchanged Bob's saturated footwear with another of his many pairs, except they were already late to the boy's scheduled soccer game and he didn't have the time to find clean ones. The contest between Bob's team and their adversary of the week began at a sadistic 8:00 A.M. Saturday. The only more fascistic sport was hockey, which scheduled its gladiatorial exchanges at nonsensical, idiotic hours and locations, like 6:30 A.M. in Elizabeth, New Jersey, for instance, or 7:00 P.M. in Danbury, Connecticut, more than a full hour away. Lloyd had actually heard of one hockey match for twelve-year-olds that had been set up for 6:00 A.M. in Rye, New York, on Christmas Day. Sports bred insanity, even in Lloyd's childhood. Now, when things were routinely insane, the situation had not improved.

Bob's shoe would simply not go on over his sock.

"What the hell!" Lloyd yelled. Lloyd tried not to yell, but he often did not succeed. Fortunately, Lloyd's children generally saw his yelling as a failure of will, not as anything to do with them personally. Lloyd had to get awfully mean in order to impress them with his wrath.

"Chill, Dad. I'll do it," said Bob.

While Bob hauled on his shoe, Steve ambled over to the doorknob of the portal that led to the garage, where his leash hung. He pensively nosed the leather loop that made up its grip, attempting to stick his head through it.

"No, Steve," said Lloyd. "You're not coming." Steve looked incredibly sad, and he paddled off into the depths of the finished basement to find some object to destroy. As Lloyd exited the basement with Bob in tow, he saw the spaniel follow them to the door, hope springing eternal, a plastic soldier tucked demurely into the side of his jowl.

At the Soccer Game

Bob was not good at soccer. He ran up and down the field in somewhat desultory fashion, attempting, as far as Lloyd could see, to be near the ball without actually touching it. This would have been fine, except for the fact that the opposing team was coached by an extraordinarily serious Latino father whose knowledge of the game and dedication to the sport was completely out of sync with that of Bob's group. By the end of the half, his son was completely winded and the other team had punched through a goal. Lloyd was wondering if he could get home for a quick cup of java and pick up Bob at the terminus of this humiliating experience. There were other parents there, however, rooting, hooting, being altogether too wholesome and supportive for Lloyd to feel he could go slinking off and leave Bob in solitary ignominy.

At the half, Barry, Bob's coach, asked his pathetic crew which of them would like to spend the next half as goalie. Lloyd, who up to this point had maintained an admirable sangfroid about the entire contest, felt every sphincter in his body tone and tighten. He knew immediately what was going to happen. Bob would volunteer. Bob would be chosen. Bob would be humiliated. And Lloyd's childhood would be replicated.

"Me! Me!" screamed Bob when the question was asked. Why? Lloyd beat his figurative breast about the question, but he knew the answer. Goalies got to wear leather gloves and a mesh pullover that distinguished them from the other players. Bob wanted to be nothing if not distinguished. He waved his arms about and went "Oooh! Oooh!" and of course Barry, whose heart was in the right place always, chose him, in full knowledge that this meant almost certain defeat for the entire team.

Bob went into the goal. Lloyd descended into hell. The score at that point was 1–0—an incredible lone point down. This was the best they had done all year. Usually at halftime, they were six, eight points in arrears, the equivalent of a forty-point deficit in football, or 260 points in basketball. So today they had been doing well, actually, even though they were losing. Until Bob went into the goal.

Lloyd watched a small, lithe whippet of a boy with nut-brown skin and legs so lean and efficient that they seemed never to grow tired—he watched this boy batting the ball between his feet and taking it confidently down the field.

"Go *to* the ball, Eduardo!" shrieked his coach, who, Lloyd noted with some pleasure, would have a bad case of vocal polyps if he kept that kind of exhortation up for much longer. And sure enough, Eduardo ratcheted up his performance one extra notch, moved into a higher gear, and began a stately but inexorable drive toward Bob, who was at that moment taking a small break to adjust his gloves.

"*BOB!*" screeched Lloyd. He could hear the desperation and terror in his voice and hated himself for it. "*Stop him!*" Lloyd received a clear, objective picture of himself standing there hollering, red-faced, on the sidelines, and he was ashamed. "*Watch out!*" he screamed again. Lloyd saw there was little he could do to stop himself. He was standing against ten thousand years of racial and cultural history with nothing more than his will. Back when his ancestors had been carefully gluing fur onto hats, this boy's progenitors had been kicking an Incan rock around. What hope did Bob have against those kinds of odds?

Bob looked up from his painstaking equipment adjustment and fixed his gaze on his father. He seemed genuinely interested in what could possibly be bothering Dad at this juncture. Wasn't he in the goal? Didn't he look cool?

Then he saw the ball headed in his direction and his entire appearance decomposed. Like Lloyd, Bob immediately knew what God had in store for him at that moment. He summoned up full understanding of the inexorable outcome of this situation, and he realized that while he might fight it, he could not change it. Lloyd saw the insight in his son, and he grieved for him. Together, they watched the lean slab of momentum drive the white sphere ever closer to its goal. Together, they beheld the white leather ball moving like destiny past Bob's legs, past his flailing arms, and into the net.

"Goooooooooallllllll!" said the opposing coach. Lloyd wanted to impale him on a tree limb.

There was more soccer for the next half hour, but Lloyd did not see it. He was in a black cloud of desperation from which no amount of effort could extract him.

"Man, that was harder than I thought it would be," said Bob as they left the field not long after. Lloyd put his arm around his son and wished there was something he could say to him that was not full of shit.

"We'll go buy comics later," he said instead.

"Can we get a drink now?" said Bob.

"Sure," said Lloyd. "I always like a drink after work."

They went to a store at the corner that sold water. There was water at home, of course, but that came without packaging. Things always taste better when they're directly marketed at you.

Nora's Science Project

Lloyd got home from Bob's soccer match at about 11:00 A.M. and was already completely wrung out. Donna was at the kitchen table, reading the Metropolitan section of the *New York Times.*

Nora was at the far end of the breakfast table, drawing a highly detailed map on a piece of unlined notebook paper. She did not look happy.

"Bob did great today!" chirped Lloyd, feeling inauthentic. And indeed, the moment the remark escaped his lips, his son skewered him with a withering glare.

"I stunk," he said as he pulled off his rubber cleats.

"Not at all!" warbled Lloyd. "You gave it your all! You hung in there! You did your best," he concluded lamely.

"I gotta get out of this stupid cup and jockstrap," said Bob. He turned and stalked out of the room. Lloyd didn't blame him. This display of gratuitous faux bonhomie wasn't even fooling himself. Like his son, Lloyd remembered how loudly he had been screaming at the crucial moment when the opposing player had sent a tracer bullet past Bob and into the goal. He felt

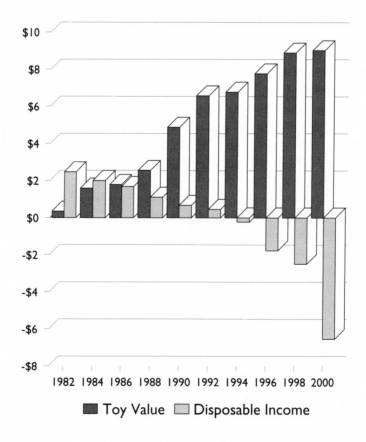

Toy Expenditures for Nora and Bob

vs. Lloyd's Disposable Income per Month

■ Toy Value □ Disposable Income

bad about that now. How much of his son's current suffering had he been responsible for? Half? All? Certainly not all.

"Hi," said Lloyd to the two women at the table. He could not have used that word about Nora until recently, but there was no doubt about it: While still a very young person and uncontestably a girl, Nora, at thirteen, had grown more angular of late. There was a more complicated and knowing glimmer in her general demeanor, and a new sardonic quality had filtered into her judgment of incidents and people. She was still amenable to silliness, though.

"Whatcha doon?" said Lloyd to Nora.

"Map of the site," said Nora. The site was a location about ten minutes from their thoroughly suburban street, a place under a viaduct on a very busy road where a small stream burbled, tall birch, oak, and maple trees swayed in the wind, and hanging vines and leaves obscured the sun. If one took the swoosh of passing cars for the onrush of wind or water, the site could seem a thousand miles and a hundred years away. Nora's class was studying this site for its natural properties, and also taking careful note of what the ravages of teenaged man had taken on the place, which was dotted here and there with plastic rings from six-packs, cigarette butts, and beverage cans and bottles. A fair amount of the litter had been left there by the students observing the shocking way that civilization had degraded the pristine nature of the site, and the area was strewn with pencils, erasers, rulers, and the occasional assignment pad.

"I've got to go down there later," said Nora as Lloyd looked over the fine, meticulous chart his daughter was constructing, detailed down to the position of rocks and tree stumps, with metrical measurements of the width of the stream and the height of the arching viaduct that loomed above. "Want to take me?"

"Yeah, okay," said Lloyd.

"And don't rush me when we're there, Dad," said Nora. "You rush me all the time and I'm afraid I'll do a lousy job. So don't rush me."

"How long you figure we'll be there?" Lloyd liked the site, but spending a full hour sitting on a rock while his daughter chatted with her pal Sophie, as had happened on a prior trip, or counted rocks and berries, as she was probably going to do today, was not Lloyd's idea of the way to spend a glorious Saturday. Spending money at the mall was the way to spend a Saturday.

"I have to do measurements of the width of the stream at its widest and narrowest part and note down a bunch of other stuff. I should be, like, maybe half an hour if you leave me and Sophie alone," said Nora.

"Okay," said Lloyd. "I'll take you. If you promise not to shove mud up your nose like you did last time."

"Dad," said Nora. But she was secretly pleased.

"Leave her alone now and let her do her work," said Donna in her lion tamer's voice. Lloyd didn't mind it, though. It was one of the things he had married her for, the establishment of order. Why resent her for it now?

Donna was sitting at the table with her hair wet and combed, a cup of coffee in front of her and the entire newspaper spread out on the table before her.

"There's a little bit of coffee left if you want some," she said without looking up. Lloyd checked his interior need mechanism and found that he did want some, so he poured himself a half a cup. He would have poured more, but there wasn't any more. He drank a mouthful. It was hot and good. He went to the table and found the milk, which was in a gallon jug. He poured a small dollop into the mug and sat down to join his wife. For a moment or two, he considered chiding Donna for making the absolute minimum amount of coffee, rather than producing more, some of which might have gone to waste. He discarded this notion for two reasons. Donna could never change this aspect of her personality, any more than Lloyd could change his propensity, which would be to make twelve cups and throw six away. Second, Donna hated to be criticized. A mean-spirited remark could well end up with Lloyd making his own coffee for a while.

"I can't believe this," said Donna, scowling at the newspaper, and Lloyd knew he didn't want to hear about it. "This child molester in New Jersey," she said now. "They let him out on this early-release work program and he got himself into a halfway house in Passaic."

"I don't want to hear about it," said Lloyd. Nora rose without comment and left the room.

"So you know what basically happened without my telling you about it," she said.

"That's why I don't need you to tell me about it," said Lloyd. He regarded his wife. She was wearing a ratty gray T-shirt with sleeves ripped up to the ball of her shoulder. The night they had first met, on a blind date, Lloyd had knocked on her door, expecting nothing but another quizzical evening of the variety he had been experiencing at that time, consisting of several hours of increasingly drunken badinage, a little tongue wrestling, a graceful exit, and sleep. Donna had opened the door to her apartment, wearing a peach-colored silk shirt with a very slight sheen to it, ultratight black slacks, and a gold necklace with a tiny diamond hanging from it. There was a slight fullness to her lips that was not altogether expected, a hint of jut to her jaw not quite in classic proportions, a slight top-heaviness in her chest, and, even then, before she had started working out, an admirable flatness to her tummy and lower abdomen. But most of all, there were her great green eyes with tiny flecks of gray and brown that took him in in one large gulp as she evaluated him for the first time and, surprisingly, found him provisionally not wanting.

"Come in," she'd said. Her apartment was furnished with a real couch and matching chairs, a glass coffee table, a neat cream-colored rug to tie it all together. It was the nicest place he had ever seen that was occupied by someone their age. Donna was then a book editor at a well-respected publishing house in town, and she made approximately sixteen thousand dollars a year, about four times Lloyd's salary as a stand-up comic and taxi driver—an amount Lloyd found impossibly seductive and astronomical.

There in the kitchen eighteen years later, Lloyd wanted to rise and rub his wife's shoulders, stick his hand under her skimpy little shirt, and squeeze her someplace. He refrained, however, because he could see that at this instant of time, his needs were not in complete synchronicity with hers. Just because you were married to a woman didn't mean you could take advantage of her at a moment's notice. He had learned that lesson in 1982.

"I don't understand what the rationale for parole is anymore," said Donna, leaning intently over the article she was reading with a dissatisfied gleam. "It's pretty clear that rehabilitation is not the issue, because there's no assumption of rehabilitation at all, just the desire to clear out correctional facilities to make room for worse miscreants."

"What's on the schedule for today?" said Lloyd. He desperately wanted to change the subject, but there was nothing he could do. His wife wanted to talk about substantive issues.

"Barry put Bob in goal today," he said.

Donna looked up. "No," she said.

"I'm afraid so."

"How much . . . I mean, how bad . . ."

"Two. Not that terrible, really. Afterward, Barry put Danny Melman into the goal and the other guys scored three on him. So it wasn't that horrendous, except, you know . . . Bob felt bad."

"Damn," said Donna. Her face was flushed with displeasure and concern. Lloyd could feel her sinking down into herself, immersing herself in her bottomless reservoir of empathy and outrage. "I remember when I was about eighteen, I tried out for the fencing club and I got in," she said. "I decided to go out for saber because fewer girls did that, and it was kind of macho because you have this longer, thicker blade and it's quite a dangerous weapon if you want it to be, and the moves are more like broadsword, with less finesse than épée and, you know, more drama?"

Lloyd wondered where this was going.

"And after we had practiced for almost an entire semester," Donna continued, blowing on her coffee and taking a small sip, "the coach decided that we were ready to compete with another school, one of those small hippie schools near Northampton. When we got there, I was really keyed up, totally nervous, felt like barfing, because, you know, I was all alone there, nobody to root for me. My entire family was down in Miami waiting for me to join them for the Christmas break like always and I didn't have a boyfriend at the time, so it was just me, and there was this girl who was going to be my opponent. She was nervous, too. I could tell, because she kept on warming up on the sidelines, doing vocalizations every time she'd lunge, like "Ha!" I could tell she was scared, because there in the front row of the bleachers were her parents, who kept waving to her with these little timid waves parents use when they don't want to embarrass their kid. I got out there under the lights and it was really weird, but everything seemed to go into slow motion for me, and every move I had to make felt easy, and slow, and I could see what she was going to do a full second before she even thought of it herself. She was sweating, and this was really, really bad in saber, or any kind of fencing, because fencing is all about form. Sweating isn't form. It's function. At any rate, we got up to about five points, and I had won them all. Then I looked right into her eyes through her face mask and I could see she was close to tears. And then this really big fleck of sweat, or maybe it was drool or something, oozed out from behind her mask and plopped on the floor, and we both heard it, but she looked down at it and I touched her again and she got mad and lunged at me and slipped on her own perspiration and went down on the floor and was out. It was a completely ignominious loss, without a shred of dignity whatsoever, and I won a blue ribbon."

Lloyd rose and walked over to the sink, where he rinsed his cup under extremely hot water and then placed it in the dishwasher. This was exercising, in miniature, an old habit he had acquired in childhood—the washing of dishes that would simply be washed again in the dishwasher.

"What exactly did that little tale have to do with the entire Bob scenario?" he said cordially.

Donna picked up the newspaper and resumed her search for aggravating news worthy of discussion. "I felt for that girl is my point," she said, "I enjoyed the winning, but part of my joy was squelched by what it did to her. I've never completely enjoyed winning since."

"Yes you have," said Lloyd.

"Possibly you're right," said Donna.

Lloyd felt very jumpy, as if he had to do something right then or burst.

"What's on the agenda for today?" he said.

"I guess you could start by taking Nora to the site," said Donna. "I'll help Bob with his black-history project. Be back here around noon so we can get them to their twelve-thirty karate class."

Lloyd went to cudgel his daughter into forward motion.

In the Garage

At the last minute, Lloyd figured he would take Steve along, because it would have been mean not to. Steve wore his emotions in his rump, and as Lloyd put on his coat and went down into the basement, which gave access to his garage, Steve's entire retro-rocket went into overdrive. Lloyd grabbed the leash and clipped it onto Steve's collar after several tries.

"Dog!" he yelled at Steve, which elicited its customary response in the cocker spaniel; Steve immediately lurched forward and then side to side, looking hysterically for one of his own species. Lloyd knew it was cruel to tease the dog, but he enjoyed doing so. What was the point of having a dog if you couldn't torment him now and then? Lloyd most liked hiding a biscuit or ball in his shirt pocket and lying down on the couch with a good book. Steve would shortly become aware that there was something he wanted on Lloyd's person, but he couldn't tell where or what it might be. He proceeded to sit attentively at Lloyd's foot, his muzzle puffed out in consternation, a motorboat growl issuing forth at very low decibel level, his enormous brown eyes beseeching Lloyd to end his misery and give him whatever it was that was being withheld. Tragically, when Lloyd finally relented and handed over the treasured object, Steve either ate it so fast that he had no memory of it or lost the ball or toy so quickly that he usually lined up immediately thereafter and took up his begging routine, this time for no particular purpose, since Lloyd had divested himself of the object in question.

Lloyd opened the garage door and waited for Nora to come downstairs. Nora was slow and tended to bonk her extremities on whatever riser, banister or chifforobe presented itself to her in transit. This time, Lloyd heard her thundering tread as it bore her down the stairs, followed by the sound of flesh hitting drywall.

"Ow!" Nora said.

"Come on!" said Lloyd, who was feeling impatient for reasons that he couldn't quite pinpoint. What was there to do, after all? "Get your shoes on!" he yelled, immediately regretting his tone. He had, maybe, what—five more years before his daughter went off to college and he lost her? What was his hurry? Weren't these the best years of his life?

"Sorry," said Nora, who came in rubbing her knee. "I hurt my leg on the stairs. I know you consider it another self-inflicted injury, but it hurts anyhow."

"No, honey," said Lloyd. He felt crushed under a weight of dank, fetid guilt. "Where does it hurt?"

"Here," said Nora, and showed him.

"I guess you're too old for me to kiss it."

"I guess so."

"Would it make you feel better if I walked into this wall here?"

"Yes," said Nora. "Yes, it would."

Lloyd quickly turned and walked directly into the door to the garage, employing the old vaudeville methodology of allowing his knee to precede him and take most of the shock, then allowing his head to recoil as if struck viciously. Nora knew the entire thing was bogus, but she got a kick out of it anyway.

"Let's go, Dad," she said.

Lloyd punched the button that set the electrical garage-door opener into action, and Steve immediately began to bark at it.

"There he goes again," said Lloyd.

"What do you suppose is going through his mind?" said Nora.

"He hates moving parts. I think he wants to bite them."

Lloyd knew how Steve felt, though. In a way, he loved his electric garage-door opener. It symbolized the arrival at a certain point of adulthood. Only substantial people of a certain social class had one. It was based on a lovely archaic principle of modernity. The electric garage-door opener could only have been invented in 1950s America, a time when better living through science and technology prevailed. When he had been a child, Lloyd had felt contempt for the Ozzie and Harriet banality of the appliance. Now he felt a grudging but unmistakable pride in it. It was darned convenient, too.

At the Site

Nora and her friend Sophie went off a bit to sit by the brook that ran through the site. Lloyd could see them at a distance, gabbing and chuckling and filling in data of some sort into their spiral notebooks. Lloyd took in the beauty of the surroundings and, within a surprisingly short amount of time, was swept by a wave of powerful boredom.

Lloyd knew boredom. Boredom was what assailed you in boardrooms, when meetings were under way from which no one but the chairman could excuse himself. Boredom came in trains on the way to these meetings, where he was trapped between two snoozing commuters who drooled and leaned against him, their heads bobbing against his shoulders no matter how hard he tried to shrug them off. Boredom arrived in long anecdotes told by Nerf, corporate tax director, interminable tales of legal precedents and hairy negotiations that could have been telescoped into efficiently entertaining nuggets but were not. "To make a long story short," he would say, and then would do anything but. Boredom came when you were by yourself in the USAir Club in Pittsburgh and your laptop was out of batteries. Most of all, Lloyd knew boredom for what it was: the inability to be with oneself, for people who are content with themselves are never bored.

Why was he bored here, at this beautiful site? The stream babbled, dappled in the morning sun. It was a rather warm spring, and the last remnants of the icy barnacles of winter were washing away in the sunshine, although the air was still just a tiny bit cool, and there was a smell of growth, of green just about to burst from branch and vine. Sparrows twittered just out of sight. The voices of his child and her friend mingled with the burble of the water as it tumbled over the rocks in the streambed. He had no work to do over this weekend. A complete paucity of required labor. None. Zilch. Nada.

Steve was standing at attention at the utter end of his leash, closely regarding a dead leaf left over from last year's autumn harvest. It moved a bit in the breeze and Steve, seized with every defensive urge that a thousand years of spaniel breeding could muster, erupted into a hail of barking, his chest expanding to maximum breadth, ears at attention, every muscle ready for action. A squirrel who had walked virtually across his muzzle just moments before had achieved no such reaction, incidentally. Steve was funny that way. Just the night before, he had turned up his nose at a plate of fried chicken livers. Not long after, Lloyd had found him nosing beneath the kitchen sink, his muzzle red with the soap from an industrial-sized Brillo, which he had been eating.

Lloyd sat down on a rock and looked at the water. He could feel himself sinking deeper, deeper into a boredom that had no bottom or end.

"Can we go now?" he yelled around the bend at the girls, who could not be seen.

"Dad!" hollered Nora in that condescending tone that children reserve for the stupider of their two parents.

"Okay, okay," muttered Lloyd under his breath. He looked at his shoes. Steve lay down in the leaves by the rock in the mandatory pose: front and rear feet lined up perfectly, head erect, nose wet and black and flexed for peak reception of odors.

On Monday, there would be many people fired. It would be a good day for firing. The weatherman said bright and sunny, with a light breeze from the southeast. Six hundred people at various work locations around the country would be told by their local senior managers that the corporation no longer required them to be present. That wasn't a lot, really, considering that the company then employed nearly ten thousand people. That left at least nine thousand with jobs that were more secure, given that the cost structure of the entire business system would now be more manageable. And the six hundred were not concentrated in any one location, either. Twenty here. Sixteen there. Forty-seven someplace else. Horrible, true. But tolerable. Except . . .

Lloyd had once been almost eliminated, and he hadn't even found out about it until later, when he was already the head of his department. He was looking at the budget for the headquarters operation, and he saw his salary listed as a general expense under the chairman's budget line. That was very strange, and completely erroneous when viewed from a process point of view. With spreadsheet in hand, Lloyd went to Burbage and asked him why his salary was not listed as a department expense but was in Chet's costs instead, and had been there for more than three years. "The only thing I can think of," said Burbage, "is that at some point you were taken off the legitimate roster and put into Chet's slush fund as a personal responsibility."

Lloyd was stunned. When would that have been? Three years ago . . . when Don reorganized his department, and . . . and he hadn't been given a title for a while . . . and his duties had suddenly been really unclear . . . and then all of a sudden things had gotten better and he had forgotten about the whole thing. He went to Fitz and told him about his discovery. "Yeah," said Fitz. "Chet and I saved your butt. Don wanted you out, and we said no, and Don said, 'Fine, put him on your budget, Chet,' and so Chet did."

Lloyd stood in the hallway then and let the feeling of having just missed being run over by a big train creep over him, and then subside. He kind of wished he had been nicer to Chet, or said thanks to him a little bit more when he had the chance to do so. I should give Chet a call now, thought Lloyd, sitting on his rock next to the stream in the middle of the site. But he knew he would not. Business friendships, no matter how powerful and authentic, almost never lasted beyond the operational viability of the association. And that "almost" was a cheat, a sop to sentiment. The reality was . . . never.

On Monday morning, he would have to tell Betty, though. He had delegated all the other executions, all 644 of them. But there was nobody who could tell Betty but Lloyd. Betty was sixty-seven and a completely decent person. The fact that she was the second secretary in a two-secretary department wasn't her fault. She did a good job answering phones. She got lunch when people needed it. She couldn't operate a computer, though. Couldn't tell one end of a floppy from another. Couldn't have that. Betty had to go.

But how? How?

"You know, Betty, you're getting kind of close to the time when people like to start to think about retirement. . . ." No. That wouldn't do. Betty didn't want to retire and go back to her room with a hot plate and pictures of her children, who now lived in Flagstaff, Arizona, and never invited her out for holidays except once, several years ago, and never again.

"You know, Betty, the separation package the corporation is offering would be enough, for someone like yourself, to chuck this aggravation and see the world." No. That was idiotic, too. Betty got nervous if the local muffin place closed for a day and she had to find another one. Betty had the same lunch at her desk every day—a microwaved yam. Betty wanted to see as little of the world as possible. The world was cold and unfriendly and filled with uncertainty. The office was better.

"Betty, we've looked at this thing a hundred ways 'til Sunday and we still can't figure out how to keep two secretaries in a department that now has only three professionals. We're going to give you a nice package. We're going to let you stay on until the end of the second quarter, which is July first. Then I'm afraid you'll have to go." Yes. That's what Lloyd would say. Lloyd sat on the rock and let that sink into his system a little bit. Then he didn't think about anything for a while.

This reorganization was only the beginning. There had been a time when things were stable. Not at the beginning of his career, of course. Like Betty, he had been the seventeenth wheel in a sixteen-wheel rig back then. And they had just been acquired by the parent corporation for which he now worked. Thousands had come and gone, but Lloyd had stuck by his desk. He had come to be one of the few who smoothed over the rough bumps of existence with other people's money. He golfed, when forced to. He ate when he was not hungry. He had friends in high places. He lived the unreflective life. And it was worth living. The air smelled sweet in the morning when Lloyd rolled down the window of his company Volvo on the West Side Highway and took a big lungful of exhaust.

Now Walt was screwing with things. He had begun to talk about growth in a way that Lloyd didn't like. Growth by revenue enhancement was one thing. Growth by selective acquisition was all right, too, as far as it went, as long as it was clear who were the Romans and who were the Gauls when the outlying duchies were conquered. But growth in one gigantic, ambitious swallow? Walt had his eye on something. Something enormous. Some big deal for which he would need not millions, not hundreds of millions, but billions, and not just 1 billion, either. Six, maybe ten billion! Maybe more! The kind of money that brings in people who want to watch it. And after them . . . the deluge.

The worst part of it was, Lloyd knew with a certitude that rarely attends adult life that he would be assigned big, important work on this deal he detested, that all of them would be required to work hard and longer and more brilliantly than they had ever worked before in pursuit of the goal that would destroy the fabric of their existence and hurl them gasping and naked on an alien shore.

And then there was Ron. Ron was his protégé, his comrade, his friend, sort of. They had worked together for several years now. Lloyd had brought Ron along, even when others said Ron was a grasping, greedy grind as shallow as a layer of ice on a mud puddle. Now it seemed as if Ron was watching him all the time. Lloyd would go to get coffee and there Ron would be not a moment afterward, pouring himself a cup and inquiring about Lloyd's most recent activity. Lloyd would be in a meeting, sitting next to Walt, and there, suddenly, would be Ron, sometimes with Doug. What was the meaning of that? Had to watch Ron carefully. Not that the corporation would prefer Ron to him, ever, if it came down to a head-to-head thing; that would be impossible, so foolish, so thoughtless, so lacking in insight. Brain-damaged. Still. The Ron thing.

And Mona . . .

Steve began to honk and hawk up phlegm all at once, his sides heaving, head bobbing. He stood and prepared to expel whatever piece of tinfoil, rubber band, plastic toy, or balloon he had gobbled down this morning. Lloyd was not concerned. Steve threw up several times a week. Sometimes it was nothing more than some of the tissue paper he liked to munch on in reflective moments. Other times, it was more interesting fare. Once it was the foot of a Barbie doll. That was, perhaps, the best. This time, nothing came up but a bit of yellow bile.

"It's all right, boy," said Lloyd.

"Dad?" said Nora. She was standing over him with a bag of leaves and a concerned expression. "Dad? You okay?"

"Sure, honey," said Lloyd. "Can we go now?"

"Just as soon as we count these leaves," said Nora. And then, "I'm kidding! I'm kidding!"

The Rest of the Day

The trip to the site was perhaps the last reflective moment Lloyd was allowed that day, and for this he was thankful. In the next several hours, the following things occurred:

Bob and Nora go to karate class. Tae kwon do, actually, a less violent, more defensive martial art invented in Korea, as opposed to the chopping, slashing, variety bred, quite naturally, in Japan. Both Nora and Bob liked their tae kwon do class, because it was run by perhaps the best teacher Lloyd had ever seen work, a tall, handsome, light-skinned black man by the name of Abiyoyo. Lloyd was aware this name had been derived from a folk song and story told by Pete Seeger that he had heard quite a bit in the early 1960s when, each summer, he attended Communist summer camp. Abiyoyo's parents must have heard Pete Seeger, too.

Abiyoyo was about thirty years of age and possessed a sense of calm and self-knowledge Lloyd envied. He ran a small, clean little dojo. His classes were always full, and always full of laughter. No matter how small, skinny, or incompetent a child was, he left Abiyoyo's class feeling strong and capable.

Slide Show Three

- Demographics
- Psychographics
- Financial Information
- Lifestyle Data
- Behavior as a Function of Organizational Life

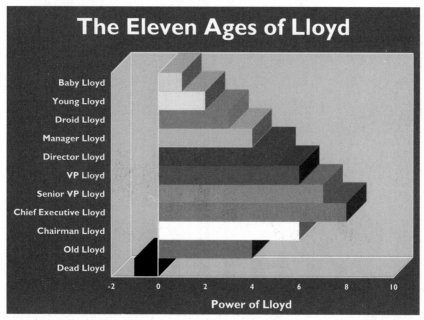

Slide 1

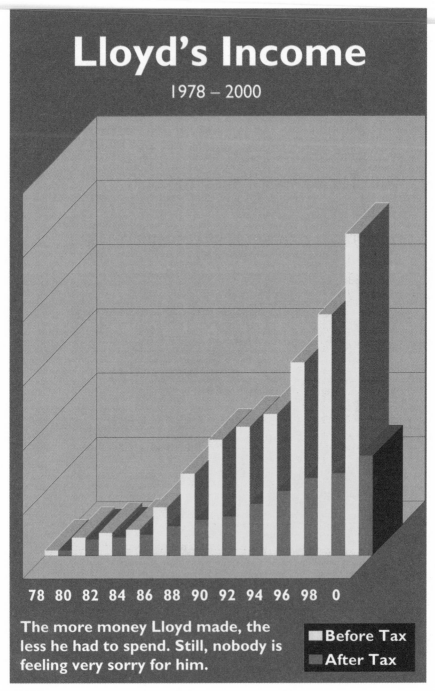

Slide 2

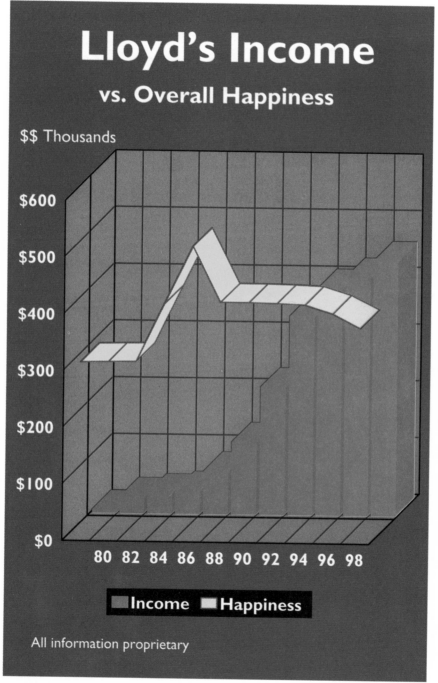

Slide 3

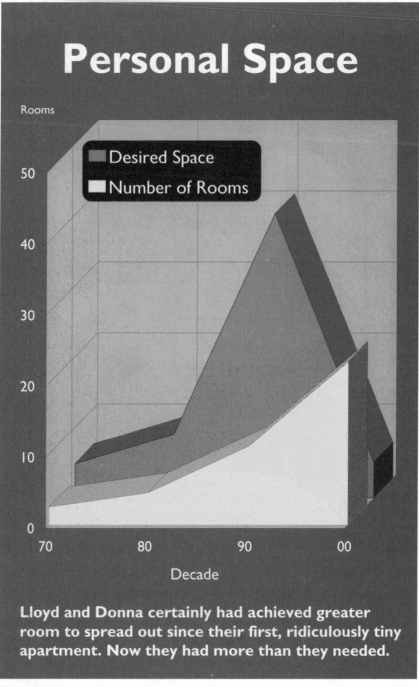

Personal Space

Lloyd and Donna certainly had achieved greater room to spread out since their first, ridiculously tiny apartment. Now they had more than they needed.

Slide 4

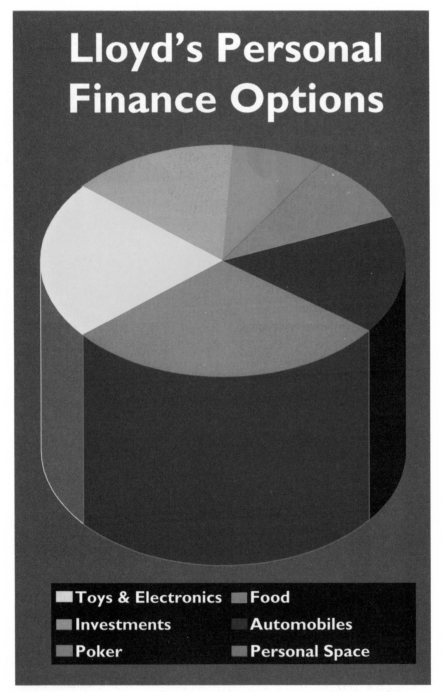

Slide 5

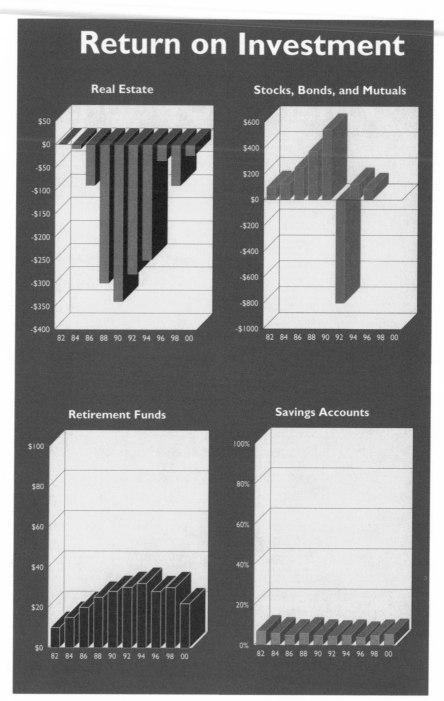

Slide 6

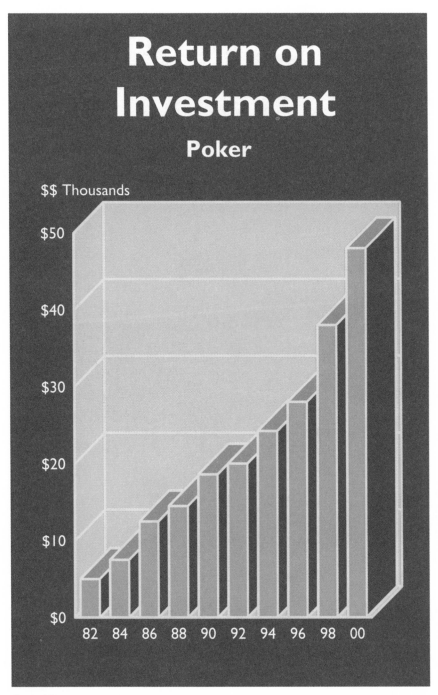

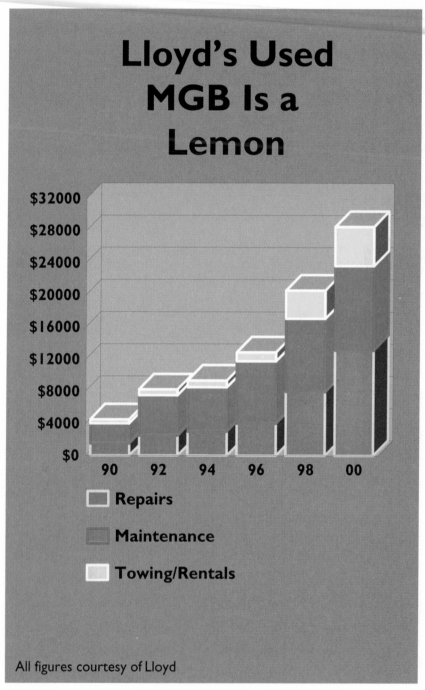

Slide 8

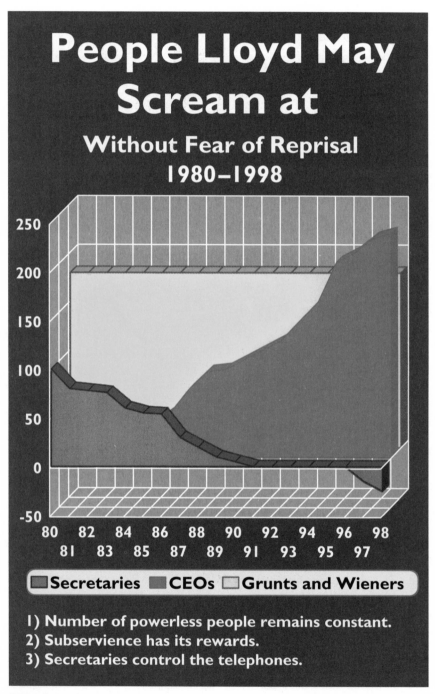

Slide 9

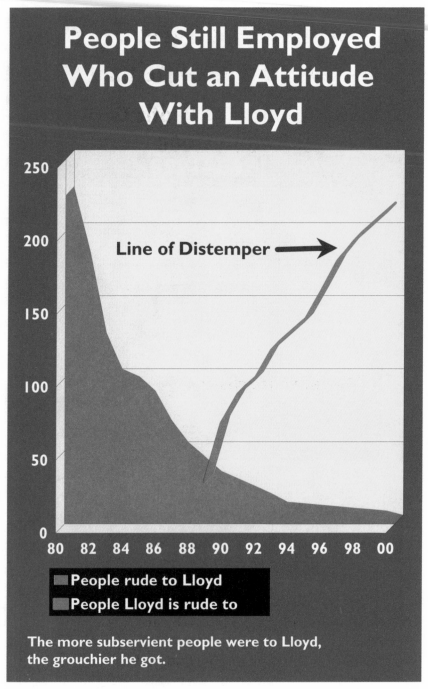

Slide 10

122

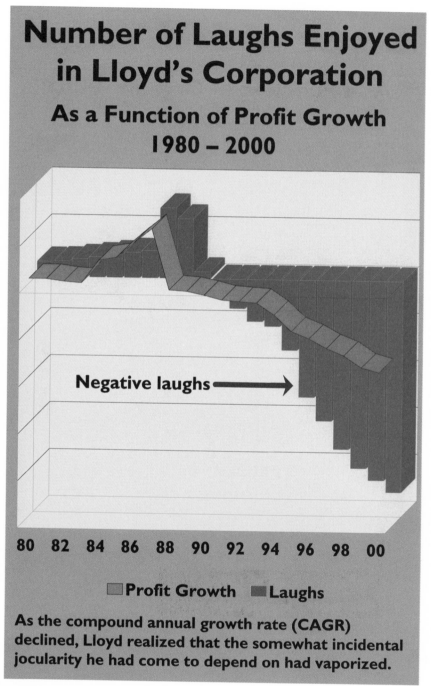

As the compound annual growth rate (CAGR) declined, Lloyd realized that the somewhat incidental jocularity he had come to depend on had vaporized.

Slide 11

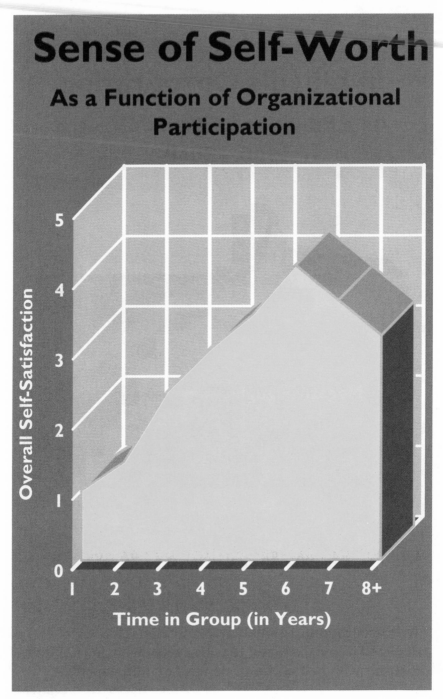

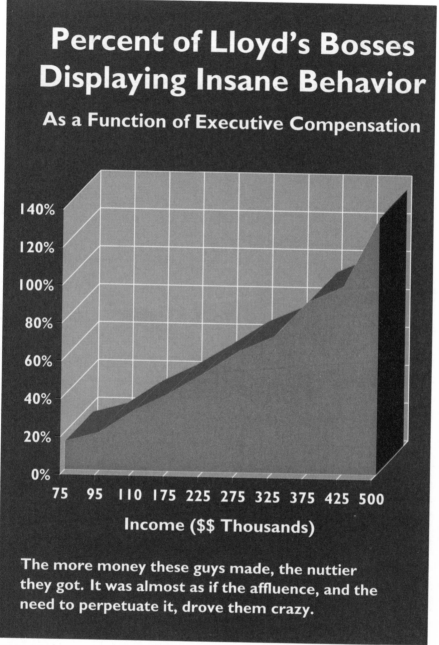

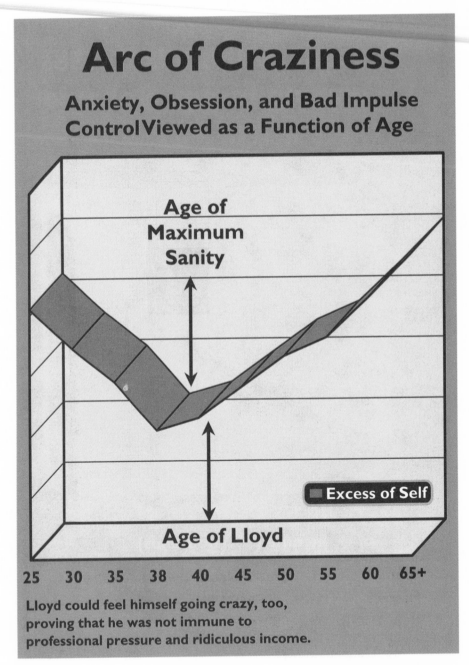

Business Intoxicants

Slide 15

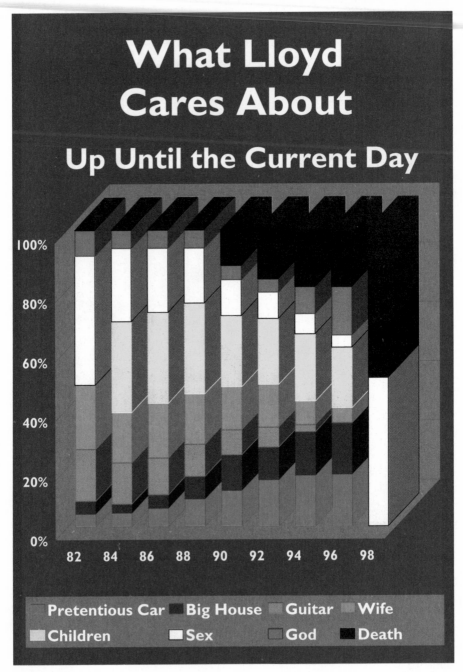

Slide 16

After a year or so of the drill, Bob seemed to slip into a groove and had now achieved a good, crisp standard and a green belt. His pride in this was enormous, as was Lloyd's. Nora came to the movement easily and had won her green belt in very short order. Both now poured out of Lloyd's Volvo with happy grins and belts flying and popped into the studio building without a word of good-bye to Lloyd.

He now had an hour to kill. In the old days, he would certainly have ducked behind the nearby train station for a quick smoke, but now he had quit and there was nothing clandestine for him to do. He could go home, he supposed, and hang out with Donna for the forty minutes or so before he had to get in the car again and head back to pick up the kids. Sometimes that worked out great, in the sense that the stolen moments they had alone turned out to be aphrodisiacal. Lloyd would get home, to find his wife drying her hair after a posttreadmill shower, wearing nothing but bra and panties and still a little moist. He would come up behind her and put his arms around her. She would then indicate whether the embrace was timely. Sometimes they even took a shower together, one of Lloyd's favorite pastimes since he discovered it with Jennifer Conley back in twelfth grade. Lloyd stood in the sunshine outside the dojo and thought about Jennifer for a couple of minutes. How she had broken his heart!

Lloyd went to the car and called his wife.

"Hi," he said. The connection was bad.

"Hi," she said.

"Whatcha doon?"

"Checkbook," said Donna. Ugh, thought Lloyd. The antithesis of a conjugal shower.

"Can I get anything while I'm out?" he said.

"Nah," she said. "Are you coming home?"

"I don't know," he said. "I thought I might just hang around and get them at the other end."

"Okay," said Donna. He could hear the silent machinations of the calculator as Donna poked at its rubber buttons. "Take Steve when you get home."

"I will. See you later."

"Did you write a check to Egghead Software for one twenty-seven-fifty?" said Donna.

"Uh . . . yeah?" said Lloyd.

"What for?"

"Two games."

"For the kids?"

"For me."

"Man," said Donna.

"It's better than having an affair with a beautiful stewardess."

"Okay," said Donna, and hung up.

Lloyd buys beer. Around the corner from the dojo was a beverage wholesale establishment. Lloyd realized it had been in the back of his mind all along; even when he was thinking about his wife, thinking about Jennifer, about soap and sex on the floor of a shower in Nanuet, New York, he was thinking about beer.

Once upon a time, there was beer. There was Schlitz, the champagne of bottled beers. And there was Bud, and Narragansett, and Carling Black Label, and also Pabst Blue Ribbon and Schaefer (the one beer to have when you're having more than one, until the nineties, when it became the one beer to have when you're trying to have some fun or some other neutered idea like that). In Pittsburgh, there was Iron City, and Iron City light, and in Denver, there was a little-known beer made by ultraconservative Americans who really knew their hops. Coors, they called it. Beer was beer. Suds. Brewsky. And Lloyd knew one thing about beer, the one thing that never changed no matter what beer you selected: There was no such thing as bad beer, if it was cold. The only bad beer was warm beer. In England, of course, they drank it warm, and it was fine, so maybe the distinction was bogus. Perhaps temperature didn't matter and, when you got right down to it, there was no such thing as bad beer at all. This Lloyd knew: He had never drunk a beer he didn't like. There was, of course, truly great beer. One summer, Lloyd had gone to Denmark. Although it was not well known, the Danes drank more beer than anybody except the Germans, who drank so much beer, they practically floated on it. Sitting in a little jazz club in Copenhagen one night, all by himself and feeling lonesome, Lloyd ordered a Carlsbad lager on tap. What appeared was the coldest, frostiest, tastiest, tallest glass of beer he had ever set against his lip. It was a glorious glass of beer. He put it to his mouth, and a tiny trickle went down his throat, and a tear came to his eye. Lloyd was then living on about five dollars a day, and the feeling of being treated to something of unparalleled superbness was so powerful that Lloyd never forgot that glass of beer, and he never forgot how a truly perfect beer experience could make a man feel.

He had searched for a similar intense beer buzz over and over again in his life, but had never quite achieved it. That did not make him sad, not at all. It simply sharpened his taste for the chase. And this store, here at the edge of this tiny New York suburb, was like the African veldt to a hungry hyena.

There was Blackened Voodoo lager from New Orleans, which Lloyd had already tasted and found a trifle sweet, but, if served cold, delicious and almost meaty enough to make a terrific appetizer. Two were most certainly a meal. There was Carlsberg Elephant, a heavy, substantial wallop of a brew that sank into one's tummy like a loaf of bread and, unfortunately, stayed there. Served cold, it was delicious. There was Foster's lager, which was average beer but came in an enormous can, which was not something to be sneezed at. When one's wife said, "How many beers have you had?" on the cusp of driving off to someplace social of an early evening, the honest Foster's husband could say "One!" and not be criticized, even though that one beer was the equivalent of two gigantic tankards of lusty ale. There was Rolling Rock, a good, honest American beer that now suffered from the fact that it was not a toy beer, but just a simple, straightforward amber glass of brew. It was good if served cold. There was John Courage, a somewhat fussy brew with an almost too distinguished complexity. There were Kronenbourg and very tall cans of Heineken, which Lloyd never chose because he knew it was the best beer in the world, was bored by its consistency. There was Red Dog, a really terrible beer that was about as complex as a loaf of Wonder bread, but had a great logo. There was Greek beer and Alsatian beer and Chinese beer and Korean beer and African beer and French beer and Moosehead Canadian beer, which reminded Lloyd of the only time he had been laid in a sleeping bag, and Mexican beer, which reminded him of the almost terminal case of dysentery he had caught in that nation. So Lloyd wandered amid the cases of beer, then bought a case of Brooklyn beer, because he had drunk a bottle recently in a place called the Bowery Bar in lower Manhattan while in the company of two young copywriters from a hip advertising agency in SoHo, one of whom had touched Lloyd's face when she said good night. At the last minute, Lloyd also bought two six-packs of Kingfisher beer from India, because it was right in front of him on the counter and was purported to be on sale. At $9.00 the six-pack, it certainly seemed like a deal.

Quick lunch at McDonald's. It was after one now, and everybody was hungry. If they got home without picking something up, Donna would insist on what she referred to as a "nice sandwich," or possibly a "nice bowl of soup." Nobody wanted that, so, without too much discussion, they pulled into the drive-through McDonald's that was about a mile or so from Lloyd's house. Bob had a Quarter Pounder with cheese, small fries and, in a stab at propriety, a milk. Nora, already beginning to adjust food intake in adult fashion, had a grilled chicken sandwich, small fries, and a diet Pepsi. Lloyd, who suffered under no such compulsion, ordered a double Quarter Pounder with cheese, large fries, and large diet Pepsi, a meal that weighed in on the ergonometer at more than fifteen hundred calories. The drive from McDonald's to home was less than five minutes, and by the time they pulled into the driveway, the kids had finished most of their fries and Lloyd could feel reservoirs of drool collecting in the back of his mouth.

Donna and Lloyd go to the Hayday. After lunch, Lloyd drove the family to a number of errands, chief among which was the assemblage of more than three hundred dollars of food for consumption over the next several weeks. On the way, they stopped off at Sweet Time, where Donna got a cup of

French vanilla goo. Steve, who ate soap pads, rubber bands, action figures, newspaper, bathroom tissue, soap, candles, and, once, an entire Playtex rubber glove, could sit for hours next to an open container of Donna's favorite lunch and not guess for one moment that the substance was edible. Donna loved it, though, because it was only eleven calories an ounce.

Hayday was a festival of food that left even the Food Emporium in the dust. Wherever one turned in Hayday, there was a little platter with food on it for tasting. In the front, where strange, recently invented space fruit awaited amid the more pedestrian kiwi, grapefruit, uglifruit, asparagus, and mushrooms the size and shape of a beret, there were tidbits of melon and whole strawberries of extraordinary ripeness and color. Alongside these offerings were toothpicks. Around the corner, where gorgeous hunks of salmon competed with slabs of porterhouse steak, veal, and venison and sprays of ultra-fresh shrimp beckoned from mounds of shaved ice, there were offerings of scallops in bacon, whitefish salad on crackers, and tiny bits of broiled chicken. Ralph, the meat man, was busy hacking up a freshly barbecued Cornish hen with a cleaver. Ralph loved meat. Many times, when Lloyd dropped by to gorge on samples, he regaled Lloyd with tales of meat past. After ten or fifteen minutes of meat talk, Lloyd would say, "Well, Ralph, I gotta run." "Come back tomorrow," Ralph would say. "I'll be braising a nice Polish kielbasa." Lloyd liked people who enjoyed talking about their work, who loved their work so much, they could actually be at rest with it enough to share it with others. Lloyd didn't feel that way about his work. Lloyd felt that way about beer.

By the time Lloyd got out of Hayday, he had eaten four strawberries, about half a pound of very interesting soft cheese from Schleswig-Holstein, six chunks of smoked lobster, three pieces of delicious dinner sausage from a small farm in Montana, ten or twelve crackers of various denominations, two fruit tartlets, and a small cup of decaf espresso, all for free, while at that moment there were probably several thousand homeless people freezing and starving within a mile of his office. In eight biodegradable bags with sturdy twine handles were:

- Two pounds of blueberries
- Three odd spiky fruitlike objects that Lloyd had never seen before
- A bunch of asparagus
- A handful of broccoli stalks
- Three kinds of arcane lettuce, none of them iceberg, some so bizarre that without a reference sheet, they could not be identified as lettuce, per se
- One eggplant, dark blue
- Four potatoes so large, they could have come from a Stephen King story
- Two smaller eggplants, eggshell white with tiny mauve dots

- One gigantic Vidalia onion
- Six smaller red onions
- One bag of shallots
- One six-pack of draft root beer
- One six-pack of draft birch beer
- One four-pack of raspberry soda
- One porterhouse steak (24 ounces)
- Two free-range chickens
- One lovely salmon steak
- Two pounds scallops
- Four thick veal chops
- One tub of port wine cheese spread
- One six-ounce bottle of designer mustard, the kind with the tiny grains
- One barbecued chicken, for later
- One bottle of red vinegar with a sprig of rosemary inside
- One bottle of virgin olive oil that cost as much as a bottle of expensive champagne
- One container of hummus, for dipping
- One container of tahini, for dipping
- One package of Syrian flat bread, for dipping
- One bottle of herring in cream sauce
- Two pounds of sweet sausage from Germany
- Two pounds of hot sausage from Sicily
- Twelve hot dogs from Pennsylvania, supposedly
- A dozen eggs
- Two baguettes
- One large bag of very wild rice
- One blackberry/boysenberry/rhubarb pie
- Two pounds Zimbabwean coffee
- A complement of crackers
- One copy of *Bon Appétit* magazine

"Uh-oh," said Donna on the way out of the parking lot. The kids were silent, completely full of food. Bob had spent a considerable amount of time by the fruit tartlets, and Lloyd had counted three that had disappeared whole into his mouth before he himself had been distracted by the herring in cream sauce.

"What did we forget?" said Lloyd.

"Milk," said Donna.

So they went to the Finast down the street and got all the real food that they had not been able to get at Hayday, including milk, orange juice, American cheese, Cheerios, and even a pound of bacon that Lloyd sneaked into a copy of *People* that he tossed on the conveyor belt.

When they got home, they found that Steve, having grown annoyed at that time he had been left alone on a weekend afternoon, had gotten into the linen closet and taken apart an entire roll of toilet paper. He lay on his side in a pile of the stuff, panting and satisfied, his tail wagging quietly in greeting.

Donna and Lloyd go to Lord & Taylor. While Bob and Nora watched a movie at home, Donna forced Lloyd to drive her to Lord & Taylor so that she could "duck in and pick up a couple of things." The horror of these shopping expeditions was, for men, that there were no chairs. You would see them drifting like vagrants from department to department while their wives grazed among the million items they must touch but never buy. This level of purgatory was minimal next to the seventh subbasement of hell into which Donna thrust Lloyd every time she entered the endless world of panty hose. This afternoon, they entered the department at approximately 4:10. They left at 5:00, after Donna had meandered past every single pair in the area. Unlike most times, she actually purchased one pair of black panty hose, which appeared much like every other pair of black panty hose she had looked at and rejected over the course of the last forty-five minutes. Lloyd was close to comatose, slightly dizzy, and nauseous, and he felt like weeping. He could spend an infinite amount of time at an electronics store, and he had whiled away entire days at the local gardening outlet. There was plenty to see at Lord & Taylor. Why did he have what was, in effect, an allergic reaction to the establishment?

"Thanks, Lloyd," said Donna as they inched out of the parking lot behind six tan Camrys in a row.

"I don't mind," said Lloyd. "I'm just happy you bought something."

Dinner with the Mertzes at Modern Pizza. Andy and Elaine. Best friends. Lloyd and Donna and Nora and Bob. Mertz children, Betsy and Allison. Betsy best friends with Nora. Bob and Allison okay together, too. Mertz a business affairs guy for the NFL. Funny. Politically incorrect, but from a sixties power base. Small family Italian place perilously close to the Bronx. Three-dimensional murals of southern Italy stipple the walls. Very-thin-crust pizza with plenty of cheese. Andy and Lloyd drink a lot of beer, then switch over to glasses of red wine. The older girls giggle continuously. The younger two have a serious conversation conducted in such an aura of excruciating privacy that nobody can hear what they're talking about. Donna and Elaine, drinking white wine, are complaining about the quality of math instruction in the fourth grade, which is inhabited by both Bob and Allison. The downtown redevelopment project is then dissected, with an attendant discussion of property values. Both these subjects—insufficiencies in the children's education and the collapse of their inner city—make Lloyd quite nervous. He and Mertz discuss arcana pertaining to cable distribution of organized sporting events, a subject, incredibly, of business interest to them both, for varying reasons. Dinner over at nine. At the end, in the parking lot, the men slam each other on the back several times, then kiss each other's wives.

Blockbuster Video. Lloyd runs in and rents one of his wife's favorite movies, *Rosemary's Baby,* the story of a wife tormented by a faithless, cruel husband in league with witches and warlocks who wish to impregnate her with the devil's seed.

Donna falls asleep in front of the movie. Eleven minutes into the movie, to be exact.

The children go to sleep eventually, too. But only when they really feel like it. Bob tosses in bed, singing and playing with his stuffed polar bears, for more than an hour, until he gets seriously scolded and Lloyd feels bad about it and gives him more kisses, which wakes him up even more, which means he needs a drink of water. Nora does not lie in bed at all. Instead, she sticks around quietly in her parents' room, sprawling with Steve in front of the TV, taking up very little space, just being in the presence of her elders. At 10:20, Lloyd walks her downstairs and tucks her into bed after having rooted around in her chaotic mess and found her teddy bear, Bentley.

And so, to bed, after one mother of an anxiety attack, triggered by that terrifying phone call from Doug.

Later, Lloyd got up from not sleeping and went downstairs. As he was standing in the kitchen peering into the basement, trying to decide whether or not he wanted a cookie, Lloyd realized that the answering machine was winking at him. Yup. Definitely a message.

Lloyd knew in his heart it was a business message. And he had missed it. He went downstairs, his chest constricted suddenly in the way only weekend business could produce.

"Lloyd. This is Walt," the answering machine said. "Give me a call if you get home anytime before midnight." It was then 12:13. Lloyd knew Walt was long ago snoozing. Walt always overestimated his stamina. On road trips, he was always the first one to fade into his room. "Call me, Lloyd," Walt said again. He sounded annoyed. "There's a lot to do and very little time," he said, and then his hallmark statement when the one gigantic dream vision of the future was pounding in his overheated brain: "We've got to get this done," said Walt.

So it *is* on, thought Lloyd. In spite of the fact that before it was all over, it could possibly cost more than any other deal in history and threaten industry on three continents; it's still alive, still plausible. The deal. The deal is on. But how? And more important . . . why?

In this month of wet drear and fecund rebirth, we find Lloyd face-to-face with the intricate politics and tactical demands surrounding The Deal, both the legitimate aspects that Walt knows about (which move slowly) and the other stuff he doesn't need to know about (which move rather quickly). Lloyd finds Ron Lemur around quite a bit, for reasons that are unclear to him. One might almost think that Ron had been engaged to keep an eye on Lloyd, although not really. Lloyd's relationship with Walt has never been better. One could say it almost approached friendship, although that would be ridiculous. In a world where affections could be terminated without cause, it was a fool who gave his heart to others.

In the course of working up the financial rationale and corporate mythology that makes all such deals possible (and in the meantime slightly braising the second-quarter numbers), Lloyd finds himself in increasing contact with Mona, senior vice president of finance and administration, whom we met in Lloyd's daydream back in January but didn't take as seriously as we might at that point simply because Lloyd was not yet sufficiently far gone.

Mona

Mona is single, dynamic, and windblown even in a becalmed environment, with a wild head of red hair that sets entire roomfuls of porcine executives on fire with ill-suppressed desire, but her true allure is in the magnetism generated by her passionate drive to make things happen. Work arouses her, in a very creative and positive way, and she is essentially uninterested in everyday life. She is all Now-and-How, quick to anger, laugh, decide. Lloyd finds himself thinking about her a lot and, worse, confiding in her. We see the extent of Lloyd's exposure at one session, very late in the day, that seems to lay the groundwork for a whole bunch of very bad stuff, depending on how you look at it.

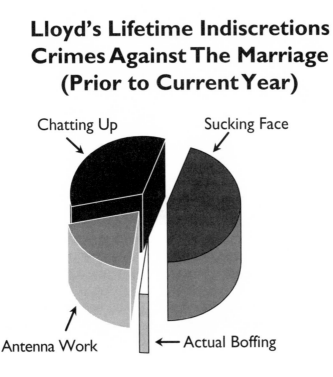

Lloyd's Lifetime Indiscretions Crimes Against The Marriage (Prior to Current Year)

Chatting Up

Sucking Face

Antenna Work

← Actual Boffing

In the Boardroom

Lloyd stood with his jacket off, both hands on the cool wood of the enormous tabletop before him. His tie dangled and beneath his nose was a large, detailed spreadsheet covered with numbers in a multiplicity of rows. His mind wasn't on the numbers at all; instead, his entire concentration was engaged in dealing with the complicated physical impressions that Mona was imposing on his biosystem.

Mona, too, was leaning over the table. She was wearing a teeny-tiny miniskirt made out of some form of endangered skin so soft and supple, Lloyd wanted to run it between his middle finger and thumb just to see what it would feel like. On her upper body was a taupe satin blouse that showed a bit of cleavage, sleeves rolled to her elbows for serious labor. Mona's fiery red hair was up today, pinned away from her neck with two wooden prongs that looked like chopsticks. Around her neck was a simple gold chain that dangled over the spreadsheet in time with Lloyd's tie.

Mona was so near, Lloyd could feel the warmth of her personal aura throbbing gently beside his. She smelled interesting, too. A hint of baby powder. Some scent, but not strong, not assertive, not fruity, not woody, not citrusy, not oily, not anything definable to Lloyd, who was bad at naming smells. He smelled her breath on the back of his neck. It was not great. Coffee in there, and tension, and a whiff of cigarette. He was having trouble controlling his breathing a little bit now, and the lower part of his torso was experiencing a familiar and completely inappropriate awakening. He had to get out of there before something started to show! He straightened up (but not too far or too fast) and pulled up one of the substantial high-backed reclining chairs that lined the table. He sat.

"The question is whether the information we have from the field is useful or correct in any meaningful way," said Lloyd.

"I wish I could smoke," said Mona. She, too, eased herself into a chair, placing her forearms on the rests and leaning back in the recliner until she was prone. Lloyd looked at her legs, long and sheathed in slightly iridescent panty hose. At the end of her legs, where shoes should have been, were feet. At the end of Mona's feet were some of the cutest toes Lloyd had ever seen. This little piggy went to market, thought Lloyd. This little piggy stayed home.

"Can we go home now?" he said.

"As if," said Mona. She lifted her right foot and put it approximately six inches from Lloyd's face. "Foot," she said.

"Unquestionably," said Lloyd.

Mona's Foot

"You like my foot," said Mona. She was stating an obvious factoid, much as she would report an EBITDA number to a group of thirsty investment bankers.

"Yes, I like your foot," said Lloyd. "But that doesn't seem responsive to the issue that's keeping us here at this point in time."

"It would be all right with me if you rubbed my foot, Lloyd," she said now. "Go ahead," she said. "Rub it."

Lloyd thought this whole thing was incredible. Was rubbing an attractive woman's foot some form of infidelity? Nonsense!

The question was, Where did you draw the line? Kissing on the lips, with minimal tongue involvement? If so, many American husbands who slept well each night were guilty and should be carted off to the woodshed immediately. Extended hugging and tongue wrangling were more problematic, but not much more, for most guys who spent more than eighteen days a year on the road. Once one used a digital extremity to execute tactile exploration on an erogenous zone, however—a finger on a nipple, for instance, or full hand engagement vis-à-vis a buttock, certainly, and most unequivocally any exploration of a genital region, naturally—the line of most sane people was passed. For some lucky relativists, actual penetration was necessary to kick off the guilt reflex, and even then there were those who believed it had to "mean something" for any substantial moral muscle to be exercised. What, then, was one to make of an offer to rub a foot safely encased in miles of synthetic?

"It would be completely inappropriate for me to rub your foot, Mona," said Lloyd.

"I would be willing to sign a written declaration indemnifying you from subsequent prosecution," she said, as if proposing an alternate payout clause in a long-term contract. If only she would stop smiling! The foot was hovering in the air in front of Lloyd. Lloyd did what he could to focus on the foot, but it was very difficult, considering that the foot was attached to a slightly plump but taut and juicy leg. Above the leg was a thigh that disappeared into a dark zone, albeit a very small one, above the thigh, under the tiny little skirt. And in there somewhere . . . a very small area . . . completely black and triangular . . . no, no. Don't look at that, thought Lloyd. That way lies madness.

"I want to rub your foot, Mona. But I'm afraid what it would lead to for a married person such as myself," said Lloyd. What the hell. Put it on the table.

"Nothing, Lloyd," said Mona. "This is just one isolated session of foot rubbing we're discussing here. No strings attached."

What a deal, thought Lloyd. How many vice presidents in the corporation would grant temporary possession of one testicle in exchange for the opportunity to rub Mona's foot? The object in question was right under his nose now. He tried not to sniff, but he failed. Incredibly, Mona's foot smelled good. Lloyd wanted not only to rub the foot; he wanted to kiss the foot. And then what would happen? A rock-hard boner had blossomed in his pants now. Worse was the fact that Mona knew about his boner. Mona knew she had elicited a huge erection in this pinstripe-suited company man who was sitting here over a spreadsheet thinking about operating profit and margins and earnings before depreciation and taxes. Maybe that's why she was smiling that horrible, decadent smile. Lloyd wanted to wipe that smile off her face. He wanted to wipe that smile off her face with a kiss—that's what he wanted to do.

"Urg," said Lloyd. He tried again. "None of this can go anywhere, Mona" was what came out.

"Oh, yes," she said. "You don't even have to articulate that thought. In fact, don't."

"But I want you to know that," said Lloyd. "I want you to know that whatever kind of enormously tantalizing cockteasing is going on here, there is not one chance in the world that it will lead to anything substantial, not physical, nor emotional, nor social, nor, like, anything like that, if you know what I mean." Lloyd was speaking, but the only thing that was going through his mind was, Foot, Foot, Foot.

"I don't want to fuck you, Lloyd," said Mona. "I just want you to rub my foot."

"Well, if that's all, then," said Lloyd.

Mona's Foot, Part Two

The ball of Mona's foot was soft and smooth, the skin under the panty hose very white and without any sort of callus material, even at the big toe and the heel, where it would have been normal to see some buildup. The nails of the toes at the end of Mona's foot were clipped very short and neat and were polished a deep Bing cherry—delicious. Lloyd wanted to pop each of them in his mouth. What the hell was he thinking about?

"Mmm," said Mona. She picked up the spreadsheet that was lying on the table and put it in her lap, resting her foot, the one not engaged, on the edge of Lloyd's chair, about six inches from his crotch. She proceeded to review the numbers on the document carefully while Lloyd concentrated on the task at hand. "I'm going to do a little work here," she said.

"Try," said Lloyd.

Lloyd took Mona's big toe between the thumb and forefinger of both hands and began gently and rhythmically to knead it between his fingers. While he was doing so, he worked a small space between Mona's big and second toe and inserted a finger into that space, too. The tender skin between a person's toes was highly sensitive. He kept up a nice firm pressure there without stretching out the panty hose too much.

Lloyd liked the space between Mona's toes, so he gently inserted all four fingers of his left hand between them while maintaining a nice rhythm on the big toe. Mona was making a big show of perusing the spreadsheet, but Lloyd noted that her legs had parted just a minuscule amount, and her tongue had slipped out between her teeth a bit. Her cheeks were a little red, too, and she was sitting 20 to 30 percent lower in her chair now.

"They're . . . hiding . . . some b-expense in these outyear . . . projections," said Mona.

"Hm," said Lloyd. "If it's in there, you'll find it."

". . . help them make their numbers . . ." she murmured, but Lloyd could barely hear her. He decided this between-toes thing was working too well. Mona's other foot was stretching out gradually, perhaps inadvertently, and was now less than four inches from a point where Lloyd did not wish it to go, a point that would change the entire nature of this . . . intercourse. He moved to the ball of Mona's foot, hoping that it would change the quality of the developing situation. The fat part of Mona's foot was fully engorged. She was arching the entire mechanism backward and offering the ball for activity. Lloyd seized the ball between thumbs and forefingers and tenderly worked it back and forth. All the tension that had built up in Mona's foot during the toe manipulation sort of melted. The foot grew quite loose and malleable and Mona's other leg retreated a tad. Lloyd thought he was losing torque and glanced across at her, his gaze, he now realized, having been on the foot for quite some time. She was looking at him across the expanse of paper, her eyes at half-mast, her mouth slightly ajar, her cheeks now redder than her nail polish, her arms carefully arrayed on the arms of the recliner. Lloyd said nothing, but he moved to the arch of her foot.

Her arch almost caused him a momentary loss of control. It was, perhaps, the most beautiful arch he had ever seen, perfectly defined, as sweeping and abruptly vertical as the vault of a medieval cathedral. He very nearly brought it to his mouth, not from any desire for Mona herself at that moment, but simply as a testament to its splendid perfection. "You have a beautiful arch," he said.

"I've been told," she said.

Lloyd rubbed the arch. "Ooh," said Mona. She put her head on the back of the recliner and closed her eyes. "That's . . . good," she said.

It suddenly occurred to Lloyd that they were completely accessible to anyone who was on the floor from two large double doors that fed onto the corridor through which all executive life must pass to get to its office. It was late, true, but still. Anyone could come in, and then what would they say? "No problem, Marv. Mona and I were just going over her foot." Or "This isn't what it looks like, Carl. Mona here just fainted and I was trying to revive her foot." No, it would be the talk of the office. The person who blundered in would see them playing footsie, literally, and immediately convey that fact to anyone within a mile of his or her reporting structure. That would be a horrible embarrassment, and worse, who knew what one of these bozos would say when drunk at a summer cocktail party and in close proximity to Donna?

"We could get caught here," said Lloyd, "doing this."

"Mmm," said Mona, her eyes still closed, her hair boiling over the back of the reclined chair like strawberry syrup over a mound of chocolate ice cream. "Would you like to get caught, Lloyd?" she said.

"Caught? No!" Lloyd practically screamed, although it was really a horrified whisper.

"Are you sure, Lloyd? Are you sure it wouldn't be just a little bit exciting to be caught rubbing my foot in the middle of the conference room? Have somebody come bursting through that door there and see us? See . . . me . . . almost flat on my back here . . . my leg between your knees . . . your hands rubbing my feet like you're doing right now, Lloyd. . . . Don't stop, Lloyd. . . . Don't stop rubbing my foot now, Lloyd." Mona's voice had grown much softer now, and kind of guttural. Her entire body had grown very, very still, and a little band of concentration knotted the line of snow-white skin between her auburn eyebrows. The spreadsheet lay in her lap now, completely inert. Lloyd had moved to the heel of her foot.

Her other foot had advanced another two inches, and Lloyd could feel it now, disturbing the air between his legs.

"Atch," said Mona.

This is not infidelity, thought Lloyd. It is simply touching another woman's foot. He had not laid a hand on her breast, although, to be completely honest, he could now see a small pucker underneath Mona's blouse that was the unmistakable sign of a nipple in full erection. He had not placed any part of his body on other forbidden portions of her body, although, to be perfectly frank, the way she was now sitting was most unladylike, in terms of how flat her thighs lay on the expanse of leather beneath them. This was a small physical game they were playing, a little dangerous, to be sure, but just a game.

"I think you'd better stop now, Lloyd," said Mona, opening her eyes and looking at him with a quiet, friendly grin.

"Stop now?" I haven't even started on the other foot, he thought. Stop now? He was aware of a piercing sense of incompleteness, a deep, painful disappointment that the harmless, intensely interesting game they had been playing could not continue. This was as alive as he had felt in American business in his entire fifteen years of history in the arena! Stop now?

"Yeah," said Mona. In most dignified fashion, she removed both feet from within Lloyd's purview and placed them squarely on the floor. She put both hands on her thighs and leaned forward directly into his face. "Unless you'd like me to take off my panty hose," she said.

"Take off your . . . panty hose?" said Lloyd. What a terrible idea! "Why would you want to take off your panty hose?"

"I don't know," said Mona. "So that you can continue your excellent work on my toes?"

"I don't think that would be a good idea," said Lloyd. "The only thing I want to do with your toes is . . . totally inappropriate. I mean, you don't want to hear what I'd like to do with your toes."

Mona was staring at Lloyd with rapt attention, and a bemused smirk played about the corners of her mouth, which was slightly open. Lloyd could hear her breath coming in shallow huffs, which he imagined were echoed somewhere . . . but where? . . . Lloyd realized the place where that whoofing noise was being emitted was himself. He and Mona were breathing virtually in unison. Their noses were not more than fourteen inches apart.

"Tell me what you would like to do to my toes," said Mona.

"It's not something we should talk about," said Lloyd.

"It can't hurt to talk about it," said Mona. "I mean, what can it hurt to talk about it? That's part of the fun. Knowing that no matter how much we talk about it, nothing can come of it."

"Nothing can come of it." Lloyd was not so sure. He was pretty sure he knew the reason why she had stopped him from continuing. Going nowhere? Like fun, thought Lloyd.

"Right. Nothing. I promise you, Lloyd. Nothing is going to happen because we played this little game tonight. I won't tell anybody. You certainly won't. There will be no repercussions, Lloyd. Think about it. Not every bad deed gets punished."

Lloyd disagreed. Almost every bad deed he had ever committed had received sure, swift retribution. No matter how hard he had tried to conceal the thing he had done, no matter how insignificant or unimportant it had seemed at the time, everyone important had found out and immediately exacted the full measure of chastisement. Panty raids in summer camp. Nights spent away from home in high school when he was supposedly at his friend's home but was really in the city with Jennifer Conley. Times he had been playing poker when he should have been at the office. Busted every time.

Mona leaned in just a little closer. "Tell me, Lloyd. Tell me what you want to do with my toes."

"I want to pop each of your toes in my mouth and pretend they're hard candy," said Lloyd. "I want to spend about two hours on your toes."

"I get it," said Mona. She looked at him for a while, and it was that searing gaze, more than any physical impression, that pumped blood into Lloyd's groin and face. He wanted to kiss her right then, but he didn't want to kiss her even more.

The air conditioning kicked on in the boardroom. It never kicked on until the temperature in the room elevated beyond a certain point. Was it possible that they had effected this change in the climate of the room?

"The only question I have is whether what you've described would go beyond the rules we've created," she said. "We've been able to have this tiny little thing tonight because we've created a very real, very objective set of regulations that allow both of us to play within the framework that limits our behavior if we're to continue to view ourselves as civilized. First, we're in the workplace. I'm a senior vice president. You're a level-forty-four department head. We have a context that can't be destroyed by our personal excesses, no matter how tempting that might seem to be. Second, you're married and very into that, not a player at all, not a sleaze—I know that, Lloyd. The fact that nothing can happen with you, nothing, you know, real . . . that's part of what makes this sort of thing not only possible but impossibly sexy." She leaned forward and put her hands on his knees, looked deep into his eyes. "Let's never let anything spoil the shallow, dead-end nature of our relationship," she said.

Lloyd wanted more than anything to take her head in his hands and kiss her on the mouth.

"Panty hose" was what he eventually whuffed out.

"Okay," she said.

Mona stood up directly in front of Lloyd. The lower portion of her abdomen was not more than a foot away from the tip of his nose. He had a mental flash of himself reaching out with both hands and grasping a buttock in each, drawing her tummy close and burying his cheek in its soft/hard surface. Instead, he made a conscious effort not to let his tongue hang out.

"I don't believe I should leave you alone," she said. "When I return, you might or might not be here."

"Um," said Lloyd.

She released her hair—cruel woman, did she not know this was her most devastating feature?—and let it pop free. She placed both hands in her mane and gave her scalp an energetic massage. When she was done, a nimbus of golden red framed her face. Her eyes were a deeper green now, the green of marble, shot with bolts of lighter chartreuse, and very wide. Her skin, always pale, was as white as an orchid, and, like a flower, under the surface of the white flesh was an almost-imperceptible tone of another color, red and pink, but just a hint, nothing you could put your finger on. . . . Put your finger on, thought Lloyd. . . . Nothing to put your finger on . . .

Mona stepped away from him and demurely turned her back. She looked over her shoulder with an accusatory gleam. "Turn around, Lloyd," she said.

Lloyd turned around. His heart was pounding horribly. Would he be the first business executive to have a coronary while trying to avoid having sex?

On the wall of the boardroom was a large piece of paper that had been torn from a big pad that their organization consultant had been using to capture ideas from a session on reorganization they had been conducting earlier in the day. The page looked like this:

Negatives/Issues

- Culture decimated
- Forced retirement of most qualified individuals
- Excessive productivity requirements
- Labor unrest
- Revenue impact
- Bad industry positioning
- Loss of customer confidence

Positives/Upside

- Improved cost structure
- Better-operating cash flow
- Possible acquisition opportunities
- More security for key players
- Actualization of senior-management priorities

The last item, Lloyd remembered, had occasioned a huge, boisterous guffaw from the entire assembly, which had included Darling, Fitz, Sweet, and, at one point, Walt, who had come in to give them a pep talk about determination and toughness of spirit and all that kind of stuff. After he had left, they had added "actualization of key management priorities" to keep them going for a while. Put into English, this phrase simply meant they had to accomplish this reengineering thing because Walt wanted them to do it. For his part, of course, Walt had to do it because Doug wanted him to do it. And up above Doug? Was there human life on that level? There were rumors there was. Something about a man named Arthur. Very old. Very removed. Someplace at corporate headquarters. Arthur. Lloyd had been with the corporation for a long time. The name had come up, perhaps, twice, always in a tone that was not only reverential but fearful, as if to talk about Arthur was to tempt fate, much as the ancient Hebrews were enjoined from mentioning the name of their God, or of writing down His name.

Lloyd thought about these large sheafs of paper covered with virtually incomprehensible consultant jottings. The drill was simple and the same in almost every corporation. The consultant came in. There was an easel with a large pad on it, like two feet wide by three feet high, filled with poor-quality paper that was clearly meant to be used and recycled. The consultant would conduct his session and fill up pages of this pad with jottings. When each page was full, it was ripped from the pad and Scotch-taped to the wall. This presented a problem for corporations that had fabric wallpaper, as the paper lifted off from the porous surface and fell to the floor, but masking tape usually did the trick. After such meetings, the consultant would look at the room, which was now lined with sometimes a dozen or more broadsides covered with untelligible gook, and say, "Well, I guess somebody better capture this work." He or she would then carefully remove the pages from the wall, roll them up into a tube, then port them away for the critical process of capture. Some weeks later, a document would come from the consultant that was inevitably superfluous to the life of the corporation, because the result of any good meeting could be summed up in three or four words, or perhaps one or two compelling ideas, such as "Cut Finance in half," or "Buy Time Warner," or maybe, more simply, "Let's meet again Tuesday." This paper Lloyd was looking at was no different. All it did was codify their indecision, confusion, and underlying despair.

"Lloyd?" said Mona.

No Stockings

Mona was sitting on the edge of the boardroom table. The panty hose, which had sheathed her legs in dark nylon—or whatever the hell they were making panty hose out of these days—was gone, possibly stuffed in Mona's briefcase.

Lloyd was worried now. The panty hose had provided some measure of security against his worse judgment. All that lay between their mutual assured destruction now was some leather, a little silk, maybe, one zipper, and ten thousand years of sexual taboos. Not enough.

There was another thing, too. A warm glow of pleasure had engulfed his entire psychosexual machinery, from his cheeks and the back of his neck to his nipples, which were sort of buzzing quietly, to his thighs and the back of his legs, which were engorged with blood and who knew what other fluids, to the more obvious regions of his reproductive system, which were now fully

146

engaged in preparing for what they believed was their natural duty. He had gone from flaccid to completely, painfully erect and back again no fewer than three times in the last twenty minutes. Right now, he was somewhere between dress-parade attention and at ease.

"Mona," he said. "You're a bad girl."

Mona lifted her leg to him again. This time, he could see her undies without any trouble, and he did not bother to avert his gaze. He wanted to touch the tiny white triangle there.

"Get over here, Spunky," said Mona.

Lloyd Balks

No, no, thought Lloyd. Boundaries. Too far too fast. Even by corrupt standards, too much at once. Starving man. Feast syndrome. Eats tons. Explodes. A surfeit of panties. Hair. An excess of hair, all over the place. Must stop now. Stop it somehow now.

"Mona," quoth Lloyd. He kept his distance.

"Lloyd," said Mona. There was a wrinkle of sternness about her demeanor now, and a certain managerial cast to her tone. "I have removed my panty hose for superior access to my toes, which you have all but promised to service. We have at least another fifteen minutes of this exquisite torture before one of us must call an end to it, but we're far from that point, Lloyd. There's no danger of you going too far because I won't allow it."

"You won't?" said Lloyd. He was amazed and surprised at the plaintive quality his voice had assumed. "I mean . . . you won't, huh?"

"Not at all, Lloyd. You think I want to get laid on the boardroom table? I didn't complete four years at Harvard and several more at Wharton and MIT in order to get pumped on my own boardroom table. This is just a tease. And if you can't do it without a lot of Sturm und Drang, then maybe we'd better call it off. But don't tell me to call it off, Lloyd. I really don't want to. It's too much fun, isn't it?"

"It's been a little slice of heaven so far," said Lloyd. And he kind of meant it. His entire system was tuned to an inaudible pitch, like the highest harmonic on a violin. He was alive, aware of every sound, every modulation in the space between them. If Mona had touched him anywhere on his body, he would have closed his eyes, rolled on his side, and kicked one leg fast.

"So you're the control mechanism here?" said Lloyd. He was stalling to see what she would do to move things forward now.

"That's right," said Mona. She leaned over onto one arm, slipping her feet under her onto the surface of the boardroom table, her entire body now off the floor. She made herself more comfortable by leaning over completely and resting her head on her hand, her arm propped up on one elbow. "I torture you. You attempt to retain some kind of control. I apply more pressure, to which you are most certainly susceptible. You cave in and begin to come on way too strong, the call of the wild having been, like, suppressed for so long, it cannot be denied anymore. This of course places the responsibility for keeping things on track completely on me, and I turn the tables at the last possible minute, to your relief and our mutual frustration. We go home, exhausted but comfortable with the level of impropriety we've committed. Honestly, the last thing I want is to create some kind of permanent discomfort between you and me, or you and yourself, or you and your wife. The only question is, Can you handle it, Lloyd?"

Lloyd sat down in a chair close to where Mona was perching on the boardroom table. What was he to do? He knew the right thing to do. He knew the complete and utter wrong thing to do, which is what he would not do, not because he was a great person, but because there was no question in his mind that he basically did not want to. What he wanted to do was a very small wrong thing. Which is what this incredible, sophisticated, fascinatingly powerful woman was offering him. Maybe that was the problem. Who was interested in something so circumscribed? If there was indeed no danger of development, what was the point of doing it?"

"I mean," said Lloyd thoughtfully, "if this thing is completely packaged and delineated by our mutual needs and limitations, what's the point of getting into it in the first place?"

"Why don't you just give yourself the pleasure of doing exactly what I want?" said Mona. He brought his eyes up to meet hers. "You're in control all the time, Lloyd," she said in that terrible, matter-of-fact MBA voice she took on when she was not to be denied. "Why not trust me and give over that control now? Then, at least until neither of us no longer wants it."

"Give up?" said Lloyd.

"Yeah, that's right. You give up control. You trust me to not take advantage. I try not to, because that's not easy. When I see you assert control, I stop you. Unless, of course, you will not be stopped. Then we see." She sat up, crossed her legs, and sat Indian-style. Her tiny skirt was now up around her waist. "Think of how many venues we have to play our little harmless games, Lloyd. Think how many offices there are here at headquarters. How many meetings we attend off-site. How many retreats and road shows we have to sit at next to each other. It's a perfect setup for two intelligent, creative people who want to torment each other but stop on the brink of having an affair that would possibly destroy their professional and personal lives."

"Nothing can be that perfect," said Lloyd.

"No, I know it," said Mona. "But when we find a hole in it, we can reevaluate. Until then . . ."

"Gimme," said Lloyd.

Lloyd seized Mona's naked foot and plunged all five toes into his mouth.

"Ah," said Mona, and settled back on the table, both hands behind her, arms stretched behind her back, supporting her weight. "Ah, Lloyd, go slow," she said.

Lloyd removed the slightly wet foot from his mouth. "Why, Mona?" he said. "You're the one who's in control." He ran his tongue roughly from Mona's right heel all the way up her arch and into the soft, supple skin between her big toe and the ball of her foot. "Oh," she said.

"Lloyd, you'd better stop. I . . . misjudged this particular exercise."

"Okay," said Lloyd. But he did not stop.

"Stop, Lloyd," said Mona. She was leaning back still. Her pubis was slightly elevated off the table now and there was a troubled look on her face. "Stop, Lloyd. Stop," she said.

Lloyd stopped. Mona instantly withdrew her foot. "That was too much," she said.

"I'm glad to hear that," said Lloyd. He had a hard-on the size of a baseball bat. He longed with all his heart to push Mona back on the boardroom table and put both of them out of their misery.

"Man," she said.

"We gonna continue to do this kind of thing?" said Lloyd.

"What are you guys doing in here? Making out?" Walt was standing in the doorway in his winter trench coat. How long had he been there?

"Going over the first quarter," said Lloyd.

"It's way too late to be working," said Walt. "Why don't you guys knock it off?"

"We will," said Mona. She did not move from the edge of the table. Lloyd stayed ensconced in the enormous comfy chair. Mona wanted to adjust her skirt but feared that such a motion would create the wrong impression. Walt was looking them over with molten intensity, but Lloyd realized with relief that he was not present with them in the room at that moment, but was beaming his physical persona in from the reality vector he was then inhabiting.

"Business could be better," said Lloyd, trying to transfer his shock at being caught and his frustrated desire for Mona into a believable expression of concern about operating performance.

Walt gazed through him. His left hand was in the pocket of his coat. His right hand, gloveless, rose aimlessly to his face and pinched his lower lip. Mona and Lloyd awaited his next statement, which they knew could come in three seconds, three minutes, or possibly three years. Patience was all with Walt. Most of the time, what came out of his mouth was worth the wait, for one reason or another.

"We could do it, you know. We could get it done," was what he said.

There was a smoldering, weighty silence, the sound, Lloyd imagined, that lava would make while cooling. Walt had left them again and was just standing there having an out-of-body experience in their presence. Lloyd's engorged projectile had gone into remission again, and he felt it was safe to stand and meander around the room, putting some distance between him and the roaring sexual engine of fantasy and flesh that was his peer and fellow vice president, who took Lloyd's movement as a fitting occasion to leap lightly off the table and go to her briefcase. When the pause had grown to more than half a minute, Lloyd could take it no longer. As Mona settled primly into one of the reclining chairs—which no longer looked quite so much like a couch to Lloyd, and more like a functional seating unit—Lloyd barked at Walt in a tone that sounded a trifle snappish to himself. "What, Walt? What is it that we could get done?"

"We could explode revenues, quadruple operating profits, and become the largest industry distribution system in history," said Walt. "In one action."

Lloyd felt tremendously disquieted by this line of discourse. Walt had been making noises like this for the past several months, but he had remained vague and grandiose, had not yet entered the strategic-planning mode that Lloyd knew would inevitably follow these sort of pronouncements. He had an urge to excuse himself on account of the lateness of the hour and get out of there, but that was impossible. Walt was on a roll. The trick was to try to make it a small seeded roll that could be toasted and eaten in a few minutes, as opposed to a foot-long French bread that would take hours to knead, bake, and eat. Lloyd was also worried about the way Mona was acting. Rather than maintaining her businesslike demeanor, one that would help Lloyd assure a brief and effective interface, she was showing all signs of total engagement. She had tucked her magnificent, long, well-muscled legs beneath her luscious bottom, which until just moments ago had been so close, and was leaning forward, staring directly at Walt's face.

"Get specific, Walt," she said now. "I've heard this from you before and I'm at the point of wanting to know what you're talking about. I know you're thinking about something. How can we help you get it done if you don't take us into your confidence?" It was as if no sensuous incidence had recently occurred at all to anyone within her social circle, let alone herself. She was completely involved in the business instant. Ready to produce ideas, paper, projections, or just brain smoke if need be. Lloyd felt admiration sweep over him for this splendid woman and, most alarming, a positive feeling of—what was that? . . . Tenderness?

No, no, thought Lloyd. God help me.

"We could buy it all," said Walt, and slammed back into his body with a tremendous crunch. Walt was home now and open for business.

"What do you mean, Walt?" said Lloyd to fill space.

What Walt was talking about was the biggest deal ever, a monster acquisition that would make them the largest multinational conglomerate in the world, dedicated to virtually all businesses in existence, and some that were not. Targets included firms in Tokyo, Berlin, and Milan, with operations in all major international landmasses, and more than 400,000 employees worldwide. The resulting corporation would be one of the most powerful human entities on the globe, more sizable and important than many governments that supposedly united people into national units, with security forces more sophisticated and potent than a good number of armies. What kind of madness was this?

"How much debt would this involve?" said Mona.

"Between eighty and one hundred," said Walt.

"Billion," said Lloyd.

"Reorganization and disposition of nonstrategic assets could reduce that number to under sixty billion within three years," said Walt. "The competitive impact would be significant, in that we would essentially control several sectors of our business completely, and certain elements of hardware production in associated defense electronics and missile-guidance systems worldwide. We could also build on this international distribution and production system to integrate the entire business food chain vertically from the smallest local elements to the macrosystems that move global markets. We're talking Rome here, guys. Rome. Not since Rome has there been a strategy like this."

"And look what happened to them," said Lloyd.

"Simple. Elegant. Achievable. We're just the ones who can do it. We've got extensive business dealings with everyone already. We know everything is for sale at the right price. We fit with them all like . . . nobody's business." Walt was not good with metaphors. This was one of his favorites.

"Does Doug know about this yet?" Mona said. She was up on her feet now.

"I've given him a little peek under the skirt," said Walt with a grim smile. "He'll need to be pulled all the way into this thing, but he's game. He's got a mandate to enlarge us. We're basically the best hope of the corporation for double-digit EBITDA increases. If the rationale is there, they'll move it down the field."

"You take care of the heavy lifting, Walt," said Mona with quiet confidence. She advanced on Walt and stood just within his aurora. "We'll handle the rationale."

"Not a word of this to anyone," said Walt, who turned and left.

Lloyd and Mona stood in the empty boardroom and looked at each other. Mona crossed to the table and grabbed her briefcase, then turned and walked up to Lloyd, standing just a little too close.

"Not a word of this to anyone," she said. Then she took his hand, placed it between her lips, and bit it, not enough to make a significant bruise, or to draw blood, just enough to leave a tiny indentation, the meaning of which would be significant only to one who was present when it was made.

"Ouch," said Lloyd.

"That's only the beginning," said Mona, and left.

"Is cleaning!" said Rosa, rumbling into the room with her cart before her like a Zamboni machine.

Lloyd stood in the middle of the boardroom. As Rosa vacuumed and fussed around him like a tornado, he existed in the calm eye and thought, Nothing lasts. Business associations. Love. The company of children. The equanimity dispensed by a full portion of mead. The peace of sleep. The friendship of men, or women. Lloyd was in a bleak mood. He tried to make himself feel worse. He thought of his children, trusting little spuds now preparing to fight the washing of their bodies and the cleansing of their teeth and wondering when Daddy would be coming home to tuck them in and kiss them good night. He thought of Donna, intelligent, contemplative, fit as a racehorse, reliant on his hard work and honesty to maintain the world they had both created together. He thought of his house, which he liked to live in very much and had no desire to leave, especially in the middle of the night, after a torrential battle with his spouse over revealed infidelity. He thought of Steve, the dog, whose life revolved around some very simple things: his dish, his ball, his family. Was he so very different from that?

While his mind spun about this constellation of fixed points, there was a bright light growing in breadth and intensity. Right now, it was illuminating his entire internal landscape. Soon, it would be all he could see. In that light, seated in glory, was a woman with skin of pearl white, a woman with flaming red hair, a woman naked, seated on a reclining high-backed boardroom chair, her arms on the arms of that chair, her carriage straight and proud, her breasts full and heavy and round, with nipples small, pink and peach, constricted with desire. The woman smiled, and that smile bathed him with a warmth that spread from the bottom of his limbic brain to the outward reach of his imagination, and silently, without voice, the woman called to him, called with a music that suffused his entire being and drove him forward into the light, into the invisible, the unfathomable, the miraculous.

And there in the boardroom, with the drone of the cleaning machinery mingling with the hum of the woman who operated it, something inside Lloyd strained, cracked, broke, and came away from its moorings, lifted from its base and went lumbering off into the luminescent unknown.

Would it ever return?

On his way home, Lloyd picked up some flowers for his wife. She was pleased with them.

June

Drift. Memory, and the memory of desire. Lloyd is long-ing, for . . . something. It's vague, but also enormous and ugly. Huge, yes. A gargantuan lodestone reeking evil light and calling, "Lloyd. Lloyd."

He is working longer and enjoying it more. He thinks about the first days of his marriage, about the first days of his career, about the way he always thought his life would go . . . and is going, sort of. And where is that, exactly? Toward comfort, respectability, moderate, even deep satisfaction on most fronts, despair and grief at intermittent intervals, with enough time in between to almost forget about the fact they were bound to happen, and eventually, like a tiny penlight at the end of a very long room, death. But so what about death! Ha! Or so Lloyd thinks.

Lloyd begins having a few pops with Ron after work on a regular basis. Sometimes Mona comes along. Occasionally, they end up at a club, listening to music. He feels some-thing beginning to break free.

Although these and many other matters of developing interest are explored in this chapter, only two things actually take place here. First, Lloyd gets stuck in an ele-vator by himself for more than forty minutes. Sec-ond, he steps off the eleva-tor at the end of his . . . ride . . . and finds a memo waiting for him. Here is the memo:*

> June 19
> Confidential
>
> Lloyd:
>   Please plan to spend the best part of July building some bridges with our German friends, who seem to need some intelligent cajoling. Tell Helen what you need about tick-ets, hotel, etc. She'll set it up.
>   See me later about your itinerary. I figure two weeks or so should do it. Plan to go alone, by the way. I believe our German friends want to deal with partners who can stand alone when need be, not with a bunch of dogs who huddle together for warmth.
>   Congratulations!
>
> **DOUG**

*See end of chapter for full text of letter.

153

Who Knows, at the Beginning of a Day, How It Will End?

Lloyd woke up that morning with a tremendous urge to mount something. Donna was already in the shower. He listened to the sound the water made hitting his wife, pouring down over her body.

He went into the bathroom and saw his wife's naked form behind the smoked glass of the shower. Lloyd considered doffing his boxer shorts and climbing into the shower with her. But the kids . . . the kids were set to awaken any moment, and Donna was already into the morning pipeline of frenetic activity.

"I have a mother of a day ahead of me," said Lloyd.

"Uh-huh," said Donna from behind the opaque glass.

"Can I come in?" he asked his wife.

"I'm shaving my legs, Lloyd," said Donna. "But you can come in if you want."

Lloyd locked the door to the bathroom and opened the door to the shower. It was very crowded in there, and his wife was indeed shaving her legs. She was bent over in the corner of the stall, facing away from Lloyd.

"I have to make lunch for the kids," said Donna. She continued shaving.

Lloyd got a good lather going, then made a great show of washing his wife's back.

"You look good," said Lloyd.

"I'm fat."

"Thank God you're still a little on the chunky side," said Lloyd, grabbing her gently but decisively from behind.

"You shouldn't get too amorous, Lloyd," said Donna. "Bob's gonna be up in a minute."

"I locked the door."

"We'd have to make it awful quick." Donna was leaning up against the shower wall now, hugging herself under the spray.

"I can do that," said Lloyd.

"Well," said Donna. "Let's try." She wrapped her arms around him and circled his waist with one of her legs.

Bob knocked on the bathroom door.

"I have to pee!" he yelled quite loudly and unpleasantly. Bob was not a morning person.

"We could tell him to go away," whispered Lloyd under the quiet roar of the shower.

"He'll get suspicious," said Donna.

"We'll be there in a minute, sweet pea." She was already out the shower door.

"Rats," said Lloyd.

Donna stepped out onto the cushy mat and grabbed a towel. "It's cold in here," she said. Her nipples were tight and erect as the tip of a baby's pinkie. Lloyd decided to concentrate on washing and calming himself down. The water was hot and good. Lloyd let it pour over his body. What he wouldn't give to be able to wrap himself in a fluffy towel and head on back to bed for a quiet lie-in. He would snuggle under the comforter while his wife took the kids to school. He would watch music videos. Later on, he would see what cartoons were on cable. When the phone rang, he would answer it, sounding enervated and dejected, as one who was incapacitated should. He would return important calls, sure. But on some level, he would revert to his original self, the nonessential Lloyd who was free to be whatever he determined was important for that extended moment in time. He turned off the water and stepped out of the shower. Donna was there doing something to her eyelashes with a gizmotic object that Lloyd had seen before.

"Hi," said Lloyd.

"Hi, Lloyd," said Donna.

Lloyd was completely engorged with blood in all his extremities. He could actually feel his heartbeat pounding in his big toe. Donna left the bathroom.

Lloyd dried himself off as Bob, having at first been thwarted from his quest, finally waddled into the bathroom and, eyes closed, took care of business. Bob did not bother to raise the seat, or aim particularly well. Lloyd said nothing, and in fact, he felt a small twinge of pride.

"Morning, geek stink breath," said Lloyd.

"Dad," said Bob cordially.

Lloyd started shaving. The events of the day ahead were daunting. Lloyd hated shaving but hated himself unshaven even more.

He got into his shirt and socks and headed for his closet. There, a number of blue suits hung waiting. He took one and a yellow-red-and-dark-blue tie that set off the whole ensemble handsomely.

By 7:40, he was in his car and headed to the station.

The Elevator to Nowhere

The elevator was a long time coming, which should have told Lloyd something. Once it arrived, it beeped angrily and slammed its doors back and forth. It was a nasty elevator, but Lloyd passed through anyway. What choice did he have? Up was where he had to be.

The first leg of the elevator's journey began with a trip through X-Land. Lloyd always thought of it as X-Land, because it was designated on the panel by an X. Rationally, Lloyd knew this meant that the elevator was traveling on an express route between the ground floor and the twenty-fourth. But he still thought of it as an undiscovered country, filled with Japanese guys smoking and drinking scotch on their way to a hypertense business meeting at which somebody would be sent back to the home country. Lloyd was happy to avoid X-Land. He considered it one of the benefits that came with inhabiting one of the upper floors.

Somewhere in X-Land, however, things began to go awry. Wrenching Lloyd's stomach from the muscular tissue that attached it to the wall of his interior cavity, the elevator suddenly bumped and lurched to a precipitous halt. Not quite a complete one, however, no, a partial halt, one that caught the mechanism up short and then allowed it to inch painfully upward one increment at a time.

"Help!" Lloyd screamed. He punched the button in the console before him. "Help!" he said again, attempting this time to be slightly more executive.

"Murf nox bleeporg frenish!" said the elevator grille.

"I'm stuck in here!" said Lloyd at a rather dramatic volume.

"Flemming breekmanish?" said the voice at the other end of the line.

"I can't understand you!" said Lloyd. "The car is, like, just creeping upward! Is it dangerous?" He was aware that his entire frame was trembling, and his head was very light, very muffin-filled. "Get me out of here, 'kay?" His vocal pitch and tone were those of a terrified eight-year-old, the age to which Lloyd usually reverted when he was truly threatened. He took a deep breath. "Are you there?" he said into the microphone box.

"Jes!" said the box. "We are having technical difficulties! Please stand by!" Lloyd was amazed by this statement, cribbed from a basic text provided by countless movies and television programs.

The elevator was now making its way upward at a speed of approximately one foot per minute. Every now and then, it gave a giant lurch, paused for a time, then continued. Every time it lurched, Lloyd screamed.

"Get me out of here!" he shrieked into the box once more.

"We are attempting to addressing the situation!" said the heavily accented voice at the other end of the wire. Sounded friendly. Like to meet the guy sometime, thought Lloyd. Have a beer. Maybe two. And a scotch chaser. Mud in your eye.

"Hi!" said the voice at the other end of the line quite abruptly.

"Hi!" shrieked Lloyd.

"We are experiencing technical difficulties," said the voice apologetically.

"Yes?" said Lloyd. "And?"

"And we are experiencing technical difficulties and are calling the company."

"Which?" said Lloyd.

"We are calling the company!" barked the voice in what now seemed to be either deeply clipped Hindi or possibly that of a recent arrival from Puerto Rico. Dominican Republic?

"This thing is not going to fall down the shaft or something, is it?" said Lloyd. He knew it was a stupid question. If it was going to fall, would the guy tell him about it? Say, "Yes, there's a good chance the elevator will fall down the shaft and you will be killed. Try to leap up at the exact moment the box hits the floor. I've always thought that might work." No, he would say, "No, no, man. You completely safe. Relax." Which is what he did say.

It was silent in the elevator. Lloyd took a deep, deep breath. He wanted a cigarette. He hadn't had one in—what, seven years? There were still times he dreamed about it. His favorites had been those with no filter at all, cigarettes that ripped the inner cortex of your lungs from its moorings and sent it drifting amid the cochlea, or whatever the hell was in your lungs. Lloyd thought about the guy he had seen in the hospital. He was missing a lung. That was worse than being stuck in an elevator. And the guy wasn't screaming. It's amazing what a person can get used to.

When he was seventeen, over the summer, he had started smoking for real. There was something about smoking when you were that age. You knew that if you continued, you might kill yourself with it in twenty or thirty years. But nobody ever died of cigarette-induced lung cancer at the age of seventeen. Or very, very few, at any rate. Fewer than died from choking on a chicken bone, probably. That was a horrible way to die. People also died of drug overdoses, sure. Or traffic accidents, jerks who impaled themselves on lampposts in the drunken dark. But smoke a cigarette and die? No way. If one was willing to bank on one's stamina to quit at the age of, say, thirty, one could smoke with relative impunity throughout his twenties, wearing black, popping a coffin nail between one's lips, lighting . . . inhaling . . . the rough, sweet scratch of all kinds of horrible irritants massaging the lungs. Gitaines . . . Gitaines were the best. Kind of roasted flavor. Camels, too. Moist and kind of loamy. And Luckys—they're toasted! Finally everyone ended up with Marlboros, though. Lloyd thought about his first serious girlfriend, Nell. The apartment in the village. Marlboros.

He realized that the elevator hadn't bumped in a while, and he looked around. He waited, holding his breath.

"Hang in there. We are attempting to address the situation!" said the box again. The elevator had ceased activity entirely. As long as the elevator did not move, Lloyd could live with this. He could convince himself that he was in a little tiny room. A waiting room. Waiting for a friend. Waiting for the *Robert E. Lee*. Waiting for Godot.

"Can you give me an estimated time of escape from this thing?" he asked the wall.

"I have someone who wishes to speak with you!" said the voice.

"Me?" said Lloyd quite stupidly.

"Of course you!" said the voice. "Hold on one minute, please!"

"Lloyd?" It was Walt's voice. "Lloyd? This is Walt here! Can you read me, Lloyd?"

"Walt!" screamed Lloyd. "Get me out of this fucking thing!"

"Yes, yes," said Walt. "Of course. But in the meantime . . . I'm here with Doug, Lloyd, and I was wondering if you had the deal papers with you."

"The deal papers!" screamed Lloyd. "Yeah, Walt, I have the fucking deal papers and I also have a cellular phone and a battery-powered portable fax in my briefcase here! Why don't we conduct the whole fucking meeting with me stuck in an elevator twenty-two floors up!"

There was a brief conference at the other end of the line.

"That will be fine," said Walt. "We'll call you from the box on the fifty-second floor. What's your cellular number?"

Lloyd gave it. He heard a click. They were gone.

Lloyd in the Elevator

Lloyd heard a creak. It wasn't a big creak. It was a small creak. A tiny little shifting in the center of the car's weight. Lloyd was sitting on the floor now and felt it very clearly in the lower part of his spine. They were inching downward.

"Eek . . ." said Lloyd. Perhaps he didn't say "Eek," exactly. He didn't *say* anything, actually. A sound escaped him, that was all.

He put his briefcase in front of him and opened it. It was full of paper. There were address books, green-lined envelopes that contained personnel forms with people's merit increases in them, memos about Finance Department reengineering, old correspondence, and an envelope containing instructions for several home samples he was supposed to have collected subsequent to his recent physical, which had taken place last week. He hadn't looked forward to the collection process.

He had not enjoyed the physical at all. The procedure in the Executive Wellness Center was a concept new to Lloyd. When he checked in, he received a locker key that was already assigned him, by name. He made his way to the men's locker room, where row upon row of deep mahogany lockers awaited crucial individuals. In the locker was an outfit that would suit either the busy surgeon or the terminally ill mental patient. Lloyd looked at it. It was in a hermetically sealed plastic bag. He referred to the instruction sheet that had been issued him at the door to the place. It instructed him to put on the gown and pants and stow all his valuables in the locker.

"Here," said a voice at his elbow, very quiet, very discreet. "This should fit you better."

"Thank you," said Lloyd. He took the plastic-enshrined package from the attendant, who disappeared as quickly as he had materialized. He stared at the package for a while, then ripped it open and started putting on the garment within. As he did so, he noticed there were two influential executives suiting up in his area. One looked to be an Indian man in his late forties who had gone completely and somewhat prematurely white. The other was a whip-lean Japanese man in his fifties with a huge shock of steel-gray hair. Both were in varying degrees of nakedness. Lloyd wondered who they were, what they made, what kind of power they wielded when they were not simply cotton-clad specimens. We're all going to die, thought Lloyd. We are all one skipped heartbeat away from a gurgling quietus on the bathroom floor. He thought of Pittsburgh.

The pants were very large and needed to be cinched up and tied aggressively simply to stay somewhere near his waist. It occurred to Lloyd that the locker room attendant had viewed him, upon entering, as an extremely fat man in need of capacious garmentage, which he was clearly not. He tied the long jacket, which mercifully closed in front, and regarded the next instruction on his sheet, which required him to give a urine sample in the test tube provided and leave it at the door for later processing. He went to the bathroom at the end of the room and, with cup and glass tubing, did as he was instructed. He noticed that his urine was darker than he would have liked, and he considered adding water to it. No, he thought. How dumb would that be? If there's something wrong with me, I want to know about it, don't I?

He left the golden receptacle in the container, upright, where it stood next to that of the Indian CEO and his Japanese counterpart. The waiting room was about the size of a hotel lobby, opulent, very quiet, with an outsized TV screen in one corner broadcasting CNN and a buffet table on the other side of the room offering a load of healthful breakfast alternatives—segmented muffins of corn, bran, and blueberry, cold cereals and milks sporting varying levels of fat, grapefruits, oranges, caffeinated coffee, hot water for a panoply of teas both caffeinated and non, and an urn of decaf coffee, which was labeled "Decaff." There was also toast and a range of interesting-looking breads. Unfortunately, Lloyd had been instructed to neither eat nor drink until he was explicitly permitted to do so. He took a seat next to a grossly overweight young business manager who was reading the *Wall Street Journal*. He, for his part, had *USA Today*. He turned the pages, not really seeing.

He resented the feeling that he was not a healthy person being given a checkup, but a sick person being evaluated. He hated being stripped down in front of these other mysterious potentates, whose actual status could not be measured because they were all wearing the same clothes.

His doctor had been a religious zealot who, while checking for prostate inflammation, had exhorted him to be more observant in his faith. About one test that Donna had instructed Lloyd to take, the doctor said, "I don't know why anybody wants to take that test. If it registers solidly positive, you're dead anyhow. If it's a low-level reading, you could start down a road with biopsies, and eventually maybe you have to have the whole thing removed.

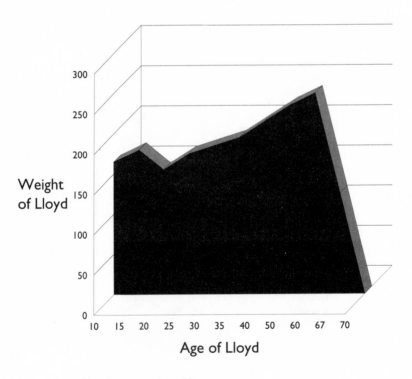

Size of Physical Plant

Weight of Lloyd

Age of Lloyd

Lloyd's not getting older.
He's getting fatter.

160

Slide 1

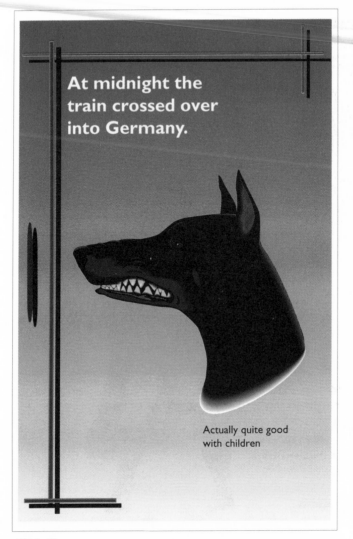

Slide 2

Lloyd goes to Germany, and then to Italy, to do business, so of course he does some. The following three slides give you some idea of what he was up to.

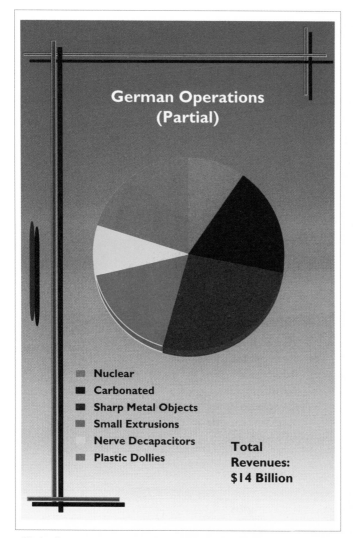

Slide 3

This was a portion of the stuff he was
supposed to acquire via merger. On the
next page is what was expected of his
Italian initiative. The essential deal was
already agreed to at a higher level, but
that didn't mean the whole thing was a
lock. Lloyd could screw it up.

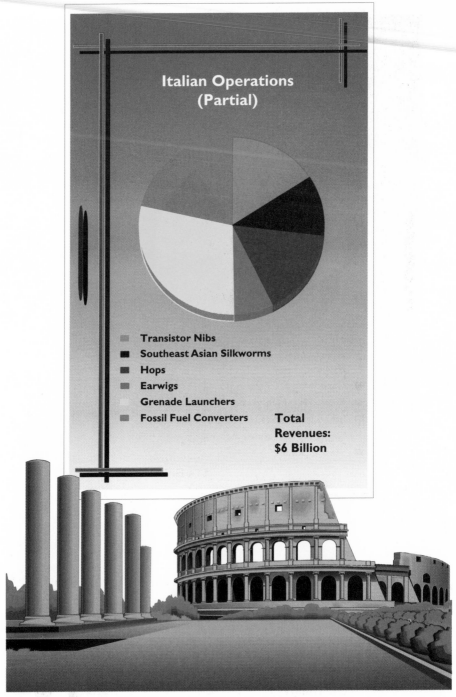

Slide 4

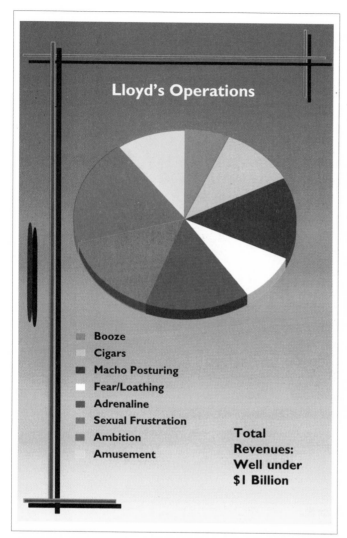

Slide 5

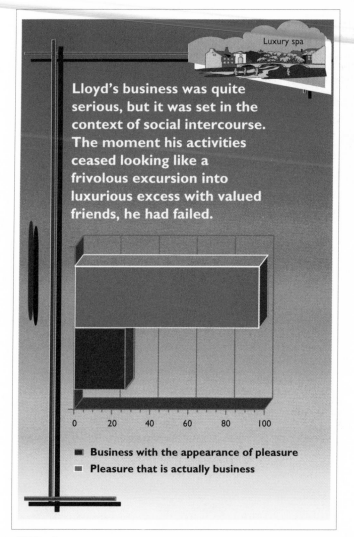

Slide 6

During the couple hours a day he's actually doing something other than eating, drinking, and recovering, Lloyd finds it necessary and advisable to spend some time with Mona on the phone, strategizing.

166

His assignment consisted of a series of ceremonial meetings, each of which would have a tiny, fragile nugget of substance hidden within the massive husk of chaff. Lloyd spoke no German or Italian, and he was sure his new partners would be constantly muttering in unintelligible gibberish behind his back.

Slide 7

Beyond that and the more duty-oriented, long-distance talks he has with Walt, Doug, and Ron, Lloyd finds the primary activity required is nothing but raw, unadulterated, exhausting jollity and schmoozing, which, in fact, is the business, since Germans, like most people, prefer to deal with those who at least pretend to like them.

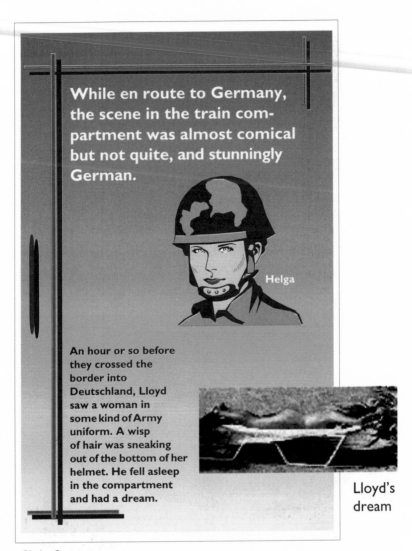

While en route to Germany, the scene in the train compartment was almost comical but not quite, and stunningly German.

Helga

An hour or so before they crossed the border into Deutschland, Lloyd saw a woman in some kind of Army uniform. A wisp of hair was sneaking out of the bottom of her helmet. He fell asleep in the compartment and had a dream.

Lloyd's dream

Slide 8

In so doing, it becomes increasingly difficult to abjure from drinking himself into stone oblivion every night, beginning at dusk and ending at the time of the night when one must either go to sleep or do something really very bad.

Lloyd was unprepared for how he was treated the moment he crossed over into Germany. He had hit London first, and the British were prim and unintrusive. When they passed across the Channel into Calais, the French begged Lloyd's pardon and generally gave the impression that they had been finely infused with garlic butter, and were now ready to be tasted.

Slide 9

At the Dutch frontier, it was much the same. The authorities were polite, perhaps even happy to see him, although that seemed unlikely.

Slide 10

Before too very long, Lloyd notices that he feels like he can do anything. The talks are going well. People treat him like a nabob. He is, indeed, an Uberbusinessmensch. He even goes so far as to begin speaking with a very slight Continental accent that he kind of likes.

Slide 11

With all restraints gone and an ever-increasing sense of his own strangeness to himself, Lloyd begins to exert his new, Teutonic personality more forcefully than he would have ever dreamed possible. This makes business go even better.

Slide 12

By the end of his trip, he has convinced both himself and his hosts that he, Lloyd, is a dynamic, rigorous, indestructible business honcho with balls of steel and guts to match. Nobody doesn't listen to what he has to say, even when it is not worth listening to.

This is heady stuff, and unattainable
at home. Lloyd is intoxicated by the
seeming fabulosity of the new he. Being a
German is fun!

He had always felt a substantial personal difficulty with individuals incapable of controlling the arrogant exercise of authority.

Slide 14

After ten days or so, he goes home and tries on his new persona. Before long, he and Donna no longer recognize each other. There is one particularly unpleasant evening that is just plain rotten from the moment Lloyd steps through the door after a nasty train ride home to the final instant immediately after the front door has slammed and Lloyd is on the wrong side of it.

Slide 15

Where will Lloyd go!? What will Lloyd do?

Slide 16

On the stoop, with his keys in his pocket, he pounds on the door until Donna lets him in. His European suavity is gone. The Ubermensch has fled. He and his wife have an intelligent and ultimately quite tender conversation over a bowl of Wheatabix. Then they both go upstairs and go to sleep. All is well. But is everything really back to normal? Only time will tell. And, as always, it does. Relatively soon, too.

And after that . . . you could possibly never . . . function again, you know? For nothing. Maybe nothing was wrong anyhow. So everybody's getting that test now. It's a fad."

"Well, so what are you saying?" said Lloyd. "I should disregard the results of the test?"

"No, you can't," said the doctor, who had a long, rather stringy beard and a rapidly balding head, even though he was possibly younger than thirty-five. "At any rate, let's not talk about that. Is there anything that bothers you about your health?"

"No," said Lloyd. "I'd like to lose a couple of pounds."

"Really?" said the doctor with some surprise, appraisingly squinting at Lloyd. "How much do you weigh?" He looked at Lloyd's chart and then did some calculations on a document in the file. "Um-hm," said the doctor. "Yup. You could lose twenty pounds."

"Yeah, sure, I could do that," said Lloyd.

"Or maybe, yeah, thirty, certainly thirty," said the doctor, still jotting.

"Thirty?" said Lloyd. "That's a lot."

"You put down your ideal weight here on the form," said the doctor. "Your ideal weight would be almost forty pounds less."

"Forty pounds!" Lloyd was really upset now. Forty pounds! Fat men have to lose forty pounds! He was certainly not a fat man. He would lose twenty pounds and that would be that.

"And your blood pressure is a little high," said the doctor. "It's one thirty-five over ninety."

"That's not very high," said Lloyd. He was starting to get a little bit pissed off.

"I think you should cut out the saltshaker, before I put you on medication," he said.

"Medication!" said Lloyd. He was shocked. "Would you like me to retire to Florida?"

"Also no canned soups, or potato chips, stuff like that. Come back next week and I'll give you the results of your test, and a tetanus shot, which you should have immediately, considering that you should have a booster every ten years or so." The doctor stood and stared blankly at Lloyd, making no move to shake his hand or place an avuncular arm about his shoulders. Lloyd realized that not once during their thirty-minute visit had the physician offered Lloyd his name.

"What is your name?" said Lloyd, who felt tempted to add, "so that I make sure not to see you ever again."

"Dr. Monsky," said the doctor. "With a *y.*"

"Well . . ." said Lloyd lamely. "Thank you, Dr. Monsky."

For the first time in his life, Lloyd now believed, he would have to take at least temporary steps to fix up his body. Before he left the lounge, he had a glass of orange juice, a small bowl of cereal, and a tiny corn muffin nuggetine. If the head nurse had come out of her glass and steel enclosure and said, "I'm sorry, sir, but it seems you need to be hospitalized immediately," he would not have been surprised. Never had death felt so close.

"Lloyd?" the elevator speaker coughed his name. Lloyd jumped. "Is there a power source near you at any location?" It was Walt's voice. He heard murmuring behind Walt, too. Who was there? Ron? Mona?

"Everything I've got here is RF and battery-powered," said Lloyd. He opened his bag and got out his gear.

In the briefcase was a variety of hardware. First was his cell phone, which was fully charged, and his laptop, with a remote fax/modem slot inserted in its available PCMCIA slot. He opened the laptop and dialed the modem into his office computer, which, like the machine he worked on here, was loaded with a program called PC Anywhere. In a few moments, he was looking at the screen of his office computer. "Give me a minute here," he said to the people on the other end of the line. He typed for a while. It was a good laptop, except that it used the detachable Microsoft trackball for a mouse. The built-in trackball of the Powerbook was much superior. The Microsoft detachable mouse always detached right in the middle of the session, requiring an immediate return to manual keystroking in the Windows environment that stopped the heart and left the wrist weak and mealy. Still, the Toshiba cost nearly five thousand dollars, loaded with RAM and ROM and portable CD player and everything necessary for a full-scale financial presentation at a moment's notice. Right now, Lloyd was accessing the Persuasion dog-and-pony show that contained the strategic rationale and the numbers-related superstructure developed in support of the deal they were scheduled to discuss. "I'm on it," said Lloyd. "Give me a couple seconds more."

"Hell, man, take your time," said Walt. "We're not the ones awaiting certain death." He heard a hearty business chuckle and then chairs being pulled out and the low mutter of business voices exchanging worthless information to pass the time. "Lloyd is a whiz on these things," he heard Walt tell somebody in the area.

Lloyd took off his jacket, folded it neatly, and set it down on the floor of the car and sat down next to it.

It occurred to him that not one person on the other end of this makeshift squawk box gave a damn about the fact that he was sequestered in here. He felt a tiny kernel of something coalesce and harden deep within his chest.

"I've got the documents up now," said Lloyd. He felt very dry. Cold inside. If this was the way they meant him to conduct this meeting, so be it. He would do it. Later, he would see them in hell. Or on the golf course. Whichever came first.

"What are the outyear projections on the revenue stream of the combined operations?" said Doug. Lloyd could seem him in his mind's eye. His jacket was off, folded neatly over the back of an adjacent high-backed boardroom chair. He had his perfectly shined shoes up on the boardroom table, a position that was itself a declaration of power, since nobody present would dare do the same with him in the room. His shoes were themselves a work of art. Three hundred dollars at the least. Their soles tan and pristine, having walked on no sidewalk, ever, because Doug went from home to car to office to corporate dining room to internal meeting areas to car and home again in those shoes, never achieving outdoor living at any moment. Doug would be running his thumb along his bloodred suspenders, too.

"Immediate revenue impact is dramatic," said Lloyd. "We're talking about a four hundred percent increase in top-line performance immediately."

"With associated debt and operating expenses, right?" said a voice. It was Ron Lemur. What was Lemur doing at the meeting? The minute Lloyd was not there, there came Lemur, suck-up that he was. Clever bastard.

"My impression is that it's all about top-line revenue and improved operating margins," said Lloyd with frosty reserve. "Those increased revenues translate to a doubling of operating profit and commensurate boost in EBITDA almost immediately, which increases our ability to borrow as well, as of course you know."

"What kind of synergies are we talking about?" said Doug. "These firms have a lot of operating locations in places that are hard to reach. We could be talking about no potential redundancies at all."

"We've got to get our arms around this thing," said Walt. "Take it up the ramp, fieldstrip it. There's no point in doing it if it's basically a wash by the time we get to the bottom line."

"I think," said Lloyd, "that it comes down to where we can produce and distribute the product through a consolidated process. That means probably shutting down eight of forty-two plants worldwide and focusing quality management in the key remaining areas."

"Eight of forty-two, with no discernible impact on revenue?" said Doug.

"Looks that way," said Lloyd.

"Good, Lloyd," said Doug.

The elevator fell about eighteen feet then, very smoothly, all at once, and then stopped.

Lloyd passed out.

The New Lloyd

"Lloyd! Hey! You all right?" It was Walt. "What the hell is going on around here!" He was screaming. "You've had that man in there for more than half an hour and nothing's going on! You!" Muttering of an intense nature in the background, and then: "Hey! You! I'm talking to . . . I'm the one who's doing the talking. Get it? Get it!" Lloyd heard it as in a dream, saw in his mind's eye a giant Roman in full metal breastplate and bristled helmet, ordering a plebeian to his death. He appreciated it.

"We're gonna get you out of there, buddy!" yelled Walt. Silence. The sound of receding voices. A door slamming.

Lloyd sat up. He felt completely devoid of blood. His head drifted, pounding, somewhere above his neck. His ears were ringing. He felt an overpowering gag reflex seize the back of his throat, a bubble rise in his stomach. "Please," he said to nobody in particular.

"I think the elevator has finally found its level." It was Doug, very quiet, conspiratorial, almost.

"Doug?"

"Do we know how to run any of these businesses, Lloyd?"

"Maybe the way to run them," said Lloyd, "is to leave them alone. They run pretty well already."

"I'm sure we could bring some management science to it," said Doug.

"Maybe." Lloyd had seen a lot of management science in merger situations. He didn't think much of it.

"You have to calm down more."

Lloyd was not sure he had heard Doug correctly.

"I have to . . . what?" said Lloyd.

"Calm down, Lloyd." Doug's voice was matter-of-fact, not soothing at all. This was not the suggestion of a friend, although it was not put unkindly. This was a command of some sort.

"I'm not sure I know what you mean," said Lloyd, even though he was quite sure what Doug meant. Why did he bother to posture with the man? Doug saw right through him.

"You worry too much. Do what you can about the things that come before you. Attempt to know everything. Don't whip yourself. Not everything is in your control. The things you can control, though . . . control everything. And relax, Lloyd. You've got the job for another six months."

"Gee, thanks, Doug."

"Be colder, Lloyd," said Doug. "You'll live longer."

"I want to live," said Lloyd. He thought of Schoendienst. He thought about his blood pressure. He looked at the six metal surfaces of the elevator, which seemed to be moving slightly toward him. And, all at once, the dam of civilization that had been built up inside his breast over the years neatly burst, and a great black ooze poured forth, bathing Lloyd's insides with poisonous liquor, sealing his vital organs shut, exploding from his ears, nose, and mouth in invisible clouds of greenish steam. And Lloyd was Lloyd no more. It was one hell of a great feeling.

"I tell you what, Doug," said Lloyd into the metal squawk box on the wall.

"Yes, Lloyd?"

"You make this deal. You purchase this thing. You put Walt in charge. We'll make you a ton of money. The vertical synergies are impressive enough, but it's the horizontal implications on both production and distribution that have yet to be quantified. More than that. If we, like, don't do this, if we chicken out of it in some way, or drop the ball in the middle, or just plain analyze it to death, we'll kick ourselves for the rest of our lives. We've got to do it. It's logical. It makes sense."

"You don't do a deal like this because it makes sense, Lloyd," said Doug. "You do it because it can be done."

"Well," said Lloyd, "that makes me feel real good."

"The essential, basic issue of all strategic actions of this type, the factor that determines the wisdom of the move itself, is management, Lloyd. The majority of mergers fail because existing management doesn't know what to do with the toy once the parent has indulged the child and given it what it wants. That is certainly true here. Unless I miss my guess, you guys don't have a single coherent plan in place about what to do if you ever get your hands on our targets. Don't you think that's rather unmanagerial?"

"Give us a couple of hours and we'll give you a plan."

"Why don't you just work on it yourself, Lloyd," said Doug thoughtfully. "There will be a myriad of management issues while we wait for guidance."

"I beg your pardon?" Lloyd was completely confused. What the hell was Doug talking about? Guidance?

"Guidance," said Doug. There was a creepy silence on the other end of the line. Lloyd said nothing. What kind of guidance? God? Was Doug a nut?

"I may want you to do some traveling, Lloyd," Doug said after a while.

"Sure, Doug."

"I'll send you some paper on it."

"Okay, great," said Lloyd.

The elevator took one great hitch downward, then began smoothly to rise upward toward its appointed floor.

Out of the Can

The elevator stopped. The doors opened. Lloyd realized he was looking at the floor, which was about six inches from his chest, at basically eye level. It took him a second or two to understand where he was exactly. His explosion of bile and adrenaline had departed. He was lighter, somehow. He felt like kicking somebody in the face a couple of times, real hard. It was a good feeling.

Lloyd hauled himself off the elevator, hoisting his body up the last two feet with a tremendous effort of will and whatever residual strength remained in his upper arms. He stood in the elevator waiting area and took a deep breath of air. Free!

Whatever had been left of the decent, God-fearing, pedestrian Lloyd had been burned clean off in the fire of solitude he had just passed through.

"Lloyd! Dude!" said Lemur, who got to him first.

"What the fuck are you doing here, Ron?" said Lloyd.

"Lloyd, man!" Lemur looked profoundly wounded. His lower lip trembled a little. Lloyd thought it looked pretty authentic.

"The minute I'm not at the meeting, you're there. You weren't invited to the meeting, Ron. You are not free to go to a meeting to which you are not invited. Do you get that? You are not an independent agent. You work for me. Yes or no? You don't work for me, you don't work with me."

"Okay, okay, Lloyd, man," said Lemur. "Gee."

"I can't feel like you're sniping at me from the bunker, son," said Lloyd.

"Okay, okay, Lloyd," said Ron. "No problem. I mean, I mean it. No problem at all."

Lloyd was impressed. This was the best result he had achieved with Ron to date. Ron had always been independent-minded, and he clung to a dotted-line reporting relationship with an executive vice president on the West Coast who nominally oversaw Ron's performance review. But his true love was freelancing.

"Okay, Ron," said Lloyd. He offered his hand to Ron, not to shake, but to kiss, with the proper amount of irony.

Ron kissed it.

And then he was in the middle of his colleagues as they strode forward one by one, sweeping into a circle around Lloyd, smiting his back, punching his shoulder, laying hands on him. Walt was there, standing somewhat apart, examining something interesting in the distance, sneaking peeks at Lloyd to see if he was really all right. Fitz, who while ostensibly checking for broken bones, inadvertently stepped on Lloyd's foot several times with suspicious force. Doug, too . . . and was Doug touching him on the shoulder? Doug touching him. He felt his body tighten like one giant muscle in spasm.

Mona stood a micron too close to Lloyd, with one soft hand resting lightly on his forearm, looking with professional concern directly into his eyes.

"Are you all right, Lloyd?" she said.

"Never better," said Lloyd.

Two Hours Later

Back at his desk, Lloyd found a memo waiting for him:

```
June 19                        C O N F I D E N T I A L

Lloyd:
Please plan to spend the best part of July building some
bridges with our German friends, who seem to need some
intelligent cajoling. Tell Helen what you need about
tickets, hotel, etc. She'll set it up. See me later about
your itinerary. I figure two weeks or so should do it.
Plan to go alone, by the way. I believe our German
friends want to deal with partners who can stand on their
own when need be, not a bunch of dogs who huddle together
for warmth. Congratulations!
                        Doug
P.S. There's no need to mention this little sojourn to
Walt. He has been told that you're off to Florida to
recuperate from your ordeal, and also to investigate the
site and setup of our executive management forum in Sara-
sota, or wherever the heck it's supposed to be this year.
Nuff said?
                        D.
P.P.S. On a more personal note, Lloyd, I would like to add
kudos for having conducted a full business meeting from
an elevator. Excellent performance. Keep up the good work.
```

And so, thought Lloyd, . . . off to . . . Germany. Home of BMWs and wursts and Beethoven. And, of course, millions and millions of Germans.

Alone in a foreign land, without his family. Without rudder or barometer. With unlimited access to plastic and not a need in the world. Traveling first-class all the way. Hamburg. Berlin. The Black Forest. Perhaps he would have some cake there.

Maybe he'd better brush up on his German. All he could come up with at that moment was *Achtung*, baby.

Perhaps that would be enough.

Lloyd now enters that magic country to which all executive travelers must journey if they wish to play where the game counts—Businessland. It matters not where this place may be on the globe of the real world, for everywhere it is the same. From the limo to the plane. From the plane to a train, perhaps, especially if one is in Europe. From the train to the hotel. From the hotel to a tall, glass tower with spare furniture and plenty of marble, or wood, or steel and glass. Men, then, mostly, men engaging in the sport of war, sometimes the sport of friendship. The days go past and each day little more of one's original personality drops away, until finally there is just the businessperson, the job, and whatever may happen in the strange place that is so far from home. You will be happy to know, right up front, that Lloyd did indeed get the job done, and that this trip of his would one day be written about in *Fortune* magazine as, "one of the most expeditious and productive international sojourns since Don Kendall served Nikita Khrushchev his first Pepsi." Would you enjoy some snapshots of Lloyd's trip?

Worldwide Market Share

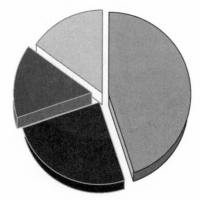

- Germany
- Lloyd's Company
- Italy
- Japan

Snapshots

1. Here is Lloyd packing. Lloyd always overpacks. For a ten-day trip to Germany, Lloyd takes:
   — 14 pairs of black socks
   — 12 pairs of underwear
   — 4 pairs of boxer shorts (to sleep in)
   — 4 white T-shirts
   — 1 pair of running shoes
   — 3 pairs of neatly creased khaki "casual" pants
   — 1 pair of tight black jeans (for Berlin club scene)
   — 20 dress shirts
   — 5 suits (black, blue, dark blue pinstripe, gray pinstripe, wrinkled off-white)
   — 1 "wrinkled" oatmeal-colored silk sports jacket
   — 15 ties
   — 3 black button-down "cool" shirts (for Berlin)
   — 8 chemise Lacoste shirts (in rainbow colors)
   — 1 pair of heavy wing-tipped shoes
   — 12 disposable shavers (Bic)
   — 2 disposable paperback books
   — 26 pounds of paperwork
   — assorted toiletries
   Lloyd still feels he has forgotten something.

2. Here is Lloyd's carry-on luggage. Lloyd is afraid to check bags, so he walks around in the airport like a camel loaded up for a trip from Jordan to Mecca. He is in considerable pain. And when he gets on board the aircraft, two entire overhead compartments are filled with his stuff.

3. Here is Lloyd's airplane seat. It is in first class. This is policy. All plane trips over five hours require a first-class plane ticket for senior vice presidents of level 3 or under, the lower grade being the superior one. Doug, for example, would be a grade-0 executive on the business unit level. Walt would be a 1. Lloyd was a newly minted 3, and quite proud of it.

4. Here is Lloyd's airline dinner, served at about midnight New York time. The sauce is very strange. The meat has attained a microwaved perfection: soft, yet grainy; stringy, but also crumbly. Lloyd believes it had once

been beef but is no longer, having mutated into a form of protein not wholly unfoodlike, but not immediately recognizable. There is also a cube of Gruyère cheese, with crackers. Scalloped potatoes, too, apparently. Quite good, really. Several moments ago, Lloyd finished a generous portion of hot nuts, which he found delicious. Now he is feeling guilty. As instructed, Lloyd has drunk a lot of water already and feels quite sloshy. He eats everything before him anyway. There is white wine and then red, then after-dinner brandy . . . as much as he wants. Strawberries with chocolate. An oatmeal cookie. Then two. Everything is free. A warm feeling of physical well-being has now stolen over Lloyd, only slightly offset by his fear of being blown from the sky by a terrorist bomb or faulty piece of replacement equipment. He closes his eyes and imagines himself, still alive, hurtling head-down toward the earth, which rushes up to join him. Then he sleeps.

5. Here's what Lloyd thinks over deep in the middle of the transatlantic night: The stewardess—no no, that isn't the correct word—the female flight attendant is quite pretty in an exhausted and slightly plastic way. Several years ago, due to lawsuits and societal changes of all kinds, the role of flight attendant had changed. Lloyd had recently been served on a flight to Jacksonville, Florida, by a fellow who looked like he could have coached college football until mandatory retirement age kicked in— a short, stocky Irishman with a fleshy, beefy, ruddy face sporting a bouquet of capillaries blossoming off his nose.

On the woman's side of the profession, things had changed, as well. Where before there had pretty much been a population of cybernetically engineered fantasy bimbos, now there is a wide range of real human beings with a variety of positive attributes and drawbacks. While many still adhere to the older, blowsier standard, the vast majority look to be indistinguishable from ordinary individuals with a tough job to do trying their best to deal with a public in varying degrees of rage, need, and anxiety. Not long ago, Lloyd recalls, a senior business executive from New York City, on a flight from somewhere in South America, had enjoyed a bit too much to drink and, when refused additional service, had defecated on the food-service cart. He had then wiped himself with the cloth napkins that had been provided for a somewhat different purpose. Finneran was the man's name. For months afterward, the incident had been the subject of hilarious debate throughout the corporation. Lloyd considers. Has he ever been drunk enough to shit on a food-service cart?

Lloyd looks at the ash-blond female flight attendant now bending over him to turn out his light. She believes him to be asleep and is trying to make him more comfortable. He lets her go on thinking so. Her right breast, sheathed in a white linen blouse and a blue starched apron that

186

runs from her knees to her chest, is mere inches from his face. The breast appears firm and not particularly large, no, but certainly ample enough to fill its allotted space. The breast bobs merrily right before Lloyd's lidded eyes. She is pretty. Her hair is a bit rumpled from long hours of toting and lifting and scurrying and, perhaps most difficult, smiling. Around the edges of her eyes are splashes of tiny wrinkles. Around thirty years old. Married. There is a ring. Kids? Sure. What does her husband do? Is she happy? Is she willing, as so many people seem to be, to destroy her happiness, at least temporarily, by an ill-considered act of sheer hedonism? Uh-oh. Lloyd realizes his eyes are open now, and staring into hers as she continues leaning over to collect some of the errant material befouling his place setting.

"Hello," she says, pausing for a moment, then keeping on with whatever fussy thing she is doing. She does not retreat, though. Lloyd finds that interesting.

"Hi," he says. He is painfully aware that he has just awakened and is not in full possession of his defended self.

"Can I get you a pillow?" she says.

"Amanda," says Lloyd, looking at the little tag on her uniform. "No, thank you . . . Amanda."

"Go back to sleep now, Lloyd," says the flight attendant. How does she know his name?

"How do you know my name?" says Lloyd. He feels naked, exposed.

"We have a little thing called a manifest, you know." Is she flirting with him? Is she just being friendly?

"Want a little more water?" she says.

"No, no."

"Club soda?"

"Okay," says Lloyd, more to break the contact than anything else.

Lloyd leans back in his hippo chair and is immediately unconscious. When he wakes up, he is in London.

6. Here is London. Lloyd has a meeting here.
7. Here is Lloyd talking with a British banker. They are resolving an arcane issue of international financing and an approach to the complicated tax implications of borrowing on a global basis. Lloyd's meeting goes well. He could fly to Germany from London but decides not to. From this time forth until the end of his life, Lloyd will avoid flying whenever possible, having received several mental images of himself distributed over acres of verdant farmland after the plane upon which he imagined himself to be flying disintegrates in midair. He decides to take the train.
8. Here is Lloyd falling, somewhere over Belgium, in his imagination.
9. Here is Lloyd in Germany.

Lloyd is in Europe on business that will redraw the map of the international corporate world. If he succeeds in the task at hand, troops of higher executives will migrate over to take his place, flags flying, papers open to signature pages, ready for notarization. So little of what Lloyd has to do concerns substance, however. No, this is about trust. Will. The high concept. Can he pull it off?

To complete the assignment, Lloyd will have to take a couple of ceremonial meetings, only one of which will have some actual substance in it. Lloyd speaks no German and he is sure his new partners will be constantly muttering in unintelligible gibberish behind his back.

10. Here is the conference room in Berlin where Lloyd meets with Mr. Horst and Mr. Jaekel, the two German industrialists who form the core discussion group from the other side. Horst is short and fat. Jaekel is a model of fitness, tall, angular, with a bony oval head on a strong, lean frame. Neither man has any hair to speak of, by design, the style in Teutonic culture this year being the power-balding dome.

At first, the meeting does not go well, because Lloyd is in a funny place both mentally and physically. He has rested relatively comfortably on the train, after being awakened by the border patrol in the night.* He checked in very early in the day, unpacked, and took a shower. Like most showers in Europe, this one was pretty terrible, a puerile trickle alternating with short, hostile bursts of superheated steam. In the middle of the ordeal, as his head was covered with lather, the water gave out altogether, except for a stone-cold dribble that Lloyd could barely feel through his hair. He sat down on the floor of the shower and waited. It wasn't like this was a substandard hotel or anything. The rate was more than four hundred dollars per night.

The room itself was fine, although a bit strange, as all rooms abroad tended to be. First of all, it smelled different than an American room. Impossible to say how. Was it the laundry soap? The disinfectant used to keep the toilets clean? The quality of the dust underneath the bed? Lloyd didn't know. It didn't smell like home, though. The minibar was amazingly tiny, filled with strange brands and foods he didn't want or recognize. Nutella, of course. Toblerone by the pound. Odd beers and bitters. A stick of sausage, another of cheese loaded with what looked like pimento. An assortment of crackers that made him feel homesick. As for the size of the place itself, it was also fine, as far as it went. Two rooms, very small, perfectly regular. One with a queen-sized bed and a television in a bureau, the other room with a love seat, desk, and telephone. The carpets were gray, the walls white. The furniture was polished mahogany, quite lovely, func-

*See visual documentation, page 176.

tional, no handles on the drawers at all. It took a minute for Lloyd to find the little indentations that made their opening possible. On a gleaming table by the window was a basket. In the basket was a bottle of champagne, several apples, some grapes, a few bars of chocolate. "Welcome to Berlin," said a note. "Your friends at Blod." There was a personal message scrawled in German. Lloyd tried to read it, then gave up.

The bathroom was the most bizarre area of all, with fixtures that could have come from another planet. It smelled weird, too. And the water tasted alien. Lloyd shaved, combed his hair, and got out of there.

12. This was the view from Lloyd's hotel room. A cat was sitting on a garbage can. It was a skinny cat. A German cat. He called, "Hey, kitty!" but the cat didn't respond. Do cats ever? Lloyd was swept by a wave of loneliness and insecurity. He took two tiny bottles of gin from the courtesy bar, poured them into a bathroom glass, and downed the contents. What time was it at home? What time was it now? His first meeting was in two hours. Lloyd called the front desk and arranged for a wake-up call, then fell asleep.

13. At the meeting with Horst and Jaekel, Lloyd feels like someone has wrapped his head in cotton batting and, for good measure, forced him to swallow some. It is only the most important meeting of his life. Is he going to screw it up?

14. The two Germans are cordial but unimpressed as Lloyd circles the issues between them and leads them on his version of the gentle gavotte that precedes all serious engagements. Horst is game enough for it, but Jaekel looks bored. Yet it is too early to lay the facts out on the smorgasbord. There must be more human interaction. Lloyd racks his brain. The taste of blood fills the back of his throat. Now what? he thinks, and in that moment, the answer comes to him.

15. Meanwhile, back at the ranch . . .

16. Here is Ron Lemur in his office in New York. He is plotting and dreaming. Dreaming and scheming.

17. Staff vice presidents reporting to the chief executive officer—in this case, Walt—make on the order of $350,000 a year. Ron sees the number in his mind: $350,000. He now makes about a hundred grand. This he considers chicken feed, and, in fairness, it is, when one considers the proximity of Ron's daily work to the top branches of the organizational tree. In addition to the $350,000, top reports also receive a bonus equal to approximately 50 to 75 percent of their salaries, and also stock options. A guy like Stein, who has been with the company for several decades, now holds hundreds of thousands of options, at varying valuations. Some are underwater, having been issued when the stock was doing better than it is today. Many, however, are worth several times their face value.

18. The way options worked is this: The option is issued at a "strike price" of, say, ten dollars, or what the company's security is worth on the day the option is granted. In one year's time, which is the first day the option can be exercised, the stock will be worth, for instance, eleven dollars. This means a fellow like Lloyd has now made, simply for sitting around waiting, fifteen thousand dollars, since Lloyd is given about fifteen thousand options every year, give or take. A personage like Stein, who runs a profit center, makes fifty thousand dollars. Walt probably can take in more than five hundred thousand. And Doug? It is not uncommon for the chairman to receive a million options, thanks to the awesome contribution he, in his excellence, has given to the company. Options need not be exercised at year-end, of course. The best strategy, if one believes in the enterprise, is to hold on to the options until the last possible minute, so they attain maximum value. Options, more than any other compensation, are a way for individuals to achieve personal wealth.

19. The concept, relatively new to polite discourse, is "wealth generation." This is a phrase that Lloyd had not seen until 1996, on a résumé of a senior officer type who had been laid off from his Fortune 500 company. "Objectives: (1) to run a major firm with international operations. (2) wealth generation." Lloyd saw the résumé while perusing the contents of Walt's desk, upside down, during an extended meeting. This naked admission was slightly chilling to Lloyd. Was it appropriate to admit that you were after personal wealth at the expense of fellow workers, shareholders, the customer?

20. Ron has no options to speak of. Last year, he was the recipient, under one of Walt's pet programs, of a one-time Attaboy award of one hundred show options, given to employees who weren't in the pool but did good work, according to their general managers. Ron hates his one hundred shares with a white-hot animus. The hundred options, in several years, could be worth thousands of dollars if the company moves up in value. But they will never be worth millions. The lousy hundred options represent all that Ron hasn't earned, all the status that has not yet come his way, the respect he so far lacks.

21. Ron sits in his office, thinking about things. It is all he can do to contain his anger. What good would a display of pique do? The organization respects people who do their thing and do not complain. There are no bonus points for emotion. Ron stands up and walks to his window. There are four plate-glass windows. He had asked for five and not gotten it. He had also asked for a lot more money. That is pending, which is interesting. Pending is not a denial. Quite a few things are interesting right now. Doug, for instance. While Walt has virtually nothing to do with Ron, Doug seems, in a weird, dismissive way, to get a kick out of

him. At meetings, sometimes, he will turn to him and, with a quizzical smile Ron can not quite read, ask him, "I wonder what callow youth might feel about that," or some such oblique, insulting query. Ron will always live up to Doug's assumption by offering the most disgustingly venal and short-term analysis of the situation. And Doug will be pleased. Just the other day, Doug had asked him to assemble an industry profile of companies with revenues of more than $10 billion. Why, Ron did not ask. But he did a good job on it. Or rather, he had Kaskowitz do a good job on it, slapped his name on a hastily produced cover page, then personally delivered it to Doug. In Doug's office, he hobnobs with Kali, Doug's gorgeous Brahman secretary. Whenever he sees Kali, Ron thinks about the *Kama-sutra*. There is no reason for this. Kali is always quite proper, even a little stiff. But since he had read the *Kama-sutra* while in college, Ron has a secret jones for Indian women, suspecting them of harboring powerful sexuality not evident from their public demeanor. Is it his imagination or does Kali actually like to flirt with him a little?

22. Ron leaves his office and makes a slow turn around the executive floor. He keeps his pad with him in case an officer walks by, so he will look busy, on the way to something. He thinks about Alix. Things are going well with Alix. If only the girl wasn't so expensive. She believes him to be a high-powered executive. He does not want to disabuse her of that. She feels him to be a man of power. When he is with her, sometimes he believes it himself. That feeling of mastery is one he can't see living without. He goes into the law library for a moment. It is quiet in there.

23. Alix is tall, and languid, and kind of loopy. So much has happened since that first night. Immediately, he had blown off—what was her name, Gretchen? Alix is all he can handle. Too much energy. Too much need. God, how many needs could be wrapped up in one woman! How many needs could one woman excite in him? And this is no ordinary woman, if there is such a thing. This is an acquisitive, aggressive woman with tremendous imagination and physicality. She wants him. She wants things for him. She wants him around. If he has drugs, she wants those. If he has a hard-on, she wants that, too. Food also. Drinks. Music. She is a thirsty, hungry maw just waiting to be fed. When properly maintained, she gives back more than any partner whom Ron has ever experienced. When deprived, however, she is terrifying. Her disappointment is a like a rock fastened to a rope around his neck. He has felt it once or twice. He never wants to again. The first thing that goes is her sexual drive. She becomes inaccessible to him. That pain is worse than a toothache. He needs to find his reflection in her satisfaction. She is all that truly matters now. Ron loves. And in spite of what you read, love is not always beautiful in people. Ugly people love ugly. And so it is with Ron.

Ron's Executive Behavior Since 1990

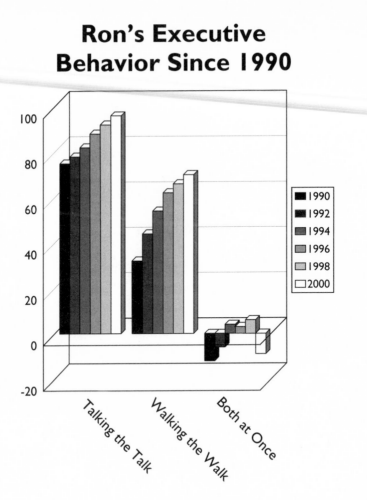

24. Here is Ron sucking up to Doug, whom he has run into on his perambulations around the executive wing. He is complimenting Doug on his tie. Doug, you would think, would hate this, and see it for what it is. But you would be wrong. Doug is very smart. Doug graduated from William and Mary, with a graduate degree in philosophy from Yale. Doug is the closest thing to a genius in the building, except for Mr. Arliss, the custodian, who, due to circumstances, never received an education and has no idea of his own mental capacity, merely thinks that for some reason he is prodigiously good at crossword puzzles. But that's another story. No, Doug is wise to Ron, aware that Ron is a terrific suck-up. The unspoken recognition that sucking up is taking place gives it its rich emotional context. If sucking up takes place and neither party is aware of it, does it take place at all?

25. "That tie is a work of art!" is what Ron says. "Thanks, Ronald," says Doug, unable to suppress his pleasure. "When I die, I'll leave it to you."

Both men laugh at this, Ron perhaps a little too loudly. That kid really knows how to play the game is what Doug thinks as he continues on his way down the hall after this exchange. That went good is what Ron is thinking.

26. Here is Ron working Walt. Walt, unlike Doug, hates a suck-up. Some guys do, but they are very rare. "Can I help you, Mr. Lemur," Walt says. Ron employs a different tactic in his approach to Walt. Ron always asks Walt's business advice on a thorny issue, gets into Walt's face with something that will dominate Walt's fractured attention for several minutes. This, employed over time, is meant to convince Walt that Ron has some substance. It almost works. But Walt is no dummy, either. The most it does is slightly puzzle him about Ron, give him slight pause, and occasionally force him to reexamine his basic assessment of Ron—that is, that Ron is shallow, ambitious, crudely intelligent but essentially second-rate, and after something in every interaction that comes his way. Walt is also not unaware that Ron is a threat to Lloyd, who he now knows has been sent to Europe on some kind of boondoggle.

27. What Walt thinks is going on: He, Walt, is working on the heart of the deal that will transform the company into the largest of its kind in the world, an enterprise that he will run, under Doug's distant supervision. He, Walt, is headed for greatness! What is really going on: something else.

28. Here is Ron, standing in Lloyd's office. He has just attempted to take a look in Lloyd's desk but has failed, since Lloyd locked his desk before he left for Europe. Frustrated, Ron contents himself with a brief session in Lloyd's chair, and an extended gaze out Lloyd's window.

29. Under Lloyd's blotter, Ron finds a note from Mona. He faxes it to himself to make a copy, then replaces it. (Don't you think that Lloyd had better come home quick?)

30. Here's Lloyd's big idea: "I had the most amazing glass of beer last night in my hotel," Lloyd says to Mr. Horst while the group is ostensibly looking over some preliminary backgrounders. The conversation in the moments before had completely fizzled and things looked so bleak that Lloyd had felt like crying. Jaekel had twice looked at his watch.

    "Yes?" says Horst, shooting an eyebrow and licking his upper lip with a plump, serrated tongue.

    "Er . . . yes," says Lloyd. "Very cold. Very crisp. Almost—I can't really find the word for it—oaty. . . ."

    "Like oats, yes!" shouts Horst, a bright light suffusing his face. "This is most often true of Bavarian beer, but also the Dutch, I think, have sometimes this quality."

    "Well, I never quite tasted anything like it before," says Lloyd. His heart is singing in his chest.

"What may I ask was the color of this beer?" asks Horst, sitting at the large conference table and leaning forward into the discussion with great seriousness.

"Dark gold shading to a kind of bronze," says Lloyd. He waits to see if this description will meet with Horst's approval.

"Yes, that would be right," says Horst, sinking into a profound, if not unfriendly, silence.

"You see, my friend Horst is the complete aficionado," says Jaekel. He does not seem in any way put out by this digression; rather, he appears pleased, as if the conversation, having meandered about with great insufficiency up to this point, has finally found its groove and taken off down the track the way God intends it to do.

"The one thing I've found difficult to find in Germany is a darker beer that's not overcome with sweetness," says Lloyd. He says it as an archaeologist might observe an interesting deficiency of a certain kind of fossil in an area where he might expect it to appear.

"Yes," says Horst. "That is very perceptive. There are areas in the East where certain developments have transpired over the course of the last fifty years to which we have not yet had sufficient access."

"Understandable," says Lloyd, and from his breast pocket he retrieves a plump, not overly long Macanudo cigar. "May I?" he asks.

Jaekel's ears perk up noticeably and seem to lift and separate from his head. His nose appears to grow several millimeters in length and sharpen slightly. "What is that?" he says. "Cuban?"

"No, unfortunately," says Lloyd. "Just a lowly Macanudo."

"Lowly?" says Jaekel. "Lowly, no. Not perhaps the best in the world. But not the worst, either."

"I figure it will sort of do until something truly remarkable comes along," Lloyd says. This is going far better than he could have dreamed.

"Something . . . like this?" says Jaekel, and produces a long, slender tube from his breast pocket. Lloyd sees what it is: a hand-rolled Dominican of Cuban ancestry that probably set its owner back at least eighty American dollars.

"Oh no," says Lloyd. "I couldn't possibly. You are . . . too generous."

"We'll see how generous we are when we get down to business!" says Horst, and the three men share the kind of laughter that binds the male animal to his fellow for life—or at least until the next negotiation.

31. Here is Lloyd with Horst and Jaekel at a bar. The table is very tiny and covered with glasses. Each holds the dregs of a different kind of beer. There are light beers and dark beers and beers in between, warm beers and cold beers and beers that once were ice cold and now are warm. Dot-

ted through the flagons of brew are occasional small shot glasses that hold schnapps. The three men are not talking now because they are too drunk. Each is afraid that if he says anything, he will spoil the mood, which is one of supremely emotional incoherence. Each man is also smoking a very large cigar, not his first of the day. The feeling of relaxation and satisfaction suffuses the entire region around the table. It is very late, and the three are the only ones left in the bar, aside from the bartender and a couple of girls sitting at a table at the other end of the room. The men pay no attention to the women there. They are only about one another. "So now," says Horst to nobody in particular, "now we must to Rome."

"To Rome!" says Lloyd.

"Rome!" barks Jaekel.

They drink, not caring from which glass, or whose.

Lloyd puts his head down on the cool glass of the table. The next thing he knows, it is morning, he is in his hotel room, and the door is buzzing.

"Room service!" says a voice.

32. Lloyd sits up. He is hungry. And aside from the coating of grunge that lines his mouth on the morning after a day of cigar consumption, he feels great.

"Bitte!" says Lloyd, feeling very continental.

33. Here's Lloyd's breakfast.

34. Here's the jet that takes Lloyd from Berlin to Rome. On the jet, they drink beer and smoke more cigars. They also go over some numbers. Here are some of the numbers.

35. The meeting in Italy goes very well, too, not because Mr. Tognazzi drinks or smokes, but because he is intimidated by the Germans and does whatever he thinks they want him to do. There are also compelling financial reasons why the merger makes sense for Rome, as can be deduced from the following exchange between the principals:

HORST

Frankly, I am rather disappointed by your skeptical attitude to the matter under discussion, Gianni.

TOGNAZZI

I am sorry. There is very little I can do about that.

JAEKEL

In the sense that you would appear insensitive to the question of leverage.

TOGNAZZI

I don't follow.

I'm sure there's no need to spell this out in any overly obvious way. We're all aware of the market implications, I think.

TOGNAZZI

I'm not sure I—

LLOYD

Is this some kind of old-world song and dance?

HORST

Hm?

LLOYD

Why don't we dispense with the niceties and let Mr. Tognazzi here know the lay of the land?

JAEKEL

What is that? An American cliché? The . . . lay of the land?

LLOYD

Er . . . yeah. It means—

TOGNAZZI

I'm sure we all know what it means. I, for one, went to the Kellogg School of Business at Northwestern University.

LLOYD

Around the time I was playing guitar on the street, I would guess.

JAEKEL

Look. It's basically a matter of market share. The new company, as we define it, will command approximately sixty-five to seventy percent of the international market for the core business operations that make up the greater part of the new company's revenue stream.

TOGNAZZI

I would have to study the numbers.

JAEKEL

Take my word for it.

LLOYD

This leverage would give the new company quite a bit of power to set prices, control inventories, and commit funds for research and development. Essentially making it all but impossible for any other concern to compete.

HORST

And that's that! Right?

Yes. I see.

Let's all have a drink now and talk in a friendly manner about this thing. This is no way to conduct business. With all this rampant seriousness about. Way too German, right? Ha!

Ha!

I agree. I think it would be appropriate at this juncture to state that we are of course aware that Mr. Tognazzi here is a man of tremendous taste and discretion who has built his operation into an absolutely essential piece in the global distribution system of which we're all a part. That this corporate realpolitik in no way reflects on our basic respect for either the man or his enterprise.

Does he talk like this all the time?

You should hear him when he's had a couple of beers!

Beers?

Absolutely.

Let's grab a bite to eat now and let the matter settle for a couple of hours. Perhaps smoke a cigar, if things go well.

Certainly. I am sorry I allowed things to get off on the wrong foot before I knew the . . . lay of the land.

All right, all right. Boy. What a bunch of kidders.

I know a place that has the most marvelous veal.

I love veal.

A real meat-and-potatoes man, eh?

Hey. You only go around once.

I know a little club we can go to afterward that might appeal to other tastes you might possess.

LLOYD

Really? Wow.

HORST

Excellent! Now we have a meeting!

JAEKEL

Nothing too participative, I trust.

TOGNAZZI

No, no. Certainly not. Propriety all the way.

LLOYD

Shall we go, then?

TOGNAZZI

Sure. Let me just say before we get excessively informal, as we are bound to do over the next several hours, that while we may come to an eventual accommodation, it will be an agreement born of some level of coercion, since it is true that you gentlemen have a tremendous number of chips on the table while I, unfortunately, have simply the inherent value of my concern to play with. For that reason, you will forgive me if I insist on obtaining that last bit of value from you in recognition of the fact that it is the realization of that value that is my responsibility, the only way I can play the one card I *do* hold.

LLOYD

That's okay, Gianni. We expect you to squeeze us.

(The men all laugh with egregious gusto. They leave.)

37. Here is the club where an extremely beautiful woman, approximately twenty years of age, wearing nothing at all except a diamond-studded silver dog collar, sits on Lloyd's lap while the three other men are similarly engaged in other locations within the club. She is tall, with very shiny auburn hair, small breasts, lean and supple except for a round little tummy that speaks of a healthy appreciation of the marvelous food and drink that characterizes this area of the world. In ten years, she will probably weigh 220 pounds and sport a full mustache. Her eyes are very large, brown, and liquid, with long, expressive lashes and slightly bushy eyebrows. Her underarms are unshaved, and as straight and sleek as is

the hair on her head, her pubic hair is tightly curled and a little wispy. If one could see Lloyd's face in the darkness, one would be amazed at its childlike expression. He is speaking to her in English, telling her how beautiful she is. "You are beautiful," says Lloyd. "You understand what it means? Beautiful?" "Yes," says the girl. "I understand beautiful." "Speak Italian to me," says Lloyd, mesmerized. "Tell me something. Anything. About you. About me." The girl speaks to Lloyd then, murmuring to him in the fluid, expressive language of Dante and Mussolini. After a time, Lloyd begins to stroke her face, her hair, running his index finger lightly down her nose, across her lips, her chin. They do not kiss, nor does Lloyd touch any other part of her body. This goes on for several hours. At approximately 1:00 A.M., Lloyd says good night to the young woman and stumbles out into the night arm in arm with his business companions. They do not speak much. All are deeply moved.

37. When Lloyd gets back to his hotel, he is in a primal zone, so deeply intoxicated that he has attained a higher level of clarity, with a tremendous ache in his guts he's not quite sure how to treat. It is still early evening in New York, so Lloyd makes two telephone calls. The first is to his wife and children. The second is not.

38. Phone call number one: Lloyd calls at a very bad moment. Donna has just experienced an unfortunate incident with Steve. As night fell not long before, Steve had become convinced that there was something of interest outside the house, in the backyard. He announced this conviction by barking vociferously at the kitchen door, interspersing his short, percussive yelps with his most menacing growling, an effect that always produced a heightened sense of seriousness to anyone within earshot. Donna realized there was something worthy of canine investigation and let Steve out into the backyard, at which point he was promptly sprayed by the skunk that had been the cause of the ruckus. Donna has just finished dousing Steve with tomato juice and giving him a bath, a process that has reportedly left the dog smelling like a rich sachet of Aveda botanical hair treatment, Campbell's tomato juice, and, powerfully declaring itself underneath those scents, skunk. Steve is, at that moment, cringing in the basement, where he will live until he is more fit for human intercourse. This fact deeply upsets Bob and Nora, both of whom get on the phone to complain about their mother, who has been so mean as to put the dog, who was upset by the entire experience already, in the cold, dark basement. Lloyd would have felt worse about this if he had not recently spent nearly twenty thousand dollars to fix up the basement, which now is considerably nicer than any apartment in which he had lived when he had been single.

"Dad?" says Bob, and Lloyd can hear the tears in his voice. "When you comin' home?"

"Soon, Spud," says Lloyd.

Nora gets on. "I miss you, Dad," she says. She then launches into a long story about her shop project, which has not been going well but is now going better. Lloyd listens. "I love you, Floradora" is what he says after a while.

"Love you, too, Dad," says Nora. "Bring me back something cool from Rome, huh? Bob, too."

"Like what?" says Lloyd. This is something he can do.

"Like, I dunno. Like earrings for me? And—hold on a minute"— Lloyd hears a brief discussion in the background—"and a skateboard for Bob."

"Right. A skateboard. No problem."

"Mommy wants to get on again. Love you, Dad." Nora makes a kissing noise into the phone. Lloyd reproduces the sound exactly in reply.

"Hi," says Donna.

"Hi," says Lloyd.

"It's really hard when you're not around here for an extended period of time."

"I know."

"I'll see you in a couple of days, then."

"I miss you, Dee."

"The house smells of skunk," Donna says.

"Don't be mad at Steve," says Lloyd. "He's just a dog."

"Love you," says Donna.

"Love you, too," says Lloyd.

They hang up. What Lloyd didn't tell Donna is how he is all roiled up by the experience of having a beautiful young woman's naked pudenda placed directly against his penis for more than two hours with nothing but a sixteenth of an inch of cotton in between. Two-sixteenths, if one counted Lloyd's underwear. What Lloyd didn't say is how macerated he is inside, a festering stew pot of guilt, desire, blasted hope, and black frustration. What Donna did not tell Lloyd is that, after three years of flirtation, her friendship with Chuck, the contractor who has just completed their kitchen and who has been a godsend since they acquired the house, has entered a new phase. Today Chuck kissed Donna for the very first time. And Donna did not resist. Chuck is six four, 240 pounds, and plays hockey with a local semipro team. A very solid guy. Three kids. Irish. A good head for business. Not a bad guy at all. Lloyd likes him.

39. Call number two: Mona is still at her desk, which is not uncommon even at that hour, when most people are with somebody, eating, drinking, turning back into somebody. After sitting with attorneys for most of the day, she is spending some time with the actual documents upon which the

deal, if it comes to pass, will be built. These are papers suffused with such prodigious tedium that it took years to train an individual to look at them for more than a few moments without falling asleep. Yet in spite of her years of experience, Mona is nodding off over the sheafs of detail when the phone rings. Her secretary, Daniel, left at least an hour before. She answers the telephone herself.

"Is this the party to whom I am speaking?" says Lloyd.

"Lloyd?"

"*Al buon gusto!*"

Mona sits for a minute and listens to the international silence at the other end of the line. "Let me guess," she says at last. "It's a quarter to three. There's no one in the place except me and you."

"Gzackly."

"How's it goin' over there, babe?" Mona is aware that something is off, that the person with whom she is conversing is not completely present in the conversation.

"Swimmingly," said Lloyd. "Outstandingly. *Bellissimo,* in other words. We have . . . closure."

"That's good." She waits.

"Oh," says Lloyd. "Is it? Is it . . . good? Is it just good? Or is it very, very good? How good is it, in other words? Perhaps it's not good at all. Perhaps it's great. On the other hand, perhaps it's neither good nor great. Perhaps it's something that will change everything for no particularly good reason, or none I can come up with at this particular moment. Do you want things to change? Why? Aren't things very good right now? Don't we have, like, this incredible racket going in the sense that we're at the top of a nice-sized pineapple instead of in the middle of a gigantic one over which we have no control? Don't we know everybody in senior management? Aren't we friendly with everybody we need to know? I understand why guys like Doug want this thing. And even Ron, who may, like, come out on top of some weird new cast of the pyramid. But why you? Why me? Why Walt? Most of all, why Walt?"

"You sound very tense, Lloyd" is what Mona says.

"I am," says Lloyd. "I am tense. I have a lot of . . . stuff . . . bottled up. Lot on the table. Lots . . . riding."

"You're in Europe," says Mona. "Can't you kick out some of the jams over there? In relative anonymity?"

"I'm very selective in the exact kind, location, and quality of jams I choose to kick out," says Lloyd. "If you take my meaning."

"Keep your nerve, babe. You the man. Everybody knows that." She is groping around now, trying to tell him what it is she thinks he might want to hear. There is something coming over the phone, dense, slightly dangerous, not related to business, unconventional, a little ugly. She likes it. "You're under a lot of pressure, Lloyd, pressure to perform duties you're not a hundred percent buying into. That creates strain. Everybody reacts to strain in different ways. Some guys like it. I like it. I like it when there's pressure and it all counts. It makes me . . . excited. Don't you feel that just a little bit?"

"Yeah," says Lloyd. "Yeah. I feel excited. I feel too goddamned excited, if you want to know the truth."

"And . . . how does that excitement manifest itself?" asks Mona. She is suddenly aware of the surface of her skin at certain points pressing a little too heavily on the fabric of her clothing. "Tell me, Lloyd. Go ahead. It's late here. The door is closed. Tell me what you're feeling right now. Hell, you called me to tell me. So tell me."

"Wouldn't you like to know," says Lloyd.

She listens very closely to his breathing. Has it picked up a little? Gotten a bit more . . . thick? Glottal? "Are you drunk, Lloyd?" she asks. "Or rather, I should say, how drunk are you?"

"What are you wearing?" says Lloyd.

40. Oh. And at 8:32 in the evening, New York time, Richard Schoendienst, at the age of forty-four, died of a massive coronary while walking his pet shih tzu, Rocco. Rick had always thought Rocco was a ridiculously funny name for a dog the size of a large hamster, but there was, in the end, something Rocco about the dog after all, for as Schoendienst fell on the Rappaports' lawn, next door to his own, Rocco set up an enormous howl that brought the entire neighborhood to the street.

The EMS unit was called immediately and responded in less than two minutes. They almost saved him, nearly consigning him to several decades of existence in a vegetative state in some expensive nursing home upstate. But Rick outsmarted them all by having an associated neurological incident approximately ten minutes after the initial attack that shut down his brain stem and related involuntary functions well before the ambulance delivered its cargo to the intensive care unit moments later. His last words were, "Ah. Shit. That hurts."

41. Lloyd is on his way home the next day, the letters of intent in the zippered compartment of his briefcase. Somewhere over Iceland, however, a small package filled with plastic explosive by Iranian nationalists detonates in the cargo area of his 747, blowing Lloyd and all other 345 passengers to sardine-sized niblets.

Just kidding. He makes it home okay.

August

 On the first week of the month, only hours after Lloyd's return from Europe, the Company begins its big retreat at an opulent hotel/spa on an island off the west coast of Florida. Lloyd and Mona find themselves in extended social discourse for days that stretch from morning breakfast through the late-night drinking sessions at the corporate "pub" set out exclusively for the use of the three hundred company executives and managers who are there to build the culture and have a good time. After several days of extraordinary arousal and denial, Lloyd and Mona permit themselves to do what comes naturally after sixteen drinks.

For the rest of the week they enjoy the sneaking around, surreptitious striving, and short, violent relief that only illicit, self-destructive activities can generate. At the same time, the management group is engaged in a bunch of team-building games that are so emotionally intense for the participating executives that their level of hedonism goes unnoticed in the stew of passionate brotherliness, inebriation, and, underneath it all, politics. Sometimes they play golf, and the level of their amity and familial bondage rises precipitously. Other times it's a friendly game of snooker.

On the final day of the meeting, Lloyd and his buddies are given a physical challenge. They are dropped by chopper in the middle of a remote bird sanctuary and told to find their ways, with one canteen and a granola bar each, back to "home base"—the hotel bar. It is very hot. They are quite thirsty.

On Lloyd's team are two other people, and Mona. The goal of their team, of course, is to be the first group to arrive, thereby qualifying for the award of one set of Ping golf clubs each—a huge gift worth thousands of dollars, but of limited meaning to Lloyd and Mona, neither of whom golf. Still. They want to win. The groups split up, with Lloyd drawing Mona as a partner, a complete accident that nevertheless has everybody sniggering. Lloyd and Mona explore the buggy, hot Florida outback together for a while with compass and map in hand. It takes them about a half hour to get lost. They get back, of course, but not before they both have a very wicked sunburn and are the talk of the meeting. Two naughty senior managers! How sweet! How rich! How flattering to the mythology of the culture!

On the Road Again

It was very early for a Sunday morning—8:00 A.M. Donna was sitting up in bed and watching Lloyd pack.

"Make sure to toss in a couple of those Lacoste shirts," she said.

"I don't know," said Lloyd. "They're a little threadbare."

"I hope that's not meant as some sort of reproach." Donna had one of her supremely expressive eyebrows going. She was sitting up a little higher in the bed, too.

"Not at all, not at all," said Lloyd.

"Because I can go out this morning and pick you up some stuff." Donna sat quietly, eyeing him with a somewhat squinty glare.

"Yeah." Lloyd stood back and looked at his suitcase. "I mean, I don't have a concept here. I have slacks, but they're not the right kind of slacks. They're too dressy. I have golf pants, but they're ridiculous. Why did I buy them?"

"As I recall, you were feeling underdressed before another one of these retreats and felt like you wanted to look more authentic."

"Yeah," said Lloyd. "But this one is complicated. There's going to be golf. Some swimming. Hanging around in informal situations. A couple of dinners where you can't wear a suit but have to look nice. I'm underpowered here."

"What time is your plane?" said Donna. She was bare from the waist up and the blanket was arranged neatly at her waist. It was already in the high eighties outside, but the room was chilled to refrigerator coolness by the massive air conditioner that Chuck had installed in the window.

"Plane's at one," said Lloyd.

"Well, that gives us a little time." Donna popped out of bed and went over to her bureau, which offered a variety of combs and a large plastic brush with widely spaced bristles. She gave her head a vigorous brushing as Lloyd watched her bottom in her tiny cotton bikinis and turned a couple of alternatives over in his mind. "Give me a minute," said Donna. She dropped her panties, then writhed into a T-shirt and a pair of spandex shorts that would have had her arrested a couple of decades ago had she been insane enough to appear in them in public. She passed behind Lloyd and gave him a swat on the bottom of his boxer shorts. "I'll take you out to the mall for one of your famous sprees," she said. My, Donna was in a good mood! Lloyd felt an overpowering wave of guilt for which he had no explanation. After all, what had he done?

The phone rang. "I'm sorry to call you at home on a Sunday at this particular hour," said Walt's voice at the other end of the line.

"Mr. Walt," said Lloyd. "The Walt man."

"Lloyd," said Walt with the utmost seriousness. "I was wondering whether you thought that we would need any kind of suit or whether a navy blazer would do."

"I'm hanging with the sport-jacket look," said Lloyd.

"I've got a couple of canary yellow and, you know, plaid summer-weight slacks for golfing, and a few khakis for afternoons."

"Uh-huh." Lloyd was shoving the entire contents of his sock drawer into his bag, the portable telephone tucked uncomfortably behind his ear. The elimination of the phone cord did not make this process any easier. In fact, it made things more difficult, since the phone itself was slippery and provided no ballast at the bottom of the instrument to keep it perched in the correct position. Now it slipped like liquid mercury through the space between his ear and his shoulder and hit the carpet with a thud. Lloyd picked it up in time to catch Walt saying, ". . . golf clubs?"

"Walt," said Lloyd, feeling kind of annoyed all of a sudden. "You know I don't golf, not really."

"It's never too late to start, Lloyd," said Walt. "I didn't begin the game until my early forties. Now I'm an eight handicap."

"Okay," said Lloyd affably. "If you want to pay the twenty-five-thousand-dollar initiation fee, and cover all my club costs, I'll consider taking up the game as seriously as it deserves."

There was one of those enormous Walt-based silences. "Yo, Walt," Lloyd said.

"I might consider doing that," said Walt judiciously.

"Really?" Lloyd was flabbergasted. "Really, Walt?"

"No!" said Walt. "Not really!" He barked out a volley of canine laughter. "Was there anything else?"

"You called me!"

"Bring some of the documents we've been working on. See ya."

Been There, Done That

Lloyd was feeling very sad. He had just returned from Europe and here he was going off again. Donna said nothing during the whole ride. She was clearly thinking about something, though. There was the ghost of a tiny smile on her face.

While they were at the mall, Lloyd purchased two perfectly appropriate pairs of khaki pants, four chemise LaCoste shirts, some colorful socks, and a nice sport coat. Out of the blue, Donna said, "I'm going to miss you, fathead." It had been many long months, perhaps years, since his wife had called him fathead. He looked at her closely.

"Miss you, too," he said. After a few moments, he added, "You know I have to go, don't you, babe?"

"We all gotta do what we all gotta do," said Donna, opting for a tan cloth belt and holding it thoughtfully over Lloyd's new slacks.

"That's deep," said Lloyd.

"Yeah," said Donna. "And wide."

Donna was wearing a gray T-shirt that, despite its shapelessness, displayed the subtle lines of her chest, the way it tapered down to her flat little tummy. . . .

Lloyd realized that he was staring at her and he quickly averted his gaze.

"Gonna miss you," he said again, a voice rather more husky than he intended.

"You really don't have to go, Lloyd." Donna was looking at him with an intensity he didn't quite get. What was going on? Wasn't this just one day of many in their long and relatively uneventful marriage?

"Ah, but I do. I do, you know." And it was true. He did have to go. He had a presentation on what had transpired in Europe. There would be discussion. Someone else could give it, of course. But then nobody would see him in the role of the individual who had been there and done that. And what if Ron in some way wormed into the role of presenter? That would be bad, very bad indeed.

"Of course you do. I know you do," said Donna.

"You can't win if you don't play."

"Yeah, I know. Hey," said Donna, "we better hurry." And something closed down behind her face.

Two hours later, Lloyd was in the air again.

Wherever You Go, There You Are

Lloyd had wondered if Mona would be on the flight, and, sure enough, there she was.

Lloyd was on the bulkhead, a position in the plane he always favored because it gave added legroom and made it just about impossible to be distracted by the movie, which was displayed for his row alone on a teensy-weensy screen the size of a postcard, approximately twelve inches from his nose. Mona was two rows back, on the aisle to the right.

The other people there were corporate faces Lloyd knew he had seen many times before, now in a different context and therefore unrecognizable.

Mona appeared in the space in front of him. Her face was sufficiently near for him to be able to smell her breath, which was cool and as fragrant as a botanical garden. "I wonder if I could made a huge imposition on you," she said to the passenger in the window seat next to Lloyd, a quiet lawerly woman, perhaps thirty, who had just settled in comfortably after a long session stowing her terrible wheeled luggage. "I wonder if you would be so kind as to switch seats with me. I'm two rows back in an excellent spot for the movie. I believe I could promise free drinks for you for the duration of this flight."

"That comes with the ticket," said the woman in a pleasant, informational manner.

"What more can I offer?" Mona moved closer, and Lloyd felt the heat radiate off her body.

"Nothing, nothing," said the woman affably. She began to pack up her stuff. "Only, maybe . . ."

"Please," said Mona.

"I'm a junior associate at Merkin, Flum, Craddox and Charbonneaux. It's a very enormous sweatshop with more than two hundred lawyers."

"You sound happy there."

"I'm interested in getting into international mergers and acquisitions," said the young woman, rising to make room for Mona. Lloyd realized quite suddenly that he was finding the woman who was interested in getting into international mergers and acquisitions very attractive. She was ambitious. She was courageous. She was reasonable and somewhat generous. She had a lean athletic body that had yet to feel the pull of Mother Earth. Now he would never see her again. Oh well, thought Lloyd as philosophically as he could. That's life.

Mona and the junior associate had now changed places. "Here's my card," said the woman. "Judy Bloom." She and Mona shook hands and exchanged cards, for Mona, too, had produced hers from a small leather case she carried with her at all times.

"Cool," said Mona. "By the way. How do you know I can help you?"

"Come on," said Judy Bloom. "Be serious."

Mona plopped down next to Lloyd. "Hi, Lloyd," she said.

Putting on the Ritz

Before long, the mimosas came. A quiet drink, thought Lloyd. A refreshing drink. Lloyd had two. Mona kept up with him. She had untied her string tie and opened one button on her white silk shirt. Other than that, she looked ready for business, as indeed, Lloyd supposed, she was.

The two sat companionably for a while. Lloyd had taken out a bunch of paper material and was perusing it perhaps a bit too seriously. Mona rummaged through her briefcase, extracted something big and fat, and began going through it with a yellow Hi-Liter. They did not speak. Each time the flight attendant came by with a trayful of mimosas, both Lloyd and Mona took one.

Pretty soon, they had each consumed four mimosas. Or was it five? Oh well. They were small.

About an hour into the flight, Mona closed the tome she was highlighting, put it carefully back in the bag at her feet, reclined her seat to maximum benefit, and closed her eyes. Within a few moments, she was asleep.

Lloyd watched Mona sleep. For the first time in the flight, he was not fearful about the idea of staring long and hard at her. She could not see him doing so. He had yearned to drink her in since they had taken off in New York, had wanted to simply turn to her and say, "Hey, don't be upset, but I'd just like to look at you for a couple of hours. Is that okay?"

What is going to happen on this trip? he asked himself quite earnestly. If there was ever a time for sober reflection, this is it, thought Lloyd as he sipped another mimosa. What a shitty drink! He rang for the attendant and ordered a Tanqueray with a couple of olives in it. Ah, now that was better. Now was the time for a snooze. It was a very deep sleep, one of those devastating naps from which one awakens with the sensation that one has been snoring, and possibly even drooling. "Snork!" said Lloyd, opening his eyes.

Mona was looking at him, her head turned a full ninety degrees in his direction. "You have very curly hair at the nape of your neck," she said.

"Oh," said Lloyd. It was all he could think of.

"I'm getting a clear impression from Walt that things are moving forward now a lot faster than anyone was anticipating," she said.

"There's so much work to do," said Lloyd. He felt very groggy. Should he drink his way out of it? Or take in more healthy fluids?

"Water?" said the flight attendant.

"Sure," said Lloyd. He hungrily drank a glass of sparkling water with a disk of lemon floating at the top.

"I drank way too many of those mimosa things," said Mona. "I suppose I was nervous. I wonder if I can sleep now that I'm up," she said.

"I can't at all, usually," said Lloyd. "But I guess it's worth a shot." He closed his eyes and feigned sleep. There was nothing more uncool than a flight companion who talked when he or she had nothing to say. He didn't want to penetrate Mona's peace of mind. Why? . . . Because he liked her. What was that from? The Mickey Mouse Club. It was what . . . Jimmie Dodd used to say. And he did like Mona all of a sudden, hugely. And if sometime over the summer she had grown a little bit plump . . . why, now he liked her even better.

Lloyd extruded one finger from the rest of his hand and very gently poked it into the soft tissue in Mona's side, right below the elastic of her bra, where the very chubbiest part of her petite newly minted love handle might be.

"Stop that," said Mona.

"Sorry. I was just trying to bury my finger into something soft."

Mona opened one eye. "Are you saying I'm fat?" she said.

"Let me see," said Lloyd. He poked her very gently one more time. This time, Mona wriggled just a little under the probe.

"That tickles," she said. "I don't like to be tickled, Lloyd. Stop tickling me."

"Really?" said Lloyd. "Really stop tickling you?"

"For the time being," said Mona, opening up the in-flight magazine.

More than half the flight was over. They had already enjoyed a tub of beverages, a wave of hot nuts, several other snacks, hot towels, and other ludicrous offerings. Lloyd had read all he intended to. And it had seemed to him that he and Mona were going to play for a while. Now . . . maybe not.

He hoped that he had not done something to annoy Mona. Made her mad. Mad woman not a pretty thing. Long week in this really pretty place. Mad Mona. Lloyd perched on the edge of unconsciousness. He saw himself beginning to float away from shore, standing in the front of the boat to make out what, if anything, could be seen of the other side of the lake. What was there? Would he be all right there?

He felt a strange sensation on the side of his head. Something was approaching his ear. Now it was in his ear. It was . . . soft and . . . wet. . . . Something was entering his ear and making its way to his brain! It was— what do you call it?—an earwig! It was in his brain! He was going to die!

Lloyd lurched up and looked around in terror, remembering after a long, vague moment where he was.

"Relax, Lloyd," said Mona from the seat next to him. She was regarding him closely, her face turned directly to him, and very close. Lloyd could smell the mint and pistachio on her breath. "It was only a dream, 'kay?"

"What did you do?" said Lloyd. He found that he was quite annoyed.

"Nothing," said Mona. "Go back to sleep."

Lloyd leaned back and closed his eyes.

After a few minutes of regular breathing, he felt something approach his ear and pause there. He kept up his steady inhalations and exhalations, even adding a low, stentorian tone now and then to complete the impression of full somnolence. Moments passed. Then here came the object again. It was warm . . . and very wet. It felt good, actually. It stayed in his ear, kind of wobbling around in there in a gentle, exploratory fashion. He opened his eyes.

"Whoops," said Mona. "You caught me." She removed her finger.

"Well," said Lloyd, picking up a cocktail napkin from his armrest with great dignity and drying out his auricular cavity. "I haven't had a wet willie in quite some time."

"Did you like it?" Mona, too, was drying off her finger, keeping one eye trained on his reaction.

"Yeah," said Lloyd. "True, you startled me. One rarely gets a wet willie while sleeping. That was a first for me."

"You really should get out more."

"This time, I cleverly pretended to sleep and so caught you at it."

"Yes. I was surprised to find you were in fact not sleeping at all, but were awake."

"You must be pretty bored," said Lloyd. "To torment a sleeping person like that. I mean, that's pretty low."

"You're right," said Mona. "I should get back to work." She briskly hauled up her briefcase, extracted a mound of paper, erected her tray table, and hunkered down.

Beyond commenting on the quality of the food and service, they didn't speak for the rest of the flight.

Pelican Island

The corporation chose the island, this particular island, because it had all the necessities a great corporation demanded of an island.

First, it was remote, far from the push and blast of the insane city that made them immediately crazy from the first bell in the morning to the last wheeze at end of day. The sun was very hot here, and the sand white. Gigantic birds wheeled overhead, diving precipitously from a great height, then rocketing off into the ether again. There was primordial silence, cut solely by the occasional shriek of a gull, the distant click of a club on a golf ball.

It was out there, this island.

The place was elegant but stark. Stripped bare. Such emptiness was vastly expensive these days. Every man and woman felt privileged to be in such a place, felt that their lives had attained a certain stature simply because they had come so far and arrived there.

The cabins booked were right on the beach, each furnished with nothing but a large comfortable bed, a small bureau with a mirror over it, and a gigantic wicker chair and hassock. There was no glass in the windows, although screens could be lowered, and a deck fronted on the Gulf of Mexico, which was luminescent, blue-green, and very, very warm. For those who tired of the Robinson Crusoe bit, there was a championship golf course.

Finally, there was the exceptional food. In the main "cottage"—a blond-wood palace that squatted impressively over a huge hunk of ocean property, there were three restaurants: one formal, one casual, the other a rough-and-tumble barbecue pit with great steaks, burgers, and dogs on the grill all day. In that same building, there were rooms and suites; there was also a library, a half a dozen or so well-refrigerated meeting rooms, a towering ballroom two-thirds open to the sea, a spa loaded with all forms of corporeal abuse, several gyms, a running track, and a cinema. Business took place there, but if one did not look for it, one did not see it.

This was the second time the corporation had gone to Pelican Island. The prior year was distinguished mostly by one display of bad behavior by several of the men, Lloyd among them. One night, drunk on tequila, they had gone for a dip in the Jacuzzi next to the swimming pool, each with a six-pack of beer within easy reach. At about three in the morning, as the crickets sang and a million stars put on a show above, Alissa Waverly, the senior vice president of public affairs, a very attractive blond woman about thirty-seven who had once worked in the Bush White House, meandered by in some state of disrepair herself, having just completed a nine-hour poker game in which she had won eight hundred dollars. Upon seeing the Jacuzzi full of drunken yahoo executives, she paused.

"Come on in!" said one, and perhaps it was Lloyd, as people later said.

"Naw," said the former Bush spokesperson.

The group in the pool then descended into pointed ribbing and catcalling, the essence of which was that no matter how they protest their equality, no woman executive is loose and courageous enough to be "one of the guys." Waverly naturally took some offense at this, and simply to prove the group wrong, she jumped into the bubbling, foaming water with her clothes on.

All this would have gone unremarked had not Walt at that moment happened by on the way to his room. None too steady himself, Walt looked over the crew, said, "Good evening, gentlemen, if I may use that term under the circumstances," and continued on his way.

The episode had grown somewhat more potent in the retelling, particularly when Waverly was promoted to an important marketing position on the West Coast. Was it possible that scandalous and licentious behavior was rewarded in this culture? Perhaps Waverly would misbehave again and give the group more information on which to base its analysis. Or maybe it would be somebody else this time around.

Sun, Sand, and Stars

On the first night of the retreat at Pelican Island, there was, naturally, a dinner preceded and followed by drinks. The drinks beforehand were held on the deck outside the dining room. Everyone was in regulation casuals: khaki pants or skirts, white or blue button-down shirts without ties, blue blazers. Lloyd had finally gotten his act together and packed this requisite outfit. He also had new sneakers he was quite proud of. They were called Simples. Bob

211

had helped him pick them out. They were olive green leather with white soles, the opposite of the ridiculous edifices of rubber and plastic that passed for sports footwear among the unfit and unathletic.

Mona was at the other end of the patio, drinking a mimosa. Like the rest of the crew, she was in khaki, but with a slight difference. On the lower portion of her frame was a pair of very short "skorts"—half shorts, half skirt. Her long, well-defined legs were tanned and showcased by her footwear, what looked to Lloyd, at this distance, to be high-platformed macramé sandals that laced up Mona's ankles almost all the way to her taut calves. Lloyd felt a string tighten in his midsection and an inexorable hand reeling it in, pulling it tight, and drawing him slowly, carefully, like a fish on a line, toward the other end of the patio.

"Have a nice flight?" It was Ron, standing between him and his goal. Ron's hair was slicked all the way back in a power-raider do only about ten years out-of-date. He was drinking what looked to be Stoli on the rocks, the drink of alcoholics everywhere.

"Yeah," said Lloyd, scanning the party for somebody more interesting, and finding her talking animatedly with Fitz in a slightly different location than before. Fitz was nodding seriously, as if the matter was of the gravest import, which cued Lloyd to the fact that it was not. When things got serious, Fitz leered. This was his all-purpose social expression. Lloyd wondered what they were talking about.

"How were the hot nuts?" said Ron. The rims of Ron's eyes were kind of pink, Lloyd noticed. There was a hungry gleam in them. Lloyd wondered if Ron was on something other than adrenaline and envy.

"Tasty, Ron, tasty," Lloyd said, and did his best to focus on the young man. "How are things with you, Ron?" he said. "We haven't had much of a chance to get down with some quality time this summer."

"Nah nah nah," said Ron, waving his hand to one side as if fending off the negative vibes Lloyd was putting out. "Not since you tore me a new asshole and then flew off to Europe!" He cackled as if he'd just related something amusing. Lloyd waited a minute to see if that was the end of the joke, then joined in with a professional chortle.

"Yeah, well, maybe that was a little harsh," Lloyd said after their merriment had eased.

"Way harsh, way harsh," said Ron forgivingly. "So anyway . . ." He grabbed Lloyd's elbow. "Whassup? . . . Got a tidbit?"

"Gosh, Ron. Are you cleared for tidbits?"

"Absolutely. Also clumps and wafers."

"Europe went well. We got a lot done. All the pieces are almost in place. But that's off the record."

"I hope you know I'm way into this entire scenario." Ron sucked down the rest of his drink and popped the lemon twist in his mouth. "And I know you are, too. Behind this thing, I mean."

"Sure," said Lloyd. Was Ron trying to find something out? If so, he was being mighty ham-fisted about it. "I'm behind it, Ron. I'm behind it to the extent that I'm behind anything I essentially have no choice about."

"How true, how true," said Ron gravely. "But a big thing like this has to create opportunities for everybody, if you know what I mean."

"I do, Ron," said Lloyd. "I do know what you mean."

"I worry about . . . middle management, though," said Ron, and Lloyd did not believe he was lying. "The big guys will take care of themselves. The little guys, I mean, honestly, who gives a shit? That leaves you and me. Department heads and their vassals can be dog meat in a transitional environment."

"I have to believe that Walt would protect us as best he can," said Lloyd.

"Or Doug," said Ron. "Doug, too, huh?"

Lloyd felt very watchful all of a sudden. "Doug, too. Certainly. There's nobody smarter than Doug pretty much on the planet, if you ask me."

"Fucking A," said Ron sagely. There was a rather smarmy pause neither man seemed capable of terminating. Ron finally came to a solution.

"Good show!" he murmured in a rather poor excuse for a British accent. He put a brotherly arm around Lloyd and drew him close. A new and slightly more human Lemur extruded through the corporate politician for a moment. "So in addition to all the hard work you put in over there, you get to have any fun? Tell me about the fun thing. 'Cause . . . if it's not fun, what's it all about?"

"Yeah. I guess I did. It's weird to be away from home for more than a week or so. You get kind of discombobulated."

"I hear the club scene is awesome in Berlin and Rome," said Ron. He was looking over Lloyd's shoulder now at the bar, although he didn't know he was doing so.

"Man," said Lloyd. He was beginning to feel the effects of the ice-cold Tanqueray he had just put down. "Wanna grab another?" he said to Ron. They made their way over to the bar, which was perched diagonally at the end of the patio, not very far from where Mona was chatting with Fitz, holding on to one of Fitz's elbows with a delicate hand. Lloyd felt a twinge of—what was that?—jealousy? tear through his viscera. Ridiculous. Put it down.

"There was this one club in Rome," he said to Ron, who leaned into both his new drink and Lloyd's conversation with equal focus. "This one extremely beautiful woman, had to be about twenty, maybe not even that. I think I fell in love."

Why was he telling Ron this?

"She was very dark and thin—you know, the way European women are before they . . . spread out."

"Haw!" said Ron.

"Anyhow . . . she was, you know, sitting on my lap. . . ." Lloyd suddenly felt embarrassed imparting all this personal stuff to Ron, who was, after all, not a real business friend at all, but just a compatriot in misbehavior, and a relatively junior one at that.

"Yeah?" said Lemur. He was drooling into his cocktail.

"Yeah, and that was about it. Nothing happened, Ron. Like, I didn't fuck her or anything."

"I thought not," said Ron. "I mean, I would have expected no less from you, Lloyd. You're so filled with integrity, it's practically running out your cuffs."

"I resent that," said Lloyd.

"My life is a mess, frankly," said Ron. He exchanged his dead drink for a live one that walked by on a silver tray. "You?" he said to Lloyd.

"Okay." Lloyd took one. "Ron, I've got to go mangle with the people."

"I moved out on what's her name—you know who I mean."

"Betsy?"

"Whatever. And there was the fabulous chick, Alix? I met her while peeping at her through our window, you know. I think I told you about her." Actually, Ron had not told Lloyd a thing. Did people still use the word *chick?* Nothing ever changes. Social improvements are essentially nothing more than fads, thought Lloyd sadly. By the time you live to be forty, you see everything espoused with equal passion. "Loved the woman," Ron was saying. "Completely impulsive woman. Tall. Sculpted. Loved that woman. Remarkable woman."

"What happened to her?"

Ron had drifted into silence, and an undefinable but real emotion had surfaced on his face.

"Nothing," he said. "Nothing happened to her. I gotta go." He turned abruptly, then turned back to Lloyd with a face full of blood and rage. "I don't need you fucking with my head, Lloyd. That doesn't come with the territory." His entire demeanor changed suddenly, and a bright, boyish smile suffused his features. He grabbed Lloyd's arm just above the elbow. "See ya, big guy," he said, and squeezed Lloyd's arm, hard. Then, clearly moved by the weird cocktail of emotions he had just undergone, he made his way, slamming backs and tweaking waists, out of the room.

Was it possible that Ron was insane? And if so, why did only Lloyd see it? Mona was by his side.

"What the fuck is the matter with him?" Lloyd said.

"Coked up," said Mona, rather matter-of-factly.

"No shit." Lloyd was amazed.

"None whatsoever," said Mona. "Excuse me." She leaned over, very close to him, and grabbed a cracker and crabmeat appetizer as it passed her. As she did this with her right hand, her left hand inadvertently brushed his leg, once . . . twice.

"So . . ." said Mona. "How ya doon so far?"

"Fine," said Lloyd. But he didn't feel so fine. Something was the matter. Something fearsomely wrong. He felt like jumping on Mona just because a small portion of her arm had touched him inadvertently. And the week was only several minutes old.

What was it this woman did to him?

"Excuse me for a sec. I gotta go . . . do something," said Lloyd.

The Remains of the Day

All people could talk about at the cocktail party was the deal. Deal this, thought Lloyd. Most of the conversation purported to come from a solid base of emotional support. Enthusiasm. Definitely not fear.

"When these things happen, the new company needs people who know where the bodies are buried," said Pogue, an accountant, whose theory was that central financial services were most prized in merger situations.

"The new organizational structure is going to take, like, eighteen months to work out," said Mosten, a director in Human Resources, who believed that HR was, as he put it to Lloyd, "the central brain-stem function of the changing corporate mind."

"We're all dead meat," said Fitz as he ate a bright red cherry from the bar dispenser, which also held olives, pearl onions, lemon twists, and wedges of lime.

"I don't know," said Lloyd, aware that he was coming off exactly like Pogue, who was at that moment repeating himself quite inanely to an entirely new group of listeners at the other end of the deck. "We're the guys who put the deal together—me, you, Walt, Mona. We thought of it. We constructed it. We made it happen. Why would they fuck with us?"

"Because they can?" said Fitz. He was scanning the area with his eyes only, like a submarine looking for depth charges in the surrounding ocean. "Or because maybe when it's all done, they'll want to run the new toy themselves?"

"Whatever independence from Chicago we've maintained over the years has completely disappeared in the onslaught of big business activity surrounding this deal."

"It was all an illusion anyway," said Fitz. His pale green-blue eyes rested with amusement on Lloyd. "Gonna get lucky?" he said in a completely different tone of voice.

"Huh?" Lloyd felt annoyed. He needed this kind of raw innuendo like a hole in the head.

"Nothing." Fitz had that obnoxious gleam in his eye that Lloyd hated, the one that a little boy might get while separating a fly from its wings. "Hey, man," he said. "Look who just came in."

"Waverly," said Lloyd. Waverly looked very good. She was wearing an abbreviated khaki skirt and a tight white T-shirt that barely covered her midriff. She was sipping on a glass of white wine and listening to Bob Darling blare something into her face from a distance of about six inches. "Wow. Look at that L.A. tan," he said. Waverly looked as if executive life on the left coast really agreed with her.

"Let's go say hi," said Fitz. He left Lloyd and crossed the room to Waverly. Lloyd saw him put his arm around Darling, leaning into the conversation with a level of interest in Darling's words that no one could possibly take seriously.

"Why don't you say hi to Waverly," said Mona, who was standing at his elbow. "She looks hot."

"I will later," said Lloyd.

"I guess she's lost a little weight."

"Yeah?" said Lloyd. "I didn't notice."

"Hm," said Mona.

"Besides, you know . . . it's possible to be too thin."

"You think?" Mona had brightened considerably. She was stirring what looked like a martini with her index finger and staring thoughtfully into its dregs.

"Oh yes," said Lloyd conversationally. "This vogue for bony women is a fad foisted upon the heterosexual public by a small group of sadistic designers who hate both genders and can't decide who to revenge themselves on first."

"No matter how hard I try, I can't drop below a certain weight."

"One eighteen?" said Lloyd, who prided himself on his ability to do this particular parlor trick.

"Yeah!" said Mona. "You never cease to amaze me, Lloyd. Can you do that for everybody?"

"Pretty much," said Lloyd. Mona had the full force of her concentration on him now. A dozen separate impulses smashed into him at once. His guts felt like rice pudding and his knees felt a little shaky. He felt *life* course through him like a popper of amyl nitrite, which was something one never saw at all anymore, although he had been moderately fond of it in the early

216

seventies. Was it still around? "Darling over there, for instance, is up to two thirty-eight, which is not so good on a man who barely clears five ten. At two twenty, Fitz is okay, since he's up around six two."

"Incredible," said Mona. "And how about me?"

"Pardon?" Lloyd was nervous.

"You said I have trouble getting down below one eighteen, which is when I'm at my skinniest, which is not now, as you must know, given the awesome powers I've just witnessed. So tell me. What do I weigh?"

"One twenty-four," said Lloyd. He shaved it by a pound, perhaps two, just to be careful.

"Thanks for coming in on the low end, Lloyd," she said. There was a ripe, curvaceous pause as they regarded each other with something altogether too benign for Lloyd's taste. Lust and teasing were one thing, and possibly just manageable over the short term. Affection, on the other hand, was out. Absolutely.

"You look nice tonight," said Lloyd. Conversely, there was no harm in being friendly. In fact, friendly and straightforward seemed the best-possible approach. It was all this circuitous and complex strategizing that was going to get them into trouble. *Him.* Was going to get him into trouble. Important to remember that.

"For a fat woman," said Mona.

"You're so pretty. Surely you must know that." Lloyd's voice was very low. It was possible that she hadn't even heard him. He took another pull on the remains of his gin. Approximately four ounces of the fragrant, bitter juice went down his gullet. When had he refilled his glass? "You're beautiful . . . is what you are," he said. "Your hair. Your hair is so amazingly . . . lush. I've never seen a color red like that. It makes me want to plunge both my hands into it and never come out. I'm sorry. Excuse me. I think I've been drinking."

"Don't you dare go away," said Mona.

"I have to," said Lloyd. "I must. I'm not in excellent control of myself and this is just the first-night dinner. I have to get back in line or I'm going to, like, spit up all over myself. The fact is, you sort of drive me crazy. There doesn't seem to be anything I can do about it."

"Calm down, Lloyd. Breathe. It's gonna be okay." Mona's cheeks, in spite of her moderate words, were as red as her hair.

"Okay, sure. Yeah, right. I will." He looked at his shoes. They were nice shoes. He liked them.

Lloyd and Mona stood thoughtfully over their drinks for a while. Although the patio was full of people giggling, snorting, and slamming one another on the backs, shoulders, and, in the case of several macho guys from Purchasing, bottoms, not one individual approached Lloyd and Mona as they stood silently drinking, staring off into the distance, munching on olives. To Lloyd, the patio area was deeply silent, as if they were in a pocket of space where no sound could intrude. It was cool in the bubble, and blue, and it smelled nice. Lloyd felt calmer all of a sudden. He also felt nauseous and light-headed.

"Er . . . I think I may faint," he said to Mona.

She regarded him with concern but not alarm. "Gee," she said conversationally. "That would be interesting. Not good. But certainly worthy of notice."

"I see what you mean," said Lloyd.

"Maybe if you could excuse yourself from the party for a few moments, we could meet in the bar off the lobby and sit in those huge deep chairs with the high backs and side wings that obscure our faces, and sip our drinks in peaceful, anonymous quiet, and have a, you know, conversation without attracting any notice whatsoever or anything."

"I'll see you there," said Lloyd. He turned and left the room.

It was hot there on the deck. Mona was glad that she had worn the light silk top with delicate spaghetti straps that she had just this week found at Bergdorf Goodman. She had noted Lloyd taking it in.

He was gone long enough. Time to follow.

"Good to get away," said a somewhat brusque, almost military voice.

"You said it," Mona replied, and turned to Walt. The commander was picture perfect in the essential khakis and fine double-breasted blue blazer with its outlandishly nautical buttons. The only special thing about Walt was his shirt, which was a gorgeous blue-gold-brown-and-yellow-plaid statement of affluence and taste by Pendleton. Walt wore no tie, and, in fact, he had liberated an extra button at his chest, creating a wholly human and nonbusinesslike air of confidence out of uniform. "It's so beautiful here," she added for lack of anything better to contribute.

"Pelicans," said Walt, which seemed to complete his assessment of the physical setting.

"Yes, sir," said Mona.

"I'm very much looking forward to your presentation tomorrow morning." Walt was drinking a brown liquor on the rocks. It looked like either watery bourbon or some form of scotch. He took a pull. "Doug should immediately appreciate the implications of the cash flow versus cost of money scenario."

"When you told me to run the numbers, I never thought it would work out so dramatically," said Mona. Walt seemed to be inattentive to the point of reverie at times, while in fact his mind was spinning, crunching, mashing the situation into comestible shape and form. She felt an intense wave of admiration mixed with something odd and slightly askew, something approaching concern. Why was she worried about Walt, who was, after all, the guy in charge?

"Well, anyway, I'm pleased that it did." Walt's eyes narrowed a bit, and he speared Mona with one of his brain-poaching probes. "You ought to use the next couple of days to relax," he said thoughtfully. "You. Lloyd . . . Fitz. Even that crazy son of a bitch—what is it? Don?"

"Ron," said Mona.

"Shifty little guy," said Walt. A different gear popped in. "We're going to be forced to the wall in the next couple of months. Everything is going to change. The whole world will shift on its axis. Nobody knows where each of us will be placed when it's over."

"I'm sure there's no need to articulate it quite so forcefully," said Mona.

"Yes, well . . . in a postmerger environment, one rarely gets the opportunity to spend a million dollars of the shareholders' money just to pamper senior management, if you see what I mean."

"Enjoy it while we can?"

"I'm going to move over to vodka," said Walt. He placed a friendly hand on Mona's shoulder. "See you later. In the pub, eh?"

"In the pub, Walt. In the meantime, don't hurt yourself too badly."

"Hey," said Walt. "There isn't a drink that's been invented that has the power to put me under." This was, of course, not true. Walt got drunk on two drinks. He was a pleasant drunk, though, and never unable to conduct the kind of business a senior executive must.

Mona eased herself from the deck. She moved down the quiet hallway, the noise of the drunken three hundred reverberating ever more softly as she went. She crossed the lobby, a huge space dotted here and there with groups of comfortable chairs. She spotted Lloyd sitting in one at the far end of the cantilevered expanse, in an area just abutting the bar. There was a table that was also a checkerboard in front of him. His head lolled backward against the chair. His eyes were closed.

Altogether, Lloyd was not someone who would stop traffic if you saw him on the street. He gave an overall impression of bigness, but he was neither outstandingly fat nor overwhelmingly tall. He had black hair that he wore combed straight back, and rather prominent eyebrows that stopped just short of bushiness. Even in this general posture of repose, Lloyd's most prominent feature declared itself: a brooding sense that every decision or situation, no matter how minor, was important. Even sitting there with his eyes closed was a big deal. There was a quality of high drama to the pastime of hanging around Lloyd. If it ceased, she would miss it. Not a big missing, but still.

Then there was the effect that she had on Lloyd. She had attracted many horny businessmen in her time, and while many had offered blandishments, very few had been chosen, and none recently. Lloyd's attraction for her was deeper, more classically . . . romantic. She felt this thing reaching out to her, and another part of the man rising up from within to bat it down, strangle it before it had a chance to effect its desires. She felt the push and pull inside Lloyd, and she was curious to see which would win.

Then there was the power she could exert over his body. He tried adorably to prevent it from showing but failed. His face flushed, not bright red—that would be crass—but a lovely rosy pink that moved from his cheeks to the side of his neck and up into his forehead. His eyes also became a problem—in the sense that he had absolutely no idea where to let them rest. His hands found his pockets, lost them, arranged his hair, tucked in his shirt, checked under his nose for any possible unsightly thing that might be there, rediscovered his pockets again. One time, at a party several months ago, she had kissed him good-bye in a wholly friendly way, and he replied in the same spirit, and she felt something surprising press against her leg for an instant. Was that where it began? Wouldn't that be too simple? Mona shook her head as if to clear some cobwebs out of her noggin, then moved a few steps closer to the supine lumpy shape of Lloyd.

Lloyd was not sleeping, but he certainly looked out of it. His mouth was a tad slack; his breathing was fast and shallow. Semicomatose, but not unconscious. Thinking things over, probably. Lloyd loved to think things over. When he stopped thinking things over, then what would happen?

Lloyd opened his eyes. Mona walked a little faster. When would she reach him? Would this lobby never cease?

As she neared Lloyd, the vast front doors of the hotel opened and a lone figure stepped inside. It was Doug. He was dressed in a white linen suit. A small snap-brimmed straw fedora was on his head. He was carrying one overnight bag, not a big one, and clearly not very heavy. He looked around the enormous high-ceilinged expanse, smelled the blond wood, the flowers that stood in a huge urn in the middle of the reception area. He went to the front desk. Either he had not seen Lloyd and Mona—each frozen in position like a bug in amber—or he chose, as executives have every right to do, not to see them. Since he did not see them, they were under no requirement to see him.

"Don't look now," she said. "But Doug is in the lobby, checking in."

"I'm drunk," said Lloyd. "I had five drinks in twenty minutes. You think I'm trying to escape from something? Or rush toward it?"

"I think it's very stressful to endure forced relaxation among people with whom one usually enjoys a strong structural grid," said Mona.

"I think it would be a fabulous bummer to see Doug at this point in time. What do you think?" Lloyd sat very still. Mona could feel his head spinning.

"Okay." She leaned forward so that she could speak even more softly. "So where should we go? I figure Doug will check in, toss his bag on his bed, and head off to cocktails with the rest of the folks. We have about half an hour until dinner. Want to go to the bar? Outside for a walk? Patio by the pool?"

"Yes," said Lloyd.

Light on the Water

Lloyd felt better. He had been light in the head for a while, that was all. He had flown, and drunk alcohol too early in the day on the airplane, and then arrived here and felt privileged, true, but also anxious about Mona. So when the time came for the cocktail party, he drank a lot, and he drank fast, and in addition there was the stress, the business pressure of a big meeting like this, much of which had been his own personal responsibility. This was his show, so it's no wonder he had felt desperately, crushingly ill.

Now things were better. First of all, he had come to a decision in his own mind, and once a man knows his own mind, he achieves a kind of peace that no amount of food, wine, scotch, bourbon, port, sangria, brandy, champagne, or heroin can approximate. At some point, while sitting in the chair in the lobby, trying not to bark at ants, Lloyd had made a crucial decision and now he was feeling very good about himself. He had decided that he would not take advantage of this situation so fraught with possibilities and danger. He would have fun with Mona, yes, but as a friend, much as he would pal around with Fitz and Walt and Burbage and Darling and even Lemur. This whole meeting was about getting close to people, so there was nothing against that in the charter. But too close, no.

The knowledge that he had irrevocably closed the door on what could have been a big mistake took an enormous weight from Lloyd's spirit. He breathed as a man just freed from prison. The sky looked full of eternal wisdom and grace. Lloyd felt strong, and right. He was pretty sure that Mona sensed this strength in him, for as they walked by the side of the pool in silence, staring at the black water highlighted with tinges of aquamarine, he felt her admiring regard bathing him from her position at his side.

"What are you looking at?" he asked her. He was suddenly filled with tenderness and the milk of human empathy.

"You," she said.

"What about me?"

"Just you," she said.

They looked at each other, hard. God, she was beautiful. Her head was tilted up to meet his. Kissing wasn't anything. Kids did it. It was fun, and healthy even.

Lloyd buried himself in Mona's mouth. Ah, Christ, he thought. Man, that's a taste you never grow tired of. How lovely and soft. How warm and wet. Her

The Battle for Lloyd's Soul
Don't Blink, You'll Miss It

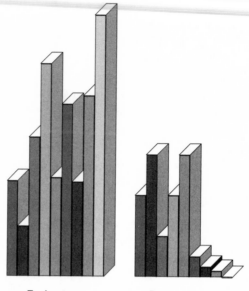

Enthusiasm   Remorse

After a few drinks, Lloyd's feelings about what
he was doing vacillated wildly, enthusiasm
battling with remorse—and winning.

tongue was down his throat. He drew it in. They stayed like that for a long, long time. After a while, they stopped, panting, and looked at each other.

"I didn't know that was going to happen," said Lloyd.

"You're a very good kisser, Lloyd."

"Yeah?"

"Oh yeah."

So they kissed for another ten or fifteen minutes. After that, fearful that they would be missed, they went in to dinner, first Mona, then Lloyd, and then, finally, Ron, who had been watching.

Dinner

There were eight people at each table, which made for forty tables. Each table had one person above the level of vice president, which meant senior vice presidents, executive vice presidents, and presidents. The two head tables

222

were stocked with one chairman each. Walt was at one, with a select assortment of common men. Doug was at the other, with the neatest collection of sycophants this side of the Iraqi senate. There was Ball, the hairless EVP of New Media, who had no real job and so resented all those who worked; Dorkin, the benefits administrator, champion of the mandatory HMO, tall and rail-thin, with one the worst combovers of the last several years; Darling, who was in the midst of designing an international sales solution for the new merged entity based entirely on commissions and so needed Doug's ear to advise him of the obstacles such a vision would have to overcome; Doug, who ate nothing but vegetables and so had his own plate prepared and brought in by special emissary; two consultants from McKinsey, young, plenty of hair, bright, small eyeballs aglimmer with synergy; Mazerowski, the executioner, about whom nothing was ever said; and Ronald Lemur, miserably dejected because Doug had, either accidentally or on purpose (Ron would never know which), seated him on the absolutely other side of the table, at a place where, due to the din of the three hundred happy campers, Ron could hear nothing of Doug's pearls and, worse, Doug could hear none of Ron's.

Lloyd was at a table in the east end of the room. He could see virtually nothing of Mona, who was in another part of the room, nothing but a luminescent wedge of Mona's hair, bobbing as she spoke to someone Lloyd could not see.

Lloyd had enjoyed kissing Mona. Kissing was not fucking. Kissing was wrong, probably, but there weren't a lot of men who would reject a bit of making out with a colossally good-looking, passionate, intelligent executive who found them attractive. On the other hand, Lloyd was quite clear about a couple of basic facts. First, things could not be allowed to get out of hand. She could be a psycho and bust up his marriage. Forever afterward, he would have to lie to Donna. He might not be able to pull it off. Suppose he talked in his sleep. Then what? Donna would scream at him and throw him out of the house. He would deserve no mercy for what he had done. Donna trusted him. He would be living in some hovel that was never cleaned because he would never clean it, and he would have cream of mushroom soup for dinner and be found in a pile of his own filth one frigid morning in February, his heat having been shut off for lack of payment because he didn't like to pay bills. All right, he would survive. He could, say, have a quick affair with the woman and that would be that. But suppose things got weird. He and Mona were friends and fellow workers. It would be a shame to mess that up. And what if she didn't like sex, really? Or, worse, sex with him? That could happen. Probably not, but it could happen. Suppose she needed a guy who could go for two, three hours. And what about AIDS? Or so many other diseases that, while they did not kill you, could be passed along to one's wife for the ultimate in unforgivable sins? True, Mona didn't look like a walking cauldron of infection, but who did? It would be just his luck. No good deed goes unpunished is what they say. Then what about bad ones?

In this way did Lloyd occupy himself while discussing the zoo in Bern, Switzerland, with Roover, Weaver, Krips, Lazenby, and Schecter, who had all been there within the last three years when they visited the company's banking establishments in that tiny, disturbingly clean nation.

By the time the ice-cream bombe landed on his plate, Lloyd had pretty much come to a conclusion: He and Mona could hang around together as might happen in the natural course of things. But he wasn't going to sleep with Mona. He had too much respect for her simply to diddle around with her in this unreal setting. That was kid stuff, and he was sure Mona would not go for it, either.

Once he had made this decision (which he had already made at least once before), Lloyd felt an enormous pressure once again slide from him, and an immediate and powerful urge to tell Mona about it. He got up and went over to her table, where she was in thoughtful conversation with Fitz. How had Fitz ended up in the seat of honor next to Mona? As the big cheese in HR, he had asked for and received, from Walt, the right to set up the tables.

"Thanks for inviting me to sit at your table, man," he said to Fitz.

"I knew you'd be over," said Fitz.

"Do you mind if I take Mona away from you for a couple of minutes? We have to go over a couple of slides."

"Gosh, that's just about the most clichéd attempt at misdirection I've heard since business school. You two. Honestly."

Mona stood and rose to her full height. There was nothing kidding about her now. She was infuriated, and righteously so. "Fitz," she said. "You wouldn't make a smarmy comment like that about any male coworker. You wouldn't dare. You're the head of Human Resources. You investigate these kinds of situations. You are supposed to be the moral compass of this corporation where relations between people are concerned. And this is what we get from you. I guess you can see how I would be pretty disappointed."

"Gee," said Fitz. "Gee, I'm sorry." He looked extremely crestfallen. "Mona. You know I'm nuts about you. In the best possible way. I was just teasin'. Come on. Lighten up." He had risen and gone to her side. He took her by her chiseled biceps. "Tell me you forgive me."

"I forgive you, you crass bastard." She took him by the nose and squeezed hard.

"Okay," said Fitz, pleased.

"We won't be long," said Lloyd.

"Er, Lloyd," said Fitz. "My presentation is on Thursday and I don't have dick. I'm gonna need you to get up one of those computer presentations and patch it into the big system. Nothing large. Just five or six overheads. Can you do that?"

"Sure, dude," said Lloyd.

"Where are we going?" asked Mona after they had made their way through the doors of the gargantuan banquet room and walked in companionable silence through the ground floor of the hotel for several minutes. They wound up in one of those anterooms off a cul-de-sac down a hallway from one of the secondary lobbies, where Lloyd had felt it necessary to lead her for their little chat.

"Right here is fine," said Lloyd. "Look. I've got a couple of things to tell you."

"Yes?" said Mona. She licked his chin.

"Mona," said Lloyd somewhat sternly.

"Yes, Lloyd."

"You . . . have a tiny piece of rum cake right . . . here." Lloyd put his finger at the corner of Mona's mouth, where indeed a crumb of pastry had perched. Her mouth opened and took in his finger. He let her. Since when was finger sucking a crime? There were so many worse things. Lloyd thought about a few of them. In the meantime, Mona was running her tongue very slowly and thoughtfully up and down his finger. Every now and then, she would kiss it gently. As she did so, she held his eyes in a hammerlock, gazing up and into Lloyd, amused, inquiring, playful. Lloyd held his hand before her, powerless to move it away. If anyone saw them! But who could possibly see them here? They were completely cut off. There was only one entrance to the area. The floors were marble, and you could hear a mouse skitter across them at a hundred yards. Mona had two of Lloyd's fingers in her mouth now and showed no signs of quitting. Lloyd had quadrupled in size and felt himself straining against the fabric of his casual slacks, which, he noted in horror, were a light khaki color.

What was he thinking about? Coming in his pants? Christ! This fingersucking thing had to stop right now. So just to get her to quit it, Lloyd put his arms around her, drew her immediately contiguous to him, planted his lips on hers—my, they were so soft!—and began to draw all of Mona's life force out of her through her mouth.

"You're so big," she said, pressing against him.

"Mm," said Lloyd.

They moved to the settee in the corner of the area. Mona sat on his lap. Lloyd kissed her some more. He tasted white wine. Underneath, a touch of gin? The memory of a cigarette smoked perhaps an hour back. Mona did not smoke a lot, but he had seen her light up with obvious pleasure now and then. Showed a lot of control to be able to smoke at will, not get sucked in and ruined by the habit. Lloyd couldn't do it. For years, he had smoked a few a day. Then he entered the corporation, still a relatively young man, and while sitting at a desk and talking on the phone all day, his habit bloomed to at least a half a pack. When he made vice president, it shot up to a pack a day. By then, everything he owned smelled like dead tobacco worms. Still, he tried to hide his smoking from Donna, who had insisted that he quit and believed he had, because, essentially, she trusted him and believed in general that he did what he said. Trusting Donna. At any rate, when he found himself walking the dog in the rain with a butt in his face one night, he decided it had to stop. He went home and told his wife. "I've been smoking for the last two years, even though I told you I wasn't. I can't stop. I'm addicted." Then he cried and she forgave him. After that, he never smoked again, except now and then he did have a cigar, which everyone in the nineties was doing, even Cybill Shepherd. He had seen her with one in the paper not long ago. A big, meaty stogie, right out there. Mmm, thought Lloyd. His thoughts drifted. Wet. It was wet and there was suction where he was. Plenty of suction. God, her tongue tasted good. This was just kissing. Nothing to it. Except . . .

Except, now that he tuned-in a little bit—how long had he been out?— his hand was between her legs. Not all the way up there, no. Not at all, just between her thighs and moving. She wasn't writhing or anything tasteless like that, but the thighs were definitely closed on his hand, welcoming it there, applying a bit of pressure on it, turning around it just a bit as she moved this way and that, looking for the best angle at which to suck his face. And what was happening with her hands? Both of them had been playing with the hair on the back of Lloyd's neck, holding his head where she wanted it. Now one hand moved and was rubbing his upper back. No, not his upper back, his lower back. No, not his lower back, either; that wasn't his lower back. She had her hand down the back of his pants about one quarter of an inch and was very gently tickling the top of the base of Lloyd's spine, inside his underwear. Still she kissed him, sitting rather primly, legs pressing lightly on Lloyd's hand, there on his lap.

"We ought to quit," she whispered after a time. "We're going to be missed."

"Yeah," said Lloyd. "Let's quit now."

They parted. Mona stumbled off his lap and stood in the middle of the little room, straightening herself a bit. Lloyd sat there, just heaving in and out. He watched Mona straighten her skirt and tuck in her shirt, and before his mind knew what his body was doing, he found himself falling in one fluid motion to his knees in front of the couch, then walking like one of the Seven Dwarfs to Mona, who watched him approach without moving, curious about what he might do. What he did was, he waddled like Toulouse-Lautrec over

226

to her, put his arms around her lower body, and buried his face in her crotch, not nose-first—that would have been shocking and intrusive—but with his cheek pressed firmly into her pubic bone.

"Ah," said Mona. "Lloyd. Stop."

"Beautiful woman," he said, hugging her. They stayed like that for a while.

"Lloyd," said Mona. She just stood there, eyes closed, very straight, her hands buried in his hair. "Get up now, baby," she finally murmured.

"Yes," said Lloyd. "I will."

Lloyd got up then, abruptly, lurching to his feet. He turned, bent over, grabbed Mona's head, hands spread to the back of her scalp, beneath her hair, embedded one last kiss deep inside her mouth, gently pushed her from him, and careened into the men's room at the far end of the area.

"Go," he said, opening the door. "I'll be along."

"Okay, Lloyd," said Mona. She pitched forward toward the hallway that would have gotten her back to the lobby, and sanity, but just before she made it past the archway, almost as if her physical being were being controlled by some larger force, she reeled into a ninety-degree turn and entered the men's room, where Lloyd was attempting to put himself together.

Mona stood in the door to the men's room.

"What are you doing!" said Lloyd, who was standing contemplatively at the urinal.

"Nothin'," said Mona. She watched him for a while.

"Mona," said Lloyd. "I think we've pushed the envelope about as far as we should this first night. I mean . . . I'm feeling a little shaky." With his back to her, he zipped up his fly. Then he turned around and looked at her. She was leaning against the wall. She looked so pretty. No! He would not start kissing her in the men's room!

"You're so sweet," said Mona.

"You're the sweet one," said Lloyd, keeping his distance. But she was sweet. He had touched the tiniest lacy edge of her bikini briefs while they were on the couch. He was sure they were white, and slightly translucent.

"Put your back against the door," said Mona. "I have to pee, too."

Like a man in a dream, Lloyd put his back against the door. Mona went to one of the stalls, dropped her skort and panties—they were white!—and sat demurely on the edge of the toilet. The sound of water running. Lloyd could not tear his eyes away. Lloyd wasn't really watching her, though. He was gazing like a medicated psychopath into her eyes. She returned his gaze. Then she daintily replaced her clothing. Checked herself in the mirror. Took him by the elbow, and, quite carefully, they exited the men's room together, crossed the lobby, where they disengaged their arms, and reentered the ballroom, where Walt's informal remarks had just begun.

"Mighty attenuated review of the slides," said Fitz when Lloyd seated himself as quietly as possible.

"Uh-huh," said Lloyd.

"What were you doing all this time?" Fitz was regarding him closely.

"We were programming transitions," said Lloyd.

Title Slide

LLOYD AND MONA TAKE THE PLUNGE: A SLIDE INTERLUDE

Slide #1

Graphic: THE HOTEL POOL.

Text: *The sun was very hot. Lloyd felt a thin film of perspiration glazing his upper lip.*

Notes: They sat by the pool in their bathing suits, stretched out in long wooden chaise longues with big firm cushions. Lloyd had big boxers sporting a riot of Hawaiian color, their size, splendor, and substantial waistband helping to create the modest impression that he was in some kind of shape. Mona had on a somewhat-demure maroon one-piece cut very high on her thigh.

Slide #2

Graphic: AN ASHTRAY ON A GLASS TABLE. IN ONE GROOVE, THE REMNANTS OF A FINE CIGAR. IN ANOTHER, A CIGARETTE BUTT WITH NO LIPSTICK ON IT. BESIDE THE ASHTRAY, THERE IS A BOTTLE OF NUMBER 35 SUNBLOCK, OPEN, A BIT OF WHITE SPUME BUBBLING OUT OF ITS TOP.

Text: *He longed to take the back of her head in his hands and bring her entire facial structure into close proximity.*

Notes: It had been hours since Lloyd had kissed her. The rest of the grown-ups were off somewhere on the golf course. Some had gone on the tour of a nearby bird sanctuary. They were sitting in silence. Lloyd looked over at her. She was lying on her back, eyes closed, breasts rising and falling with the rhythm of sleep.

Slide #3

Graphic: REVENUE GROWTH 1996 VERSUS 2001, AFTER ACQUISITION OF MULTIBILLION-DOLLAR PRODUCTION BASE.

Text: *So that's what he did. . . .*

Notes: They were on the second full day of the trip. After the remarks on that first night, Lloyd spent quite a bit of time at the pub with Mona, Fitz, Waverly, and an assortment of party players, and all of them drank and played cards and smoked cigars, including the women, who proved that the fad was not the denatured pastime it was being portrayed as in the media.

Slide #4

Graphic: MAIN STRIP. LAS VEGAS. NIGHT.

Text: *AAAhhhhhhhhhh, Lloyd thought. At last.*

Notes: There was a lot of mutual bonding and physical touching among associates, although none of it inappropriate. The contemporary executive worker is far too sensitized to the issues of harassment for that, especially in California, where a cross word to an obnoxious person may generate a multi-million-dollar lawsuit. Lloyd knew of an occasion in their San Francisco office where a woman who periodically began morning sales meetings with the announcement that she had "fucked her brains out" the night before later sued the general sales manager for creating an unfriendly working environment where such statements were all too welcome. She won.

Slide #5

Graphic: SUNSHINE. A LONG DRINK IN A TALL GLASS. LIPSTICK ON A STRAW.

Text: *Her mouth tasted sweet and redolent of citrus, which was not surprising considering the number of margaritas she had recently ingested.*

Notes: A hard-on in a swimsuit is not easy to conceal.

Slide #6

Graphic: LLOYD'S ENTIRE FAMILY IN A PICTURE TAKEN DURING THE LAST FAMILY VACATION. THEY ARE LINED UP AT THE EDGE OF THE GRAND CANYON. THE PHOTOGRAPH WAS SNAPPED BY THE FATHER OF ANOTHER FAMILY THAT HAD LINED UP TO SEE THE VIEW AT THE SAME TIME THAT LLOYD, DONNA, NORA, AND BOB HAD REACHED THE FAMOUS PRECIPICE. LLOYD IS AT ONE END OF THE LINE, DONNA AT THE OTHER, BOB AND NORA IN BETWEEN. THEY ARE ALL SMILING. A TINY LICK OF FLAME EATS AT A CORNER OF THE SHOT, ALTHOUGH PERHAPS THAT IS IN OUR IMAGINATION.

Text: *"Let's go to my room," she said.*

Notes: There was an empty lot across the street from Lloyd's office window. While talking on the phone, Lloyd could look down on it, which he did for hours at a time as he wrangled with the wide variety of business issues that made up his day, each of which was different while being essentially the same. The question arose at a staff meeting: Are there rats in the empty lot? Debate raged. Dienst, a senior staffer who had been there since 1957, said no. Ruhalter, a more junior type who tended to see the dark side of everything (and therefore deemed himself a realist), maintained the opposite point of view just as vehemently. They settled it, finally, one soggy July afternoon when not much else was going on. At the company's expense, they purchased a four-pound hunk of aged Gouda cheese. Lloyd insisted on Gouda, since it was the cheese that, while he was eating it, always made him feel most like a rodent. He assigned Ruhalter to go across the street to the place where a board fence separated the sidewalk from the empty lot, and Ruhalter threw the chunk of Gouda over into the abyss. Then they all repaired to Lloyd's office with coffee, diet sodas, and Perrier and waited. In approximately twenty minutes, there was activity around the edges of the area, shadows and dust amid the rocks and garbage. Moments later, they arrived in earnest, the smallest first, then the largest, some as big as cats. The junior associate rats picked and nibbled around the edges of the cheese. The senior officers, who were already quite fat, tore at the younger, weaker ones, driving them away. Then the four or five of the most enormous fell upon one another, biting and scratching, all the while eating, stuffing their cheeks with as much cheese as the others would allow, fighting when necessary over the remains of the hunk, until, at last, there was only one, a gigantic specimen with jet black hair and a tail as long as a human arm. As the others receded, he took the still-not-inconsiderable lump of Gouda, now covered with dirt and gravel, and hauled it off to a corner of the lot, where he and it disappeared into a dark space beneath an adjacent building. The group hung around together somewhat disconsolately for several minutes after the little scene was over. A joke was called for, but if any joke was to be made, it would be Lloyd who should have made it, and since he chose not to, it was clear that none was appropriate. Thankfully, in the second minute of the silence, Lloyd's phone rang. It was Walt, who wanted to talk about bonuses. "Get out of here, guys," Lloyd said to the general assembly, and they vaporized like mist over a pond at morning.

Slide #7

- - - - - - - - - - - - - - -

Graphic: LLOYD, APPARENTLY THINKING WITH HIS BIG HEAD, BUT ACTUALLY USING A LOT MORE OF HIS LITTLE ONE.

Text: *Lloyd thought it over.*

Notes: None. The situation pretty much speaks for itself.

Slide #8

Graphic: An enormous spreadsheet with every calculation in the universe jammed into it.

Text: *"Okay," he said. "As long as we make it to the three o'clock workshop on the tax implications of international acquisitions."*

Notes: The ramifications of global revenue generation are not simple to understand, and the need to do so for each member of Walt's staff was imperative. Each of them had basically been trained for domestic waters. Now they would have to swim with the Japanese, Germans, Italians, Arabs. They would have to understand what games were being played in a wholly new framework, know how to order food that would not poison or gag them, ponder the implications of transactions in four different currencies. Those who could not do so would end up in Boise or Dubuque instead of transnational cities like Berlin, Paris, and New York. Consequently, each and every one of them was boning up on the necessities as fast as possible, and nothing, not even pleasure, could get in their way.

Slide #9

Graphic: Weather map of the world photographed from a weather satellite miles out in space.

Text: *"Hey!" said Mona. "I wouldn't miss it."*

Notes: So this is what happened:

They decided to leave the pool separately, for reasons that might be guessed at. True, Lloyd had a towel around his waist, disguising the drama of his condition. But to be caught together at this juncture? Call it unnecessary.

Mona left first, crossing the lobby on her own, languidly, pausing to look in the glittering shop windows that dotted the lobby. At Gianni Versace, she paused longer than usual and then went inside. She emerged five minutes later with a shoe box in an exquisite over-the-shoulder shopping bag. Inside the box was a pair of red Manolo Blahnik pumps she'd had her eye on since the evening of their arrival. They were horrendously expensive. Buying them had set the last mooring of propriety loose inside her. She felt wanton.

Lloyd left the sundeck some time thereafter. He, too, did not rush, but for a different reason. A riot of warring emotions struggled for dominance in him. On the one hand, he was driven mad with turbulent priapic desire. As a physical being, she inhabited his dreams. But if physical qualities had been the decisive factor, Lloyd would have succumbed to temptation years and years ago. No, there was also the matter of Mona's playful, intelligent spirit. The woman loved to play games, but also to be stone-cold serious and indulge in speculative discourse. And she was smart, of course, smarter than Lloyd maybe, and certainly better at numbers.

She was also quite vulnerable, as had been evidenced by her reactions when Lloyd happened to touch her feet, or kissed her. When he touched her, Lloyd felt something open inside her, something she was yearning to turn inside out and give him, whole. This unfolding inflamed him even more painfully and inexorably than the color of her hair.

And yet, what of Donna? His wife was certainly equal in beauty to Mona. He saw the way men looked at Donna. She was certainly just as bright, and more witty, too. He had found her not simply interesting but also fascinating for more than a decade. Was this not the basest form of betrayal? Of course it was. No amount of rationalization, self-delusion, false hipness, or moral relativism could change that essential truth. This was about to become the biggest lie, the most terrible breach of another person's trust he had committed in his life.

Of course, it was also true, thought Lloyd as he waited for the elevator at the most distant end of the lobby, that there was no real reason why Donna should ever find out. This was a thoroughly mature affair he was about to embark upon, if that was indeed his intention, which it certainly seemed to be, considering that he was standing there waiting for the conveyance that would deliver him to its door. Mona would tell no one. It would be injurious to herself for her to do so. Also, she was a mellow person, Mona was, a soft and generally nonpunitive kind of woman, whose overall personal aura was one of acceptance, friendliness, and a lack of bitterness and guile, a willingness to take things as they came, with open arms, her hair flowing around her shoulders, lips slightly pouting, moist with lip gloss and longing, firm, ample breasts with small declarative nipples yearning for the touch. Lloyd shook himself. This was supposed to be his thoughtful overview of upcoming life choices?

The elevator arrived. Lloyd stepped inside.

No, there was little chance he would be discovered if he was careful. Mona was discreet. Mona was healthy, too. They had discussed the matter pretty frankly, in a philosophical sort of way, in a conversation they had shared about life in the nineties on the chaise longue that very afternoon. Mona revealed that she had lived with several men over the course of the last ten years, had been tested before and after each relationship had ended because she was morbidly afraid of disease, and stayed away from one-night stands. In closing, Mona said informationally that the last of her relationships had ended politely about ten months prior, just before she began to find Lloyd interesting in, she admitted, a somewhat clinical way. She did not miss romance, she said, when it was not available. The work was so all-encompassing. Her life at the office was inexorable. There were other passions that had taken her over.

So Mona was not a physical danger to him. Nor a social one. When either of them chose to end it, it would end. It could end right here, after just this one time. But that would be a shame. There was so much to the woman. So much to find out. So, in sum, it was pretty obvious that the only one who could hurt him in this affair would be himself, Lloyd, if he went and did something stupid like fall in love with her. Actually, he already was sort of in love with her. He thought about her, even when he did not wish to. He had dreams about her. When she entered a room, his heart leapt. When he saw another man engaging her in conversation, he was smitten with torrential jealousy and a desire to wrench his adversary's windpipe from his throat.

Most frightening of all was the possibility, and not a remote one, that, if after they had conducted their affair for a while, he found he did not love Mona, he could succumb to crippling, lacerating guilt that would destroy his peace of mind and drive him to confess. How would he feel about the despicable treachery of his own actions? Would he not feel the need to punish *himself*? He was suddenly seized with a desire to call Donna, tell her about the whole thing, and throw himself on the receiver until it punctured his heart.

But here he was at the door already.

He knocked.

Slide #10

Graphic: THE COMPANY LOGO

Text: *Toward a New Tomorrow*

Notes: We will now take any questions you may have.

Terra Incognita

She answered the door in one of the plush terry-cloth robes provided by the hotel with a reminder on a little cardboard card placed around the hanger that those who wished to procure such succulent articles of clothing could buy them at the hotel shop. In other words, don't steal them. Lloyd had never stolen one, primarily because he was afraid it would show up on the final tab, which could, possibly, be checked by Accounting. He was even relatively nervous about the $8.95 he spent on the nightly movie in his room. Lloyd liked to do things by the numbers. Or so he told himself.

Mona had brushed her hair and had put on some subtle scent Lloyd could not name. It was the smell of Mona. She said nothing, just simply stood in the door to her room in her white, white robe. Behind her, sun poured into the stark blond-wood interior. They were up rather high for this particular hotel, the fifth floor, about treetop level, and the sound of the wind in the trees mingled with the summer country noises of this enclave so far, far away from home. The sunshine, the cool breeze with the smell of mango carried from the tropical region just a couple of hundred miles south, a bowl of fruit on Mona's credenza—these all came clear behind her as she looked openly, speculatively, and really quite lovingly at Lloyd.

"Don't be nervous, Lloyd," she said. "This isn't a performance review."

"I know," he said, and stepped inside. "I can't help it, though, if I'm nervous." He took off the towel from around his waist and tossed it on the floor of the sink-and-mirror setup outside her enormous bathroom. "This is nicer than my room," he said.

"Want a look around?"

"Okay," said Lloyd. She was playing some kind of game. Whatever it was, he felt himself relaxing within its confines.

"This is the tiny little room outside the bathroom," said Mona, sweeping her arm gracefully around the area in which they were standing.

"Very nice," said Lloyd.

"Here is where you can wash up on the way to or from the bathroom, or simply pause for a moment to brush your hair. Would you like to brush your hair?"

"No, thanks."

"No, but honestly." She was grinning at him. "You should brush your hair."

Lloyd looked in the mirror. His hair was swirled around the top of his head like a Carvel soft ice cream recently poured out of the machine and coated with liquid chocolate. Lloyd took up the brush by the side of the washbasin and ran its stiff bristles over his head. It felt good.

"Better?"

"Yep," said Mona. "Now this is the bathroom, where, as you see, there is a lovely sink once again, a huge mirrored area, and"—here she turned and gestured to the bath/Jacuzzi that took up about half the room—"here is an amazingly hedonistic device that calls for occupation by more than one person."

"Almost immediately," said Lloyd.

"No, no," said Mona. "We have to show you the entire place before we are sure you will like it."

"But . . . I already like it."

"Now out here, we have the living room and study, which, as you see, is quite capacious and luxurious and also has a couch and home entertainment center and many places where the busy young executive can relax and shed the tensions of the day just past." She had moved into the central room and was standing there in her puffy bathrobe, which, he noted, was now a tiny bit open at the neck. "I'm not wearing any underwear," she said.

"Come over here," said Lloyd.

"And finally," said Mona, moving elegantly into the last room of the suite, which Lloyd could just glimpse from where he was standing. "Are you coming in, Lloyd?" Lloyd went into the bedroom. "This is obviously the bedroom, which is not fancy but, in its own way, is the center of the entire space." She was right. The bedroom was deeply, spiritually perfect. In the center, up against one immaculate white wall, was a pine bed with a thick box spring and an even thicker mattress on it. On the bed was a rough spread the color and consistency of oatmeal. Above the bed was a small mirror. On the floor was an oval throw rug of many colors. The doors, which went from floor to ceiling and were made entirely of screening, opened onto a tiled balcony that looked over the golf course, outbuildings, and, in the distance, bird sanctuary, and, way off, almost like a whisper in the back of the mind, lay the Gulf of Mexico. It was silent and bright, and so very clean.

Mona took off her bathrobe. She was naked, as truly and completely naked as anyone Lloyd had ever seen. She shone in the radiance of her nakedness. Christ, thought Lloyd. This is what it's all about. The tremendous banality of this thought struck Lloyd dumb. He sounded like one of those politicians who are constantly elevating something convenient into what it's all about. One day, it's the family, for example. The next day, it's putting in an honest day's work for an honest day's pay. Then next thing you know, it's a naked woman. Maybe the truth is that it's no one thing that it's all about, thought Lloyd. Still, fuck it. It was how he felt. For once in your life, go with how you feel, he told himself. It will be all right.

"Christ," said Lloyd. "You are what life is all about."

"You think I'm beautiful," said Mona. It was not a question.

"Oh yes," said Lloyd. There was nothing in the universe but her beauty. He took the three steps that placed him directly within her luminosity, and he put his arms around her. Her skin was cool and dry. "You're so beautiful, Mona. You're so beautiful, I don't know what to do."

"Do nothing," said Mona. "You don't have to do anything."

He was mesmerized by her breasts, which were putting off an intense glow in varying shades of pink. Her hips were full, and below her waist, a small tummy declared itself. He ran his hands down her arms and drank in the entirety of her physical being. Her knees. Her knees were dimpled and her legs were turned slightly inward, giving her a gentle pigeon-toed stance that tore directly into his heart. "God," he said.

"Come here, Lloyd," said Mona. She stretched out her arms and took him in. "Don't you think you should take off those stupid trunks?"

235

"Yeah," said Lloyd. Without thinking about it too much, he slipped his fingers into the waistline of his shorts and pulled them down, stepped out of them, and tossed them aside with his toe. He stood in front of her, aware that his stomach wasn't quite as flat as it should have been, that the backs of his thighs were perhaps not as firm as once they had been, that his back, since 1989, had hair on it. She didn't seem aware of any such thing. She grabbed him by both shoulders and held him at arm's length.

"You're cute," she said.

His penis stood before him like an exclamation point. He would have to put it somewhere real soon.

"Come on, Lloyd," she said. "Put it in me."

So he did. It was so easy. What had all the procrastination been about? They should have been doing this for the last six months, since the idea had first occurred to them! Why did people postpone happiness?

Mona simply leaned back and let the bed have her, pulled him down on top of her, and wrapped her legs around him. There was nowhere else. Here was where he belonged.

"Ah," said Lloyd.

"Yes," she replied. "Oh yes."

Her breasts were both soft and hard at once, and crushed beneath him. He lifted himself up on his arms and looked down at her. Her loveliness was blinding, oppressive. He could look at it no longer. He descended into her, inhaling her scent, gorging on the intense splendor of her eyes, her skin. A tiny ridge of fine ruby blond hair ran from just beneath her navel and, delicately thickening, into the curly mystery below. He ran his finger down this mighty tributary. She closed her eyes.

"Mmm," she said.

"How could you possibly not be married?" said Lloyd.

"I don't really know," said Mona. Her eyes stayed shut. No vapor marred her brow. "I've been in love. I've lived with people for a bunch of time. I just never got married. I think I will. I'm only thirty-five, you know."

"Only thirty-five," said Lloyd. "How pretty you are in every way."

"You are, Lloyd," said Mona. She opened her eyes and looked at him with the eyes of a person awakened in the middle of a long, pleasant dream. "You're so pretty, too."

"Me?" said Lloyd. "I'm . . . pretty?"

"Oh yes," said Mona. "You have such soft hair at the back of your neck. And your back is so . . . strong." She had shut her eyes again. Slowly, as she and Lloyd moved together, she extended her legs to their full length, then folded them behind his back, wrapping him in a tight embrace. He was so deep inside her! How deeply could one person go into another and still be a separate individual? Lloyd could feel them picking up speed. He wondered if they should be. He thought about asking her about it. He didn't want to mismanage her orgasm the very first time around.

"Go faster, Lloyd," she said. A wrinkle of concentration had appeared between her eyebrows.

God, thought Lloyd. Let this be the first of many, many times.

"Come inside me, Lloyd," she said.

"I hope you've taken the necessary precautions," said Lloyd.

"Started taking the pill again . . . last Thursday."

"Last . . . Thursday?"

"Yes."

"Why . . . last Thursday?"

"Decided . . ."

"What?"

"Decided," said Mona. . . . "Must have you. Lloyd."

"Oh!" said Lloyd. And he shot a bolt of bright blue light inside of the space they both inhabited.

"I love you," said Lloyd.

"I love you, too, Lloyd," said Mona.

After that, they sort of dozed for a while. Then they took a couple of baths. By that time, it was nearly six. Lloyd went to his room, showered, changed, called home, and went down to dinner. It was hard for him not to whistle on his way through the lobby to the dining room. That would have aroused suspicion. Nobody whistles in business.

Payback

On the bus going to the airport at the end of the meeting, Lloyd sat by himself way in the back by the rest room. There was beer on the bus, and many of the executives were sort of polishing off the buzz they had maintained for nearly five days running now. Nobody felt much like talking, though. Lloyd's sunburn hurt. Somewhere up near the front of the bus sat Mona. Lloyd imagined that her sunburn hurt, too. Lloyd closed his eyes and put his head back. He missed her. The twenty minutes since they got on the bus had been just about the longest time they had been apart in the last seventy-two hours.

During that time, Lloyd had bent Mona over, turned her upside down, flattened her, lifted her, mashed her, and crushed her in the following locations, given here in chronological order immediately after that first incident (beds excluded):

- ✓ In the bathtub in Lloyd's room, both standing and seated.
- ✓ On the patio of Mona's room, after dark, while reclining in a cold wrought-iron chair.
- ✓ Behind the soda machine at the swimming pool at 3:00 A.M., where improper placement of the gigantic dispenser left a small corridor that just fit two.
- ✓ In the elevator on the way to breakfast, as it inexplicably broke down and stopped between floors.
- ✓ In the audiovisual booth at the back of the presentation room, when both were there long after anybody else, rehearsing for Mona's financial presentation the next day.
- ✓ In the deep woods off the seventh green of the championship golf course as Mona and Lloyd, neither of whom played the game, took a break from tooling around the area in the little cart they had essentially stolen from in front of the clubhouse; this was most particularly dangerous, since they had stashed the vehicle somewhat carelessly behind some bushes and, at that moment, several midlevel managers from the Northeast region were trying to chip out of the rough.
- ✓ On the floor of the anteroom of Lloyd's suite, right inside the door, since it had been three full hours of dinner, speeches, and drinking since they had had any access to each other at all, unless you count the hour or so spent at the pub, seated at a table across from each other, with both of Mona's naked feet in Lloyd's enraged crotch.
- ✓ Under a mangrove tree in the bird sanctuary, shortly before they realized that they were lost and began to hike back to civilization in the broiling sun without any sunblock.
- ✓ On the beach at 5:30 A.M., where the two went to watch the sun rise on their last day together, walking to the farthest end of the strand, far, far from the hotel, and collapsing behind a gigantic outcropping of rock. Sad and a bit spent, they bid farewell to the Florida Gulf Coast.
- ✓ Fully clothed, upright, standing with their carry-on luggage in the alcove of Mona's suite. Immediately thereafter, they parted and made their separate ways to the airport jitney, convinced they had fooled everyone.

This may not be a complete list.

Sitting on the jitney, exhausted, depleted, and a little bit sore, Lloyd closed his eyes. The knowledge that their perfect little week was over hurt him badly. Not that their relationship was ended, of course. It would just be more difficult. They would find a way, though. Love always finds a way.

It had been an excellent retreat for everybody. Ron had found face time with Doug, and he used it to trade several interesting industry facts he had accumulated, including some intelligence on other executives Doug had implied he might like to see. Walt had shot his best round of golf ever, a 78, from which he earned more than three hundred dollars in bets. Fitz spent five days in mutual teasing with Waverly that had resulted in about twenty minutes of harmless tongue hockey that satisfied them both without threatening either. Darling had won at poker and sold his marketing plan to Walt, who approved a 42 percent increase in his budget basically to get Darling off his back. And Lloyd and Mona had gotten significant business accomplished as well, as we have seen.

For Lloyd, however, the best was yet to come.

After almost an hour of flouncing and jouncing, Walt approached Lloyd, who was giving a very good impression of a man sleeping, plumped down in the seat next to him, gave him an enormous paternal squeeze on the shoulder, and said, "Lloydmeister." Then he stared at him for a while, and Lloyd knew that Walt was thinking of the white-hot romance he had enjoyed in the summer of 1979, in the eighth year of his marriage, with a corporate communications consultant who was then servicing his little corner of the firm. The thing had been a sharp, vivid pain smack in the middle of Walt's life, but he had overcome it, and now it was one of his most treasured anecdotes. He placed a hand on Lloyd's shoulder.

"Lloyd," he said, growing rather misty, "I'm gonna make you executive vice president of this corporation. Would you like that?"

"Well, is there more money?" asked Lloyd. It was not as stupid a question as one might think. The building was full of people with big assignment portfolios that came with negligible tangible reward. Lloyd did not wish to be one of them.

"A little," said Walt. "Probably in the nature of fifteen percent. Couple more options, maybe."

"I would, Walt. Damn right I would," said Lloyd, pumping Walt's beefy paw.

Thank God, they did not hug.

September

Lloyd is like a teenager again, finding out what the thing can actually do. He's never been so besotted with his own amoral bestial power. Life is good! *Arrrgh!*

Underneath it all, however, the man is consumed with self-disgust and paranoia. How could he possibly be getting away with this? How could there not be consequences? Thus begins a series of mysterious ailments attacking Lloyd out of the blue: Salmonella, after a plate of clams that didn't taste quite right; skin cancer, after thinking about the amount of sun he had just taken at Pelican; baldness, although he was not yet bald per se, ipso facto, he does have a lot less hair than Fabio. At the same time, for some reason, his own wife has never looked better. What a woman! He is constantly considering resumption of a better life, but always decides against it. He is tormented, miserable. He has never been happier.

And then along comes Doug.

Venues

- In the multimedia suite at 201 Park. Five minutes. Right after lunch. Danger Level: 9.8.
- In Roy Schwab's office while Roy is visiting his estranged wife in Sacramento. On the trip, Roy and his wife effect a reconciliation that is mysterious to them both.
- Lloyd conducts an entire meeting with three members of the Quality Council who pop in from Toledo unannounced as Mona crouches beneath his desk in the crawl space allowed for his knees. Fortunately, the wood of Lloyd's desk extends all the way to the floor in front. Was it designed for this reason? His fly is open. Mona, terrified, does not move. It is the closest they come to getting caught. To date.

Clobbering Time

Lloyd?" It was a voice on his internal executive line. Who could it be at this hour? "Hello? Lloyd?" the voice said, very dry, very calm. "I know you're in there."

"Yes, sorry," said Lloyd. "I . . . was trying to place you."

"It's Doug, Lloyd," said Doug.

"Doug!" exploded Lloyd. "Well! . . . Hi!" What a fatuous thing to say!

"Hi, Lloyd," said Doug. "I was wondering if you could come up and see me for a minute."

"Yes!" said Lloyd. "I mean, sure!"

"It's about some stuff that happened at the retreat on Pelican Island," said Doug. He gave the phrase "retreat on Pelican Island" the flavor of a title, and a slightly ridiculous one at that.

Meanwhile, Lloyd's small intestine had encircled his stomach and begun to squeeze. "I've got to sit down," said Lloyd to himself, and he was already sitting. His head was spacious and empty, nothing at all in it. All there was was the fear.

"Hello? Lloyd?" said Doug.

"Yes indeed," said Lloyd. "Ah . . . what kind of things?"

"Well," said Doug confidentially. "I hear there was an awful lot of screwing going on while people were supposed to be off golfing and having a tour of the bird sanctuary. What do you think about that?"

"I . . . I . . . I . . . don't think anything about it," said Lloyd. His voice was coming from very far away, small and quizzical, like the halting voice of an eight-year-old-boy caught setting fires in the ravine behind the school.

"Well, anyhow, I know you and I haven't put our heads together for quite some time, and we're overdue for a substantive meeting overviewing your European experiences. I hear you did quite well over there."

"Yes?" It was all Lloyd could come up with.

"Oh, yes," said Doug. "But that's a big ball of wax and I figure this little thing here is something you could probably help me with. I mean, you being kind of the community conscience, in a way, the public face of the corporation and all."

"I just try to articulate the views of those far more worthy than I," said Lloyd. It was an answer on the verge of insubordination, but it was the only one that, after severe reflection, came tumbling out. He held his breath, and he heard Doug chuckle.

"That's a good one, Lloyd. Ha," said Doug. "'Views of those far more worthy than I' . . . ha ha. I like that very much." It seemed like a genuine laugh.

"So, Doug. You . . . want me to come up now?" Lloyd held his breath. Could it be that he was off the hook? That his presence was no longer required?

"Well, I suppose you might have enough time for a quick pop behind the soda machine, but try to hustle on up here right after that, huh?" said Doug, and hung up.

Sayonara, Bud

Lloyd sat at his desk and thought things over. This was very bad. Someone had observed them in all kinds of unthinkable positions. Doug had mentioned the soda machine! Was it possible that was just a lucky guess? Lloyd remembered the minutes he had spent sandwiched between the side of the Coke machine and the wall of the pool area. He had lifted Mona's towel—under which she was blessedly naked—hitched her up around his waist, and, using the smallness of the space as leverage, entered her at a perilous angle, which could have injured him had she fallen or become wedged in an inopportune stance. She was sucking on his ear. A bird cried in one of the palm trees nearby. It was a perfect memory. Afterward, they bought a Coke and shared it while sitting in complete solitude by the edge of the pool, wrapped in enormous, thirsty towels, their feet in the bathtub-warm water.

But what if they had not been alone? How would that have changed things? What kind of slime would have stayed up late enough to watch them, intruding on the spell they had created? Taking notes. Reporting on them for personal benefit. Ratting them out. Not only destroying the magic that set that night apart but visiting almost-certain havoc on their careers with the one person with whom it really counted. Not Walt . . . but Doug. Doug.

It could only be one person.

Lloyd called a number he knew by heart. "Hi," he said into the phone. "Doug knows." He listened for a while. "I'm going up to see him now," he said. "No, he doesn't sound angry. He sounds . . . bemused. I think he's got something on his agenda. . . . Uh-huh." Lloyd listened for a while again. "He suggested I might have time for a quick pop behind the soda machine, but he asked that I hurry on upstairs right after that. . . . Mm-hmm. No, I'm pretty sure he's got to be referring to the soda machine by the pool at Pelican. . . . Yeah, hon. That one. . . . No, babe. I don't think there's a place like that around here." Lloyd looked at his watch and smiled. "Which?" he said. "The one on thirty-four or thirty-seven?" He stood and wrestled himself into his jacket. "I'll meet you there in ninety seconds." He hung up.

He was in Doug's office in seven minutes exactly.

Big Girls Don't Cry

Mona sat at her desk and stared into space. She was jittering with terror. Her life to that point wavered before her inner eye. She saw herself as a little girl, crouched over her kitchen table in Winnetka, Illinois. It was the late 1960s, and the smell of burning leaves wafted in through her kitchen window. It was a smell no longer available in the modern world, for the burning of leaves outdoors had been banned in most communities. There were good reasons for it, just as there were excellent justifications for the banning of smoking in public places, and the elimination of beef in corporate lunchrooms. But leaves burning had been her favorite smell, once upon a time. The nutty, crisp smell, borne always over air just piped in from Canada, the knowledge that with the burning of leaves and the advent of cooler air there would soon be toasty sweaters and pumpkin pie. Pumpkin pie. Mona put her head down on her desk and wept.

It had been a while since she had cried this hard. How long? Years? Yes, years, certainly. Decades? No, thank God, not that long. There had been that time when she was a young associate—not that long ago, really—and Mortimer had made fun of her in an open meeting for an analysis that he had instructed her to present. Mortimer. He was gone now. A consultant to nobody in particular, he dropped in now and then to "see how she was doing." Didn't he know that she hated him? Perhaps he did. Perhaps he didn't care. Hatred was not the worst thing one could feel about another person in business. Pity, yes. Maybe pity was the worst.

But what was she crying about now? She sat with her head buried in her arms, tears coursing down her cheeks. Fuck it, she thought, and gave herself over to it. Behind her eyes, there descended a blackness so complete, no thought could enter.

Would love end? That was the idea that surfaced when the night parted just a bit. Yes, that's it. That must be what she was crying about. Not fear. Not resentment. Just an unwillingness for life to move on. For things, as they always did, had to change into something else, not always better. Things end. Even the best things. Especially the best things.

She rose and wiped her face with the back of her sleeve. Then, holding her waist with both hands, she bent in half and hung down, her head nearly touching the floor, flopping down between her legs, her red hair hanging down and making a pool between and about her feet. Then, just as suddenly as she had gone down, she stood and flipped her mane backward. This functioned to array her tresses in splendor around her shoulders like an auburn and crimson halo with just a touch of gold.

"Well," she said into the empty room. "Whatever."

She left her office and went to meet Lloyd. Not long after, she took her post downstairs at a small table in the bar at Palio, a gorgeous site lined with outrageous murals and callow media buyers.

She waited and drank Sambuca and coffee, and after a while, just coffee. By the time Lloyd appeared, she was on her fifth cup.

Try to Run

Doug was standing in the middle of his vast, sparely opulent office, staring at a video image on a forty-eight-inch screen. It was sports of some kind. Soccer? No. Rugby. Doug was tuned into some satellite transponder beaming in programming from Oceana. Lloyd's mouth was very dry.

"Would you like a soda or something?" said Doug. He looked perfectly cordial. "Anisette? Or . . . scotch? I understand you're a very big scotch drinker."

"I'm not a lush or anything, Doug. I'm sober much of the time."

"Yes?" said Doug. He looked disappointed. "I like a drink in the middle of the day myself." He went over to a closed bookcase and opened the cabinet door. Inside, there was a bottle of Laphroig, a single-malt scotch whiskey meant to be drunk neat. Doug poured himself three fingers into a large slab of glass. "Want one?" he said.

"Sure. Yeah." Suddenly, Lloyd did want one, more than anything in the world. A huge pool of viscous brown fluid in a ten-ounce glass. Relaxation. Relief. Doug handed over Lloyd's drink. It gleamed in the light. Lloyd knew everything would be all right.

Doug went behind his desk and sank into his gigantic black leather recliner. He leaned neatly back and placed his perfect feet on the top of his black onyx desk, which was not a desk, really, but a large slab of highly polished stone. Lloyd sat in a smaller, more upright wooden chair with an upholstered back and seat. He did not, as yet, feel like lifting his feet off the floor. He took a tentative sip of the Laphroig. Doug did the same.

"Sorry I honked your horn a little back there on the telephone," said Doug after a while. "I couldn't resist. It was . . . too tempting. I know . . . so much." He was silent then, and Lloyd discerned a strangeness in his physical demeanor. It seemed that Doug's frame was at intervals quivering slightly. He would then go stone cold again, ruminating over his glass of whiskey, after which he would once again fall to quaking, if only briefly. It came to Lloyd that Doug was laughing, not out-and-out guffawing, but dedicated to the repression of a massive attack of mirth. Lloyd didn't know what to think. On the one hand, Doug was terrifying him. Who could possibly know what a senior executive of Doug's size was capable of doing in an extreme, shapeless situation like this? On the other hand, it was all Lloyd could do, once he recognized Doug's physical manifestations, to keep from collapsing into merriment himself. What would he be laughing about? His life was disintegrating!

"I don't know what to say, here, Doug" was what Lloyd finally thought to say. He knew it was lame, but he put a lot of feeling into it, and it had the added benefit of being completely true.

"Oh hm," said Doug. He closed his eyes and shook in silence. "Haw," he said, and then, finally, he ejected a noise that came very close to "Oh hoo hoo hoo," rose, and left the room entirely, disappearing into the depths of his private bathroom, shower, and nap area.

Lloyd sat very still, staring at the carpet. It was a very deep Turkish baby with plenty of weft. He took off a shoe and pushed his toe into it. It was nice. Every now and then, he took a thoughtful pull on his scotch, which featured a peaty, oaky radiance Lloyd loved. When it was gone, he got up, poured himself another, only slightly less ample than the first, and reseated himself.

Doug reentered with an empty glass, went to the bottle, then resumed his place behind his desk. "A couple of years ago, I had a crisis in my marriage," he said. "You know how that goes. There was a little director of something in Marketing. She was responsible for packaging of customer incentive plans, I think. She was . . . adorable. Thought I walked on water. It was pleasant, being adored. At that time, my wife still viewed me as human, which was a liability, considering how elevated I had grown at work. I found it difficult to go home and return to flesh-and-blood status. Sally was her name. Sally was . . . lovely. Not beautiful, mind you, but . . . young. Youth is beautiful, I think. Inherently. At any rate . . ." Doug rose and strolled over to the window. Below, the park was fully engaged in molting from the green of summer into the many-colored coat of autumn. "Sally was the first, the first time I . . . strayed. And she was the sweetest. It ended when her job was eliminated. I asked her whether she wanted me to intercede, but she said no, that such an action would compromise me and she didn't wish to do that. I suppose she thought that once she no longer worked at the company, we could be more free in our engagement. The opposite was true, of course. We had no social infrastructure to bring us together and it ended essentially the moment she walked out the door."

Lloyd looked down at his glass. It was empty. He put it on Doug's desk.

"Put a piece of paper underneath the glass, Lloyd, for God's sake," said Doug. Lloyd hurried to do so. Doug got up and disappeared behind Lloyd. A moment later, the bottle appeared over Lloyd's shoulder and decanted another four ounces of scotch into his glass. Doug disappeared behind him again. "The next time around, it was not so perfect," he said. Lloyd could hear that Doug's voice came from slightly less altitude, and he turned, to find him sitting now on the couch that was the centerpiece of the talking pit that faced his desk at some distance. Lloyd got up from his chair with the full intention of joining Doug over there, then decided to stand quite still for a while instead, since his head was refusing to remain firmly seated on his neck. "Margaret," said Doug. "She was a senior vice president at a management-consulting firm a couple of blocks away from here. She came in to pitch us some business, and I can't explain it, but it was like something base and thrilling inside me responded immediately and directly to her. I knew she felt the same way. For years, we regularly got together. Perhaps not with the frequency of you and your good friend . . ." Here Doug once again fell to a suspicious coughing that Lloyd was pretty sure covered some other expulsion he did not wish to advertise.

"You'll excuse me if I don't consider the fact that you've had me under surveillance to be quite so amusing," said Lloyd.

"Yes, I can understand that. But I had to know, Lloyd. I had to know if you were a player. Whether the facade of decency that most men maintain had cracked and the real person inside you was in danger of coming out. It's lonely, Lloyd, being the only person in a group unconstrained by conventional frameworks and morality. I wanted to see if it was possible that I might have some company. I wonder if I have."

"I'm not quite sure, Doug," said Lloyd, flopping down on the other end of the couch and setting his head down on the backrest. He closed his eyes. "I'm not certain how far gone I am yet."

"But while we weren't your equal in frequency, I will say we were in our own way daring and creative. I think you would be impressed. I'm not going to enumerate. Oh what the hell. Maybe just a little. We would wait until Myrtle went home for the night and Kaskowitz, that huge brownnoser, saw that he wasn't going to outlast me, and Vincent, the shoeshine man, was done on the floor for the evening, and the guys in the A/V suite had packed it up, and then Margaret would come up in the service elevator, and I would let her in, and we would have the run of the place. I don't believe there's a major office in this executive suite we didn't explore."

"You never took any risks during business hours, though," said Lloyd. He felt a twinge of pride and turned to face Doug, who he saw was leaning up against the back of the couch as well, his head back, his eyes trained on the ceiling.

"No, Lloyd," he said. "But then . . . we never got caught, either."

There was a thoughtful silence between them. They sipped. They considered the issues.

"So . . . what happened with, you know, Margaret?" said Lloyd at last.

"Nothing," said Doug. "I still love her. I love her more than I've ever loved a woman, I think, if that doesn't sound unacceptably dramatic. But I decided that to break up my marriage would be a tragic betrayal of a person whom I still consider my best friend, my companion. I love my wife, Lloyd. I love her a lot."

"Oh yes," said Lloyd. He lay there in silence for a time, feet splayed out. Doug said nothing. "Boardroom table?" said Lloyd at last.

"Oh, absolutely. Many times. With the entertainment center going full blast and the electric curtains open to greet the night."

"Cool," said Lloyd.

"At a certain point, we just couldn't go on. Once I decided not to leave Winnie, it didn't seem an acceptable alternative. I suppose we could have tried. But the honesty, the freshness would have gone out of it, and I would have lost whatever was beautiful and necessary in the affair entirely. I prefer to suffer without her, rather than lose her. I'm aware that I sound incredibly corny. But love is corny. Love is sentimental. You have to have a little room in your life for sentiment."

"You still love her. But . . . you don't see her," Lloyd said. He was feeling the alcohol now. "That's . . . a tragedy." He felt like crying.

"We get together for lunch now and then. But we don't venture beyond. She understands. She has a husband, too. Grown children. It's better."

"Pretty tough, though."

"Yes," said Doug. He sat up and ran his fingers through his ample white crown of hair. "Sure it's hard. You have to be hard to earn the right to be soft, you know what I mean?"

"Sure, Doug. Hard as nails. Ram-tough. That's us."

"What are you going to do, Lloyd? Are you going to wreck your life? Or are you going to work toward some form of accommodation? I'm not advising you one way or another. Sometimes devastation is the only way to effect quality improvement."

"I haven't decided yet," said Lloyd. "I'm having too much fun."

"And your wife?" said Doug. "Can she possibly not be aware of the situation? At the last holiday party, she struck me as an intelligent, highly evolved woman."

"I don't know," said Lloyd, and the full weight of sudden understanding slammed into him like a freight train into a car stalled on a railroad crossing. And he saw. Everything. How could he have been so blind?

Try to Hide

He had returned from Pelican Island in a frenzy of riotous emotion: excitement, sexual triumph and regeneration, horror, remorse, fear of discovery, a yearning to confess. None won. He plumbed the behavior of his wife for some wick that would set one or another choice within him afire, but he found none.

"I'm home!" he shouted up the stairs, his luggage arrayed around his feet like the gifts of the Maji. On top of one pile, there was a box for her.

"Hi!" she said, skipping down the stairs to greet him. She was wearing the tight ribbed brown stretch pants with stirrups at the bottom. On top, she wore a large sleeved mohair sweater in bright red. Her hair was wet and combed straight back. She looked quite nice to Lloyd, and he was impaled by a sharp, bright icicle of longing. She kissed him briefly on the side of his mouth, making it one of those half-lip, half-cheek jobs. Meaningless. Perhaps she missed his mouth. She tasted of mint and a hint of facial soap. "How was it," she said. "Good?"

"It was okay," said Lloyd. He had called Donna dutifully throughout the trip and honestly and completely reported most important anecdotal material, with certain obvious exceptions. Why hurt her about something that was essentially meaningless and therefore basically none of her business?

"Did you get me anything?" said Donna. There was a light, slightly teasing tone to her voice that Lloyd couldn't quite place. Where had he last heard his wife speak like this? When she had gotten drunk at his thirty-sixth birthday party. Had she been drinking now? He stepped close to kiss her again, and he found her staring appraisingly at him from very close up. "That's quite a tan you've got there," she said.

"I got stuck out in the sun by the bird sanctuary when we had the wilderness experience on Thursday," said Lloyd. "I was out there with Burbage and Finster and Wieseltier and Bradford and a couple of other senior types and it was incredibly hard out there—I mean hot, hot out there, and we got lost and had to find out way back without, like, paths or anything. It's a wonder I'm not in the hospital, actually."

"Does it hurt?" said Donna. She was touching his face with two fingers, very lightly, watching the impression her touch made on his skin.

"A little," said Lloyd. He used the opportunity to investigate his wife closely. "Have you been drinking, Donna?"

"I had a glass of wine," said Donna.

"At . . . four in the afternoon?"

"It's almost five," said Donna.

"Okay," said Lloyd. He decided to drop it. Who was he to criticize another person's drinking habits? "I got you this." He picked up the box and offered it to his wife. She sat on the floor and opened it very carefully, saving the gold elastic that trimmed its corners, neatly folding the fancy tissue, gently removing the green silk bathrobe with exquisite red, blue, and emerald stitching in the shape of a dragon on the back. When worn, it would be very short and very smooth, falling to the exact point where Donna's legs terminated and her buttocks began.

"It's nice, Lloyd," she said. She did not look up. After a while, she held it up in front of her and regarded the back. "I'll get quite a bit of use out of this," she said, a remark that now struck Lloyd, sitting in Doug's office, cringing under the full weight of his horrible suspicion, as a very odd comment indeed.

"Well, I'm glad you like it," said Lloyd.

"I'll just put it back in the box now," she added hurriedly. Almost as if she was afraid that Lloyd would ask to see it on her.

"I got some stuff for Spud and Theodora, too," he said, dragging his bags up the stairs. He realized he hadn't heard the kids yet at all. "Where are they?" he said.

"Nora is playing tennis with Jenny. Bob is over at Kenny's riding his bike. They'll be back in a little while."

"You want to go out to dinner?"

"Yeah. Okay." She was rearranging the bottles of perfume, eau de toilette, deodorant, and hair spritz on her dresser. Did it seem a little bit more crowded than he remembered? The room . . . smelled funny. What was that smell? Paint?

"Did you . . . have the room painted or something?" he said. No, it wasn't paint. It was—

"Caulking," she said. "It's . . . caulking."

"You caulked?"

"Chuck did. We were getting a ton of air round the base of that window and, well . . . I thought it would be a good idea. . . ."

"It is!" said Lloyd. "It is a good idea!"

"Anyhow, it's more economical." She was staring out the window now, peering at the situation outside with intense interest. Lloyd came over to look, too. A black squirrel was sitting up on their lawn like a prairie dog. Other than that, nothing much.

"Sure," said Lloyd. "It's a fine idea. Did he do the rest of the windows?"

"Yeah."

Lloyd had gone back to unpacking. He threw a ball of laundry into the hamper. "How much?"

"How much what?" said Donna.

"How much did he charge us?" Lloyd replied. Had his wife grown stupid all of a sudden? Was he speaking Farsi?

"I don't know," said Donna. Then, after a pause, under her breath, she said, "Nothing."

"Nothing?"

"Nah." Donna let down the venetian blind. "It was no big deal. He was putting in the new garbage disposal and just, like, before I even knew about it, it was done."

"Yeah," said Lloyd. For some reason, he felt as if he were walking very gingerly around a sleeping beast that, if awakened, might eat him. "But . . . it took his time and all . . . these guys, their time is valuable. At least they seem to think it is."

"Well, you know." Donna was sitting on the bed now. The remote for the television and VCR dangled from her hands. "Last year, we gave Chuck's name to Rosemary and Howard, and they ended up paying more than fifty grand for that renovation. I guess Chuck doesn't feel he has to charge us for every little thing. We're long-term customers."

"Okay."

"I don't understand why you're quizzing me about everything!" said Donna. She got up and left the room. Lloyd heard her light footfall tripping down the stairs. All was quiet in the room. He grabbed the remote and put on something to keep him company while he finished unpacking. Women were so weird sometimes.

Break On Through to the Other Side

Now the whole situation came clear to Lloyd as he sat contemplating Doug's betrayal, and his own, and that of the weasel who had been spying on him in hopes of bringing him down. Donna and Chuck. Chuck and Donna. He thought about Chuck, large and gentle, but also strong enough to crush Lloyd's head between his palms as if it were an acorn. Donna had almost begged him not to go to Pelican. She hadn't screamed or anything, but for her, that was about as close to beseeching as it got. And he hadn't listened. It was his own heedless lust that had driven him to make sure that nothing disturbed his sordid little trip. But when you got right down to it, really, what difference did it make? He couldn't stay home every day for the next twenty years. Eventually, Donna would have been tested, and she would have failed, as had he.

Lloyd thought about Donna laboring under Chuck's enormous body, the two of them sweating in his bed, bathed in the bright sunlight of a late-summer afternoon. He used the image to torment himself for a while, and he felt a glowing ember of rage spring into flame, first blue, then white, then nothing more than a translucent shimmer of intense heat in search of an object to incinerate.

"Lloyd?" It was Doug, looking him over strangely. Given Doug's seeming ability to divine his thoughts, Lloyd took pains to arrange his face. "At any rate," said Doug, looking into the depths of his drink. "If you would prefer to avoid conversation about your wife, that's all right. What I mean to say is that I understand completely. Not that you require my permission to avoid unwelcome intimacy. I've made a career of it myself."

"I see," said Lloyd judiciously, but he was just treading water. Where had they been in the conversation? Oh, yes, Doug's tragedy. Not his. "You seem to feel pretty sad about the whole experience," Lloyd continued. Doug gave all appearances of accepting this observation as an appropriate one, so Lloyd pressed on. "I wonder if you've done the right thing. You love this person. Maybe you ought to be together. I don't know." Doug nodded, taking it in. Thank God they seemed to be off Donna. That was good. He knew that if he started speaking about her, he would lose his mind or, much worse, his composure. "In the sense that you didn't completely deconstruct your life based on your personal needs of the moment," he added with something of a flourish.

"God, Lloyd, you can really sling that hash," said Doug. Lloyd took a quick look at him to see if he was angry. No, Doug appeared as serene as always. More than anything, Doug seemed tired. How long had it been since he had shared his thoughts with a business associate in this manner? Never? "Do you think this liaison you are now experiencing is a grand passion?" he inquired. "You two seem to be thoroughly committed to exploring the limits in this matter."

"Excuse me, Doug," said Lloyd. He stood up. "I appreciate the tolerant view you've taken of my actions. But your remarks have dredged up an incredible load of . . . material that I have to digest, and at least a couple of things that I really should be doing immediately. So if that's all . . ."

"No, Lloyd. I don't think that's all," Doug said. "Sit down."

Lloyd sat.

"First, I am sorry that I employed the methods I did to have you observed. But I needed to know what you were up to. If you were merely diddling another senior officer, that would have been one thing. I am satisfied that you are, in your private as well as your public life, pushing the barriers of what is possible within the framework of a business existence. That's the kind of person I need on my side, Lloyd. Working hard to move the overall scenario in the proper direction, not encumbered by the petty conventionalities of other men or women. At lower levels, business structures need orderly, conventional people. At our level, Lloyd, only borderline personalities will do."

Lloyd found himself staring into Doug's face. In one convulsive moment, they both exploded into laughter and then it was over. The two men stared at each other for a moment, then each selected a minute object at some distance that suddenly could not be ignored. They stayed like that for a while.

"What are we to do about Mr. Lemur, then?" said Doug.

"Right now, I'd say we had a choice."

"Describe it to me."

"Well, Mr. Lemur, as you call him, is way too marginal for middling status. We both know that. He fancies himself an ultrasenior officer in the body of a cocaine-sniffing, butt-kissing vice president without portfolio. You can either promote him to a level where his demented character can breathe a little . . . or fire his ass into next Wednesday."

"Honestly," said Doug. "If I were you, I would elect the latter."

"Me?"

"Sure."

"You want me to fire Ron? After all he's done for you?"

"He did nothing for me. Everything he did was for himself. I needed him. He did what was required. There's nothing special about that. But if I were you, and were looking for a free hand to do what had to be done over the course of the next couple of months, I wouldn't want somebody around whom I couldn't trust."

"Gee, Doug." Lloyd was stupefied. Was this the way Doug repaid loyalty? If that was true, Lloyd would have to watch him very carefully.

"Go ahead and handle the Ron situation as you see fit," said Doug. He rose and went to the door of the conference room that abutted his office, opened the door, and took a suit jacket from a hanger behind it. He then focused all his attention on the task of putting it on, checking for creases, removing invisible dust and lint, making sure it sat right. Lloyd watched him and allowed the pounding surf of conflicting emotions wash over him. After a while, he went to the plate-glass windows that faced south and watched a pair of cruise ships jockey for position on the Hudson. Before long, he felt Doug standing behind him.

"Don't be too mad at your wife," Doug said softly. Lloyd did not turn around. Amazingly, he felt a bauble of moisture forming at the inside corner of each eye. He blinked them away, suppressing the urge to screw up his fists and rub them into his hot little eye sockets. "The same impetus that has driven you to explore your options here, with . . ."

"Mona," said Lloyd.

"Of course. Mona. Impressive woman."

"Yes."

"The same impetus that has driven you to explore your options with Mona has made you inattentive at home, more prone to drift off, to avoid emotional engagement that before was a matter of course. Without perhaps being consciously aware of this drift in you, your wife most probably felt somewhat untethered to the reality that you forged together over the—how long have you been married?"

"Fifteen years," said Lloyd.

"Well then, the reality that you forged together over the fifteen lovely years you have been married."

"Doug." Lloyd allowed the quart of battery acid that had risen into his throat to subside a little. "Doug, I can't talk about this now. It's too painful."

"How do you think Walt is doing?" said Doug.

"Walt?" Lloyd once again felt the shepherd's crook wind around his neck and yank him hard in another direction. "What about him?"

"Walt is a great operating officer," said Doug. "There are times I wonder whether he's going to be all right when the trumpet blows and we head into the field with our new friends and adversaries."

"You've left me behind completely, Doug." All Lloyd wanted to do right now was get away. What had he done? Let Doug into his deepest thoughts and feelings, this executive who could use people and throw them away like confetti into the air surrounding his ongoing parade? What was he being used for now? As some kind of tool against Walt? Never!

"Never mind," said Doug. "We'll catch up on that later."

"Except to say that Walt is doing great, I think, just great," Lloyd said. "If there's a guy who's going to be absolutely necessary around here to keep the machine running in a productive way as we piece together the corporation downstream, it's going to be Walt."

"No doubt about it," said Doug. "Shall we go? Or would you like to sit here by yourself for a while and get the feel of the office?"

Wondering what the hell Doug was talking about, Lloyd preceded his commanding officer out of the executive suite and down into the lobby, where Doug went south and Lloyd went to the riotous bar at Palio, where he found Mona totally zonked on fear, Sambuca, and caffeine.

Ecce Homo

Lloyd went through the door to the bar and scanned the room for Mona. He saw her in the corner at a table too small even for her. She looked, in fact, quite tiny, sitting there in the farthest remove of the enormous high-ceilinged room, which resounded to the threshhold of pain with the noise of high capitalism in the throes of drunken self-regard.

"Hi," he said, standing over the her, watching her hair play in the muted lights of the lounge. Above and all around them, garish titans in red and blue on rearing, frothing horses bestrode the walls.

"Hi," she said, staring up at him with a calm in which he was certain no reliance might be placed. "Are we fired?"

"Nah," said Lloyd. "Gimme a minute." He went to the bar and ordered two Bombay Sapphire martinis from a bartender who clearly found himself superior to the majority of his clientele. Lloyd was not sure the guy was far from wrong. The average age of the customers in the place was twenty-six. Well dressed. Well scrubbed. At a bar, certainly, at the end of a long day, but not kicking back completely, not at ease. Working still, Lloyd thought, as he watched them braying into one another's faces. Didn't they know that within an eye blink they would all be a pile of bones moldering in the soggy earth?

Wow, thought Lloyd. I must be more upset about this than I thought. He took a traveling sip from the pregnant top of the glass on his way back to the table. Yum. A couple more of these and he would certainly start to feel better.

"I'm not drinking anymore," said Mona, taking the glass. "I've been having coffee instead. Until you got here, at any rate." She took a hefty pull from the tall, sweaty glass. "Oh that's good," she said, and drank the rest.

Lloyd watched as a bolt of color shot up her neck and into her cheeks. "You look so beautiful," he said, aware that he could not touch her in this site only three and a half blocks from their office. Or could he? It was mighty dark here.

"You do, too," she said. She had kicked off her shoes and now extended her legs beneath the table and rested her feet on his chair, between his thighs. The tip of her big toe stretched very slightly and found its mark. "It's dark," she said, giving him a smile full of so many different colors, it came out pure white. "Go on," she said.

"Doug seems to have elevated me into some kind of spooky fraternity," he said. "He referred to you as, I believe, an . . . 'impressive woman.' Yes, that was it."

"Do you think I'm an impressive woman?"

"You know what I think."

"Tell me, Lloyd."

"Mona," he said, leaning forward across the table as if he was about to impart a serious business secret. "You're making me want to fuck you right here. Is that what you're trying to do?"

"Not at all," said Mona. "Let me tell you a secret." She removed her foot from between his legs and leaned forward across the table, cupping her hands in the traditional method of imparting something one wished secreted from prying ears nearby. Lloyd leaned into the secret and offered his own ear for its reception.

"Yes?" he said.

"It's something like this," said Mona in a moist, dark whisper. Then, with a very somber expression behind her hand, so that anyone who viewed their table would think they were two investment bankers in world-shaping discourse, she placed the greater part of her tongue into Lloyd's ear, wetting it thoroughly and reaming it out as a child would clean the bottom of a dish of chocolate pudding.

"Mmm," said Lloyd. "That's interesting."

"I thought you'd find it so," said Mona, sitting up primly and placing both feet square on the floor in front of her. "So what are we going to do?"

"Do?" said Lloyd. "You affect me in such a bizarre way, Mona." It was true. There were so many intelligent things he should be doing. Firing Ronald Lemur, for one thing. Ron was sure to be back at the office right now. Or he could go home and deal with things. Things weren't getting any better while he sat here getting an ear job. He should get going. Instead, he was operating on pure instinct and unexamined impulse. It felt good. But where was that taking him? His wife was porking the contractor, could be doing so at that very moment. That was a bad thing. He would have to put a stop to that. "I should go home, Mooner," he said.

"How am I supposed to relate to Doug when I deal with him in a business setting?" said Mona.

"Normally. Show no weakness or vulnerability. Pretend he doesn't know, but give off a whiff that you might possibly know he does. Be yourself. Be confident, dry, and secure," said Lloyd.

"Lloyd, stay with me a little bit. I need to come down. Get myself back to some kind of stasis. I feel like I've been . . . peeled away. This is like some kind of alien invasion. They came in and, like, snatched my body. I'm trembling. I don't want to be. I'm sweating. I never sweat. I feel like I've been busted. I was busted once by the California Highway Patrol while riding in a carful of pot-smoking grunge musicians. I had been hitching. I was clean. But they locked me up anyhow. I was never so scared in my life. I was by myself in a little cell in the jailhouse. In the next cell, there was another woman. I couldn't see her. I could just hear her voice. She kept saying, 'Hey, honey. Whatcha in for?' It was creepy. Her voice was like a voice from a prison movie. But it wasn't a movie. It was real."

Lloyd kicked off his Gucci loafers and placed his feet up on Mona's chair. "Come on. Relax," he said. His big toe stretched forward beneath her skirt in the darkness below the table. "Tell me," he said. "I want to feel your pain."

"This isn't exactly the kind of thing a woman gets promoted for, unless it's the chairman she's having the thing with."

"Uh-huh," said Lloyd. He stretched his foot forward just a tad, touching silk.

"Lloyd!"

Mona looked genuinely shocked. But why? Hadn't she just been doing the same thing to him? What a nutty woman!

"You keep talking," he said, leaning back seriously in his chair and regarding her with professional interest while keeping his toes on point and moving ever so slightly. It seemed to be having an effect on Mona, whose mouth had parted, revealing a micron of tongue, and whose position in the chair had shifted imperceptibly for the better. "That's what I want you to do," said Lloyd. "You keep talking, and I'll keep listening just like this, and you see if you can get where you need to go without getting caught. How's about that?"

"I dunno," said Mona. But she had made up her mind already.

Some women Lloyd had known would have required a more pristine setting, a greater variety of stimulation. But, looking in her vast liquid eyes at this moment, he saw very clearly that it just might possibly be accomplished and, later, be something to talk about and, even later still, remembered.

Mona primly adjusted her skirt so that nothing inappropriate was in evidence from any available angle. "You might use your right leg. The one next to the wall," she said, opening her purse and fishing out a Marlboro. "That would make the deception virtually complete."

Lloyd did remove his left leg, which had been the slightest bit visible, from its warm and friendly cubby and replaced it on the floor, slipping it into its loafer. He slid the other foot from its shoe and carefully inserted it into the tight circular tunnel made by Mona's teeny skirt. If Mona felt the reintroduction of his toe, she didn't let on. She was smoking now and looking at him. "I love to smoke," she said.

"This is basically what I need to do, right?" said Lloyd.

"Mm-hm," said Mona. She was studying the crowd a bit. She removed a fleck of tobacco from her tongue. "Yes, uh-huh," she said. "That's an interesting point you're making."

"Should I make it faster?"

"No, no," said Mona. "I don't think there's any reason to jump to any premature conclusions."

"Good," said Lloyd. They thought about things. "You're a lot of fun, you know that?" he said after a while.

"I . . . was shopping in Dean and Deluca and saw the most amazing cheeses," Mona observed. "Waiter!" she said abruptly. Lloyd froze. The waiter approached. Oh, thought Lloyd, she wants to play rough. "I'll have another martini. You, Lloyd?"

"Sure," said Lloyd. He was curious to see if she could hold her face steady under the circumstances. "You know?" he said to the waiter as Mona shot him an eyebrow and sucked just a little too hard on her cigarette. It was almost gone. She was certainly smoking it very fast. "It's very crowded here for a midweek night."

"Yeah," said the waiter. "It's a zoo. It's basically always a zoo at this hour."

"What kind of gin do you have, actually?" Lloyd said.

"Whatever you want, really."

"Umgh" was what it sounded like Mona said.

"Yes?" Lloyd asked her.

"I . . . would like to make . . . that . . . a vodka martini," she said to the waiter.

"Stoli?"

"Some of that cranberry vodka. That's nice, right?"

"The flavored vodkas are very popular. You want that?" The waiter was getting impatient with all these questions.

"Yes," Mona said. The strain was beginning to tell on her, but she was holding up remarkably well, considering.

"Be right back," said the waiter.

Mona had lit a second cigarette from the first and was regarding Lloyd intently, the cigarette demurely propped between her fingers. Every now and then, she took a drag. Otherwise, she had grown rather pensive. Lloyd took this opportunity to take several memos from the briefcase that sat immediately next to his chair. Mona watched him as he did so, only leaning back slightly at one point and uttering a comment that sounded suspiciously to Lloyd like "Oog."

"Our drinks should be along soon," said Lloyd by way of response. "Until then, perhaps you'd care to comment on the implications of this." He turned the fattest memo in her direction and deposited it on the table in front of her.

"I . . . see," said Mona, pausing then for an embarrassing amount of time for somebody who was supposed to be a quick study, then adding, "Arghh."

"Would you rather not converse at this point in time?" Lloyd inquired politely.

"Your drinks," said the waiter, setting the beverages down in front of them, first Lloyd's, then Mona's. "Try it," he said helpfully.

"I . . . believe . . . I . . . will," said Mona. "She took a tasteful sip from her new beverage. "Per . . . fect," she said. "Pardon me. I have a minor speech defect that makes it difficult for me to express myself quickly, particularly when I'm drunk."

"Hey, I had a stammer myself when I was a kid," said the waiter. He showed no signs of going. A gorgeous rash had spread out all across Mona's neck, cheeks, and brow.

"Well . . . tank oo," she said.

"No problem." The waiter left.

Mona took a large swallow, set her glass down, and, without any urgency at all, rested both hands on the edge of the table. "Tell me a little story," she said.

"Once upon a time," said Lloyd, "there was an extreme woman. That was the only word for her. Everything she did was extreme. First of all, she was extremely beautiful."

"Glurg," said Mona. "I mean . . . oof."

"On top of that, she was also extremely intelligent, and extremely competent in everything she put her hand to."

"I'm not sure I can do this, Lloyd," said Mona. "I'm gonna show something soon for sure."

"Want me to stop?"

"Mf."

"Hm?" It was possible that at some point in his life Lloyd might have had more fun than he was having at that moment, but it might have taken him a quarter of an hour or so to come up with it.

"Gonna, you know . . ."

"Nah," said Lloyd. "You can do it."

Mona looked up at him then, and her eyes were totally open, unguarded. "Lloyd," she said very softly, and then added, "Ah."

"An extremely wonderful, desirable, lovely, utterly fabulous woman," said Lloyd. They were quiet for a while. Lloyd took a sip of his drink. "And she lived happily ever after," he concluded.

"I would die for you, Lloyd," said Mona, so softly that Lloyd almost didn't catch it.

"And I you," said Lloyd.

He reached across the table, found her hand, and brought it fiercely to his lips in a bottomless kiss from his soul.

Lock and Load

After they had reached whatever new plateau the recent intercourse had revealed, they sat for a significant time, sipping their martinis, listening to the noise around them.

This little interlude between the fear before and the confusion that lay beyond is so complete and without flaw, he thought. Things are rarely so perfect in this life, and when they are, they seldom come again, or stay that way for very long. One had to shut out the knowledge of impermanence if life was to be enjoyed at all. Lloyd did so by ordering another martini.

They drank and Mona smoked a few more cigarettes, and they did not talk at all, because the noise around them was so intense that after a while it wasn't worth the effort, and when it seemed absolutely right, when staying put for one moment longer would have been pushing it, Mona, without additional comment, collected her stuff, put down her plastic, paid the tab, and got her coat. Lloyd got himself together and followed.

It was still relatively early. Lloyd was drunker than he had planned to be. In the plaza outside the bar, there was a statue of an elephant perched on a globe. Lloyd had no idea what it meant, but he had always liked it. The total structure stood some eight feet high and was made of unburnished bronze. The elephant was of the Indian variety and was dressed for success, or at least for work. Lloyd and Mona regarded it calmly for a while, as a way of remaining together without staring into each other's faces or touching.

"Well, I guess I'll see you tomorrow," said Mona finally, with some regret. She turned to face him, remaining several paces away. Lloyd saw her eyes were sort of red.

"Yeah," said Lloyd. He wanted to take her in his arms and press her head to his chest, but he thought better of it. "I never thought this would end up with me loving you," he said. He hadn't known that he would. It simply rose like a bubble from the bottom of an active tar pit. "It's extremely inconvenient. I think about you all the time. I stay later at the office than I should. I don't ever want to be home. I want to be with you. I want to be with you all the time. I can't imagine how this will end."

Mona had thrust both fists into the pockets of her coat and was taking inventory of some invisible aspect of her shoes. "Well," she said again. "We'll see." She kissed the tips of her index and middle finger and extended them nonchalantly in his direction, turned, and made her way across the plaza in the direction of Fifty-first Street.

Lloyd stood in the middle of the outdoor atrium and felt about six tons of aloneness descend at the speed of light from directly above him and knock him flat. He withstood the blow, but just barely. All of him, except for a tiny nugget of superego that kept him decent at times such as these, wanted to drop his briefcase at his feet, lean back to face the sky, and howl out his desire and despair like a solitary dog at the edge of the universe, lost and far from home.

Instead, he figured he would go back to the office for perhaps just a minute or two to pick up his messages and make sure nothing had exploded in the two hours or so he had been away. It was late, of course, but also kind of early. There was plenty of time for him to get home, after all. The night was young and he had a strong feeling that there was a piece of unfinished business hanging somewhere in the middle of his chest—something he could get done before the end of the day so that he would not have to do it tomorrow. Oh, yes, he could fire Ron. That would be a good thing.

And then he could go . . . home.

The image of Donna and her powerful, masterful boyfriend rutting about in the rumpus room leapt from the stream of his imagination into the bright, clean air of his conscious mind like a salmon vaulting from the murky depths of a river into the late-afternoon sunshine.

There were plenty of people about, even though it was getting on toward 7:00 P.M. Come to think of it, there were always tons of folks about at all hours now, working on the deal, laboring over all the peripheral financial and legal documents, presentation graphics, E-mails, hard-copy memos and the like for which the deal created an immediate, constant, and pressing need. One could pop into the office now at any hour of the day or night, even on weekends, and find a buzz of people rocketing back and forth with an air of great self-importance and an urgency approaching terror.

Lloyd ran into the object of his quest in the coffee antechamber outside the congregation area immediately adjoining the large conference room. He approached his quarry from behind, very quietly, and was gratified to see that he was about to catch it unawares.

"Ron," said Lloyd.

"Whoo!" said Ron. He leapt about ten feet in the air, turning at the top of his entrechat. "Lloyd, man!" he said when he hit the ground. He appeared intensely uncomfortable and, unable to meet Lloyd's eyes, attempted to sidle past with an additional grunted semigreeting and shoulder squeeze intended to carry him beyond its object and into the larger meeting region, where Darling, Sweet, and Fitz were indulging in some postconfab interface.

"No, Ron," said Lloyd. He put out one arm and stopped Lemur short. "I wanted to talk to you for a minute about your incredible acts of weaseliness and perfidy."

"Hm? I . . . what?" Lloyd was not surprised that Lemur was semi-incoherent. The boy was paralyzed with the inevitability of what was about to happen to him, for if Lloyd was still here after what Ron had reported to Doug, then Lloyd was a very powerful player, and a grave danger to any of his enemies. Even Ron, in his haze of ambition, narcissism, and sociopathology, had to be vaguely aware of that.

"Doug told me, Ron." Lloyd watched him very carefully. He was curious what Ron, who lived in the margins, would do when confronted with something that came barreling down the pike directly at him.

"I was only following orders," said Ron. He glanced upward from his cringing young executive routine to see whether Lloyd had enjoyed this witty evocation of a prior totalitarian regime. Lloyd was careful to show no emotion at all. "In the sense that I would do exactly whatever you asked me to do as well, Lloyd. At my level, it's not really possible to pick and choose your assignments."

"Certain assignments can be issued only to specific kinds of people," said Lloyd. "There isn't an individual on our entire eight floors here, Ron, who would have done what you did. Only you. You . . . have disappointed me, but not surprised me."

"I don't really understand what you're talking about, Lloyd, man. Seriously. I mean, I don't know what you think it was I did exactly. What I'm trying to say is that it was truly minimal. Doug asked me to get a lookout, and I kind of did in a very general way, but nothing specific. There was a lot I could have done but didn't is what I'm trying to get across here. You have to believe me. Doug is persuasive, but there's nothing I would do to destabilize you in any serious way, man. This was a kind of opportunity to provide service on a very elevated plane, and I'm sure you would have done the same, which is not an admission, because I have nothing to offer in that regard, but an explanation of sorts, and I hope it helps to clarify what I'm talking about."

"Well, Ron, it really doesn't." Lloyd placed a soft but incontrovertible hand on Ron's near shoulder and guided him several yards farther from the action. Ron seemed powerless to resist. "Step this way, please, you sniveling sack of shit," said Lloyd.

Lloyd felt a very strange mélange of feelings roiling within him. There was fear there, fear of proximity and violence. This was a desperately intimate act, suddenly. The naked individual was abruptly visible before him, and he was equally bare before the creature he was about to kill. Beyond the fear, there was anger, anger at the other for what he had and had not done. There was a tiny gobbet of pity there, too, but Lloyd quickly pushed that back under. Anything else? Yes . . . pleasure. That was there, too. Pleasure, excitement, and anticipation. The sensation that, in spite of all the transient negatives, this little piece of expiation just might end up being fun. Maybe that was the worst thing of all.

So Lloyd walked down the hallway with Lemur, and they both were silent for a time. Ron waited, frozen inside. Lloyd reflected. It turned out it was hard to fire somebody face-to-face. Much easier to eliminate his job in search of excellence, or Quality, or productivity, or some damn thing. Different to watch a person take the cut directly, see where it hit him, how deep it went in, at what angle, how much blood it drew, how much bile, how many tears.

"I beg your pardon, Lloyd, I really and truly do beg your pardon, actually," said Ron.

He was completely cowed now. Something in Ron was waiting to be fired, had been waiting to be fired for a long time. Possibly since he was old enough to conceive of such a thing as Ronald Lemur, and what it meant to be that thing called Ronald Lemur, he had been awaiting this moment that would, in a terrible way, validate his entire worldview of himself. This wouldn't stop him from disintegrating, though. Lloyd decided he would give him a chance to do so, since it might help feed his rage and give him strength for the task that lay ahead.

"Doug made me do it, Lloyd. I swear," Ron was burbling as Lloyd escorted him down the hallway. "Doug is a very powerful person, Lloyd. You know that. He commands loyalty. He told me that he needed to know where you went when you disappeared from business meetings all the time. I mean, you look like you're ducking out to make a phone call or something, but dude, you're gone for such a long time, man. People wonder. Is it the size of your tanks, man? Or whassup? That's what Doug wanted to know. So I get out there and see that sometimes you head for open water and cop a breather, stuff like that, man, but lately some other times, here comes, you know—"

"Mona."

"Mona, yeah, right." Ron had grown very sincere. "And so it came to the point, Lloyd, that I had told Doug about you going out to do work in some outlying area, or slipping away to buy a magazine in a hotel lobby, or just going back to your office and, like, returning phone calls. And he was interested, you know, not negative or anything, just . . . interested. And then one day, boom, I see you guys are suddenly together, and I had this very rich story line that suddenly fell into my hands. And I couldn't, like, just continue to tell Doug the same boring thing when this most incredible development was happening right in front of my nose! It's your fault, man, for being so amazingly interesting!"

"The thing is, Ron," said Lloyd, attaching his hand to Ron's elbow and continuing their little stroll away from the common area, "you're done. You have no friends. You have no supporters. I was the last person to regard you as anything but a worm, and obviously I've changed my analysis of the situation. Doug will not protect you. He finds you repellent, which you are, and he gave you up to me. What you need to understand, Ron, is that Doug feels more negative about what you did in this situation than about what you think you saw me doing."

"I know what I saw you doing, Lloyd," said Ron. "And you rule, man."

"Ron," said Lloyd. "I hope you agree with me when I say that the quintessential business relationship, particularly between a manager and his subordinate, is built on trust."

"Are you firing me?" said Ron. His eyes were as big as golf balls.

"Yes, Ron. You are a pox on the senior management of this corporation, which is a team moving forward together to face and conquer the future. You are not fit to be on that team. You're fired."

"Please!" said Ron. He looked as if he might begin to sob now, big, greasy tears that would spring from his eyes in freshets and go coursing down his cheeks. "Please, Lloyd, man! I misjudged! I made an error! I freely admit that. I do. But this job, this job is my life, Lloyd. It can't be replaced by another job. This is my whole . . . frame of reference, Lloyd, man. It's everywhere I want to be. I don't want to be anywhere else. If I can't make it here, I can't make it anywhere."

"You're fired, Ron. I don't want to work with you anymore, and I'm the only one who ever did. I was your one potential rabbi around here, and you fucked with me. And that I do not forgive."

"Please! Lloyd, man!" Ron screeched. Fortunately, they were in the waiting region outside the Legal Department's conference room now, a small enclave with a magazine table and several hard-backed chairs. Ron sank into one and put his face in his hands. He began to cry. It occurred to Lloyd that Ron was inappropriately strung out even for a person in this situation. His nose was running very slightly. "Lloyd," he said, quieter now. "Lloyd, man. Please reconsider. I'll do whatever you want. I will be your fucking slave, man. I will be more loyal to you than a dog, man. There is nothing I won't do. No place I won't go. Instead of incurring an enemy who will hate you for life and curse the ground you walk on, you will have a friend willing to circle the wagons around you, take a bullet for you, and work his fingers until they're basically bloody stumps. You will have me, all of me, whatever. Whatever, man. I mean that. Let me stay, Lloyd. Please, Lloyd, man, please. I got no life, man. I need this place, man. I need it here. I have a crummy MBA and exactly one job to show for it. I've invested my entire career in this organization. I'm part of a generation that's virtually unemployable. I can't fall out of the system. I'll never get back. Please, man. I'm begging. Okay, man? I'm begging you!"

It was pretty clear that this had to stop. "I see that," said Lloyd. He looked at the pathetic thing that Ron had become. Tears streaked Ron's face. He showed no signed of ceasing his blubbering. What was Lloyd to do? He thought it over.

Ron did have a point in one very specific area. The fact that he would represent a slave for life did little to sway Lloyd, although it was almost 25 percent of a consideration. Ron would make a good spy, serf, and functionary—that was true. He was smart. He was without moral compass. These were strong positives in a subordinate. But how was Lloyd ever to know that the fatuous nitwit wouldn't turn on him the moment a more powerful guru surfaced? That was unlikely, of course. Lloyd was getting to the point where there were few superior shepherds around. Unless something extremely untoward happened, in other words, Ron could be trusted within reason to act as an efficient, if somewhat risky, tool. On the other hand, with a host of foreign players entering the arena, Ron would have to be watched very closely, each and every day. If some potent Japanese, German, or Italian conquering type glommed on to him, he could become a liability in a hurry. Still. Wasn't that true of just about everybody? Darling, certainly. Sweet. Even Doug, if his position was threatened, or he found someone who superseded Lloyd in his fickle estimation. Many of the others, with the probable exception of Fitz, Mona, and Walt, would bear ongoing scrutiny. Ron could provide that.

But that wasn't the only reason he found himself looking down speculatively at Ron's sweaty whorl as the boy sat staring at the carpet, trembling. It was the phrase "enemy who will hate you for life and curse the ground you walk on" that Ron had blurted out almost without the intention to do so, or the awareness that he had said it once it was swept away in his river of entreaty.

Lloyd considered it . . . an enemy for life—one with certain knowledge of behavior that could explode his life at a moment's notice. . . . Ron didn't get that yet; it hadn't come to him, and once it did, wouldn't the balance of terror subtly shift? Wouldn't it be best to move now, before it appeared he had been forced to do so?

"You're fired, Ron," said Lloyd as a miserable sob racked Ron's frame. "But . . ."

"But?" said Lemur. He rose to his feet and faced Lloyd.

"Call it probation, Ron. As far as I'm concerned, you are terminated. Your separation date is . . . December thirty-first. This makes you ineligible for any bonus or stock option for this year, unless you are reinstated by that date."

"I understand," said Ron.

"Nobody will know of this conversation except for Fitz."

"Fitz!"

"That's right. He's the control of this particular little experiment. Both he and I will be keeping an eye on you, Ron. Both he and I will have the ultimate say about your situation when December thirty-first rolls around. Until that time, you have no status as an executive in this corporation. You are simply my vassal. You get that?"

"I do, Lloyd. Thank you, Lloyd."

"Remember, Ron. Not a word of this to anyone. Not to Doug. Not to Walt. If I see the slightest bit of sucking around with anyone but me, anyone at all, you're out of here with the kind of severance that will keep you going for about six weeks. Fitz will back me up on this."

"I may have a little trouble with that," Lemur said. His eyes were now locked on Lloyd with a spooky intensity, as if he felt that to break contact would be to lose the lousy but lifesaving deal he had now found offered to him. "Sometimes I find myself sucking up to people who can't even do me any good, just because they're wearing a better suit than I am. Give me a chance to sort of break myself of the habit, Lloyd. I mean, cut me some slack if you can. I get it, the general scenario you're laying out here, and I have no problem with it. I'm fired. But there's a way back. I intend to take it, man. You won't be sorry. The day will come when you'll thank yourself and me, too. I promise that. Thank you, Lloyd. I mean it. Thank you. I realize what I did was inexcusable from your point of view and I'll make up for it, I swear, Lloyd. I swear it to you on the life of my children."

"Ron," said Lloyd. "You don't have any children."

"Obviously, man. That was a joke."

Lloyd stretched out one hand and grabbed Ron's nose rather roughly between his index and middle finger.

264

"Ow," said Ron.

With Ron's nose in tow, Lloyd lowered his arm, forcing Ron to his knees.

"Don't fuck up," he said.

"I boht," said Ron.

"Because this is your last chance."

"I dow it."

"Good, man, good."

Lloyd released Ron's nose. Ron climbed to his feet. His face was wet with tears and mucus from his nose, which was now running freely.

"Lloyd, ban," said Ron with genuine affection. "Danks, ban."

Lloyd turned and strode up the hall, away from Ron and back toward his office.

"Lloyd!" It was Ron calling after him. "I want to be you when I grow up."

"Remember, Ron," said Lloyd quite softly, although his voice penetrated all the way to the end of the hallway. "You are not rehired. You are fired. Your last day of work is New Year's Eve. You have until then to prove to me that you are a human being."

Lloyd was gone.

"We'll see about that," said Ron. He wiped his nose on the sleeve of his white shirt. "Ow. Motherfucker," said Ron. He turned and headed for the men's room, where he washed his face and wiped his nose again. Taking the paper towel away from his face, he saw his nose had begun to bleed. "Motherfucker," he said again. It took a while for him to get it to stop. Cleaned and dried, Lemur stood in the middle of the bathroom and ran his situation over in his mind. It was bad, but not as bad as it first had looked. In fact, it was almost fine. He removed the small plastic handgun he had secreted in the pocket of his pants, hefted it for a moment or two, replaced it, straightened his jacket and vest, left the bathroom, got his coat from his office, and went to the elevators, where he found Fitz waiting for the last ride of the day.

"Lloyd told me of his decision," said Fitz.

"Lloyd's my God," said Lemur as Fitz gave him a speculative, narrow glare.

The elevator arrived. They rode to the ground floor together in silence and parted without further comment.

The Mudroom

Lloyd let himself in through the basement door and took off his shoes in the mudroom. It was very late. He hadn't meant to go drinking with Fitz, but that was the way things had worked out. They had met on the street outside the office. Fitz was disgusted, waiting for a Town Car that had not materialized.

"Come on," Fitz had said to him. "You look the way I feel."

Lloyd thought about it. He had laid in a reasonable base already. Three martinis—could it possibly have been four?—had established a mean foundation on which he could certainly build a productive evening. True, his session with Ron had worn his edge off a bit, but nothing that couldn't quickly be reestablished. Lloyd imagined a cold frosty one and a bowl of nacho chips and his mouth began to water. "Maybe just a quick one," he said to Fitz.

They had caught a cab to the East Side, where there was a restaurant called Rosa Mexicana that Lloyd had always liked a lot. They made their own guacamole there, right in front of you, with a certain amount of flourish and hoopla. Made you feel kind of special, for a couple of minutes—like you were at the center of a very small and inconsequential universe.

Lloyd realized now, sitting there with Fitz, that he was not just drunk; he was dejected. When did that happen? He had been so happy before. When was that? He and Fitz spent some time discussing the effects a change of ownership would have on their executive pensions, but Lloyd's heart wasn't in it. "Excuse me," said Lloyd, and went to phone Donna.

"I'm stuck here," he said when Donna answered.

"Where is here?" Once again, her voice sounded slightly thick, and a portion of her seemed engaged elsewhere.

"Drinks with several bozos," he said.

"Well," said Donna. "Bozos would certainly supersede everything."

"I'll be home as soon as I can. Then maybe we could, you know . . . hang out or something." Lloyd was suddenly smacked broadside with a powerful wave of longing, regret, sadness, and a terrible, destructive nostalgia that almost, but not quite, made him want to speak of things best left unsaid. "I miss you, Donna" was what he eventually choked out.

"Oh," she said. There was another long pause, in which he could almost hear the muscles of her throat working as she forced back something equally enormous. "Lloyd," she said. "What is to become of us?"

"I love you, Donna," said Lloyd. There was a man next to him at the adjacent phone station blaring economic analysis into the receiver. Lloyd glanced over at him to see if the fellow was spending any of his attention noticing that there was a grown business executive to his left on the verge of tears.

"Lloyd come home soon. I need you," said Donna, and hung up.

Lloyd came back from the phone/bathroom enclave and sat opposite Fitz. "I'm totally fucked up," he said. "I mean . . . totally." He began to collect his stuff. "I gotta go."

"Tell me about it," said Fitz. His large, intelligent face was very close to Lloyd's, and his eyes were wide open now, far different from the squinty scowl with which he had favored Lemur. "No, I mean that not as a linguistic space filler," he added. "I mean . . . tell me about it."

"Aw, fuck it," said Lloyd. The waiter arrived with two gigantic frozen drinks in goblets the size of Frisbees. Lloyd took his and gulped about half of it in one swallow. Immediately, a horrible pain invaded his sinuses. "Nasal freezer burn," he said.

"Yeah," said Fitz. "Life's a bitch."

"I love my wife," said Lloyd.

"Sure you do."

"But Mona . . . I think I love her, too. I'm happy when I'm with her. She's such an incredible fox. She's funny. She's warm. She accepts me. She's a party. The woman's a one-man party. I had to live almost forty years to discover I'm a horrible person. How do you think that makes me feel? I don't know what to do. I'm at a complete loss, man."

"I envy you," said Fitz. He was drinking his drink more slowly, to avoid the pain that Lloyd had recently encountered, but he, too, was making awesome headway through the towering beverage. "You're having an adventure, man. That's all. Don't take the whole thing so seriously. It's one of those things you'll look back on and smile about. Unless you do something idiotic."

"Go on," said Lloyd.

"Like, I'm pretty sure you're thinking about making a clean breast of the whole stupid scenario."

"Well, actually . . ."

"If you don't mind, as your friend, let me advise against that. Honesty is an extravagance in the real world, Lloyd. It's something you might enjoy for a couple of hours, but later on, you'll be sorry. I promise you. That's what happened with me and my first wife, Lloyd. It was terrible. I was having a wonderful time. Out late a lot. Working like a dog. Limos back to Chappaqua from the city whenever I wanted. What's a blow job in a limo? Nothing! Less than nothing. But I had to start feeling all remorseful about the ragged edges of my life, man. And I talked to my wife. Why? Not to make her feel better. To make myself feel better. We decided that we had a whole lot of symptoms that something deeper was wrong and we should probably deal with those in marriage therapy, and that was that. Pretty soon, I was living in a tiny apartment on Ninety-seventh Street and she got the house, and that was the end of my first marriage." He drank some more. "Fucking marriage therapy," he said.

"But now you're better off, right? I mean, you and Janey are happier than you could ever have been with—what was her name? Sorry."

"Dorrie."

"Dorrie, yeah."

"Yeah," said Fitz. "I'm a lot happier."

They both drank for a while.

"Truth sucks," said Fitz after a time. "Unless you want to blow up your life, and your kids' life, don't give in to it. Be a man. Live with what you've made as long as you have to, and then if you're really sure you want to leave your home and your kids and your dog, whom I happen to know you love, then you can always do it. But don't make Donna do it for you by telling her a bunch of stuff she doesn't need to hear about. In my opinion, that would be a disgustingly self-serving act."

They finished their drinks and ordered two more.

"I have to go," said Lloyd.

"So go," said Fitz.

And yet they did not leave.

"There's something else," said Lloyd.

"Well?" said Fitz.

"Aw shit," said Lloyd. "It's probably nothing."

Can This Marriage Be Saved?

Two hours later, he stood in the mudroom and tried to remove his shoes without falling over. He had spent another forty minutes with Fitz, missed the 9:27, and been forced to grab the 10:03, which had deposited him at the station at 10:45, putting him in the mudroom at approximately 11:00 P.M. Both children were asleep. The night was shot.

"Hi, Lloyd." It was Donna. Lloyd stood up with one shoe on, one shoe off. "I'm happy you're home." She looked happy. Expectant. As if she'd recently resolved an issue that had been troubling her. Free, somehow. Daring. What had happened?

His wife was wearing nothing but panties and a pair of white tennis socks. This was a look that Lloyd liked a lot. Donna wore the tiny socks at night to keep her feet moisturized. Donna was big into moisturizing. Lloyd couldn't see how it did her any harm. Usually, she wore a robe with the socks and panties. Now she didn't.

"Whatcha been doon?" said Donna.

"I couldn't get away," said Lloyd. He looked his wife over. She looked nice. "What are we dressed for this evening?" he said.

"We're dressed for the mudroom." Donna was just standing there. Her hair was extremely messy, as if she had just awakened when Lloyd's car had pulled into the driveway. Her body, as always, was a newly minted marvel to Lloyd. Venus on a cold linoleum floor.

"How's Noodles?" he said.

"Good. A ninety-six on her sequential math unit test."

"Bob's bug project?"

"A *VG*-plus."

"Why not an *E?*"

"Handwriting."

"You must be cold." Lloyd took off his topcoat and placed it around Donna's shoulders as a prelude to escorting her up the stairs and back to bed.

"Not cold," said Donna. She threw the coat on the ironing board, turned, and, leveraging herself with both arms behind her, hoisted herself up onto the top of the washing machine. "Hang up your suit and tie, Lloyd," she said.

Lloyd regarded Donna very narrowly. What the hell was this? He took off his suit jacket and pants and hung them on a hook near the secondary refrigerator.

"No, no," said Donna. "On a wooden hanger, Lloyd. That's your good suit. We didn't spend nine hundred dollars on a suit so it could end up in a pile in the corner of the basement. On a wooden hanger in the closet."

There was a closet in the basement. Lloyd went to it and carefully hung his suit up in it to be worn another day. He returned to the mudroom, to find his wife still demurely seated on the top of the washing machine. He noticed a small step stool was placed strategically at the base of the machine. Had he ever seen that before? Maybe. Lloyd climbed the miniature stairway and faced his wife. He was not surprised to find he was in a perfect position to embrace her in a number of creative ways.

"Hi, dummy," she said.

Lloyd thought about it. They had been married . . . how long? More than a decade, certainly. Made love hundreds of times, maybe thousands . . . thousands! And not once had she ever felt the need to encounter him in the mudroom in this way. True, they had lived in this house for only six years. And before that? The only similar episode had taken place in the front seat of his old Ford Fairlane someplace in West Virginia, on their way cross-country. He smiled at the memory now. That was a pleasant incident that had never, for some reason, been replicated. But this was entirely new behavior.

Why had he never noticed that step stool before?

He took her about the hips and slid her underwear down over her ankles.

"All right," he said. She put her arms around him and took him in.

"This is something different," Lloyd said. He was amazed. Something different. Now.

"Yes," said Donna. She wrapped her legs around his waist and he almost lost his footing, but not quite. At the last minute, his knees held. It seemed very important that he accomplish this engagement without spitting up all over himself. Things were going fine so far. His wife's face was very close. Her eyes were closed. He closed his, too. He smelled the alien smells of the mudroom. The smell of shoes. Detergent. Clean laundry. Dried mud. The aroma of wool saturated with rainwater and dried out again. A rich, loamy smell, the mixture of dozens of conflicting smells. There was another scent, as well.

What was that? Dog? He opened his eyes and looked down, to see Steve sitting in the corner of the mudroom, gazing at them expectantly.

"Oh, Lloyd," said Donna. But was it Donna, really? His Donna? She was acting with far more abandon than he was used to, she in her birthday suit and teeny white socks. Outrageous! This was somebody he didn't quite recognize. Who was it? Ah yes. He knew it now. It was Chuck's Donna. And this was one of their places.

Afterward, they remained much as they had been, he standing, she reclining on the cool porcelain of the White-Westinghouse washer.

"Donna," said Lloyd. He buried his face in her neck.

"Hm?"

"Is there something you'd . . . like to tell me?"

She made some kind of a noise then. What was it? He couldn't quite place it. Annoyance? Shock? Fear? "What in the world would make you say that?" she said.

"I don't know."

"No, Lloyd," she said. "There's nothing I want to tell you."

"Okay," said Lloyd.

Donna put on her underpants. There was an old T-shirt on top of the ironing board and she put that on, too. Then they went upstairs, brushed their teeth, watched the end of *Seinfeld*, turned out the light, and fell asleep, or pretended to, she staring into the darkness with her eyes wide open, he curled up facing away from her, wondering whether her attempt to re-create her lover in him had been a success for either of them.

October

One autumn afternoon, while golfing badly on a course just outside Washington in exurban Maryland, Lloyd drinks a little too liberally from the beverage cart. On the eighth fairway—actually the rough down to the right of the green behind some trees and a little bit of water—Lloyd, supposedly frustrated by his lie, loses it. He throws a golf club into a clutch of bushes and cannot retrieve it. Actually, it was sadly not Lloyd's golf club at all. It was one of Walt's. Lloyd had borrowed the new Ping when Walt was forced to take a particularly untimely call from Chicago.

Now Walt's club is gone. Lloyd sits in the deep underbrush where his club should be and has a lot of trouble not crying. His foursome meanders around yelling for him. After a while, they zoom off in their carts to scour the countryside for him. When they do find him, they are righteously pissed, Fitz going so far as to cuff Lloyd smartly across the front of his nose with a golf glove, which does not feel amusing at all. The four continue their round in a surly mood that lasts for almost one full hole. By then, Lloyd's malfeasance is legend. On the sixteenth green, after Lloyd sinks an uphill putt that fades into the hole from the right most poetically, Morgenstern actually gives Lloyd a furry smack on the cheek. Lloyd feels good. He senses something shift within himself again . . . and *pow.*

Lloyd is a new man, the old man. He wants back into the whole honorable person thing. Can it be done? How much lying will be necessary to preserve his honor? Can he battle the temptations of business life? What do you think?

Quite naturally, he begins his campaign of renewal by studiously avoiding any but the most rigorously businesslike opportunities with Mona. Is she not the source of all his trouble?! When she is scheduled to be at a meeting, he sends others to handle it. It's what he has to do. Suddenly Mona finds herself in a world almost exclusively without Lloyd. Where she is, he isn't, as much as possible. A lot of the time, it's not, of course. Often Lloyd finds himself sequestered with his hot and sweaty friend for long hours, poring over intensely detailed documents in an atmosphere of high mercenary excitement. The Deal! It's good! It's all Lloyd can do to keep the better part of him, which feels like a small, feeble echo of its evil counterpart, in control. Mona is confused, sad, and a tiny bit angry. Lloyd is frightened, mostly. When were feelings supposed to enter this thing?

□ Hope

■ Despair

271

No Mo' Mona

Lloyd considered both sides of everything. On the upside, he had gotten laid more in the past eight weeks than in his entire life. Getting laid was good.

In addition, he had had sex in a wide range of creative ways and locations: sitting down, standing up, on couches, under tables, on washing machines at midnight, under a tree in the middle of Central Park, sideways, upside down, and backward, of course.

On the downside, he lived in fear that one night he would blurt out the wrong name, either to his wife or his lover. He walked around in torment much of the time. Whom did he love? With whom did he want to be married? The image of somebody's buttocks, moving generously between his hands, plagued his imagination in meetings almost continually. But whose buttocks were they? Donna's? Mona's? Or somebody else's? How far gone was he? What, exactly, lay past Mona? Massage parlors? Assignations with young acupuncturists in the back rooms of overheated suburban malls?

What was real and what was not? Was Mona any less real because their relationship was essentially built on fantasy? Wasn't his marriage built on shifting ground, as well?

Lloyd stared out the window at the people moving about in the highrise tower opposite his office. One of the spaces belonged to a tremendously important men's magazine. The editor had recently come out of the closet. Lloyd wondered if he was happier since he had allowed his true self out. Possibly. But the revelation of one's authentic identity did not always solve life's problems. If it did, would not truth always bring happiness? That was absurd. Truth, quite often, brought misery and death, usually in that order.

There was no question, however, that he would have to make a choice. Men didn't simply go about obsessively fucking two women for months on end and not resolve some internal problem that cried out for solution. A man felt guilt for the bad things he did, the betrayals of trust he visited on his spouse. A man ought to decide which way his life would go, then set off down that road willy-nilly.

And what of Chuck? He had tried several times to bring up the beefy subject with Donna, but the truth was that he sort of couldn't. What if she had been humped for the best part of a summer by this fellow who knew more about wiring than Lloyd ever would? What could she say that would make him feel anything less than one inch . . . tall?

- "Gee, Lloyd, it didn't really mean anything." In other words, it was about sex and nothing but. Disgusting, horny woman!
- "Actually, Lloyd, I was in love with Chuck for a while, but now I'm over it." Who cared if she was over it? Unfaithful whore!
- "I didn't want to talk about it, Lloyd. But yes, I love him!" Christ. That would be the worst of all.

No, Lloyd didn't want to hear anything about it. What would he say in return? Would he be seized by the desire to confess his own deception by way of revenge? Then what? They would cry and be reconstituted, like orange juice? Did he want to be forgiven? Did he want the books to balance? Right now, in a weird way, he was sort of ahead. Freud had always made huge hay out of his continuous inquiry into the fabled issue of what women might want. But what did men want? Were they not as opaque as their female counterparts? Perhaps even more so, since they knew so little about themselves?

Maybe he had been wrong about Chuck. He saw no evidence. Perhaps he had been there and had now gone. Or Donna had thought about the possibility, then decided against it. Why not let sleeping dogs lie? Wasn't it possible that he might put the pieces of his humdrum bourgeois existence back together again? If he wished to do so, he would have to ramp up an excellent strategic plan and execute it with distinction, as Walt would put it.

And what about Walt? This whole situation with Mona was bringing him closer to Doug. Doug was weird about Walt. He didn't want to be unfaithful to Walt, though. Not Walt, too.

He would have to stop seeing Mona. He would have to stop drinking, since whenever he drank, he wanted to see Mona. He would have to stop hanging around the shop after work, since staying around when the halls were empty and underlit was a sure invitation to the big craving. He would have to begin telling his wife more about his thoughts and feelings, about his day, his fears, aggravations, and dreams. He would have to eat more carefully, since that was what Donna quite rightfully demanded when they were together, although she could not control his actions when they were apart. He would have to be content with less adventure, because it was in the search for adventure that the doorway to misbehavior opened.

Lloyd put his head down on his desk. Stop seeing Mona. That would be impossible. He saw Mona every day. Stop wanting Mona, that was it.

No More Mr. Nice Guy

Lloyd began implementing his new strategy the very next day.

At lunchtime, long after he normally would have dropped by, he looked up and in his doorway stood Mona. "Nooner?" she said. Was there something a little brittle about the request? Lloyd just looked at her, smiling credulously. God, she was beautiful. How was he going to resist? No man could!

"Come on, Lloyd," she said. "I'm not going to bite you . . . off." Lloyd was suddenly rock-hard beneath his desk.

"Gotta . . . bang away at this here," he croaked, brandishing a sheaf of documents that had been lying near at hand.

"Why ignore me like this, Mr. Lloydnik?" Mona said as Brad Forshinsky, the MIS technician with hair erupting from every available cornice of his ear, strode by outside Lloyd's office on the way to the fax machine. "You can't ignore me, you know. There's no reason you should. I'm free of disease. I'm not going to tell anybody. I'm not going to sue you for sexual harassment. I'm not going to boil a rabbit in your convection oven."

She stepped across Lloyd's threshold and took a seat on the edge of one of Lloyd's visitors' chairs. "We don't even have to make love for a while if you don't want," she said in the same light tone she would assume if the two were talking about relative debt loads. "We can just . . . mess around . . . you know? A survey in *Forbes* said that about thirty-four percent of all people have had sex at their place of employment, you know, Lloyd. And, like, seventy percent of all people have thought about it."

"I don't want to think about it," said Lloyd. "I don't want to think about it every minute of every day. I want to go back to sexually repressing at least a small portion of myself."

"Lloyd," said Mona. "There are no small portions of yourself." She smiled and went to the door. "I'll get back to you later in the day to take your temperature on the whole thing." She was gone.

Off to what he considered an excellent start, Lloyd upped the reduction of stakes at a meeting the very next afternoon. The gathering, which Lloyd had been dreading, concerned the discrepancy between their benefit structure and those of the American subsidiaries of the new company they were positioning themselves to acquire. In previous months, this had been a rather unpleasant subject to Lloyd, who hated the fact that they were about to create at least five separate castes of workers, each of whom—except for senior management in New York and a couple of lucky grandfathered employees in odd locations—would be able to look up the organizational ladder to hated individuals who enjoyed more rights and privileges than they. When he first heard about whole groups of workers who would have, for instance, no pensions, he was bereft, and he stalked about, inflamed with righteous disgust. After having lived with it for a few months, however, he now found it somewhat easier to deal with. He kept his appetite, in other words. Establishing firm have-not classes was one way of creating the famous operating efficiencies that were the business rationalization Wall Street demanded of all merger situations. When the last bell rang on postindustrial capitalism and there remained but one prodigious corporate entity on the planet, security analysts would still be demanding head-count cuts to boost margins.

Lloyd sat, as always, at the end of the table, just off to the left of Walt. The endmost seat at the other end of the gigantic teakwood expanse was reserved for Doug, who had chosen not to attend this festive session. In days past, Lloyd might have made sure he was seated close enough to Mona to feel her knee beneath the table to his left or right, or to send her a tiny note now and then that might make her smile or blush. At this opportunity, however, he selected a spot two seats to her right, just out of reach of any personal extremities either might have chosen to employ to establish physical contact. This seemed to perplex Mona for a moment. Then she took out her pad, put it in her lap, and began to doodle, as was her custom. Lloyd snuck several sidelong glances at her, but she failed to make eye contact, and after a while he allowed his mind to wander, as it was supposed to do during the metaphysical suspension of time and space that was the normal business meeting.

For the greater part of the hour or so that was taken up by this particular gathering, the group heard from Mrozek, the senior vice president of Benefits and Compensation, a horrible young woman with a face like a buzz saw and a business suit of such sadistic severity, it made everyone in the room with her feel small and inhuman. Mrozek worked for Fitz, who disliked her intensely but was forced to keep on promoting her for reasons that were opaque, even to him. On the occasion, Mrozek was going on about the principle of what she referred to as "differentiated employment status," a notion that was then making the rounds among professionals who were in charge of rationalizing institutionalized injustice. At this task, she was second to none in the corporate structure. Lloyd did not listen. He thought about Mona two seats away and wondered what color panties she was wearing. No, no. Stop that. He closed his eyes for a moment and almost fell asleep. No, that would not do, either. He stood up thoughtfully and, as if seized by a concentration of brain activity so intense that it could not be contained in a stationary form, perambulated a bit. He went to the window and regarded the city spires. He turned and looked over his compatriots around the table; he liked them all from the bottom of his soul. They were what made the job worth doing! What was this meeting about again? Oh, yes, giving people the absolute minimum for the maximum of output. A tough assignment. Thankless. Morally deadening. Yet here they were about it! What a troupe. He found himself regarding the table from directly behind Mona. Her head was bent gently downward, her red hair glowing gently in the overhead light. It took a conscious effort of will to restrain his hand from stretching outward and stroking her. How adorable she was. How like a child bent over her work. He inhaled gently through his nose and, yes, there was her characteristic scent. A noose slipped down around his heart and pulled tight. What was he doing, cutting the bands that held him to this woman? He would have to reconsider. Nobody was asking him to commit to Mona, least of all Mona. He was simply manufacturing false problems for himself. Wasn't that always the case with people in general? How many problems did we all simply drum up to keep our minds off deeper things? What deeper things?

Lloyd realized he was standing in the middle of the conference room, staring into space and woolgathering. Had somebody addressed something to him that he had failed to catch? He stared at the collected executives.

"I'm sorry," he said. "Was somebody talking to me?"

"Damn, Lloyd," said Walt, who was looking him over with some interest. "We're talking about a matter that in its execution will have a profound impact on the personal compensation of everybody in this room. I would think you'd find it of some interest."

"Actually, I don't." Lloyd meandered back to his seat and plumped himself down. "With all due respect to Mrozek here, this is exactly the kind of issue that I don't believe any of us need to hear about. It's repulsive. Okay, we're going to strip a whole bunch of people of secondary medical benefits. Thirty percent of the workforce won't have pensions. In so doing, we'll cut overhead by twenty percent and produce the kind of operating performance the analysts expect in order to justify the deal. But do we have to sit here and listen to it? Why does everything have to be a meeting?"

Something interesting was happening to Mrozek. Her throat was working up and down and she was obsessively cleaning her glasses.

"Well, Lloyd," said Walt. "I'm inclined to agree with you, but Louise here has developed a presentation for our review and I guess she worked pretty hard on it, and we probably ought to have the manners to hear her out."

"Fuck that," said Lloyd, and got to his feet. "Haven't we all come a little bit too far down the road for these kind of niceties?" Jesus. Who was this speaking? "I'm sorry, Walt, no disrespect to anybody here—I really mean that—but come on. The kind of shit we're planning, the implications on so many people, the brutality of it, the insanity of it, the scope of the suffering it will inflict, the grandiosity, the viciousness . . ." He picked up his pad and went to the door. "Well, look," he said. "I've had it. I'll do whatever is necessary to make this thing happen. It was your idea, Walt, and it's gonna happen. But I'm not going to be polite about it. I'll see you guys later." Lloyd left.

There was a relatively extended silence inside the conference room. "You don't have to go on today, Louise," said Walt to Mrozek after a while. They all simply sat and kept each other company while the clock ticked on. Nobody made a move to leave. Mona sat and drew. Pictures of puppies, mostly. Whenever she was upset, she drew puppies. What was the matter with Lloyd? He had refused to sit next to her; then he had hung around behind her, impaling her with his gaze. Didn't he care at all for propriety? Must everyone know about their situation? And what about his tantrum? Bizarre. Suddenly, the idea of being by herself outside the conference room was unutterably terrible. She huddled within the group for warmth.

"I understand what Lloyd is talking about, though," said Walt into the void. "We're working on a project that basically blows up the world as we all have known it, and to a certain extent loved it. Lloyd feels that this development has destroyed the fabric of our world and made certain social obligations not only unnecessary but hypocritical. I respect his feelings. As always, Lloyd's feelings, while inelegantly put, are genuine and reflect a common reality we're all dealing with. Lloyd feels the future pounding down the track at all of us, feels it acutely. But I guess I should make quite clear that I profoundly disagree with Lloyd's reaction to this reality, and I plan to tell him so. In my opinion, it is during times such as these that the insincere, empty, form-based interactions among us make all the difference, keep us functioning as a cohesive group that has meaning to ourselves and others. It's when the external structure breaks down that cordiality, friendliness, and just, well, good manners become crucial. We may not be together this time next year. We may not survive as an organization, or a management team. The actions we take may impact with enormous negativity on us and everyone we come in contact with. But we're going to remain civilized while it happens, goddamn it, and I'm going to insist on that. Now let's shake hands all the way around and call this meeting over. What do you say?"

Walt rose, as did they all. A number of small sidebars erupted for a few minutes as people took the opportunity to touch Mrozek, apologizing for Lloyd, commenting on her truncated presentation, checking to see if they were each all right with the others. Finally, all juice having been extracted from the interface, the room cleared, leaving no one but Walt, who stood kneading his lower lip and looking out the window, and Mona, who sat still, working over her pad.

"He's flaking out," said Walt to the general ether.

"Yes," said Mona.

"I wonder if there's anything you can do for him."

"I don't know. I wonder if I'm in some way the cause."

"No, no," said Walt. "You're terrific."

"You think so, Walt?" Mona realized she was quite upset. She kept her eyes on her pad and kept on sketching until she felt Walt's large, warm hand resting on her shoulder.

"Yes, I do," said Walt. "You're absolutely outstanding. You're a huge player in all of this, and we need to keep your focus, your judgment, right up in the middle of our sights throughout this process, or we're sunk."

"Well, thanks, Walt," said Mona. She felt the sadness and impending hysteria that had been building inside her ease, and with that relaxing came a rush of loyalty and love for the man behind her. "Thanks very much," she said. She made a great show of putting the cap on her Mont Blanc pen, which she hoped signaled the end of this intensely personal conversation. The message must have been adequately conveyed, since Walt took the opportunity to produce his roomy, crisp handkerchief and began to blow his brains out. Mona collected her stuff and went to the door. "See ya," she said.

"Yeah, definitely . . . er, say . . ." Walt looked uncomfortable.

"Yes?" She was stuck, like a fly on flypaper, in the goo of Walt in the midst of difficult self-expression. Mona knew this could take full minutes, even a quarter of an hour, but she was required to wait. She suddenly became aware of the fact that she had to pee worse than she had since a hayride almost twenty years ago when, miles from any convenience, she had been forced to hold her water for a full hour of exquisite discomfort. She had never come closer to wetting herself than then, but the urge, quite improbably, was almost as imperative at this moment, and none the less urgent because it was so unexpected and sudden.

"I wonder if you've noticed that Doug never attends a meeting that I have called personally," Walt was saying.

"I hadn't. Noticed, I mean," Mona said. This was entering uncharted territory for a high middle manager. This was ultrasenior stuff, made of the exquisite paranoia only the most elevated could experience.

"Well, he doesn't," said Walt. "And the fact is, I haven't had a one-on-one talk with the guy for almost eight weeks. Do you think he likes me? I mean, is there some problem here? What's your opinion?"

"My . . . opinion?" said Mona. She leaned against the wall and held her legs together—with taste and discretion, she hoped. It was obvious she had to speak clearly and with the force of truth, or else this conversation could extend until it became necessary for her either to declare her physical requirement or lose control. "My opinion is that Doug likes nobody and is loyal to nobody. He's as cold as a snake and completely calculating. He's completely invested in consolidating his power, which means that you're probably threatening to him because people are loyal to you and, you know, love you, Walt. If I were you, I'd watch Doug really carefully and make sure my exit package was real rich. Because when we get down to the point where there are too many big-time senior managers around, Doug will certainly try to take you out, and he'll definitely try to use those nearest and dearest to you to do it."

Walt's eyes had grown enormously large during this screed. When it was clear that it was over, he continued to stare at Mona in complete silence, although his right hand did find its way to his lips, where they began to work.

"And now I have to go, Walt," said Mona.

"Yes," said Walt. "And thanks. You don't really hear that kind of talk around here anymore. Or anywhere. I believe I'll . . . take it to heart."

"No, Walt. What I really meant was . . . I really have to go."

Who Can Stay Mad at Lloyd?

By the time Lloyd got back to his office, he was pretty sick and tired of everything. He had been out walking and had bought a tiny cellular phone he didn't need. In fact, he found it ridiculous. He had seen guys in the middle of an intersection, standing in the center of huge granite lobbies, even cruising on a boat down the Chicago River during last year's big convention, jabbering on the gizmos, which were no bigger than a pack of cigarettes. Big dudes, tiny phones. He got one and charged it to the company.

Walt was waiting in his doorway when he returned, just standing in the door to Lloyd's office, munching on a bread stick. This was, of course, instead of lunch. Later on in the afternoon, Walt would break down and have a cup of steaming-hot soup, usually cream of something, slurped while leaning over his blotter, his tie slung over his shoulder or, sometimes, tucked between his second and third buttons.

"What do you know," said Walt.

"Nothing, Walt. I know nothing," said Lloyd. He hung up his coat on the back of his door and went to his chair, but he did not sit until Walt indicated whether this was a sit-down or stand-up affair.

"You're a little on edge, Lloyd," said Walt, and began his customary investigation of all things great and small in Lloyd's menagerie of knick-knacks, toys, office supplies, awards, and outright junk.

"Yeah, well. I hate Mrozek. She's a slime. It's one thing to screw with people. It's another to do a slide presentation about the benefits. Self-satisfied crap. I'm through with it. I haven't got the energy to pretend anymore. I'll do what's necessary. Just don't ask me to take one micron of unnecessary nonsense."

"How are you going to function, then?" said Walt. Lloyd looked to see if this had been a Waltean witticism, but he couldn't tell. "The inability to sustain meaningless crap and self-satisfied bullshit is a huge liability, Lloyd. Where would we be without unnecessary nonsense? How are we to limit ourselves to the nonsense that's necessary? Sometimes you can't tell until later."

"I . . . Um," said Lloyd. He couldn't quite tell where Walt was going, but he kind of liked it. It was clear there was going to be no screaming.

"You want to get rid of Mrozek, then?" Walt peered at Lloyd over the small statuette of the Pillsbury Doughboy Lloyd had picked up on a visit to Stapleton Airport in Denver for about sixteen hours one winter morning.

Lloyd was uneasy. "Nah," he said. "I mean . . . that would be up to Fitz, wouldn't it?"

"Oh, Fitz," said Walt. "Fitz is fine, but he's not going to be playing a major role, you know. Not in the near term, at any rate. There's a guy at Phlegle whom we'll be picking up in the merger, and our friends in Germany say he is the ultimate Human Resources asset and he'll be making most of the big calls when things settle in."

Lloyd was swept with a terrible grief that smote him amidships, then passed. "Uh-huh," he said.

"Well, okay, then, we can leave Mrozek for another day, if you want, Lloyd. People look to you to put a gloss on things. When you fail to do so, it makes the rest of the group extraordinarily nervous. Please try to play out your expected role, even if that role is in a state of constant redefinition. It's part of what's required of you, of all of us. Get me?"

"I get you, Walt. Sorry I lost it back there."

"No big deal. We're all . . . on edge." Walt entered slightly deeper into Lloyd's den. He seemed, quite uncharacteristically, to be uncertain how to proceed.

"Sit down, Walt." Lloyd didn't really want Walt to sit down. Once Walt took a chair, it could be hours before Lloyd's day broke free into sunlight. Still, if what Walt needed was a substantial dynamic exchange, that was what Lloyd wanted him to have. He was aware that the Walt who was coalescing in front of him was not the executive Walt, or even biz Walt, but the core Walt underneath, which powered all the others. What was up?

Walt put his hand on the back of one of Lloyd's visitors' chairs, which, for him, was virtually the equivalent of lying prone and kicking off his shoes. "I suppose it's no secret that Doug and I have . . . issues," he said.

"Issues?" Lloyd wanted to be out of there more than anything. He picked up an ancient Rubik's Cube he kept on his desk for just this purpose, leaned back in his reclining chair, and attempted to unlock its puzzle one more time.

"Don't kid a kidder," said Walt. "The guy doesn't like me, does he, Lloyd?"

"I don't know if Doug . . . likes . . . anybody," said Lloyd, feeling like a liar. He knew one thing. Doug liked him. What did that say about him? "He has massive respect for you as a business thinker, strategist, and idea guy, Walt, that I can tell you."

"Yeah," said Walt, looking dubious. "That and sixty grand will buy me a BMW, and not a very good one, either."

"Look. Most of the ideas that have put Doug in place, that are motoring this situation, are your ideas, Walt." Hadn't he said that to somebody recently?

"Don't remind me."

"And there are a lot of people in this place who know that, who are dedicated to you, and even if Doug is nervous about your power, he has to know that he's not any kind of an operator. You're the guy who makes the team run, Walt. Without you, what have we got around here but a bunch of assets and nobody to run them?"

"I appreciate your attempt to butter me up," said Walt. He was looking Lloyd over with laser intensity.

Lloyd wondered what Walt was seeing, and he did what he could to lard himself over with a patina of neutral disinterest before something funky began to show.

"But . . . I wouldn't turn my back on him," Lloyd blurted. God, he hoped the offices weren't bugged. This wasn't the first time he had wondered whether the boys in Chicago had taken the ultimate security measure. "He's asked me several times . . ."

What Lloyd was about to say was that on several occasions, Doug had asked him, "How do you think Walt is doing?" which really meant, "Don't you think Walt is superfluous at this point and that your loyalties would be better placed with me?" On each occasion, Lloyd had defended Walt without undue heat, conveying the unarticulated response: "It doesn't matter how Walt is doing, day to day. As long as he is here, he's my boss and I am loyal to him. Which doesn't mean I don't like you, Doug. I do. You're the greatest. I mean that." This exchange had taken place no fewer than three times, most recently in September at the historic Just Two Guys Talking About Life session.

"Yes? What!" he hissed. Walt's eyeballs were several yards from his face proper, only inches from Lloyd's, vibrating on muscular cords that hummed with the tension.

"He asked me several times . . ." Lloyd paused again to think it over. "He asked me several times if I thought that you liked him."

"If I . . . liked . . . him?" Walt's eyes popped back into their sockets. He turned the concept around in his mouth like marbles. "Of course I like him. He's terrific. Why wouldn't I like him, if he liked me?"

"Well, that's my point exactly," said Lloyd. The last thing he had wanted, it turned out, was to precipitate a direct confrontation between Walt and Doug, one that Walt would most certainly lose. Or at least that is what Lloyd told himself. "It's a period of transition you both have to negotiate. You need each other and are trying to find a way to get along. It's only natural there's a little pinch and pull at the beginning."

"'Pinch and pull,'" said Walt.

"Absolutely."

Walt stood. As he did, Lloyd saw his military dignity once again reassert itself. "Thanks, Lloyd," he said. "This whole conversation has been hands-in, correct?"

"Correct," said Lloyd. He got up and walked Walt out the door of his office and down the hall to the point where Walt would have to take a separate corridor to the elevator. During the long stroll, the two men said nothing. Lloyd longed to put his arm around Walt's shoulders as they made their way in silence, and he would have, too, except for the fact that he didn't.

"I want to get together with you on the out-year cash-flow situation," said Walt as they parted.

"Yes," said Lloyd. "I think some of our assumptions could bear looking into."

Mona Weighs In

Lloyd spent the rest of his day returning phone calls from a wide variety of extraordinarily bizarre people and several crushingly normal ones, including:

- ✓ A woman from the equivalent of National Public Television in Japan who wanted to know where in the corporation she could find someone to help her uplink transmissions from Arizona to her home base in Osaka. Lloyd, of course, knew nothing about this but had to pretend he did until he could figure out a way to reroute her call so that it wouldn't come back, which he did by sending it down to Engineering, a black hole from whence no light, once trapped, ever emerged.
- ✓ Three students from New York University, one right after the other, each of whom was doing a research paper on something completely unrelated to Lloyd's area of expertise but who could not be shunted off to anyone else, since there was nobody left who could address that area of expertise after the McKinsey Company got through with their work-flow analysis last February, and Lloyd had implemented it.
- ✓ No fewer than nine regional managers who needed sales updates in order to complete their monthly review reports.
- ✓ The corporation's investment banker, formerly with the Clinton administration, calling in from Montana, where he was on perpetual working vacation, who needed to talk through some issues pertaining to his role in upcoming negotiations, but, unbeknownst to him, he had no role.
- ✓ More stuff like that.
- ✓ And Donna, who called to say that the weather report was calling for several inches of freezing rain and she hoped that Lloyd would be home at a

good hour in case there was any sort of flooding activity in their neighborhood, because if there was, their house would most surely be the one to go
under.

✓ Not Mona.

That part about the flooding was ridiculous. They had experienced a couple of wet nights in their ten-year tenure in this house, but nothing that could
approach a flood. Their basement had never seen water. Their driveway
slanted downward and was extremely near two storm drains, true, but if
those storm drains were kept clear, there was no need for concern. Of course,
it was warm for October, and the leaves had not yet been collected, but when
you got right down to it, did Donna need a rational reason to obsess about
potential negatives? Not at all. Donna was tormenting herself about the worst
possible eventuality that could come to pass. Still, there was no point in leaving the woman alone and terrified, particularly when he had nothing to do
this evening. He would go home, be a good husband. Being a decent person
wasn't as hard as he had thought!

He spent the rest of the day not calling Mona. He now only thought
about her once every three or four minutes, while at the beginning of the
workday, he found her in his mind virtually every second, even when he was
talking to other people. He was sure that tomorrow would be even easier.

At 5:30, he looked out the window and noticed that the sky was darken-
ing quite threateningly. "Wow," he said to Roover, one of the numbers guys
whose job it was to attend all mass executions, count bodies, and search the
pockets of the dead. "It's nasty out. I'm gonna take half a day." He collected
his briefcase and coat, grabbed an umbrella, and headed for the elevator,
where he found Mona standing thoughtfully, her own coat slung over her
shoulders, a wad of paper in her hands.

"Hi," she said.

"Oh! Hi! I didn't see you!" said Lloyd. Why was he speaking so loudly?

They got into the elevator and rode for a while.

"You didn't call today," said Mona after a time.

"No, I, er, well, it's . . . nuts out there."

"Uh-huh."

She wasn't buying it. Lloyd wasn't quite sure what he was selling, but she
wasn't having any.

As they got off at the ground floor, Mona put on the gas and headed for
the glass revolving doors.

"Hey!" said Lloyd. He ran after her and she stopped, not quite looking
directly at him, but attending in a distant, preoccupied way. He stood close
enough so he did not have to shout, then said very softly, "Are you not speaking to me or something?"

"No, I'm speaking to you. It's just that I don't have anything to say. That's permitted. This is America. People are free to have nothing to say. It's the national pastime, come to think of it."

"That's better."

And she was gone again, headed for the doors, which she entered and spun around, and before Lloyd could say anything, she was outside and headed down the street.

"What are you doing?" Lloyd caught up, spun her around, and seized her by her shoulders.

"You're making a scene, Lloyd. This isn't some kind of dramatic interchange. It's just me going home from work."

"What do you imagine is happening?" said Lloyd. He was furious. "Why are you treating me like this?"

"I'm not treating you any way, Lloyd. You're suddenly unsure of our friendship. You're paranoid. You're nervous around me. We don't need that. I don't want to be the woman you can't get out of your hair. We can be business friends. And you won't be threatened anymore. Because from now on, you'll have nothing to fear from me. You want it to be over. It's over. That's the beauty of a silly little affair. Either of us can end it if we want to. You want to. That's that. Have a nice evening."

"No!" said Lloyd, much more loudly than he intended. "No," he said more softly. He leaned into her face so that he could taste the atmosphere around her body. "I was wrong. I don't want it to be over. I want it to be happening. I want it to be like it was before. I want you. Don't do this to me."

"Now, now you do. Now you do," said Mona, and Lloyd could see there were big translucent tears in the corners of her eyes, which were directed down the avenue, as if taking inventory of the big buildings. "But later . . . you won't. Don't lie, Lloyd. If I come forward, you will go back. If I back up, you will come forward. It's a baby game. I don't want it. I care too much. Can you understand that? I care too much."

"Can I understand it?" said Lloyd. He was outraged. "Can I understand it?"

"That was the question, yes."

"Of course I understand it! It's simple!"

"Explain it to me."

"Please don't do this to me, Mona. Please don't push me away."

"Lloyd! Mona!" It was Darling, plump and greasy, making his huffing way from the office to the train station. Lloyd and Mona carefully drifted apart, changing their body language imperceptibly but immediately mutating into simple business associates. "What a day," said Darling.

"Go away, Bob, we're having a proprietary conversation," he said.

"What a kidder you are, Lloyd, you fucking scumbag," said Darling, and, slamming Lloyd on the shoulder, he continued on his way.

"I got a little squirrelly for a couple of hours, sweetie," he said. "I'm married. I have kids. I feel myself growing so close to you. There's nothing I can't imagine doing with you. Suppose I really love you? I mean, what then?"

"Well," said Mona. "Maybe we have to make sure a tragedy like that never happens."

"We can do it. We'll keep things light. You said it yourself. It can be done."

"Yeah, maybe. But maybe not by us. Has that occurred to you?"

Lloyd wanted so very much to touch her arm, to burrow a hand beneath the soft wool of her shirt and feel the supple cool skin of her waist. Vaguely remembered colleagues walked by them on the street. He attempted to look businesslike instead.

"It's occurred to me. Of course it's occurred to me. But we have to try."

"I don't want to try." Mona pulled herself up to her full height and for the first time focused on Lloyd. "Let's give your life a chance to work itself out, Lloyd," she said. "And mine, too. We've had fun. Let's give it a rest now before we start to hurt each other. I know I can hurt you if I want, but I don't want to. And I know that you don't want to hurt me, Lloyd, but I know, I really and truly know very deep down in my heart, that you will, Lloyd. You will hurt me. So go home to your family and let me go home to . . . this very excellent Czechoslovakian movie I rented last night. I'll walk on the treadmill. I'll eat junk for dinner. I'll be alone. I think it sounds kind of nice."

"Mona." His heart hurt. It hurt so badly. He wanted the hurting to stop. Maybe he was having a heart attack! Was this what it felt like?

"If you find, on the other hand, that you cannot live without me, then that, too, will tell you something, won't it?"

Lloyd said nothing. He looked at the woman who just a few hours ago had been his for the taking. She was so distant now. Out of reach. He ached to take her in his arms and draw her tongue into his mouth, to grasp her bottom with both hands and draw her lower torso to his, to kiss her neck and hear her say, "Oh" in that voice of quiet surprise he loved so much. What had he done! He had destroyed his own happiness again! Fool! Dummkopf! Idiot!

"Yes, Mona," he said. "That will tell me something."

"Shall we . . . shake on it?" Mona stuck out her hand.

"Why do you torment me?"

"Shake my hand, Lloyd. Be a man. Seal the deal."

Lloyd seized her hand in both of his.

"Marry me," he said.

The Flood

Lloyd was floating in a deep blackness. It was comfortable there. A good sleep, what can replace it?

"Lloyd!" It was a high-pitched scream. "Lloyd! Lloyd!" Behind the noise, another one. What was that? A whooshing, or . . . a rushing.

Rain, that's what it was. No, but this was not just rain. This was the sound of a river flowing. Pretty rain. Nice rain. Snuggle up against the cold.

"Lloyd!"

He sat up.

"You gotta come quick! You gotta come quick!"

It was Donna, in the doorway to their darkened room, pulling on a down jacket, her hair still bundled up in the bun she kept it in as she slept, her face stark white in the night-light from the hall. Now she was pulling on boots. Not one part of her body was not in motion. She was sobbing.

"Lloyd, it's the rain. It's coming down the street in, like, rivers. Half the driveway is full of water, man! Oh, man, man, this is terrible. This is horrible. Will you come on, Lloyd! Come quick." She bustled away and down the stairs, muttering, "Oh, man" obsessively under her breath. Lloyd hadn't heard Donna say "Oh, man" since 1978, when he had upset her so badly—what had it been about?—that she had exited his car while it was in motion. She had just become so sick of him, she couldn't bear to be in the same space with him for a moment longer, so she opened the door while they were moving down Mass. Avenue at about fifteen miles per hour. If he hadn't slammed on the brakes, she would have simply dropped out the door and rolled away. He had pulled her in and slammed the door shut. What a nut the woman could be! It was one of the moments in which he started loving her quite seriously for the first time. A woman who would step into moving traffic to get away from him!

Lloyd turned on the light and felt like dying. He had been up late, until 1:30 A.M., thinking and smoking a cigar in the garage. What in the world was he going to do? He had returned home, to find that his wife had just roasted a chicken. Bob and Nora were at the table, cordially discussing foods they liked and didn't like, one of their big subjects. Donna was slicing and doling things out. It was a scene of peace and, in a quiet way, joy. Family! What was its equal?

What had he done? He had asked Mona to marry him! He had blurted out that amazing statement, and she had simply stood there, allowing her hand to be held in his in what was fast becoming the traditional crummy politician's two-fisted handshake.

"Say something," he'd said finally.

"I will," she said; then she turned and one hand flew up and fluttered in the air above her head. "Taxi!" she called. She had been looking, at least peripherally, for a nice new one pulled right up and she hauled the door open. Lloyd could not believe she was slipping away at this critical juncture.

"Hey!" he said.

Mona was half in the cab and half out. "I will marry you, Lloyd," she said, "when you have asked me to do so three times. This first time counts, but it was impetuous. The idea that you would never touch me again had a powerful effect on you. That's a valid measure of something. I'm not quite sure what. We'll table it. The next time you ask, you'll know what you're doing."

"Marry me," Lloyd blurted. What was he doing!? Was he drunk?

Mona seemed shocked. She looked at him thoughtfully.

"The next time . . . you had better be for real," she said, slipping totally into the cab and slamming the door.

Was it possible he really and truly wanted to marry the woman? Earlier, he'd half-sat, half-stood, leaning on the hood of the Camry and smoking. Marriage to Mona, what would that be like? It would certainly involve:

✓ Living in an apartment in the city again, albeit a much nicer and roomier one than he had ever been able to afford in his previous lifetime.
✓ Dealing with the disapproval and jealousy so many of their common friends would feel toward him, and, somewhere, his own disapproval toward himself and self-loathing over his lack of character.
✓ Eating in trendy downtown restaurants that drizzled a variety of balsamic liquids over everything from greens to meat and piled strata of food in vertical formations, even at breakfast, at least this year.
✓ The possibility—actually, the probability—that within a year or two he would be a father again, adding an entirely new family unit to the planet, forcing him to draw on reservoirs of youth he barely knew he possessed, and perhaps didn't.
✓ A fresh start and immediate postponement of the inevitable decline into fuddy-duddyness, inexorable decay, and death.

"Woof." Steve had been staring at him from the door to the garage. Lloyd took a puff on his big creamy Macanudo and regarded the little cocker spaniel, who returned the gaze without expression.

"It's a cigar," Lloyd told Steve. Steve looked uneasy. His rump jiggled a little to signify that his tail was on the verge of wagging. "It's bad for you, but sometimes you have to do things that are bad for you just to stay in fighting shape."

"Roo," said Steve quite distinctly. Steve was the only dog Lloyd had ever had who watched television, particularly enjoying shows where animals attacked people. He was also the only dog Lloyd had known who had ever actually said "woof." Lloyd didn't want Steve to start howling, though. That might bring attention down to the garage, followed by a horrified lecture on the evils of smoking. Donna didn't care that much, but the kids were out-and-out prohibitionists on a wide variety of vices and excesses.

"Steve," said Lloyd. "Go get your hedgehog."

Steve smiled, stuck out his tongue, and darted out of sight. He would be rummaging through every room until he found it. Lloyd carefully put out the cigar, stowed it in the bottom of a wine bottle in the plastic garbage can set aside for recycling, and went upstairs. Not long after, he dragged himself up to bed. Now it was not even two hours later and he was up again, the essence of cigar coursing through his body.

He was awake, although not really, stumbling around bumping into things, asleep on his feet. He attempted to yank on a pair of socks, hopping on one foot, slammed into his dresser, and fell over, completing the task while lying on his back on the floor. "Lloyd! Help!" came a thin, reedy cry from two stories below. Lloyd jerked into full consciousness, pulled on his pants and a pair of tall rubber boots they kept in the back of the bedroom closet, and went downstairs. As he descended, the sound of rushing water grew louder. It was everywhere. Outside, in the street. Downstairs, coming through the attached garage from the basement. Water, water everywhere. And not a drop to drink. He went downstairs to the basement, which was still dry, thank God.

Donna was in the mudroom, eyes wide, her head whipping back and forth like that of a small forest animal caught between two predators.

"I called the fire department!" she cried. "What are we going to do, Lloyd? We have to bail! We have to bail out the driveway!"

"Okay," said Lloyd. They each grabbed a plastic bucket. Lloyd opened the inner door between the mudroom and the garage. An inch of water covered the floor. The sump pump in the corner was working hard—he could hear that—but there was no question that the water was not only penetrating but rising. "Can we open the door to the garage?" he said.

"Yeah, but then what? We don't want to let all the fucking water from the driveway in!"

"We can go around the front," he said.

"Oh, man. Oh, man," said Donna.

Steve was standing at the top of the basement steps, a look of intense anxiety and anguish on his face. "Woof?" he said.

"Out of the way there, Steve," said Lloyd as he went past.

"Oh, God! Oh, man! Oh!" said Donna when they beheld the driveway. It's no big deal, thought Lloyd. He had seen bigger collections of water, certainly, at some point in his life. The rain pounded down on them. Lloyd had put on two heavy coats and a Yankees cap. He felt pretty dry. Donna was in a long yellow slicker and a baseball cap that said NO FEAR on the front. It didn't seem to be doing much good fending off either fear or rain. The combination of slicker and cap made her appear all of fourteen years old. "We gotta bail!" she said again, but she did nothing. Her little pail hung limply at her side. Lloyd tossed his aside.

"I'm sure the fire department will be here in a minute," said Lloyd, although he was sure of no such thing.

Donna walked purposefully down the driveway and waded into the pool of water. She bent over and began to root around in the deepest part of it, looking for the grate that, if clogged, would stop the water from draining and heading down the pipe that went beneath the garage and into their excellent sump pump. A thick rivulet of cold rain had set up shop at the base of his neck and was making its merry way down his spine. A flutter of terror passed through Lloyd. He had several crucial meetings next week. He could not get sick.

"Lloyd!" screamed Donna from the bottom of the lagoon. "Do something, for Chrissake!" She came up with an armful of wet leaves that must have weighed a ton. Lloyd saw a torrent of water coming down the street and heading directly around a colossal pile of leaves that had collected directly in front of the storm drain that was supposed to collect water before it passed by their driveway.

Donna came up with another load of crud and dumped it to one side of the driveway. "Can I get into the garage?" Lloyd shouted over the storm.

"What?"

Lloyd realized it was impossible to hear at any distance. The noise was deafening. It was like being in the middle of a tornado. Maybe they were in the middle of a tornado! What good would their efforts do then?

"Where is the fucking fire department? Where are they!"

"I know!" Lloyd said, and took off for the side door to the house. He entered the kitchen, went down the steps to the basement, and entered the garage from the mudroom. The water in there was not too bad. Two inches, maybe. As long as the sump pump kept working . . . *Crack!* went an apocalyptic flash of lightning directly overhead. Lloyd waited. *Boom!* went a biblical crash of thunder.

"Christ," said Lloyd.

He grabbed a pointed shovel and hoofed it back up the stairs. On the way out of the front vestibule, he considered, turned, and headed up the stairs. Bob was in his bed, sitting up. "Is there a man here?" he said. He was half-asleep. Even as a tiny boy, he had been afraid of nocturnal intruders, whom he called "roberts."

"No, baby," said Lloyd, shoving Bob's stuffed bear back into his arms and helping him lie back down. He covered him up and kissed him lightly on the lips. "It's just wet out. Go back to sleep." Bob rolled over on his side and was asleep before Lloyd was out of the room.

Nora, too, was still in bed, but her eyes were open. "Are you all right, honey?" Lloyd said.

"Mommy's voice is very loud," said Nora.

Lloyd smiled in the darkness. "Yes, it is, darling," he said.

"Is the water in the basement?"

"No. I don't think we'll get that bad."

"Well," said Nora, rolling over and pulling the covers up to her chin, "make sure to get the shoes up off the floor of the mudroom." And she, too, went to sleep. What a healthy reaction, Lloyd thought. The house is on the verge of floating away, and the girl is worried about her shoes. What does that represent? A sense that no matter what chaos is going on outside, inside their home everything would work out basically okay? Would he be responsible for destroying that idiotic assumption? What kind of loser was he?

He went downstairs and headed for the front door. On the way out, he ran into Steve, who had been sitting in the vestibule wondering what to do next. Upon seeing his heavily coated master brandishing a pointed shovel, Steve decided to play the watchdog in his own unique and typical way: by barking at people who were *leaving* the house.

"Go upstairs, Steve," said Lloyd to the dog in a low but very serious voice. Steve immediately packed up his diligent watchdog act and trotted wearily up the stairs as if he were a sentry just then relieved of duty after a long shift.

Lloyd stepped outside into the rain, but now it was not rain anymore. It was an omnipresent environment suffused with violent horizontal moisture. This was not rain. This was the end of the world.

Lloyd looked up at the sky, into the maelstrom. He felt very small and very, very silent in the middle of the cacophonous din.

"Donna!" he yelled at the top of his lungs as he ran around the side of the house to help her. He found his wife toting a bucket of water up the driveway, crying. He dropped the shovel and went to grab the bucket, took it from her, and carried it across the street, where he dumped it. The water gurgled around for a second, looking for someplace to go, then turned and headed back across the street and down Lloyd's driveway. On his way back, he took a look at the pond there. It was larger, not a lot, but enough. Donna had picked up the other bucket and was headed back into the marsh, which was now strewn with floating leaves.

"We're not going to make it!" screamed Donna. "We're losing it!"

"The sump pump is working fine," said Lloyd over the racket, but it was true: The stream that had been coursing down the block was now inundating their driveway.

"We need to call Chuck!" Donna screamed as she hauled another weeny load of water up the incline.

"For what?" said Lloyd. Instant anger, he felt it, warming him, making him sweat under his soaking layer of clothing.

"For . . . for . . . I don't know what for!" Donna yelled. "Maybe he has a generator with an auxiliary pump! Maybe he knows . . . something! Maybe . . . I don't know! He'll put a stronger fuse in the socket, or find a clog we can unplug, or . . . anything! Chuck will know what to do, Lloyd! We have to call him now!"

"*No!*" Lloyd shouted with a ferocity he had not experienced in several decades. He suppressed the urge to strike her, grabbing her by the shoulders instead. "We do not need Chuck, goddamn it! No Chuck! No Chuck at all! I can fuck this thing up all on my own!" And he thrust her from him, picked up the shovel, and marched off to the Matterhorn of leaves that was blocking the storm drain.

"All right, Lloyd," she said very quietly, and Lloyd could hear her in spite of the wind, the howl of the water, the occasional clap of thunder.

After a few minutes, Donna looked at her bucket, looked at the ocean it was meant to drain, looked back at her bucket again, then put it down and walked slowly over to Lloyd, who said nothing. She began to kick the leaves nearest the gutter into the yard, helping Lloyd create the alley he was constructing.

"Go inside, Donna," said Lloyd.

"No, no." She kept on kicking.

Lloyd dug on. He was aware that suddenly the nature of the water flow had changed. It was no longer a flat sheet rolling evenly down the street in discreet rivulets. He was now standing in a wave tank, with progressive waves of water sloshing up to the level of his ankles.

"This isn't rain," he said. "It's a water-main break or something."

"What if the lights go out?" said Donna. "We've had blackouts before, but never in a rain like this. What if there's no electricity and the sump pump stops working?"

"The sump pump isn't going to stop working!" screamed Lloyd over a particularly vicious roar of thunder. Why did Donna always have to imagine the worst? And even if the worst was what relentlessly always happened, what good did it do to anticipate it? Why not imagine the best and be continually surprised when it failed to appear?

"If it did, though," Donna said, and Lloyd could only just make it out. "If it did, the car would be underwater in fifteen minutes. What if the sump pump goes out, Lloyd?"

Lloyd kept on digging. "Get out in the middle of the street and kick the leaves into a little dam just beyond the storm drain!" he bawled at Donna. "We're going to direct this fucking torrent into the storm drain!"

"Yes!" said Donna. "Good thinking, Lloyd, good thinking." She waddled out into the middle of the street and began to do a crazy dance in the pounding rain, the water swirling in frisky eddies about her feet, her ankles, some splashing as high as her calves. She absentmindedly removed her cap and put it on backward, skateboarder-style. The rain, which had previously been cascading into her face, began chuckling down her back instead.

"What is this, your homeboy from outer space look?" said Lloyd, pausing in his work for a moment. He couldn't keep himself from grinning. She looked so goofy. She smiled back at him. They stood there for a time, stuck like that. Finally, Lloyd bent back to the job, feeling lit up. Just a smile, that was all it was. Now it appeared as if they were making some progress and the downpour seemed slightly less vicious. Could they be turning the corner on this nightmare?

"This is working, Lloyd," she said. "See the water going down the drain?"

"We gotta keep it up," he said.

"You've never had any trouble in that department," said Donna, and Lloyd looked at her sharply. What was this now? Coquetry?

"Come on over here and help me finish this part of it!" Lloyd said, more because he wanted her right next to him when the water punched through and began its maiden voyage down the sluice.

"Yes!" said Donna triumphantly. She jumped up with both feet together and came down with a splash. "Yes, yes, yes!" she said, and hopped over to where Lloyd was just shoveling the last impediment away from the storm drain. With a chortle and a gush, the water filled the alleyway, then headed immediately and helpfully right where it was supposed to go into the storm drain. They stood together but slightly apart, water dripping off them, for several minutes without speaking, watching the deluge that had been headed for their house get sent underground to be dumped out about a mile later in the woods across the street.

"Let's see how the driveway is doing," said Lloyd after a while.

"Sump pump is really hauling ass," said Donna thoughtfully.

"It's still possible that the water table under the house is rising," said Lloyd calmly. "It shouldn't be a problem as long as the power holds."

"No?" said Donna. "It shouldn't? I mean, you really think it shouldn't?"

"Well, we're not going to call fucking Chuck about it, if that's what you're thinking about," said Lloyd churlishly.

"No, we're not going to call Chuck about it. I didn't suggest we had to call Chuck about it," said Donna. "You don't have to be so touchy about Chuck, Lloyd. I didn't say a thing about Chuck. There's no reason to get so nutty about it."

"Uh-huh," said Lloyd.

"Really," said Donna. She moved very close to him on the right but did not touch him. The rain had picked up again and it occurred to Lloyd that it would perhaps be smarter if they went inside for a while, except for the fact that the pond in the driveway seemed to be growing in spite of the rerouting of the flow. Still, through the garage door windows, Lloyd could see that the inside space was generally pretty dry and the big automatic door was keeping most of the water out. The pump was working. And the whole thing about Chuck seemed to have mutated somewhat.

"Let's go in and have a drink," said Lloyd.

"It's nearly four in the morning. Don't you have to go to work in a couple of hours?"

"I guess. I could use a drink."

"Fine," said Donna, taking his elbow with her hand. "Let's go in and have a drink."

"Unless God is completely against us, I think it's possible we just might be all right," said Lloyd.

"God is not completely against us," she said.

That's when the lights went out.

The Darkness

There was a crack first, then a thud, but this time the hollow, dull reverberation was not thunder. It was the sound of light departing from the world around them. They stood for a nanosecond, trying to ascertain what exactly had just happened to them. All around, the sky was gray, the first suspicion of dawn still hours away. The air was gray. The rain was gray. The hulking shape of their house and those of their neighbors rose up in the murk, gray and lifeless.

"Mom! Dad!" It was Bob's voice, impossibly distant, up in his room. Steve began to bark.

"We have to call Chuck now!" screamed Donna directly into his face.

"What's Chuck going to do? Connect downed power lines? What is Chuck, some kind of fucking miracle worker?"

"Lloyd!" Donna was tearing around the side of the house toward the front door. Lloyd followed. She was babbling. "We have to call Chuck and tell Chuck that the sump pump is going to go out in a few minutes when the auxiliary battery gives out! We're cooked, Lloyd!" Lloyd stopped listening. This Chuck thing was out of control.

He followed Donna into the house. She had already set up a number of large flashlight lanterns, and the living room and kitchen were lit by an eerie flicker. "Oh, man. Oh, man." Donna was at that again. "It's gonna be a flood, Lloyd! What are we gonna do?"

Lloyd thought of several things. Move out? Go to a hotel? Call Con Ed? Sure. Sit on hold, punching response numbers and listening to company announcements for the next several hours. How about the fire department? They'd been an awesome source of assistance up until now.

"I'll call Chuck," he said. With stone in his heart, he dialed the number that was posted on a magnetic card stuck on their refrigerator. He hated to do it. But it was just possible that Chuck would know something that could help them out. Also, if he heard his wife talking to the guy, he just might kill her, or at least say or do something that could not be taken back later.

"Call Chuck," said Donna, quite nonsensically, since he was doing exactly that.

"Where is the fucking fire department!" screamed Lloyd, slamming down the phone.

"They're not coming! You have to call Chuck!" said Donna.

"If you love Chuck so much, why don't you marry him!" He was petulantly close to telling her all about Mona. That would teach her about fucking Chuck!

"I don't love Chuck, Lloyd. I just thought he might know something about keeping the backup battery on the sump pump charged, that's all, but you insist on taking everything the wrong way. Why do you—I mean, I don't know why you do, because I keep trying to tell you that I don't love anybody but you, Lloyd, because I don't, I don't." Suffused with a cocktail of fear, frustration, and confusion, Donna burst into tears again. He felt like crying himself, but he didn't. Chuck would not cry.

"I love you, too, Donna. Stop crying," he said, and put his arms around her. God, she was cold, and small, too, much smaller than Mona. Had he ever really noticed that before? In so many ways, she was much larger, except in this body here, which was really quite delicate, and fragile, and vulnerable, and, after all, put into his care. "It'll be all right," he said. "Nobody ever died of a blackout. Nobody ever drowned in a garage with two inches of water in it."

"Maybe it's three by now."

"It could be three feet by now. It doesn't matter. We'll make it through okay." He picked up the phone. "Go upstairs and tell Bob and Nora that everything is all right. Tell Steve, too. He looked very nervous last time I saw him." Donna lingered. "Go, Donna," said Lloyd. More than anything, he didn't want Donna to hear him talking to Chuck about his lack of expertise as a home owner and problem solver.

"Okay, okay," said Donna, and left.

It was odd. Whatever chill had frosted up between the two of them had burned off, just like that. Amazing how easily that was done, thought Lloyd. Why couldn't it be permanent?

"Hello, yeah." It was Chuck.

"Chuck, this is Lloyd. You know. Lloyd."

"Yeah, Lloyd, yeah, gimme a minute." There was the sound of somebody waking up enough to talk. "Raining like a bastard out there," said Chuck informationally.

"Yeah," said Lloyd. He was aware that he was involuntarily pitching his voice slightly lower in an attempt to be macho in this humiliating pinch. "Imagine what that rain could do to our garage and basement if the power went out and the sump pump went off."

"Jesus," said Chuck.

Lloyd heard the sound of Chuck's wife in the background. Did she know? Did she suspect? What did she look like? Would she like to have an affair with a clever, powerful businessman in the prime of his life? Wouldn't that be a nice change from her husband? Lloyd thought about inviting Chuck and his wife over for coffee. They could sit in the cold, dark house and look one another over by candlelight, which usually shows middle-aged people to good effect.

"You got that backup battery on it, but it's not going to last that long. Is there water in the garage?"

"Not much. Maybe an inch or two, or three."

"Get the battery up on a cinder block, then connect it to the battery in your car. You know how to do that, Lloyd?"

"Of course I fucking know how to do that, Chuck. I mean, what do you take me for?" Lloyd was filled with a wrath so thick and full of sulfur, it could have bubbled up from the center of the earth. In a calmer voice, he said, "Remind me, Chuck. I mean . . . I used to do it, like, every day, practically, but it's been years."

"Yeah, it's red to red and black to black. You got cables, right?"

"I guess." It had been years since he'd used those, too.

"Just don't stand in water while you're playing with the cable. Put down blocks."

"I'm wearing rubber boots. Will that help?"

"I'm not sure. I don't think so. But it can't hurt, I guess. So . . . if you have any problems, you can call me back, okay?"

"Okay, Chuck."

"Oh, and open the garage door when you're ready to start the car. You don't want those fumes building up in there. Those could kill you."

"Thanks for telling me." The guy was obviously being nice. There didn't seem to be any subtext in his voice. Was it possible he was not, and had never been, boning Donna?

"Tell me something, Chuck. Do these kind of fucked-up things ever happen to you?"

"Sure, man," said Chuck. "It's no big deal. You can handle it."

"Thanks," said Lloyd. "I'll call you back if I get killed."

"You do that," said Chuck, and hung up.

Lloyd was scared. So much could go wrong, and clearly, adequacy in these areas was important to Donna, practically an aphrodisiac. He did not intend to fail.

He met Donna in the doorway to the kitchen. She had taken off her hat and was standing at the head of the stairs to the basement.

"What did he say?"

"Who?" said Lloyd.

"What did Chuck say?"

"About what?" said Lloyd.

They looked at each other.

"What are you giving me a hard time for?" said Donna. "Chuck is a good friend. He's a very sweet guy and that's all I care to say about it. I don't ask you where you are when you're traveling all over the place and working with all these people I have no idea about. Marriage is based on trust, Lloyd. No trust, no marriage. Even where two people haven't earned it, there has to be trust. And sometimes if you can have trust, you don't even need a very good marriage. I'm exhausted and a million gallons of water are coursing under the house and you want to have some kind of come-to-Jesus discussion, Lloyd?"

"I don't think so. I think you've said about all there is to say, whatever it was you just said."

"Now what did Chuck tell you?"

"About what?" said Lloyd.

"I'll make coffee." Donna slid by him and into the kitchen. Still wearing her slicker, she began fussing with the coffee equipment. Was it possible that Lloyd had imagined the entire affair between Chuck and Donna? That the feeling between the two amounted to nothing more than the affection of two people thrown together who had agreed, silently or otherwise, to keep the physical expression of their feelings at bay? Were they constantly immersed in the dance of attraction and denial, fighting their baser selves at every pass? What about the step stool? It was obviously a Chuck-inspired item. The concept of an industrial-quality step stool was about as native to Donna's mentality as a gene splicer. This did not mean, however, that the step stool had, in fact, been used for any salacious purpose.

He could find out, of course. He could ask, directly, which was something he had quite deliberately avoided. Donna, too, let it be said, had not issued a flat denial of misbehavior. She had merely asserted, over and over again, that matters pertaining to Chuck were not in a realm that need concern Lloyd. Why not? Because they did not exist? Not necessarily. Because they did not threaten the marriage? Perhaps. Lloyd's friends at the office included many guys who believed that sexual favors received in certain personally defined circumstances did not necessarily count in the big ledger. Under this basic moral tenet, if such individuals were asked by their wives whether they had at some point been unfaithful, they could, without conflict, say no, even if they had been getting their helmets polished on a regular basis, as long as the offending action, say, took place far from home, or involved an expensive call girl one would never see again, or stopped at a rigidly defined level of engagement, or transpired while exceedingly drunk. They lived with themselves, these men, and so did their wives, and no one was any the wiser, or the least bit unhappy.

"Lloyd," said Donna after perhaps half a minute of watching Lloyd muster these ruminations. "I don't think I have to remind you that we have no electricity and the garage is right now probably filling with water and it's only a matter of minutes before our sump pump goes and our entire house floats away."

"I'm going," said Lloyd. He paused at the top of the steps. "Kids all right?"

"In what sense?" said Donna.

Descent into the Pit

Lloyd went down into the dark cellar. Lloyd's lantern cut a decent slice in the murk but did nothing to illuminate the space to his right and left. The possibility that he would screw things up in some very basic way flashed through his mind, and he banished the thought. Did Chuck feel negativity when he was about to change the berl on a flange connector?

Lloyd boiled with rage. Why was this happening to him? Very vaguely, he recognized that it wasn't, in fact, happening to him personally, but to the entire tristate region, or at least their county. Darkness. Water. Electricity. Who ever thought he would be called upon to jump-start a battery again? He had people to do that. Sometimes it came down to personal responsibility, to the point where you have to take a situation into your hands and resolve it yourself. That's the difference between management and work. Lloyd hated work. That's why he made such a good manager.

Lloyd opened the door between the mudroom and the garage. He hooked the lantern onto a metal clasp that hung on a piece of beaverboard attached to the wall. When Lloyd was a child, he had loved the entire concept of beaverboard. Thin pressed-wood paneling pierced with regular holes. Beaverboard. Maybe it was the name. Why was it called beaverboard? Did beavers make it? Did beavers use it? Did beavers know there was a special board designed with them in mind? Lloyd shook himself. Would Chuck be woolgathering? Never! He snapped to and got busy.

He went over to the pit in which the sump pump was gurgling along. There was no question that it was dying. The water had reached to the top of the pit. Also, the battery that was now supplying its sole source of power was making a high-pitched whining noise that was clearly meant to be some sort of alarm. Amazing testament to the force of the storm, that Lloyd had so far not noticed this piercing bleat. He moved a small switch on the housing of the battery and the noise ceased.

He was standing in about four inches of water now. He thought that battery-powered electricity could not course through his body and leave him a french fry. But there had been times in his life when he had felt more secure. The idea of calling Chuck and asking him to come over and do this popped into his mind, but he seized it forcefully and tore it to shreds.

Lloyd's teeth were starting to chatter. It was extremely cold in the garage, and the freezing water around his feet didn't help. He popped the trunk of both cars and looked in. No cables. He leaned into the trunk of their Camry, hung his head, and wept. He pounded the small spare tire for a few minutes, screaming obscenities over the din of the typhoon. Then he stood and pulled himself together. They had cables. He knew it. And as soon as his mind settled on that concept, he noticed that in the back of the garage, on two great hooks that hung from the wall, there was a bright new set of battery cables. Why had they bought them and hung them on the wall? Was there any purpose to having them on the wall of the garage, when he or Donna might be out on the road somewhere with a dead battery? He was glad to see them anyhow. When this was over, he would pick up a few more and stock his vehicles with battery cables. There would be no place that he could look from this time forth when a pair of battery cables would not immediately proclaim itself to the naked eye.

He unraveled the cables and attached one end to the heavy-duty Energizer battery that sat on a cinder block right next to the sump pump. A rush of pride swept over his bosom. He went to the car and popped the hood. So far so good. He went around and regarded his battery. It was a good battery. Nice battery. In an act of what felt like incredible daring, he swept over to the ends of the cables, seized them in his hands, and plunged them into the guts of his car. Sparks flew.

"Aiee!" screamed Lloyd. But he did not die.

He took a breath. All was silent. The cables were in place. Lloyd felt in his pocket. His keys were there. A miracle. He carefully climbed into the driver's seat, put the key in the ignition, and, with a prayer on his lips, turned it.

Vroom! went Lloyd's car. Immediately, the green light on the sump pump's battery housing flashed bright green. Triumph! The pride Lloyd had felt before had been nothing, a mere hiccup. This emotion that now engulfed him was something else, which might be accurately described as humility in the face of his own greatness.

Lloyd went to the back of the garage and, with a massive heave, lifted the electric garage door off the floor and up. This was no easy feat. The door was heavy. Even Lloyd knew that one did not run a car in a closed garage. Not by accident, at any rate. The reservoir in their driveway was now released to fill the available space, which it did, spreading out comfortably into the garage like a fat man on a big couch. The water gurgled and moved on in. Lloyd was surprised to see that he was not immediately overwhelmed like the Egyptians by the angry Red Sea. The tide simply rose about his legs to about the level of his calves—to the center of his car's hubcaps. Still not high enough to flood their basement. This was good news. Things were looking up! The rushing sound continued, however, almost as if their home had been constructed not on land but on a bridge over a great big river.

Lloyd was tired. He climbed into the cab of his Camry and sat there. He had done it. With the storm drains working again and the pump doing its job, there was little chance that the wet garage would turn out to be anything more than an inconvenience. The lights might even come on before morning. Why not think positively? Positive thinking got results.

Lloyd turned on the car radio. He had eleven speakers with excellent bass response, and bass was what rock and roll was all about. Whatever vestigial remnants remained of Lloyd's former coolness resided in this car stereo. Right now, he had Warren Zevon on. He turned it up. "I'll sleep when I'm dead," said Zevon. Who could argue with that?

Lloyd closed his eyes and floated in the music. He thought things over. Love and marriage. Love or marriage. Choose. If you snooze, you lose. Women. So many women. Some essential quality in all women that is wonderful. Love women. Possible to love all women in the body and soul of one woman? Yes, yes. And then more than one woman? Want her, definitely . . . but which? And if not one, why not . . . all? Lloyd closed his eyes and smelled Mona—the profound mix of cigarettes and a clean soap thing, and underneath, an inextinguishable undertow of flesh. So much red, too: red lips, red cheeks, red nipples, and, of course, the red hair. Impossibly red. How could he possibly never see that totemic body ever again? Ridiculous. And the other . . . his true beloved. Impenetrable woman. Totally known, completely unknown forevermore. Like he, a prisoner of marriage, but good company, too. Sex with one woman, over and over again, and in some profound way, always good, and different, and eminently conceivable. Lucky man. Fuck it up, why don't you. And then there were the others. Why stop at two? Beautiful, extraordinarily interesting women were everywhere around at this stage of Western civilization. If there was one thing in which this civilization was accomplished, it was in the production of exemplary women. Fit, with gleaming hair and sophisticated makeup, dressed to impress in a wide variety of relatively informal duds. Women dressed up were engaging, of course, but women in unexpected states of relatively revealing informality . . . inescapable. Kris, down the hall, with pitch-black otter-sleek hair, very depressed, very serious. What would that be like? Eleanor, Darling's assistant, here only five years after having left the former Yugoslavia, six feet tall, very big all over, but not one bit fat. One time, Lloyd had seen her devour the best part of an eight-inch fruit and custard tart at a breakfast meeting. It had been part of her job to supply the gathering, which was at 9:00 A.M., and the tart was a relatively strange choice, bagels being the appropriate one. Lloyd had watched her slice a generous slab of the pastry and, with great delicacy, devour it, then repeat the process two more times. The first piece interested Lloyd. The second grabbed his complete attention. On the third piece, he found himself aroused by this frank expression of unashamed appetite. In this age, when women were consigned to eat mostly greens and monkfish! Here was a woman who would be very soft to the touch. And he would never know her. And how many others would never be part of his life? Starting way back. Girls in camp he could have had but hadn't. Girls at college? At one of his jobs or another? How many had he wisely disregarded? How many foolishly cast aside for some imaginary cause or a couple of good ones?

How many had he loved, really and truly? Ten? Four? One?

So warm and comfy, this car was. Slosh, slosh. He was in a boat on the water. He saw it from a great distance, and then he was in it. It was a blue boat, with tough synthetic carpeting. Could he have a beer? The cooler was empty. Awful thirsty. A little nauseous, too. But warm, absolutely, all roasty and toasty. Hunker down. Settle . . . in.

At the center of it all, there was a great silence. That was why it was so important to build a moat around the silence, and fill it with noise, and live on just the other side of it. Yep, he thought. Quiet down there. Nice place to live.

Down below, there was a small figure, gesticulating. "You!" she hollered. Yep. A woman all right. Naturally, he would have to stop. "Hey!" she yelled. What did she want? Suddenly, his craft, which was, after all, just himself, was seized by a terrible trembling, as if a cosmic force had wrapped him in an ectoplasmic Baggie, tied it tight, and swung it about its gigantic head. "Ach," said Lloyd. He didn't seem to be able to react.

"What the fuck are you doing?" said the ectoplasmic bag, which seemed somewhat out of character for a force of nature. "Lloyd! Wake up!" it fairly screeched. Then the vague presence began to haul at him as if he were a sack of laundry, sort of pounding on him and howling. "Lloyd!" And "Oh, man. Oh, man." Lloyd became aware, someplace in the mud flats at the edge of consciousness, that his entire body was being transported now and that he was no longer in an airborne boat at all, but, in fact, had tumbled over the side and hurtled right into the water.

Lloyd began to swim. He was a pretty good swimmer, although he had never learned to dive. This had prevented him from getting his junior life-saver's card, but so what? Lots of people hadn't. He could swim like a bastard, though. That's what he should do now. "Oh God!" said the force that was pulling him out into the open air. Wow! How sweet it was! Where had he been before? Underwater! That was it! He was drowning! He didn't want to die. More than anything, he didn't want to die. He would live! "Breathe, Lloyd!"

It was Donna screaming. Lloyd opened his eyes.

He was lying in the driveway, faceup, staring into the rain. The image of himself swimming in the gushing driveway imprinted itself on his mind as if illuminated by a strobe. Yes, he had been swimming in his own driveway. A huge bolt of nausea coursed through him. He rolled over on his stomach, raised himself to his knees, and puked up a small mouthful of bile.

"Lloyd!" said Donna. She threw her arms around his shaking back and firmly planted her cheek on his. "Oh thank God, Lloyd!" She was laughing and crying at the same time. What a night it had been for Donna. Poor Donna.

Lloyd remained on his knees, his hair in his face, panting and wheezing.

"What'd I do?" he said at last. "Kill myself?"

"The door was open!" said Donna. "But you were sleeping and very, very pale and you weren't breathing, Lloyd. You weren't breathing! I don't want to live without you, Lloyd!" Donna pressed into Lloyd's body. Lloyd felt her warm self beside him.

"You don't have to, Donna," he said. "I'm not going anywhere."

"Lloyd!" she cried. He didn't mind. She loved him. His wife loved him after all. "It was a water-main break! There's no water pressure at all now. Nothing coming out of the taps at all!"

"That's okay," said Lloyd. He was having some trouble breathing. His chest hurt. "I've had enough water tonight to last me for a lifetime."

They both cracked up and sat together in the driveway. He drew her close to him, and the rushing water at the bottom of the driveway eddied and swirled around them. The dark house rose above them. Somewhere, a dog barked. Steve, with relief at having something productive to do, replied.

It was forty-eight hours before the electricity came back on, very early Monday morning, just in time for them all to shower, dress, and meet the new day as if nothing at all had happened over the weekend. By then, Lloyd had the mother of all fevers. Every bone in his body felt brittle and overheated, but he took three aspirin, two doses of NyQuil, and a thermos of tea and honey and drove in anyway. What could he do? He had places to be, people to meet, and the illusion of indispensability to maintain to a wide variety of people, not excluding himself.

November

The strategic alliance of the corporation with the Axis forces is almost complete. Or is it? After lots of light and heat and noise, it's very quiet now. *What's going on?* is the key phrase heard throughout the core team. And it's agreed. Nobody knows. Something about the Deal, whatever it may be, has gone defunct.

Having spent months fearing and hating the stupid Deal, Lloyd finds himself bereft at the idea that it has stalled in some way. Through the intricate and cordial procedure by which he establishes contact with Doug, he reaches out for an answer, and finds that Doug has . . . gone on vacation. He is not there. No Doug. Can he be reached? He is on his farm in Baja, California. He is communing. Does Lloyd wish to interrupt whatever he, Doug, has chosen to do at this time of intense business engagement? No, Lloyd does not.

"You're supposed to be my pipeline, Lloyd," Walt says to him at least five or six times a day. He closets Lloyd into one-on-one meetings at lunchtime, long, long meetings where they both do little but obsess about various permutations in their common fate. "Work out an options page based on various assumptions," he tells Lloyd. "Post Deal, with control. Post Deal, no control. Post Deal, if No Deal. Possible alternative partners if one should fail, or two. Have them on my desk with financial backup tomorrow. I want to show them to Doug."

"Doug is in Baja, California."

"Call him."

"What exactly should I be, you know, asking him?" Lloyd says, a little too quickly. Has some . . . eagerness . . . some ugly swatch of his corrupt understructure, of his more than pristine relationship with Doug, peeped through? Maybe. Walt looks at him a very long time. "I gotta go, Walt," Lloyd says at last.

"Yeah," says Walt. "Go."

That afternoon, Lloyd calls Doug. What he finds out is very interesting. And Walt even hears about a good deal of it.

302

The Global Traveler

Off to Japan

November eleventh: Lloyd, Mona, Ron, Walt, and Doug go to Japan and find out what Doug has known all along: The Japanese will not be part of the deal.

The association collapses around the huge hardwood conference table, which seems to grow larger as the meeting progresses. The ostensible issue is control, which devolves into a discussion of the eventual name the new corporation will take and where its nominal headquarters will be. The Japanese politely request, then strongly suggest, then insist that the name be a rather inhuman amalgam of the Japanese, American, German, and Italian brands, exactly in that order. The resulting moniker would come out sounding something like Nipnokwolligieri. No one finds that acceptable, even after several branding consultants are called in (by the Japanese) to demonstrate how catchy the pronunciation of the new name would be and how well it would look on packaging and in corporate iconography.

After a time, conceding defeat, the Japanese then politely suggest a truncation of the ridiculous designation—eliminating all names but their own. This suggestion does not meet with a high level of acceptance, and it sort of poisons the environment for the subsequent issues. A similar unsatisfactory transaction takes place over the proposed logo, which, no matter how many times it is batted around the table, seems to come back flaunting a gigantic rising sun. At this point, Lloyd takes the liberty of pointing out some facts:

Lloyd's Facts

- They, the Americans, and not the Japanese, are putting up the most capital, and are, in fact, buying their competitors. In short, this is not a merger. It is an acquisition.
- They, the acquisitors, already have a company name, which is one of the most widely recognized names in the world.
- Their company logo is one of the most widely recognized company logos in the world.
- Fully 80 percent of their revenues are in nations that speak English as a first language.

• The Japanese are contributing nothing but debt and some derivative technology that could be purchased elsewhere.

After Lloyd's little speech, it's time for lunch. The Japanese serve raw shrimp and carp that has been boiled alive before their eyes, then plunged into cold tofu.

Lloyd has rice.

Walt, for his part, is not good in these sorts of meetings, which rely on a surfeit of hypocrisy until common ground is ascertained. He makes a few perfunctory statements at the beginning, each of which is far too direct and easily understood. When the general drift of the Japanese argument becomes clear, his jaw quite literally drops, slowly but perceptibly, in shock, then anger. By eleven in the morning, he has attained the red glow of pique that Lloyd knows makes it impossible for Walt to speak. By midafternoon, he is so purple, Lloyd is concerned about him. For more than four hours, he says nothing. Then the meeting breaks, with nothing at all decided.

They agree to set up several "working groups" to "resolve the key issues" (as Doug puts it cheerfully), shake hands to a ridiculous extent, bow like those little stork toys that one can set to bob their beaks into a glass of water perpetually, and part. Both sides know they will not see each other again.

Vastly disappointed, the group sits down at a small bar just down the street from their hotel in Osaka and begins to drink. In an uncharacteristic act, Doug, who normally never relinquishes his aura of calm and control, joins them. "Set 'em up, Joe," he says at one point to the geisha who is serving them, and he winks, and Lloyd, with a surprise that approaches terror, realizes that Doug is drunk. If they lose Doug's aplomb, what will they have left?

All around them at the bar are thin, intense Japanese businessmen drinking scotch and smoking one cigarette after another. The din is terrific. Each drink costs $18.50.

It is a kind meeting, almost silent. The grief is terrible. Could the structure of the deal be falling apart? Without the deal, what would they talk about? What would they do every day? What would be their dream?

After some reflection, and about sixteen ounces of scotch, several points become obvious to Lloyd:

Points That Are Obvious to Lloyd

• For the Japanese, the deal killer had nothing to do with control, or corporate nomenclature. They had to get out of the deal in a way that would, somehow, retain face.
• In actuality, they did not join because, not to be impolite but merely accurate, the entire Japan, Inc. metastructure is yesterday's history; as a nation, they are too deep in debt to maneuver, overextended in an ocean of busi-

nesses they know nothing about, their stock market and real estate portfolios wobbling toward the end of the century.

- They have no money, per se, as in cash, having expended it during the last
decade or so on global domination that never materialized.
- In this deal, they were hoping to cow everyone into servility and then
leverage what they now owe into another asset that could throw off operating cash flow to keep their debt afloat for the next five years.

Ugh. Gross, thinks Lloyd. Who wants to be someone else's cash flow?
Certainly not Doug. Once again, he feels a wave of respect and fear course
through him at this new insight in the mind of his chief operating officer.
Doug's brilliance was to know all these points without speaking them, to
allow the Japanese to exit the deal on their own terms, waving their own
rationalizations. In this way, they could come to the table in the future, either
as partners or customers, and not feel they had unfinished business to negotiate, or a revenge agenda to pursue.

When they can drink and eat no more, the group departs for their rooms
to pack for the corporate jet home.

At 3:00 A.M., Lloyd's phone rings. Disoriented, he wakes up, to find Mona
beside him, sleeping peacefully. Where is he? Where is Donna? What time is it?
Is his wife in the next room? Is he going to be caught? How did he and Mona
get to sleep together? They never get to sleep together. They always have to settle for a quick pop. Not that that is bad. It is good. But isn't he supposed to be
stopping that? Isn't that the best for everybody? Is this the new leaf he is turning over? Where are they? Has anyone seen them? The walls are thin. They
aren't really walls at all. Has anyone heard them? Has he done it again? Told
her he loved her? Promised something outrageous? He racks his brain. Nothing.

The phone is ringing. Ringing and ringing. Actually, it isn't ringing, really.
It is buzzing, kind of. Purring. A strange noise that speaks immediately of the
fact that he is not at home, where phones ring in ways you can identify. This?
This could be an egg timer, a clock alarm, a pacemaker malfunctioning in the
middle of his chest.

At last, Lloyd realizes where he is, and why it is Mona sleeping beside
him, her bosom rising and falling with the rhythm of drunken slumber, and
not his wife. Is this what he wants forever? Maybe! Maybe . . . not!

"The rest of the gang are going back tomorrow morning. Today, I mean,"
says Doug. His voice sounds thick, strange. Lloyd hears a movie on in the
background of Doug's room. It sounds like . . . Jean-Claude Van Damme
talking. That Aznavour/Chevalier sound. So Gallic. *Boom,* he hears in the
background. "I'm not going back?" Lloyd asks Doug.

"We're not," says Doug. "Just fail to make the plane, Lloyd. You can
do that."

"Where are we going?"

"We're going to Beijing, Lloyd," says Doug. "Good night."

The line goes dead.

Beijing! Lloyd has always wanted to go to China!

He watches Mona sleep for a good long while, thinking about anything that enters his brain. Just before dawn, he climbs on top of her and holds her very, very close. She does not say no.

The China Card

Lloyd goes. He never sees much of China, but will come away with a new partner.

In this acquisition, and its meaning for the corporation down the road, Lloyd has an opportunity to see the miraculous compatibility between corporate capitalism and the brand-new breed of socialism sweeping the world.

Here are his conclusions:

Things That Corporate Capitalism and Chinese Communism Have in Common

Thomas and Lenin

1. Totalitarian in structure and tone.
2. Unapologetically hierarchical.
3. Individual must sacrifice for good of collective, except when individual is of superior rank.
4. Entrepreneurialism is encouraged, except when it threatens status quo.
5. Intellectual property belongs to the people (i.e., the state or the corporation).
6. Minimal concern for human rights; resistance is punished with draconian speed and efficiency.
7. Ruling class is, for the most part, very old.
8. Ruling class eats very well and is quite sophisticated in its habits and tastes.

9. Those closest to the means of production have least power/money.
10. Bad Human Resources departments enforce inhuman policies with Orwellian command of seductive rationale. Both systems deeply loathe trade unionism.

In this merger of two centralized nation-states, Lloyd is struck by how mysterious and beautiful the union between East and West in the new millennium will certainly be. Although, of course, the marriage will take some getting used to on all sides, with the greatest difficulties being felt by those not in possession of a calling card and limousine.

Lloyd, as he did in Japan, has problems with the food in China, if it can indeed be said to be, in fact, food. At the state dinner that takes place on the evening of their arrival, Lloyd is presented with a variety of dishes set out on a large lazy Susan in the middle of the table. The problem isn't the choice, per se, it's the fact that Lloyd has no idea what each dish is supposed to be. There is something that looks like the hoof of a farm animal, and a tiny bird that tastes very gamy, not to mention chewy. Lloyd can only imagine what it is. There are small chunks of very tender but stringy meat that Lloyd desperately hopes is not dog, and some gelatinous cubes that defy classification. The requirement at this gathering is for the Americans to eat something of everything without complaint, and to keep conversation going while doing so. Not for the first time, Lloyd thinks about George Bush, the former President of the United States, who hurled quite dramatically on a fellow dignitary at an important state dinner on his trip to the Orient, if one may be permitted to use that term these days without prejudice. What an occasion for merriment that incident had been! Lloyd now understands what had happened to the President, who had probably, while exhausted and stressed out, been required to put a disgusting, terroristic object in his mouth, one designed to make him as uncomfortable as possible. His mind did not complain, but his body had refused to do the job and had expelled the hated, writhing pellet.

But still, Lloyd eats what is expected.

The Chinese have much to get used to, as well. Toward the very end of the evening, their host, who appears to be a very high party potentate, embarks on a long commentary concerning American television, which he feels is licentious and destructive and affords certain individuals unwarranted access to the minds of the impressionable, as he puts it. As he warms to the issue, he slips from Chinese, in which he has been conversing all evening with the help of an excellent translator, into English, which he speaks quite well. He is slightly younger than many of the dignitaries who have been presented to Lloyd, many of whom appear to be Galápagos tortoises dressed in comfy pajamas.

"Your Mr. Bob Costas said many insulting things about this government for which he was never punished or even adequately reprimanded," says the nabob, his voice rising in pique. The incident that he is referring to took place several years in the past, when NBC sports commentator Costas had used his position at the Olympic desk to chide the Chinese for their record on human rights.

"We live in a different society than you do, Mr. Liu," says Lloyd, who is uncomfortable having the Chinese executive's face so close to his. The man smells of cigarette smoke and wine. For his part, Lloyd has been drinking heavily and puffing on a big meaty stogie for the last half hour or so, and he can't possibly be making a good impression at this distance. "Our citizens basically get to say whatever they want to say, and that goes for people on television as well, for the most part. That's particularly true of guys like Mr. Costas, who are paid to tell people what they think. They work off the tops of their heads and are, in fact, more valuable because their views are coherent in that context. We may or may not agree with his position on human rights. . . ."

"Oh, I'm sure we're all a lot closer in the room than we dare hope," says Doug equably.

"But we can't prevent him from speaking without changing our basic rules of conduct. In other words, whether we like what people on television say or not, there's really nothing we can do about it. We have no mechanism to make him censor his own views, or punish him for them, least of all guys like him. I mean, he's a star, for God's sake."

Lloyd can see this last observation does not sit well, for the official's face fills with blood and his neck swells up ominously. "If he is a star," the man screams, "he should be pulled down from the heavens!"

That is the end of this discussion, since there doesn't seem to be any point in pursuing it.

The potential international incident does nothing to derail the new partnership, which gives Doug several great things he wanted and couldn't get from the Japanese:

- Cash with no debt attached to it
- Access to Hong Kong as a very lucrative captive market
- A partner who doesn't claim to know everything about capitalism
- A partner who doesn't demand control of the name and logo
- A huge aftermarket for defunct products and second-generation technology

- Possible location for extremely low-cost production facilities (and no unions)
- Good public-relations pop for globally obsessed financial media and generally anti-Japanese consumer media, and for the public as well, all of whom are more cordial to incursions of American capital into formerly Communist territories than they are to successful aggression by legitimate, obnoxious global competitors.

On the Way Home

As he sits in the 1948 Mercedes-Benz that takes them to the airstrip and their corporate plane ride home, Lloyd is worried about the twelve or so hours that lie ahead. Certainly, the conveyance itself is comfortable enough—a taut little Gulf Stream that shoots itself out of a cannon on takeoff and never looks back—and they are exhausted. It's doubtful that Doug will want to make the ride a hard one. A little downtime is what they need.

But what if Doug wants to talk about manly things? That will be even worse. What will he tell Doug about Mona? That he has asked the woman to marry him? That since then nothing has been said about the subject but that something deep and sad has sprung up in the ground between them, a tropical bloom of great fragility and beauty that sprouts from a plant but once a year, and then only briefly?

Will Doug be sympathetic? Of course. And that will be the most revolting development of all—using his life to generate business points with the big boy. Yech.

But when they finally get on board, things are exactly as Lloyd has wished. A huge brown drink is placed in front of them both. Doug says, "That went well," loosens his tie a tad, leans back on the miniature couch that serves as a recliner, closes his eyes, and sleeps for more than eight hours, uninterrupted. Lloyd drifts in and out and has a good chance to think about things. He is aware of a very deep feeling of missing something. He is homesick. But homesick for what?

He remembers the feeling from his first years at summer camp, when he cried himself to sleep each night and was never sure if he would wake up in a pool of his own pee.

But which home is it that Lloyd is missing now? Is it Mona? Donna?

It is Steve. When Lloyd closes his eyes, it is not the red hair of his lover, which had, just a night or two ago, hung down into his face as she loomed above him in that Osaka hotel room. It is not the blond aura of his wife, either, the smell of meat loaf cooking, the pitch of her bottom as she bends over to feed the fish. It is not Nora, nor Bob, burbling at the dinner table with optimism and humor and hunger for whatever is put on the table. He sees each of them in his mind as he closes his eyes, and, yes, a shaft of sharp regret smites him in the center of his chest. But he can tolerate it. He will see them soon. He has presents for them in his baggage, stuff they will love. The thought of giving them their presents eases the tang of the homesickness for a moment, but not for long.

No, when he closes out all extraneous input, the image that comes immediately to mind is that of Steve, his cocker spaniel, the most recent in a long line of beloved dogs, Steve, who watches television like one of the children, waiting for a dog to pop up that he can bark at, Steve, who eats chewing gum off the street, munching on the filthy wad for hours, never relinquishing it no matter how aggressively his mouth is probed for it, Steve, not the smartest dog Lloyd had ever owned, although definitely not the stupidest.

What is Steve doing in his imagination? Just sitting there, being a dog. Waiting for an excuse to do something—drool, wag, steal an English muffin. More than anything, Lloyd wants to go home. For the first time in a while, Lloyd knows where home is, even if it is for the stupidest of reasons he could ever possibly have imagined. Home is where his dog is.

Somewhere over Alaska, Lloyd begins to cry, and Doug, who has been awake for several minutes, has the good taste to keep his eyes firmly shut. Which, of course, does not prevent him from seeing everything, as is both his nature and his function.

When it seems safe to do so, Doug opens his eyes, ascertains that Lloyd is awake, and raises some salient issues they need to touch upon before they set down at Teeterboro Airport in New Jersey several hours hence.

A Précis of Lloyd's and Doug's Business Conversation on the Plane

- The consultants will be delivering their report upon everyone's return to New York, sometime after December first.
- Immediately after their findings are filed, a new organizing structure will be put into place, incorporating existing management as well as new blood from the parties that will be acquired in the deal.
- Lloyd will have a central position in a new centralized management function that will have control over all operations worldwide, and will include several division presidents and key organizational staff. In exchange for this position of importance, Lloyd will be expected to remain loyal and faithful to Doug, who is now his Lord and rabbi, although certainly a nondenominational one.
- Walt's position is unclear, but he can probably stick around for as long as he likes before being transitioned in a completely appropriate way. Lloyd

thinks about that one for a good long time while pretending to work over a memo. He decides to say nothing. There will certainly be a time for him to say something. Until then, it might be smart simply to watch and wait, which is what Lloyd decides to do right now. He implements this plan immediately.

- A large number of senior middle managers will have to be neutralized and heaved elsewhere by the end of the year so that the company can avail itself of restructuring money available during the calendar year but not after. Those who remain into the New Year will also have to be paid different severance and will enjoy a continuation of benefits for another full twelve-month period. This is clearly not in the best interest of the company, so the need to move swiftly on the list of forced retirees is clear.
- Doug will give Lloyd the list and Lloyd will act on it.
- It is better to fly slightly drunk than totally sober.
- Lloyd can certainly take a long weekend to relax before the shit hits the fan.

Lloyd sits next to Doug and lets the full import of this nightmare scenario sink in. He imagines himself anywhere, anywhere but here. . . .

> *. . . The sand is pink. There are grand buildings. The rooms are small, the food mediocre. The crowds are devastating. It is a place that he not only chooses but chooses over all others, gladly, greedily, without hesitation or shame. And so, now that all the partnership agreements are complete and he is about to be instrumental in the destruction of a fair number of his closest professional associates. Where are ya goin'? The answer comes back, loud and clear:*

We're Going to Disney World!

So, on the day after Thanksgiving, Lloyd wrests himself away from the monstrous chores that lie ahead and takes his family to Disney World in Orlando, Florida, a monument to everything excessively American, built over a hot and muggy bog.

In the end, they all have a very good time at Disney World, except perhaps for Lloyd, who never fully relaxes. This is in large part because he never unplugs, which is one of the big mistakes of all executives and self-important people constantly in pursuit of the myth of their own indispensability. Lloyd is the nitwit with the cellular phone in one hand and the FedEx envelope in the other, standing in the middle of Main Street while the rest of the world passes by on its way to Space Mountain.

On the other hand, Lloyd feels neither here nor there. He and Donna seem to slide along on parallel planes, neither fighting nor connecting very well. He misses Steve, and Mona, too, although not necessarily in that order.

At the Japanese pavilion at Epcot, Lloyd and the gang have one heck of a great meal. Lloyd has to smile at the discrepancy between what he is eating here in Florida and what was forced upon him while over in Osaka.

They have shrimp, too, just as Lloyd had eaten in Japan, but here it is cooked and served with a tangy cocktail sauce instead of being alive, cold and writhing in whatever passes for pain in a brainless crustacean as it is ripped, living, from its comfortable shell.

Yet although they do not seem to relate to each other in any but the most superficial, connubial ways, the five days in Orlando have a strange effect on both Donna and Lloyd. Donna grows ever more silent. Lloyd, for his part, begins to feel an intense sadness, a great perception of something irretrievable.

While attempting to enjoy the cool birds on Discovery Island, Lloyd receives a phone call from the emperor of Japan, who is begging to be let back in on the deal. Lloyd says no, but his composure is shot for the rest of the day. Lloyd realizes he would probably feel better if he were back at his desk, attending to things, rather than here, trying to pretend he is capable of having a good time while not in pursuit of some metaobjective.

On the last day of his relaxing time away, the line for It's a Small, Small World, Lloyd's cellular phone rings. A twelve-page fax from senior management awaits him at the courtesy desk just outside the ice cream stand on Main Street. Seating himself outside of The Pirates of the Caribbean, Lloyd gets with the program, and the program isn't pretty. By the time they return home, it is done.

All but the execution.

December

A new corporation is being born! Doug, as always, sums it up best. "There will be winners and losers in the new operating environment," he says. And nobody doubts him, which is good, because he really means it.

Lloyd takes out every living thing within a hundred miles, completing the internal aspects of the Deal in the name of Doug and all that is Doug's from Chicago to Berlin to Rome and then home by way of Beijing. Lloyd's building, which had once housed hundreds of souls, is down to about a hundred and twenty, a lean team of super-executives manning skeleton crews of scared, vacant support staff and the odd director-level wage slave.

Lloyd is aware of the incremental weight of the pressure growing on him. He feels the corners of his mouth instinctively turning downward, leaving him with a perpetual scowl. He feels slightly nauseated all the time. He hates his hair.

And there is so much yet to do. In advance of the coming deal, Lloyd continues to implement the corporate transformation to the new, more elegant paradigm, laying waste to the countryside right and left, downsizing, reorganizing, building profit margins, spending tons of corporate money on his gluttonous, hedonistic, increasingly haute bourgeois life. Can't be helped. Must be done. Achieve productivity. Rebuild competitiveness. Play golf. Eat outrageously. Drink!

Stock Price as a Function of Corporate Disemployment

☐ Employees at Headquarters

■ Stock Price

Other Considerations

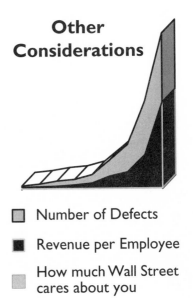

☐ Number of Defects

■ Revenue per Employee

▨ How much Wall Street cares about you

Confidentially . . . You Stink

Like many business executives, Lloyd found the high concept of cutbacks to achieve operating efficiencies quite palatable. At the same time, the prospect of actually firing an individual himself filled him with a level of fear and disgust usually associated with the concept that a public surface on which one was about to sit was teeming with microbes.

For most, the personal aspects of firing somebody, especially someone with whom one has been friendly, were extremely taxing, to say the least. The most bizarre tales about such incidents circulated throughout the company, never verified but always taken as fact, and they could well be believed. Lloyd believed them. There were stories about guys who fully intended to truncate another man's career, then ended up promoting him. Senior officers, slated for extinction, who instead went on for years and years without portfolio simply because there was no one with guts enough to heave their victim out the window and onto the beach.

These days, Lloyd sympathized with those who had to fire people, not the fired people themselves, unless of course those who lost their posts were owed hefty severance that was, for some reason, denied. That scared and enraged him more than anything else. Beyond that, he had other things to think about.

Just not this month. As Doug's key agent (read buttboy), it was Lloyd's duty to explore operating implications with those targeted for review. Lloyd woke up every morning with a ball of suet in his stomach that never dissipated until very late in the evening, dissolved by guilt, exhaustion, and vodka. But he did what he was told. That was business, nothing personal. Then why did it feel so personal?

It had not been easy. Nofziger, a large beefy fellow with vast expertise in federal regulatory policy, wept, his head hanging between his knees, occasionally raising his big fleshy face to stare with open incredulity at Lloyd. After that session, Lloyd had gone out to lunch by himself and had two martinis in quick succession. This had made him feel better for about an hour, after which he had fallen into an ill-tempered funk that made him yell at several innocent clerks who had done nothing more than wander into his vicinity. Several days later, Lloyd had been required to terminate, essentially without cause, Brassard, a Frenchman in charge of international development, who was no longer of high priority and who listened with mounting horror, then shook his tiny fist and threatened, then fell silent and refused to move. Lloyd had had to call his secretary, Ms. Wozniak, a formidable Eastern European washerwoman type, who retrieved him and led him back up to the office that would soon be scheduled for repapering. Just as bad were the scenes with Darling and Burgess and Sweet and the rest of ultrasenior management, who themselves were safe but had to be told the eventual staff levels of their departments. All left shaking their heads, pale but too frightened to demur. The substance on the wall was no longer handwriting. It was blood. Lloyd told himself that in accomplishing his assigned function, he was, in effect, saving the New York office from complete extinction. This made him feel better.

There were two that Lloyd saved for last. There was Ron, naturally. That would be bad. And then there was Walt. The assignment in regard to Walt was odd and complex, not involving any determinate fate, per se, but delivering quite a heavy blow in its own right. Lloyd didn't quite understand it himself, and he wasn't sure it should be his job to convey it anyhow.

He would leave it for later. Ron could come first.

There were several excellent reasons, Lloyd reflected, for firing the massive nexus of greed, silk, tweed, malice, and pretension known to the world as Ronald Lemur. So, on that first Thursday in December, with a sky above as flat and gray as wet slate and tiny gobbets of snow and sleet spitting down, Lloyd thought these rationales over as he geared himself up to the proper level of intention necessary to get the job done right.

Once upon a time, way back in January, when the world was a more innocent place, Ron had been content to suck up, to advise, to tag along in hopes of acquiring glory by osmosis. He had been a knowable quantity, and not without talent, if never brilliance. Now, things were different. There were some scenarios under which Ron, if left unwatched in a friable environment, could ascend to something approaching power, particularly in the kind of moral and functional vacuum that exists after any substantial merger. Ron was somewhat insane, and he looked good in a suit. He would get along quite well with the Japanese, German, and Italian types who would soon be tiptoeing around. Yes, Doug was on Lloyd's side. But what was that worth? They had all seen just how much loyalty and emotion meant to Doug. Finally, there was the knowledge that, in the long term, Ron and he could never coexist in the same universe. As someone born in the seventies, Ron was part of a generation that hated its boomer elders and longed to unseat and, if possible, disgrace them. Several times in his career, Lloyd had been smoothly betrayed by twentysomethings in whom he had invested trust and affection. He didn't mean to be on the wrong end of such a transaction again. Lloyd knew that Ron had taken to passing clever, sardonic remarks about him to people he thought would appreciate them. One of them had not, and had conveyed it, as a courtier would carry a jewel on a gigantic cushion to his master, to Lloyd.

Lloyd had taken the guy, whose name was Bergelind, into his office and had done him the extreme courtesy of sitting on the far side of his desk while he received the information. He had then spent several extended minutes of quality time with Bergelind, and he'd put his arm around the guy as he ushered him out. Bergelind was fairly glowing. Lloyd noticed he had the power to do that to people now—to confer extreme pleasure or distress with the most minimal of gestures. What he did mattered. That made him feel good.

It was Bergelind's tale that had at last convinced Lloyd that he had nothing to be ashamed of, or sorry for, by executing Ron, and that in point of fact, that job would be done well if done quickly.

The following morning, Lloyd called Ron into his office, shut the door, asked Ron if he was comfortable, then informed his business friend and associate that his next assignment would be to open the company's new one-man office in Beijing. He would be stationed there for the indeterminate future. This was the ploy, worked out with Doug, who found it very amusing, that Lloyd had cooked up to ease Ron to the right conclusions. By any measure, it was a bad break for Ron, although the money was very good, because the Chinese, at least those on the interface between totalitarian government and mercantile capitalism, were not pleasant business partners, prone, as Lloyd had recently seen, to displays of righteous temper, and to retreating to their home base with your ideas in hand and no intention of paying for them. The Chinese had a thing about copyright. They didn't recognize it. It made them pretty tough to deal with. Still, they did make excellent partners in one respect, because there were so many of them. Crack that market? Make history. Pursuit of this grail led to the famous school of business thought that had destroyed more than one entrepreneur—that if you sold only one shoe to every person in China, you could make about $6 billion. The only trouble was that very few Chinese were willing to buy one shoe. Lloyd was pointing out these and other interesting facts about life in China as Ron gazed at him with slightly parted lips. He was breathing heavily.

Ron was scrambling around inside himself, searching for any recognizable impulse or coherent thought to guide him as to what to do next. He noticed Lloyd's tie, which was slightly askew, and considered informing Lloyd about it. He decided against it. The hell with Lloyd. Let him go to his next meeting looking like that! Ha! Ron watched Lloyd's lips move. Blah blah blah, he thought. What a bozo. Fucking boomers. So pleased with themselves, with their putative hipness, their power. One day they'd be dead and guys like him would be running the joint. Only not this joint, obviously. Smug motherfucker. Wipe that satisfied plump grin off those liver lips. Yeah. Okay. Now there was something he could grasp onto, nurture as a familiar friend in these transitional times. Hate. He let it glow, and felt the burn.

What would Kurt Cobain have done in this situation? Ron thought. "Oh I don't have a gun," sang Kurt. But he had lied. Kurt would have been about his age, had he not blown his own head off. Ron thought a lot about Kurt Cobain. But not now. There would be plenty of time for that later. Now he should attempt to focus and do a good spot-situation analysis for preliminary review.

Obviously, this posting, involving a long trip to a place where people eat all of their fish, including the head and egg sack, was strictly unthinkable. This was basically a job for somebody they wanted outside the corporation. That message was clear. But were they firing him? Was that what they were telling him here?

"What if I choose not to go to fucking China?" said Ron.

"We've worked out a package that we think is generous, given your age, your position, and your length of service," said Lloyd with a suspicious lack of warmth and empathy.

Lloyd's coldness was a screen for the roiling stew pot of emotions bubbling away inside him. Of course, on one level, he was sorry to fire Ron, even though Ron was a pusillanimous worm, but, as far as he could see, his job was to do it anyhow. Because he had to, you know. For those who are interested, here was Lloyd's rationalization framework, which he leaned on while dealing with Ron:

> There's nothing I can do about it anyhow because Ron's a jerk and it was bound to happen to him eventually. When you get right down to it, that's the way the cookie crumbles. A guy has to be able to do this now and then. Those who can't don't get to play at the big table. Besides, if I don't do it, Doug's going to. That's gonna reflect poorly on me as a manager—people will think I find something shameful about it, and that will make them doubt themselves, and resent me. He'll be better off in a new place anyway, where people appreciate him. Not firing him would be unfair to him, really. Besides, I hate the little fuck.

"So, Ron," said Lloyd after a few moments in which the object of his scrutiny did little but huff vaguely in his chair like a little engine idling at the station, "I don't want to be a dick about it, but you're going to have to make a decision on this thing pretty much on the spot, man. I'm sorry, but that's the way it's gotta be."

"But you will anyway," said Ron.

"I will . . . what?"

"Be a dick about it." Ron was glaring at a point across the room just past Lloyd's elbow. "To the best of your ability," he added.

"Look, Ron," said Lloyd, "there's no particular reason we need to be strictly adversarial on this. You've got a bunch of options here and I'd like to help you choose among them. Each of them have their good points."

"Its," said Ron. "Its good points."

"That's what I mean," declared Lloyd. "You're a smart guy with a tremendous command of grammar, a quality not all that common in people your age." What was Lloyd talking about? Lloyd looked down at his hands. They were shaking slightly, and moist. Suddenly, he was alive with terror, every nerve jangling in its sheath. It began to seep through his wall of determination and self-justification that the individual opposite him in this meeting was fully engaged in reciprocating this act of destruction. He could do it, too. Ron certainly possessed knowledge that could be injurious to Lloyd.

"Don't take this too hard is what I'm trying to say, Ron," said Lloyd, placing a fatherly arm on Ron's shoulder. "You're a fantastic guy with tremendous assets, and whichever way you decide to go here, I'm sure you'll be a success. Don't let this moment define your career to date or your perception of your future."

"Don't fucking patronize me," Ron said, using a shake of his shoulder to remove Lloyd's hand. Ron's emphatic rejection of Lloyd's hand felt like an act of stark violence, breaching the veil of hypocrisy.

"I'm not taking this very well at all," Ron observed calmly. Was this an apology? A threat? Ron's face maintained its cast of belligerence. Lloyd found he trusted Ron's calm even less than he would an emotional outburst.

"No, you don't seem to be at this moment," Lloyd said. "But I have a lot of confidence in your maturity and ability to withstand a tough setback like this and come roaring out of the chute almost immediately." Lloyd stopped, aware that he felt absolutely no confidence whatsoever in this very quality in Ron. Ron had no maturity. Ron had no ability to bounce back. Ron was rigid and brittle. It was the official nature of his title, role, and uniform, conferred by the corporation, that lent him whatever outer shell of humanity he was capable of presenting.

"Well," said Ron. He rose from his chair in which he had been sinking ever deeper. He put his hands in his pockets. "I don't want to go to China. This we know. I'll leave my reasoning for you to figure out, Lloyd. I reckon even a dumb, mean fuck like yourself can figure out a no-brainer like that one."

"Sure," said Lloyd evenly.

"Of course, I'll expect you to go to bat for the kind of termination agreement that will give me ample opportunity to sit around for a while and do a complete personal ascertainment of options and strategies."

"Sure," said Lloyd. "You're entitled to four months. We'll get you a year."

"Two years!" screamed Ron.

Lloyd wondered if he could get Ron two years. He probably could. There were policies in these matters, but only when the corporation wanted to assert them. In this case, with Doug well aware of issues pertaining to Lloyd's personal security, some of which Doug had himself created by employing Ron as a spy, there was no doubt that Lloyd could pretty much write any deal he wanted on the back of a napkin and make it stick. But did he want to?

"We'll see," he said at last. This seemed to assuage Ron, who was now ambling laconically around Lloyd's enclosure, touching Lloyd's knickknacks, picking them up and putting them down, paging thoughtfully through some of the confidential papers in Lloyd's pile and otherwise insinuating himself on Lloyd's private domain with a creepy, confrontational air of insouciance. Lloyd allowed him to do so. He hoped that Ron would now depart and free them both.

"No," said Ron at last. "No, I'm not feeling well, not well at all. I don't feel . . . closure. I . . . didn't see this coming. That's my fault. But this, you know, wasn't part of my scenario at all." He ceased his intrusive inventory as abruptly as it had begun and walked to the door, opened it, and leaned in the doorway, staring at Lloyd. There was another icky hiatus in the fabric of existence. Lloyd waited it out.

"Sorry things had to work out this way," he finally said.

"No you're not," said Ron.

"You're right," said Lloyd. "I'm not. You're a disloyal, shallow guy, Ron, and I've tried to invest emotional capital in you, but you're not worth it. The thing is, I fought for this China assignment for you. You won't believe that, but it's true. Doug and Walt simply saw you as one more body to get out of here. But I said no, let's give the guy a sentence in Siberia for a while; there are opportunities there; he can make a success out of himself and maybe grow a little, you know, turn into a human being, or at least something that can pass in our world for a human being, which is not a very high bar, as you know. But you chose to see this offering as an insult and a termination, and that's fine, Ron, that's fine. It's worth sixteen months of salary to get you out of our lives so we can move on and try, in the future, to surround ourselves with people who conform to a different paradigm of social and personal interaction. People who are fun to be with, and who could possibly, at some point in time and in some conceivable venues, be considered, in even a marginal way, friends."

"And benefits," said Ron.

"Hm?"

"Sixteen months of salary and benefits."

"Write what you want in a letter. I'll do what I can to make it happen."

Ron stood in the doorway to Lloyd's office then, but he still did not leave.

"You think you've got the whole thing worked out to your satisfaction, don't you, fat man?" he said.

"Fuck you, bozo," said Lloyd. "Your entire package hangs by a string. Don't pull it."

Ron left. That afternoon, without ceremony, he cleared out his office and disappeared without a trace. Lloyd dropped by at the empty enclosure later that day, when he heard that Ron had gone completely. The office looked much as it had before. The Knoll furniture of which Ron had been so proud stood, clean and restrained, glowing slightly in the early-winter light, which was already beginning to fade. Lloyd realized how little of Ron had been necessary to complete the office. He had been in it for more than three years and had been able to evacuate the space in less than an hour. There had been no pictures to remove, no personal objects to pile into a crate, no extensive towers of magazines, papers, or files to categorize. Ron did remove the small box of backup floppies that had contained his most private documents. The wooden rolltop cube that had contained them was gone. Also missing was the six-inch-tall glass obelisk on a black marble platter that Ron had won in recognition of his putative marketing skills. He had been proud of this *objet,* viewing the inherently meaningless bauble as proof of both current and future standing in the organizational tree. Other than that, nothing was out of place. Its master gone, the office sat calmly, a little expectantly, more than ready to accommodate without nostalgia or regret anyone who was assigned it. Lloyd stood in there for a long time, searching for a scent, a mood, anything that would give him an indication of what to feel about Ron's departure. All he could feel was relief, with a small undercurrent of something indefinable just below the surface, something dank and noxious. But he would worry about these heebie-jeebies later, if it became necessary to do so. He feared it might, for some reason. He didn't want to think about that reason. He didn't want to think at all, come to think of it.

He went back to his office and called Mona. He got her voice mail.

Bad Karma, No Sutra

This did not surprise him. Mona was nowhere she was supposed to be anymore, ever. Of course, nobody was. That was what was so strange about this whole merger environment. Just a few days before, he had asked Arlene to find Darling. The matter was trivial, which still didn't mean, however, that the need was not acute. But Darling was nowhere to be found. He called Walt, who usually knew where people were.

"Walt," he said into the phone when Bridget, Walt's person, had put him through.

"What's goin' on," said Walt.

"Darling," said Lloyd. "Can't seem to scare him up. Need him badly."

"Rangoon," said Walt.

Lloyd was relatively flabbergasted. "Really?"

"Supplier issue in the synthetic extrusion products group," said Walt, as if either of them knew what the hell he was talking about.

"We're buying that?" said Lloyd. "We're buying that somebody in Burma needs Darling in person to adjudicate some business issue in a language he doesn't understand in a place where he'll be even more offensive to people than he usually is?"

"Is that where Rangoon is?" said Walt. "I thought it was in Indonesia."

"We'd better learn this kind of stuff almost immediately, Walt," said Lloyd, and felt a tremendous rush of affection for the man. In a world monumentally replete with bullshit, Walt was a tower of authenticity. And what was his reward? Well, that was still unclear. Lloyd would have to see to things, that was all.

"It's quiet around here these days," said Walt into the silence.

"Yes," said Lloyd, adding, as he had waited the greater part of his life to do, "It's almost . . . too quiet."

"Ha," said Walt. There was another silence. "What movie is that from?" he added cordially.

"I don't know," said Lloyd. "Almost too many to mention. Lot of Westerns."

"Yeah," said Walt. "You don't see so many Westerns around anymore. The last one I saw was this terrible thing with Sharon Stone where she was the sheriff. I don't know why we rented it. It was dreadful. She's cute, though."

"Oh, no question," said Lloyd.

"Before that, I rented one that was terrific," Walt continued.

Lloyd looked at his watch. He was fifteen minutes late. He wasn't quite sure at that moment what he was fifteen minutes late *for* precisely, but a nugget of anxiety was beginning to strangle him. He coughed slightly to reposition himself.

"Which one was that, Walt?" he said.

"But you're busy," said Walt.

Had Walt, in his mind's eye, seen Lloyd look at his watch? How could that be possible?

"No, no," said Lloyd, and he meant it.

"That one with Clint Eastwood," Walt continued. "*Unforgiven.* Man, that was something."

"Yeah, I loved that," said Lloyd, and he had, too, but Walt was no longer in his listening mode. Lloyd drew over a large pile of documents and began signing things without reading them as he listened to Walt play out this string.

"It's about this guy who's hired to do a job," said Walt, "which is a violent, messy, morally equivocal job, but somebody's got to do it, so why shouldn't it be him? And then things fall apart. The authorities are worse than the criminals and Eastwood comes down on all of them, Lloyd. He's like the wrath of God, and I think what it's all about is that when the bona fide order of things gets screwed up, it comes down to individual men and, you know, women to take it upon themselves to set things right no matter what the cost to themselves."

"Yeah," said Lloyd. There was a thoughtful pause on both sides.

"Well," said Walt peremptorily. "I'd better get with things."

"I'll let you go."

"See ya," said Walt, and hung up.

It took five minutes for Lloyd to snap to after that. Then he went down to Fitz's floor. Fitz was out. Nobody knew where he was. He went back to his office and thought about the many people he could call. None of them was someone he wanted to speak with. So he simply sat in his office and allowed his spirit to sink lower and lower until it was all he could do to keep from crying. Then he went home.

A week or so later, he looked back and asked himself what had made him feel so sad. He couldn't remember.

Besides, things were a little more lively now. Darling was back. Sweet was cutting his usual high profile at business gatherings. Fitz roamed the hallways with his small Styrofoam cup full of tepid oatmeal, moping, trying to scare up a good fight. But not a gleaming, auburn hair did he see of Mona. Was she avoiding him?

He monitored the feelings inside himself: exultation, anxiety, anticipation, anger. What was he to do with all these feelings? He dialed Mona again and got voice mail. He hung up. Lloyd looked at the pictures on his credenza. The kids. So cute. So marvelous and resilient. They couldn't get along without him. They were perhaps the only entities in his entire life structure who couldn't. He thought about Donna. She could get along without him; he wasn't kidding himself about that. She could get along on a desert island, as long as it had no mice or bugs. If he left, she would grow strong on her hatred of him. If he died, she would thrive on her memory of him. She would miss him, of course. Who could not? He had his moments. But live without him she would, and well, too. For some reason, it was a thought that gave him no pleasure. He picked up the phone gingerly. It had been months since he had called his wife in the middle of the day for no reason. He had once done so without fail every morning and afternoon.

He dialed Donna and got the answering machine. He hung up.

After the flood, they had gotten along quite nicely for a time. She had been attentive, so much so that Lloyd had found himself somewhat suspicious of this tenderness. He had shaken off the feeling. So much of this life was ruined when people refused to accept the pleasure that circumstances and fate offered them, Lloyd told himself. Embrace joy, that was the ticket. And he certainly felt joy in his wife and his children. Why was he thinking about whether his wife could do without him? She didn't have to! Why should he succumb to the natural tendency of people to destroy their own happiness? It was such a cliché. Couldn't he be among the first to rebel against that convention? He would. He had decided that now, irrevocably. Yes, he could push the envelope now and then, find out what was on the other side of the moat of bourgeois life. But no tectonic changes in the arrangement of his plates was either called for or appropriate. He jumped into the pool of unknowing for a while, and had himself a nice little swim. Now it was time to leap out, towel off, and head back home.

He called his wife and got the answering machine. He hung up.

Which in itself was no reason he couldn't admit his own somewhat ambiguous feelings. Feelings never killed anybody. And his genuine feeling was, at that moment, that he missed Mona, and that was that. It was important to admit it to himself. This regeneration of the core structure of his existence would be meaningless if it was built on denial. So he would not deny it. He would play through it. That was the answer. To his own self be true. Full speed ahead in the whole truth thing.

He picked up the phone and called Mona. He got voice mail. He considered E-mailing her, but he had just read an article in *Fortune* warning busy communicators about the fragile quality of network security. E-mail messages were available to any systems operator looking in, and they were stored in a mainframe somewhere in Connecticut for years. He called Mona's number again and listened.

"Hi," said Mona's voice. "I'm out of the office right now, but please leave a detailed message and I'll get right back to you." The voice of the Meridien cyborg operator came on then, giving him a raft of information he neither wanted nor needed, stuff about press this and wait for that. Then there was a beep.

"Hi," he said into the phone. "I'm in the office right now, so please accept this detailed message and get right back to me. Please get back to me. Thank you. That is all." He hung up.

Lloyd decided to take a ride to Mona's floor. She occupied the corner office of the finance area several stories below Lloyd. She was, as Lloyd suspected, at her desk. The secretarial bay outside her compound was empty, which explained her reliance on voice mail.

"I find you at last," said Lloyd.

"Yes," said Mona. She looked nonplussed. "I'm in the middle of an attempt to justify the one-hundred-million-dollar shortfall in operating profits," she said. "I wonder if there might be a better time for us to resolve our differences, Lloyd."

323

"I wasn't aware there were any," said Lloyd. He was enraged. The woman had been here all the time. And what was she doing? Working. It was outrageous!

"Oh, come on," Mona said quietly.

Lloyd closed the door. "What do you want from me, Mona?" he said as sternly as he could. How had she come to occupy the higher ground? Well, he would take care of that quick!

"I want nothing, Lloyd. No. That's not true. I want something very specific, and easy for you to grant. I want you to leave me alone."

"No," said Lloyd. "No you don't."

"Yes I do."

"No you don't."

"Yes I do."

"No you don't."

It didn't take any particular gift or intelligence to prevail at this line of dispute. After a while, Mona simply was still, gazing with grim intensity at the forbidding spreadsheet before her. Tuning him out, eh? Well, two could play this waiting game.

Lloyd realized that he was terrorizing the woman, but he couldn't seem to back off. He longed with all his heart to climb into her chair and maul her. He did not, however. There had been a recent case of sex discrimination chronicled in the *Harvard Business Review,* one in which a senior manager of many years had attempted to mount his longtime mistress for perhaps the thousandth occasion, and, being rebuffed, had prosecuted his intent until he was knocked over the head with a Rolodex. The court had decided in that case that there was no excuse for the male to assume that prior activity was a justification of future excess. The woman was found a credible victim of sexual assault in what was the final transaction between the two, and her lover was adjudged an enemy of the people and exiled to his home, forever. Several newspapers applauded this righteous upholding of the public weal, particularly the *New York Times,* which used the incident to explore the changing standards of acceptable male behavior in the workplace. Lloyd did not wish to become an object lesson, so he kept his hands off Mona.

"Mona," he said.

"What." She continued working.

"Please look at me." His heart was an aching hole in his chest.

Mona looked up. Her eyes were opaque, calm. "I'm looking," she said. "What I see is you, Lloyd. So perhaps it would be better for you to leave."

"You hate me."

"Yes, Lloyd. I hate you. You wanted me to say it and I've accommodated your desire, once again. Now get the fuck out of here. I mean it, Lloyd. There's a heavy crystal award to the right of my telephone. I believe you have one, too, as a result of our partnership on the Smart Shopper program back in 1996. If you don't change my feelings almost immediately, or at least get out of the line of fire, you're very likely to have a second recognition of your excellence in marketing right in the middle of your prefrontal lobe."

"Mona, honey," said Lloyd.

"Five."

"No, goddamn it," said Lloyd, and he crossed Mona's office in a flash. He was amazed at his agility. He seized the marketing award just as she moved to it. His hand closed over hers and they stared at each other over the hard glass object. "No," said Lloyd. "I want you to talk to me. Then you can hit me if you like."

"I can hit you if I like right now," said Mona. She then drew her left hand, which was not involved in the tug-of-war for the bludgeon, back quite smartly and cuffed it into the side of Lloyd's head, hard.

"Wah!" said Lloyd. He immediately let go of the glass pillar and smote his own head in sheer surprise. Mona had struck him in his most vulnerable spot!

"Shut up! Shut up!" Boy. She was mad.

Mona threw the projectile to the floor and, with all her weight, shoved Lloyd with two strong arms, one to each side of his chest. Lloyd tipped backward, caught the back of his calves on the arm of Mona's reclining minibarge of a chair, and fell backward. *Sponk!* was the sound his head made on the side of the credenza that abutted Mona's desk. A blossom of sprung metal exploded behind Lloyd's eyes, and then a pincushioned blackness descended on his mind. His thoughts receded to a glowing ember but did not go out entirely. He was floating. It was light up here, and he looked down and saw the top of his head. It had a tiny bald spot in it. Not too bad, really. He was sure he could comb around it.

"Lloyd. Get up, Lloyd." It was Mona. Her voice was coming from very close. "Open your eyes, Lloyd."

"I'll be all right," said Lloyd.

"Come on, get up. You're not scaring me and I don't feel sorry for you."

"Wow," said Lloyd. He sat up and immediately felt very nauseous.

"Sorry," Mona said. She dragged herself over to her couch and threw herself onto it, facedown. "Sorry, sorry, sorry."

"That's all right," said Lloyd. He was still quite groggy. He looked at Mona's back, the curve of it moving into the lower part of her spine. . . . My, she's a fine-looking woman, thought Lloyd. He saw a tiny cornice of her earlobe poking out through the lush plume of her hair, and he wanted to take it between his teeth.

"Stop ogling me, Lloyd," said Mona from beneath her face, which was still pressed into the upholstery. "Even now, you're relentless."

"Come over and comfort me," said Lloyd. Mona sat up. Lloyd searched her expression for a sign of something subtle. None was evident.

"I can't see you anymore, Lloyd," Mona said.

She was calm, but Lloyd didn't want to probe that very much. She was wearing a pair of what looked to be very sharp pendant earrings. Lloyd had a mental impression of her removing them, clutching them in upraised fist, and driving them forcefully into the soft meat of his eyeballs. He shook it off.

"I can't see you anymore," Mona said again. "I can't really sort out the way I'm feeling about you. It's very intense. I don't like it. It's so predictable. Like, I had my hopes up in a weird kind of way, and now I feel really stupid about it, but I can get over that if you just let me alone, and we can all get back to normal real soon. 'Kay?"

"'Kay," said Lloyd. He rose with marginal dignity to his feet, careened around a bit, then headed for the general vicinity of Mona for what he hoped would be a somewhat more tender good-bye, at least for now. "The thing is," he said, "I can't help how I feel about you. I know it was wrong for me to talk about marriage and stuff, but I wasn't ashamed to do whatever I could, say whatever I could, to make you understand how much I really do love you, darling, how I think about you all the time and can't get you out of my thoughts, how you torment me awake and asleep, how I never want to come to grips with the idea that we'll never make love again. I think that'll kill me, honey. I mean it."

Mona had been listening thoughtfully to his pitch, as if considering it from a number of angles for any possible flaw. As he brought it to its rousing conclusion, however, Mona's expression shifted suddenly, her face turned beet red, her head snapped up to attention, and she seized him by the throat and shook with all her might.

"Ack!" said Lloyd.

"You . . . bastard," Mona observed darkly. Then, as the spasm passed away, she let Lloyd go, shoved him rudely away from her, and went behind her desk once again. "Go away, Lloyd."

Lloyd went. Women!

That's All, Folks

Ronald Lemur sat staring out the window of his apartment, which, unless he could think of some way to pay the maintenance and mortgage, would soon be his no longer. That was likely to affect him quite profoundly, not just for the obvious implications vis-à-vis the issue of shelter but also because he now shared this opulent space with Alix, who had fought him for months on the issue and had only recently agreed to, as she put it, "give up some of her life for a little bit of his." It wasn't the cohabitation that had been difficult for her; it was what she considered the inexorable pull of middle-class existence that would end, for her, in a renunciation of ambition and the issuance of 2.3 offspring, a golden retriever, and a Volvo. Ron kept on telling her that she was wrong, and she was, too. He wanted a Mazda Miata, one of the little red ones with the optional roll bar and the CD player in the trunk.

He needed to be with somebody. When he was with somebody, it made him feel less insane, and that was good. The feeling of encroaching madness hit him with increasing regularity. Alix broke it for him. At least he didn't hear the voices anymore, or at least not so loudly.

Ron inhabited eighteen feet of cubic space and mulled things over. He had taken just about all he could take at this point in time, all kidding aside. It wasn't so much that Lloyd had fired him. He had done that before, and Ron had dealt with that. He had convinced Lloyd to give him another chance, another chance to be what Lloyd wanted him to be. And he had done his best to be somebody different. That is why he had failed. People who succeeded in business were those incapable of being anything but themselves. They were people who broke molds, not those who fit into them. He had forgotten that. Now he was well and truly fucked.

Ron listened for the door. Alix would be home soon. She would be surprised to see him there. He never got in until well after 8:00 P.M., usually finding her sacked out on the couch in her underwear, full of chardonnay and Häagen-Dazs. Yet here he was. "Hi, honey," he would say, "I'm home. Forever." She would be happy, Alix would, at first. She always said his hours were bad. She always said a corporate job was no way to build either decent dharma or serious wealth. Now he would have the time and opportunity to go back to business school for that degree in economics, which she believed was his destiny in this particular incarnation. Then he could join an investment bank and make a $10 million bonus at the end of the year, retire at thirty-five, and become a spiritual person. Then they could move to an enormous bucolic estate in northern Westchester, one that placed them firmly in the ruling, rather than the middle class, and breed. Then he could die.

Ron went to a tall bookshelf in the corner of the living room. In his early twenties, Ron had gone with a girlfriend to a flea market outside of Peterborough, New Hampshire. They had looked at the waffle irons and dolls, the old quilts with somebody else's germs and fluids all over them, moose heads that had been separated from their owners before Jayne Mansfield had lost hers; they poked around in the jewelry cases a little bit, and when they were ready to leave, Ron spotted a trunk underneath the display table of a guy who was selling old Superman comics. In the trunk were piles of books from the nineteenth century—books by Emerson and Melville, Thackeray and Thoreau, Dostoyevsky and Hawthorne. Ron bought the entire trunk. Since that time, he had collected books, not a great many, but now and then, always books of great physical beauty, in good condition, by the top authors of the Eurocentric, phallocentric Judeo-Christian cultural base. When he acquired one, he would dust it off lovingly with a special solution and cloth he maintained for that purpose. Then he would find the new book its proper place in strict alphabetical order with its fellows. If it was a particularly fine book, he might take it down once or twice after that, to read the information on the title page, sometimes even dip into an introduction or preface. Then he would dust it off again and put it back.

On the top shelf of Ron's book collection was a two-volume copy of Sir Henry Stanley's African journals, in which he described his search for and discovery of Dr. David Livingstone. Ron had always loved this book, because it was very fat and smelled of old bookstores; it had a feel of mystery and the purity of unspoiled times. He reached now for volume two.

When he had gotten involved with Alix, she had said to him, "I'm not seeing you anymore if you keep putting that poison into yourself." Since she was the only truly special thing that had happened to him since he had been hired by the corporation—she loved to have a couple of martinis and walk around his apartment in nothing but her panties; she had small, high breasts that moved with her without a lot of bounce and fuss, and a bottom to match—he could certainly give up cocaine for this woman. And he had, for a time. But she was not with him all the time, and when she wasn't with him, life seemed dull and insufficient. So Ron had translated her demand from one to give up cocaine as long as she was with him to the requirement to give it up *when* she was with him. This meant he needed a place to put a stash when he was, for some reason, alone.

The Stanley book was perfect. So one afternoon when she was out running, he had taken the book down, hollowed out with an X-Acto knife a small section in the middle of volume two, and placed his eight-gram supply into the well. He had dusted off the book and placed it lovingly back onto the highest shelf, one she could by no means reach without benefit of a sturdy chair. She had shown no inclination to explore the collection in that manner, and he felt extremely safe.

Ron stood on tiptoe and with the end of his finger dislodged the critical volume of African lore, carefully removing it from the shelf and conveying it safely down. With some internal ceremony, he transported it to his living room coffee table. For Ron, the taking of his drugs was all about ritual, one of the last rites he himself could perform, day in and day out.

Ron opened the book and gently removed the treasure that lay between pages 318 and 342. It was a good-sized pillbox. With great tenderness, he removed the container and held it in his palm. Somewhere in his mind, monks were chanting. He took the box in his stubby fingers and delicately flipped it open. Within lay eight grams of delectable cocaine.

Ron thoughtfully placed his right index finger into his mouth, only slightly moistening it. He waved it in the air to minimize any unwanted wetness, then lightly dipped it in the cocaine. It came up coated with white. He regarded the object of his affection gently, then stuck the finger up his nose and rubbed the remaining crystals along his gums.

"Gnarf!" said Ron. God, he loved cocaine. It was, of all God's drugs, the tastiest. People thought you needed to shoot it, boil it up in order to achieve the great rush of supreme power the substance could, if properly abused, convey. But no, that was not true. It was the tingling of the lips, as well as the buzz to the brain, that made it the stuff upon which dreams were made. Ron checked his watch. The Alix monster would be home soon. If she found him with his nose in a blender, that would be bad. He had better move quickly.

Eight grams. That was a lot. Ron dumped about a quarter of the pillbox onto a cable guide that was lying on the table. The rest he fastidiously packed back into its container, put the container back into its literary hiding place, and transported the book to the bookshelf, where it was once again ensconced in a place of honor. With a dexterity born of practice, he then removed a credit card from his wallet, replaced the wallet in his back pocket, seated himself before the tiny pile of joy, and began to chop up the trove into a fine, delicious dust. Is that not what we all, eventually, will be? He longed to lean down to the top of the table and kiss it. But he did not. There was a proper way to do these things.

He separated the supply into eight chubby lines, removed a twenty-dollar bill—he never snorted cocaine with any smaller denomination—then sat on the floor, crossed his legs, and eliminated those mineral deposits one by one.

Cocaine is a natural substance. It comes from the earth. In the act of inhaling two grams of the stuff, Ron, in his own way, worshiped the earth, from which we all spring.

He sat up on the couch and closed his eyes. He felt like barfing.

Alix Returns

There was a rustle at the door, a key in the lock. Ron licked his index finger and rubbed it vigorously under his nose. Then he sat completely still, waiting for her to enter. He considered doing a thorough D&C of his nose, which suddenly felt jammed full of hardening material. But he refrained. He might be deep in the most profound pit of despond, but he'd be damned if his woman would catch him with his finger up his nose. That was out. He stuck his finger in his ear instead. Boy, that felt good.

The door opened, and Alix came in carrying her briefcase and a number of neatly wrapped Christmas presents. She looked good. Her skirt was gray wool, pleated, and very short, and it matched her thick gray woolen stockings. She wore a crisp white man-tailored shirt, set off by a very cool pair of red-gray-and black paisley suspenders. On her feet were a pair of lunky Doc Marten boots that were so ugly, it took a truly beautiful pair of legs to carry them off. She was smoking a cigarette with no hands, since they were completely full. The butt jutted out of her pouting red lips, one eye squinted against the assault. She was not supposed to be smoking. Part of her agreement with Ron was that she was to give up cigarettes, in exchange for his renunciation of pot, speed, 'ludes, Xanax, Prozac, cocaine, whiskey, gin, and vodka (before 7:00 P.M.). All in all, she had found the quitting harder, since she had actually accomplished it, or so Ron had thought up until now.

Alix did not notice Ron at first; instead, she was fully engaged in the chore of opening the door, closing the door, and entering her living space, all without dramatically spewing her possessions all over the floor. Ron himself kept up his stoic posture, after a while even ceasing his breathing in an attempt to prolong this moment of anonymity. When he was a child, Ron had dreamed of being invisible, of surreptitiously watching girls pursue their lives. This was almost as good. Hell, it was better. Alix, her vision somewhat obscured by her purse and boxes, hustled into the kitchen, where she disappeared from Ron's view. After a few moments, she reemerged into the living room, where she thoughtfully strolled to the door of her bedroom, still oblivious to the presence of Ron, who continued to sit quietly on the couch. As she went, she unclasped the front pincers of her suspenders and threw them over her shoulder. Her skirt immediately dropped to the floor, where she stepped out of it. Humming, she went into the bedroom.

A marvelous electric quiet settled on the living room. Ron just sat there, letting the cocaine flow through his system, feeling the pounding of blood in his veins, the ringing of his nerves in the cochlea within his ears. She didn't know he was there!

Very quietly, Ron leaned all the way back on the couch, reclining sensuously across its back, and slowly, slowly rolled off into the area behind the seating unit. As he fell, he made a distinct bump. "What is it?" screamed Alix from the next room. She came in wrapping a robe around herself. Ron couldn't see this from his niche in the dark area next to the dust pussies just behind the settee, but he could hear the silk whisper as his beautiful, lithe six-foot lover drew the wrap around herself. "Who's there?" she asked. She was frightened. He was sorry about that, but there was little he could do. He couldn't pop up now, out of nowhere. She already considered him something of an oddball. He didn't need to augment that perception now, when he needed her belief in his credibility more than ever.

330

"Is that you, Ron?" She was coming closer.

"You!" shouted Alix, who still could not see him. "I have a gun and I'll shoot! Don't think I won't!" How stupid, thought Ron. To have left his gun on the night table!

"I'm gonna shoot you, motherfucker," said Alix in a small, determined voice. And for the first time, he believed her.

This conviction built size and body weight as he distinctly heard a very small click in the center of the room, which was where she would be if she was advancing slowly on him in her sheer silk bathrobe that, when cinched around the middle, came just to the tops of her thighs. He should probably do something about the situation now. Even if she did not shoot him, he was up for looking pretty ridiculous when she found him balled up behind the couch.

Ron considered several options. He could be asleep. No, not believable. Why would he be sleeping back here? He could be looking for a contact lens, except he didn't wear them. Maybe he had started wearing them. That was possible. He could be honest and say he was completely wrecked on Colombian sinus cleanser, but that would annoy her a lot. Of course, she had been smoking. He had her there. Still, cocaine was worse than smoking, even though the underlying broken promise was the issue, not the stimulant. She was getting closer.

And suddenly he knew what to do. Wasn't that always the case? When push came to shove, his brilliant, facile mind always came up with a solution that approached, if not surpassed, perfection. Why? Because he was the man! Suffused with the potent self-regard that often comes with a noseful of Incan pep rally, Ron executed his new strategic plan.

"Oh, my," said he, very low, so softly that only someone who loved him might hear.

"Ronny?" Alix's head appeared over the back of the couch. "Honey? Whatcha doin' down there, baby?"

"Oh, muffin," said Ron, and began to cry. It wasn't real crying; he knew that. It was sobbing without tears. Alix watched him, shocked beyond words. In all the time she had known him, Ron had expressed only two emotions: lust and anger. She liked the lust, except when it came to the acquisition of brain enhancements, which, except for white wine, she had come to detest. She feared the anger. What could possibly have made him so angry? Sometimes she feared there was simply nothing. Nothing but anger and the desire to quench it in physical pleasure. Now here he was huddled behind the couch in a fetal position, his body shaking with uncontrollable grief. She put the safety back on the handgun she had almost shot him with, then put the gun gingerly on the glass coffee table and turned back to minister to this wrecked husk of what was once a man she knew, sort of. That is, she knew him well enough . . . well enough to proceed. Who can really know anybody in this world?

She discovered that, while she had been turned away to stash the weapon, Ron had risen shakily to his feet.

"Want to tell me about it?" She knelt on the couch and leaned forward to put both arms on his shoulders, which placed her head at about the level of his chest. He looked down at her.

"Yeah," he said, maintaining a somber and shaken tone. This was very well begun!

"Come over, baby."

Ron regarded her for a moment, then he leaned forward, headfirst, bent at the waist, and rolled over the back of the couch, landing somewhat ingloriously sprawled across several pillows, his head jammed up against a bolster. This unorthodox method of vaulting the gap between them did not seem to bother Alix. She was already prepared to believe that something was awry in Ron's mechanism.

"That's good. Now sit up," she said. Ron sat up. "Want a drink of water?"

"Water?" said Ron. He had set up a nice shaky thing going on with his hands, sort of a light palsy that leant him an even more fragile and pathetic air. He had to be careful not to push it, though. He didn't want the woman to think he was having some kind of neurological incident. He just wanted her positioned correctly for future steps that might have to be taken, either by him or by her, or possibly by them both.

"What?" she said flatly. "You want a drink?"

"A small one," he said. "Stoli. Rocks. A twist, maybe. If it's okay." She looked him over. This gave him the opportunity to run both hands through his massively thick, shiny head of hair, of which he was justifiably proud.

"Whatever it is, Ron, it won't help things to get smashed," said Alix. But she rose and went into the kitchen, where very shortly Ron heard the refrigerator open and the clink of ice in a broad-bottomed glass. He let his eye wander across the expanse of the coffee table, looking for telltale signs of drug ingestion that might get him busted at this most delicate time. There, on the magazine he had cut his stuff on, was a fine, generous residue of molecular ash. She must not see it. He picked up the issue and very quietly and unobtrusively licked it with his entire tongue, from top to bottom, until it was quite wet, but also clean. Then he replaced it in the middle of the stack, just as Alix returned carrying his glass.

Turned out she made him a nice hefty drink. Ha ha! This was okay! Ron's mood was picking up, but he did what he must to prevent it from showing. It wouldn't do to get all jolly now, not while he had her all limp and squishy in the relentless grip of his sorry situation.

"Now," she said, and although there was patience and sympathy in the word, there was also a disquieting undertone, an evaluatory edginess, a soupçon of "This had better be good" beneath the glossy sheen of empathy. Fine. He would make it good.

He leaned back on the couch, put his head back, and closed his eyes, as if looking at her while he told her would place the matter the one final notch above the threshold of tolerable pain.

"Lloyd . . ." he said.

"What about Lloyd?" said Alix, her eyes narrowing ever so slightly. Based on Ron's portrayal of the last several months, Alix hated Lloyd. Lloyd represented all that was selfish, heedless, corrupt, and grotesquely successful in the boomer mentality. Lloyd was exactly the kind of person who kept worthy members of the upcoming generation sucking wind and begging for dimes. Lloyd blew.

"Lloyd took me out," said Ron. He fell silent. A shaky sigh rocked his entire body. For good measure, Ron interjected a little squeak into the end of it. He opened one eye slightly to see if this touch had gone over the top. He didn't want Alix to think that he was feeling sorrier for himself than she was. He had to be brave.

"Took you out?" said Alix. "What, to lunch?"

"Fired me. For good. Made me an offer I could do nothing but refuse. Same thing."

Alix rose to her feet and looked down at Ron. He felt her towering over him and opened his eyes to take her in. Her mouth was open in an O of shock and rage. "What!" she said.

"Called me in about ten this morning. I knew it wasn't going to be good." Ron pulled himself into a sitting position more seriously to address the demands of conveying this information. He wasn't too sure it was going all that fabulously all of a sudden. Alix's reaction was skewed somehow, too dramatic for complete control. If he didn't harness it in some way, it was possible she was going to call for an action or reaction that Ron would find difficult, considering all he really wanted to do was lie on the couch and wash down cocaine with vodka for the next couple of months. "Sit down, baby," he said. Alix sat. She was vibrating like a wood saw Ron had seen played at a county fair once. This guy had drawn a bow over the stainless-steel tool and the thing had sung like a whale. It was weird. How had he gotten it to do that?

"Ron!" screamed Alix. "Focus!"

"Oh," said Ron. She was scaring him. This was his life they were talking about. Where did she get off acting as if it were her own? He was staring at her with an expression of dismay and subtly attempted to increase the amount of woundedness he was putting out.

"I'm sorry," she said. "Just tell me what happened, Ronald."

Ronald?

"I went in and . . . You know how strange things have been around there for the last couple of months, with crazy rumors about the merger and what was going to happen with various departments, like who would be running things and everything, and where functions would be located, and who they would report to. So I was kind of prepared for everything. Except what Lloyd does is, he closes the door and he's like, 'Congratulations, Ron, you're going to be heading up our satellite office in China.'"

"China!"

"Beijing. And I'm like, Wow, man, that's no offer at all. That's like a one-way ticket to nowhere. And he's like, Well, short of that, we've got a package put together for you and sayonara, baby, and that was pretty much all she wrote."

Alix once again rose to her full height and crossed her arms in front of herself. This pushed up her breasts very high and revealed a lovely expanse of plump, juicy bosom to Ron's view. He tore his eyes from this distraction and made them concentrate on her eyes, which were viscous and opaque with rumination.

"And you just took it up the ass, I suppose," she said.

"I beg your pardon?"

"You just bent over and took it," she said again.

"Hey now," said Ron.

"Well, bullshit on that," said Alix and went into the kitchen. He heard her open the fridge. He heard liquid being poured. She returned with a large tumbler. It appeared to be filled with ice and white wine. Quite a massive drink. He reached forward, picked up his own glass, and emptied it. Alix sat, this time right next to him on the couch. He could smell her heat. He longed to lean forward and put his head against that amazing chest, but he did not. He did not want it to appear that he was taking the wrong aspect of this woman seriously. What might she do to him? His life was now in her power, that much was pretty clear.

"You know a lot about Lloyd and he can't just up and hump you over this way without considering the alternatives," said Alix. She rearranged herself on the couch, turning and leaning back on the armrest, her legs across Ron's lap. "Think about it," she said.

Ron was pretty sure she wasn't wearing any underwear. He kept his hands in his lap and felt his head spin. In about fifteen minutes, he would need another hit of weasel dust if his entire mind-set wasn't going to decompose and fall in upon itself. Fifteen minutes. That was a long time in some situations, no time at all in others.

"Are you listening to me, Ron?" she was saying.

"It's true," he said. This seemed like a good all-purpose reply to a woman in the middle of a comprehensive screed.

"What is?" she said, checking to see if he was listening.

"It's true that I know a lot about Lloyd he would prefer to keep hidden."

"Yes," she said. "That's either worth something in severance or, if you leverage it properly, it might be enough to keep you on board for a while longer. Either alternative is preferable to a trip to China. That would be difficult. I hear they have all kinds of retrogressive attitudes about women."

"Wait a minute," said Ron. His entire system was spinning like a top now. This was sometimes what cocaine did to him. It was the one aspect of the drug that he didn't like. If it got worse, he would not vomit, per se; he would be attacked by a bout of dry heaves that would leave him wrung out and ashamed. He could feel them starting now. "Huark," he said, and leaned over from the waist to wait for them to pass.

"Although I can't imagine they would send you there and then refuse to arrange for you to live like a mandarin in your new location," said Alix thoughtfully. "We could get married. Or not. It might be cool, China." She swung her legs around, rose elegantly, and went to the bookshelf, where she got down Ron's gigantic *Hammond Atlas of the World*. She sat down again at the end of the couch and opened the book to the map of China.

"Hroof," said Ron. The heaves were coming somewhat more slowly now, and not so violently. He straightened up and tested the air at head level. It was okay. What was Alix talking about? Going to China? He wasn't going to fucking China! At least he didn't think so.

"Have you given them a definitive no about the China thing?" Alix said.

"Well, pretty much." Ron took a couple of breaths. "I told Lloyd to go fuck himself and then I cleaned out my office."

"Hm," said Alix. She was looking at the map of China. "Well," she said. "Here's how I see it. You have three alternatives. One: You terrify Lloyd enough to force him to reinstate you with, like, a better situation and everything. It'd be tough, but it's my sense that you have a lot of raw data on Lloyd and he's not the kind of guy who'll tough it out and put everything he's earned in the lifestyle department at risk."

This was certainly true. But did Ron want to become a blackmailer so that he could go back to the place that had wrecked him? The extortion part wasn't so bad; he could get his mind around that. But the telling part, the writing of letters to the wife, the kids stripped away from their father, as he had been . . . Ron shivered inside his nausea, and listened.

Alix went on. "Two: You basically pursue the same agenda, but with an eye toward a big payday that can set you up to take the time to go back to business school and finish what you started at Wharton."

Ron shivered. He had been accepted at the world's greatest training ground for asset managers, attended two days of orientation, then deferred his attendance. He never wanted to go back there, never. There were no laughs at Wharton. Business laughs, maybe, the big round kind, filled with heavy gas and meat. But no real chuckles. And drugs? Forget about it.

"And three," said Alix with a mysterious little smile, "we could go to China!"

Ron's face hurt. "Ahdowanna gotachina," he squeaked out.

"Well, that still gives you two alternatives," said Alix sweetly.

"Maybe I . . ." Ron gulped down some air and tried to right his writhing brain stem. "Maybe, I'll just take the year they give me and hunker down here with you and get another job at some point and leave this whole installment of the miniseries, like, behind?" Good Christ, Ron thought. I'm uptalking. I conquered that in my late teens, when I realized I could never get a job by turning every statement into a question. Now I'm at it again. More than anything, he wanted Alix to go take her shower so he could toot up again. But she wasn't moving.

"You could do that," said Alix. "But I would be very disappointed in you if you didn't turn this opportunity into some kind of victory."

"This is an opportunity?"

"Sure, Ron," she said. She took the atlas back to the bookcase and put it up on its shelf. As she did, her bathrobe rode up on her back, revealing the tops of her legs and the first suspicion of the splendors of her bottom.

"You're right," said Ron. "Let me get my shit together and decide on one of the three ingenious alternatives you've offered."

"No, no," said Alix, still gazing at him with cool dispassion. "You do what comes naturally. But I will tell you that I perceive this to be one of those karmic moments in your life when the decisions you make will determine everything, forever. Choose truthfully. Choose wisely. I'll see where you choose to go, and then either I'll accompany you on your journey or I won't." She went to the door of the bathroom and turned on the light. "I'll tell you one thing," she said. "I don't see myself going through this embodiment with a loser. I'd be with you if you were poor, or crippled, or dying, or bravely fighting for your dream in some way, even if it was a tough way. But I don't see myself accompanying you on somebody else's road."

What the fuck was she talking about? She slipped the bathrobe off her shoulders and onto the floor. Her nakedness was always such a shock to him.

"I'll go to China with you," she said. "I'll go to Wharton with you. And I'll stay here while you gut it out with those pricks at the office. But you're nearly thirty, and I won't feel good standing by and watching you wash all your achievements down the drain because you can't grapple with a monster of your own devising." She went into the bathroom, closed the door, and turned on the shower.

A tremendous wave of shaking seized Ron's body and would not let him go. He looked at his gun on the table. It was small and made out of plastic.

The Hours of the Deal

Business Meeting
Circa 1242 A.D.

From its birth in deep winter to its final fruition some twelve months hence, the deal engages the full range of activity on the part of all citizens in the corporate village.

Commuting

6:14 A.M.
Opposite the Train Station

Every weekday, in rain, sunshine, snow, and darkness,
corporate players make their way to work, one train at a time.

Breakfasting

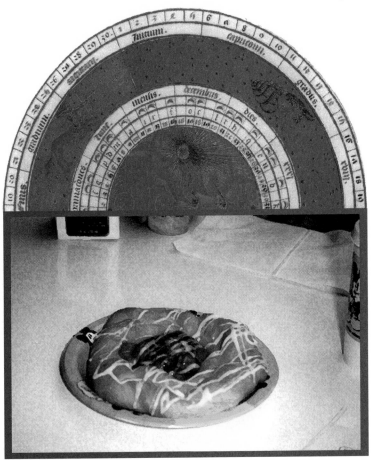

The deal begins at a breakfast that Wiedemeyer and Sweet have at a Greek coffee shop. The former is chief financial officer of a gigantic investment banking firm. "I see no reason why a well-engineered effort couldn't manage to snap up all serious global competition in your sectors by this time next year," says Wiedemeyer as Sweet pays the check. Sweet stows the comment away without being aware he has done so.

339

Planting

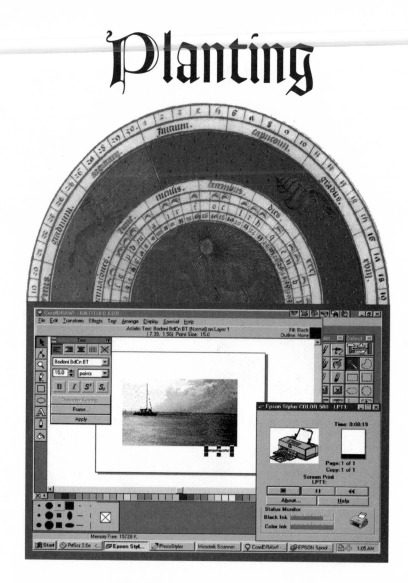

On Lloyd's Laptop at the Time

At a meeting with senior staff, Sweet mentions Wiedemeyer's remark when he realizes that he has nothing
else to talk about this week. The comment occassions
a fair amount of laughter around the big table, except
from Walt, who does not laugh.

Crunching

Working People Producing Value

A group of low-level finance droids work through the night on the eighth floor of headquarters, which in corporate terms is the subbasement of the infrastructure. The numbers show that with the cost of money factored in at a reasonable level, and certain key divestitures providing crucial capital, the deal may just be possible.

Meeting

Good Placement
at a Business Meeting

Lunching

Somewhere in the European Community
Asset Value: $1.5 Billion

Over sandwiches in the boardroom, the final valuation on the prospective property is hammered out. In the end, the process is almost a wholly scientific, objective one, give or take a couple hundred million.

More Meeting

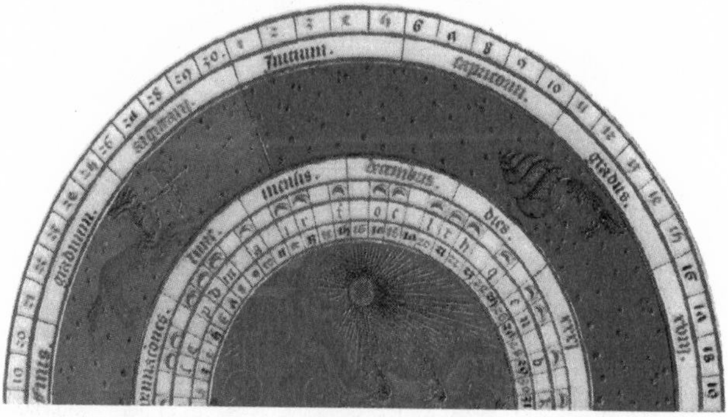

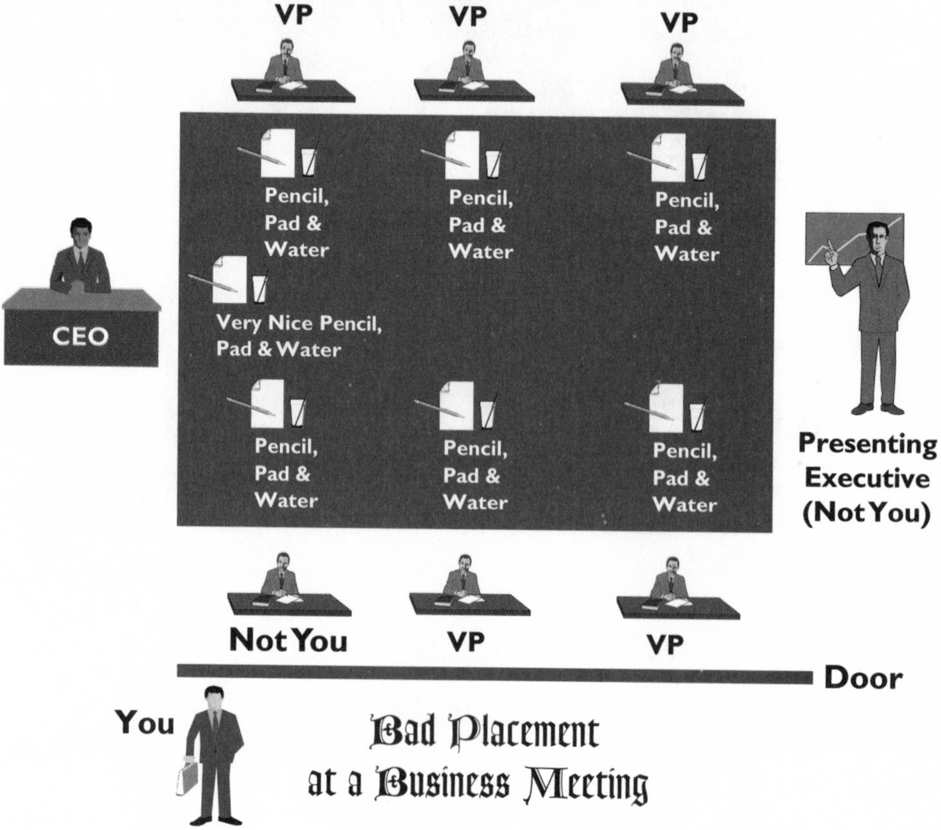

Bad Placement
at a Business Meeting

Teleconferencing

Cost of Teleconference:
$3465.45 plus refreshments

Executives from the corporation make contact with a small group of outside parties interested in the deal. Surprising agreement is achieved almost immediately, until cooler heads plead for time to consider the implications on personal wealth.

Still More Meeting

VPs

CEO

Pencils,
Pads &
Water all
around

No Pencil
No Pad
No Water

You

More VPs

Worst Possible Placement at a Business Meeting

And of course there are a lot of meetings. So many.
Enough to drive a person . . . mad! Mad, I tell you!

Flying

Lloyd Lands in London
6:00 A.M. Local Time
Midnight Lloyd Time

Sometimes you've got to be the visiting team.

Negotiating

✦ Hatred Between Primary Negotiators
◼ Level of Fundamental Agreement

Endless hours of wrangling deliver the deal into the hands of the lawyers, but not before the various chief financial officers determine to tear out each others' livers if and when they have the chance.

Golfing

Pebble Beach
Horst and Fitz

On a crisp day in September, on the eighth fairway of the most beautiful golf course in the world, the two men come to a tacit agreement about the division of tax liabilities that at long last puts the transaction on a very fast green.

Closing

The Sign of the Dove
12:20 A.M.

Eventually, even lawyers must agree to suspend disagreement.

Merging

Merged Entities That Survive Over a 10–Year Span

The New Corporation Is Born!

The shell cracks and out pops a tiny beak. And then —
here it is! Wet and ugly and sort of slimy, but beautiful in
its own way, too, and oh, so fragile. Come on, baby,
quack for Papa!

Rejoicing

Tomorrow, of course, Wall Street will begin looking for how we're going to achieve those key operating synergies we promised in the press release, but until then, Hurrah!

The gun would comfortably conceal itself just about anywhere. He picked it up and put it in his pocket. How easy it would be to blow my brains out, he thought. And if that was easy, how much more difficult would it be for him to hobble his enemy?

When he was sure the shower would continue for some time longer, he gingerly pulled himself together and, with great dignity, crossed the room to the bookshelf, reached up, and once again delved into the mysteries of the Dark Continent.

Home to Roost

By the second week of the month, Lloyd was relatively sure that somebody was stalking him. It seemed that this person, if indeed it was a person and not a figment of his imagination, was embarked on a program of intimidation, unless it was the stalker who was scared, too scared to check in with whatever brief that needed to be prosecuted.

Lloyd felt the creature, saw it in his imagination as a figure out of an expressionist vampire film from the 1920s—following him just out of sight, ducking into the shadows whenever he turned quickly, a set of footsteps tapping off into the distance just as he drew near. The stalker persisted in calling at odd hours and breathing wetly into the receiver, menacing him with guttural imprecations on the phone and, most frighteningly, over the Internet, at the office and at home. E-mail would come in at two, three in the morning, vaguely advising him to put his affairs in order, since his inevitable undoing was close at hand. Lloyd tried to view these missives in a humorous light but failed.

It's Ron, of course, thought Lloyd. Who else could it be? Mona? Gavin Snedekker, whom he had terminated last month for no cause other than the guy's age, although they would, of course, dispute that calumny in court? Walt? Was it possible that Walt had heard about his ordained destiny and did not trust in Lloyd's ingenuity enough to suspend his outrage for even a moment? Any of the two thousand people from around the nation who had some reason to wish Lloyd ill, considering how much productivity he had found over the course of the last several months? No, it was Ron, almost definitely. But every time he turned quickly to see the substance of the shadow on his tail, there was nothing there. He considered the things that Ron knew about him. He wondered how he had dared to be so brutal to the boy. He tried to call Ron several times but only got his machine, which had a weird message on it. The phone would ring three times and then answer, but rather than a voice instructing you to do the necessaries, there was the brief noise of a fax machine accepting a call (one of the most annoying sounds in the contemporary universe) and then a beep. Lloyd did not leave a message.

Lloyd started taking radio cars to every destination, no matter how nearby.

Finally, one cold night in mid to late December, as Lloyd hunkered down over the third-quarter numbers at 9:30 P.M., the only one in the enormous forty-six-story high-rise spire, deep in the silence, silence outside the vast plate-glass windows, silence on the city far below, the phone rang. On the other end of the line was the man himself, breathing. Lloyd knew it was Ron because he knew Ron's breathing, the little hitch in the top of the lung, the click of how Ron cleared his throat when he was massively affronted or enraged. "I hear you, Ron, man," Lloyd said at last.

Nothing. Only breathing. Lloyd hung up and thought things over.

He gave the appearance of working for another five, six minutes, most of which was spent sitting very erect, staring straight in front of him, a pencil between his teeth. Then he put on his jacket and got out of there.

The next morning, as Lloyd purchased his stale croissantlike object at the corner deli, he saw Ron, standing in his Burberry topcoat on the opposite side of Fifty-seventh Street. Ron was staring at him. There was no expression on his face whatsoever. After a few extended moments of this, Lloyd decided to speak with Ron. Hell, they were two men. They could work it out. But when he hit the crosswalk, he saw in the other man's eyes such an overwhelming expression of revulsion and irrational hatred that he paused. Lloyd also noticed Ron had thrust his right hand into the pocket of his overcoat. What could that mean? Lloyd stood at the crosswalk for a long time, looking at Ron, who was looking at him. Neither moved. Lloyd came to the conclusion that he would not cross the street after all. Instead, he went back up to his office, doing his best to savor the time before the day came screaming down on him like an enraged bird of prey.

As he got to his desk, his phone rang. He did not answer it.

On the night before Christmas vacation, Lloyd received a box of cow offal in the mail. Was *offal* the right word? Cow guts. Rotton cow guts, bought from a butcher, allowed to decay, then stuffed into a corrugated cardboard box and mailed overnight to him. It smelled really bad. Was this the stuff that gave you mad cow disease? Almost more horrible than the steaming material itself was the concept of the imagination that had thought of this thing. How the sender must hate him! Not a calm hatred, either. A bright orange one, capable of violence and admirable creativity.

That night, Lloyd talked to his travel agent. By some miracle, or due to someone else's tragedy requiring last-minute cancellations, there were four seats on the first plane out to Puerto Rico that coming Friday. Two adjoining deluxe rooms at the finest hotel on the island could most certainly be arranged. It would cost. But what was money for? This was a question Lloyd often asked himself. So far, fortunately, he had always been able to provide an answer.

It's been quite a ride over the last twelve months or so, thought Lloyd as he prepared to leave his office that Thursday night in late December of the year 1999. The next time he opened that door, it would be a new corporation, a new millennium, a whole new world. That's the way things go, Lloyd mused. He shrugged. The holidays always made him philosophical.

Lloyd stood in his old office and felt the history there. The stone peach on his blotter, whose weight more than one executive had hefted to his or her surprise. The plastic fish that was actually a pen. The human energy of a billion phone calls. Lloyd stood in the office and felt them all. The myriad lights of Manhattan winked on in the early-evening dusk. Tomorrow, it would be winter. It was done. The year was wrapped. He had won. He closed the door behind him and spoke aloud to the empty hallway.

"Don't look back," he said.

It sounded like a cliché. Fortunately, there was no one left to hear it, or abuse him for it, so the resonance of the idea rang like bells within him and rocked him to the bottom of his soul.

"Good-bye," said Lloyd.

No one answered. There was no one there. Walt was in Florida, with his aged dad. Burbage was at home with his wife, weighing his alternatives, which were few. Darling was out getting drunk with vendors. Fitz was shopping for Christmas, nursing his tender postvasectomy groin with shots of bourbon every couple of hours. There were no friends here. There was only silence.

"Congratulations on your promotion, Lloyd," said a voice to his right and down the hall. It was Iris, Morgenstern's secretary.

"Thanks, Iris," said Lloyd, and then, inexplicably sadly, he added, "Sometimes things don't go the way we want them to, Iris."

"We have to move on, I guess," said Iris.

"Yes," said Lloyd. "Merry Christmas to you, Iris. Happy New Year, too."

"You, too, Lloyd. See you in the year 2000, huh?"

"Yeah," said Lloyd. Hoisting his shoulder bag, he turned and walked without pause down the hallway and to the elevator bank. In twenty-four hours, he would be on the beach in Puerto Rico. Let Ron follow him there!

Beyond the Envelope

It was dumb luck—to be hanging around in the newsstand, waiting for a clear shot at Lloyd, and happen upon a chance remark like that. Dolores, the woman behind the counter, with whom everyone in the building maintained cordial relations, said to Lloyd, "Have a good time in Puerto Rico!" as he smugly purchased the potent mints he liked to chew and swallow in meetings, making a loud crunching noise Ron had always hated. Puerto Rico. Ron had never been there. He went to his old travel agent and arranged the necessaries. There was a flight out tomorrow, Friday. He would take that. When he got to the island, he would find Lloyd. It wouldn't be hard. It wasn't a big island. There were only a few five-star hotels. Lloyd would probably be traveling with his children. There were only a few places that would be wholly suitable for children. There were even some that had long river pools you could go tube rafting in. He had seen one profiled on the Travel Channel one night at 3:00 A.M. while he was up, wide awake after a four-gram night, grinding his teeth and waiting for the horrible moment when the birds began to sing.

Ron was a little upset with himself. It had been over a week and he had yet to work up the proper approach to Lloyd, one that would ensure his success. The trick, as far as he could see it, was to threaten Lloyd with disclosure on the Mona issue in such a way that his blackmail produced a positive outcome for him, Ron, rather than simply a negative one for Lloyd. Hurting Lloyd was easy. Helping himself, that was the tough part.

Each night he would return to the apartment, to find Alix doing yoga on the floor, eyes closed, breathing with the regularity of the lunar tide. As he entered, she would open one eye slightly and regard him with the detachment of Buddha.

"Well?" she would say.

"We had a couple of good meetings," said Ron on the first day. "They're batting around a couple of alternatives," he said on the second. But the third day, he simply smiled demurely and said, "I don't want to talk about it at this point in time. I don't want to jinx it." This seemed to satisfy her, at least so far. But in very short order, she would begin to smell something inappropriate. Then he would have to come up with something satisfactory, or she would once again become involved, this time in a very big way. Ron thought of himself wearing blue pajamas and one of those straw hats that come to a point on top, pedaling a bicycle to his tiny office in a cornice of the Forbidden City. Ron thought of himself in a small, hot room at Wharton, surrounded by nerds even younger than himself. Ron thought of himself hanging from a light fixture in his kitchen.

"I'm going into the bathroom to read for a while," he said, taking a book from the shelf.

"Okay," she said, then added, "Boy, you sure are interested in Africa."

It was true. He was interested in nothing but Africa. And Africa was running out. And there was nothing he could lay his hands on to procure subsequent trips to Africa. If access to Africa disappeared, it was quite possible that he would go insane.

Why, suddenly, was he afraid of Lloyd? Lloyd was unprepossessing. For his part, Ron was never at a loss for words. Why was he finding it impossible to walk up to Lloyd on the street and talk the issues out?

One thing did come to mind. When he was trailing Lloyd in this way, remaining a mysterious figure on the edge of Lloyd's imagination, Ron felt something that was utterly absent in every other social situation at this stage of his vastly shrunken game. It came to him as he felt the plastic weapon in his pocket. Power. In the sudden lack of definition that marked his new existence, in the towering anguish and fear and unrequited wrath that coursed through his system throughout every waking minute, this sense of power was there to guide him, mold him, use him for its own purpose. He would wait. The power would speak inside him, move his hand. Then, and only then, he would act.

Hasta la Muerte, Baby

Lloyd sat by the pool at the hotel in Puerto Rico. It was nice. He dozed. But what he dreamed of was not palm and coconut. No, no. He was back at the office.

It was something about his blotter. His blotter was a beautiful thing, made of supple leather, with cushy borders on the side into which he could stuff notes, invitations, and other small bits of paper, sometimes in perpetuity. Not long ago, he had discovered a note to himself dating back to 1986. The writing was faded, in a hand he recognized as formerly his own. Underneath the blotter were many phone messages, important letters, personal junk that did not belong on his desktop but which he could not bear to throw away. In the dream, he looked beneath his blotter and was horrified to find that there was nothing at all there. "There is nothing at all here!" he screamed to himself in the dream. Mona was in the doorway to his office. "Oh, I cleaned up under there," she said. She was munching on a message slip, which stuck out of the corner of her mouth. She was smiling.

"You what?" Lloyd yelled as loudly as he could. Her mouth opened, and it was bright red. "It's the message," he told himself, but it certainly looked as if her mouth was filled with blood.

It was hot in his office. So hot. He felt sweat beneath his arms and the top of his head glowing beneath the incredible force of the sun. What was the sun doing inside his office?

He woke up and looked around. Ah yes. He was not there. He was here. He did what he could to bring his mind up to speed with his body and, thanks to the fact that it was their second full day here, he almost got there. So far Lloyd, Donna, Nora, and Bob were enjoying this unexpected, total withdrawal from their frame of reference. There was a pool—and oh, what a pool! Millions of gallons of pure, azure water distributed over several acres of tropical vegetation. In the middle of the main pool area, there was a snack hut with big fruity drinks pouring out of it at all hours of the day and night. There was no time, it seemed, inappropriate to the consumption of such gigantic beverages. Was not fruit the backbone of any healthful diet? There was also the ocean, incomprehensibly vast, pounding with the rhythm of the spheres. Distributed about the property were all sorts of sensational restaurants, each of which was more difficult to book than the next. That was all right. The snack bar was loaded with food and there was a family-style eatery in the main hotel that had unpretentious fare with large portions (for Lloyd and Bob), a pizza oven (Nora), and a salad bar (Donna). Everything here was nice, and normal, more normal than reality should be, or ever really was. Imagine that. Normal. Lloyd liked it.

Over the course of the first day or so, Lloyd and Donna drank a great deal. It seemed to Lloyd that things were very slightly improving between them. After the first day, when Donna accidentally dropped his cellular phone into the Atlantic Ocean, Lloyd took no calls, save one with Walt, which he placed himself. "Get off the phone, Lloyd," Walt told him quite sternly. "Take a walk on the beach with your wife." Then Walt hung up. So Lloyd took a long, virtually silent walk with his wife. That evening, they had impossibly corny lobster thermidor in the large restaurant over at the companion hotel. Everyone dressed for dinner, even though they didn't have to. Lloyd imagined he saw the ghost of Perry Como ordering a Manhattan at a nearby table. Lloyd remembered watching the Perry Como show with his father, back in the late 1950s or early 1960s. Perry Como was not like Andy Williams, whose life was touched with tragedy by the rotten finger of the sixties. Perry Como wore cardigans, sang nicely, and was very neat.

The kids chattered and sang and ate all their food. Nora was in that splendid mood where she was too happy and at one with the family even to pretend to coolness, very young, completely uncondescending to her brother and, better still, her father. Bob took the opportunity to put bread sticks up his nose. And Donna . . . Lloyd looked Donna over. She was very quiet for a happy woman. Her hair was washed and blown straight. She was regarding the menu seriously, looking, Lloyd knew, for a dessert that was either too good or too virtuous to resist. Her dress was cut slightly low in the front, and he watched her breathe in, breathe out, chest rising and falling. He was swept by a devastating bolt of affection for her. He took her hand and was torn from stem to stern with remorse.

The next morning, Lloyd felt lighter. What was the point of revisiting all the woe he had attempted to inflict on his family, himself, their collective existence? It would be selfish and unforgivable. So he shrugged on a gaudy coat of jollity and, with his uncharacteristically thoughtful wife in tow and his children burbling along behind, got an early start down by the pool.

An hour of lounging behind him, Lloyd got up, grabbed his tube, and headed for the ramp that led to the headland of the synthetic river. He would find Bob and Nora and dunk them. They would scream and complain. A beverage cart trundled by, filled with various forms of medication. Lloyd thought it over and rejected it. It was possible he could stay completely sober for his entire stay here. There was no reason he couldn't.

Donna lowered her book and peered at him over the tops of her Wayfarers. "Goin' swimmin'?" she said companionably.

"Great rapids up near the top," said Lloyd.

"I'll go in later," said Donna. "I don't want to leave the chairs unattended at this hour." Lloyd knew she was 100 percent correct in her strategic assessment of the situation. The competition for good pool chairs was intense here. People came down from New York, Chicago, Los Angeles to escape the insanity and pressure of urban life. They got down to this bucolic tropical arcadia and immediately started stabbing one another for deck chairs. Positioning was all-important. One needed to be just this side of the pool, not too far from the bar but not too close to the sand, equidistant from the water slide and the volleyball courts, beneath the shade of the palms but not in some off-the-path cornice that was too dark, a spot that was private but not lonely, bright but not blazing, hot but cooled by precisely the right amount of breeze, and so on. People set their alarms for the morning rush and thundered down with the sun to reserve their spots with as many personal belongings as their ancestors had carried away from their little European villages three generations ago. They then sat in their locations for the rest of the day, jealously guarding their turf like one tribe of gibbons protecting their juicy pile of mangoes from another.

So Puerto Rico was like everyplace else. You learned and played by the rules. You fought for yourself when it was necessary. The rest of the time, you tried to have a little fun.

"So I'll see you in a little while," said Lloyd to Donna as he headed off to the top of the river pool on this, the second day of their impromptu vacation.

"Don't be gone too long," she said.

"You think . . ." he said. He started over. "You think we'll have a chance to be alone at any point on this little excursion?"

"Sure," said Donna, sizing him up with eyes narrowed by the glare of the sun. "I'm sure we're both going to need showers later."

Lloyd went off to find the kids, humming a little Puerto Rican tune. On his way, he saw an interesting thing: some guy, way up on the top floor of the hotel, on the balcony of his room. He was wearing a ridiculous felt chapeau and a hotel bathrobe that looked to be stuffed with something, so enormous did this fellow's girth appear. Most odd was the fact that his face was completely obscured behind a pair of high-powered binoculars, with which the guy seemed to be regarding the pool, the beach, and, most particularly, him.

A cool wind swept under the palm trees at that moment, and the sun went behind a cloud. Lloyd shivered and ran for the relative warmth of the water.

Meanwhile

Getting the plastic gun and pillbox full of drugs by airport security hadn't been very difficult once he had set his mind to it. The airport security people on the X-ray machine at La Guardia had been looking at someone's baby pictures, laughing and kidding with one another in a language other than English, although he couldn't for the life of him figure out which. They didn't even glance at the luggage he had fed into the conveyor belt, his heart pounding in the roof of his mouth. Fine, thought Ron. It was nice to see that sometimes things went as they were supposed to.

Once in Puerto Rico, it didn't take much effort to see where Lloyd would be staying. As Ron had suspected, this was not a very big island, as witnessed by its dinky Third World airport. There were just a few places hereabouts a senior-type guy could live the good life with wife and kids in tow. So Ron tried a couple of locations, keeping his good friend Paco waiting by the curb of each with his motor running. He felt a little bit odd, dressed as he was in full business regalia, but it gave him credibility while he was making inquiries. At the desk, he would offer an official-looking manila envelope (stuffed with in-flight magazines) and ask whether he could drop off this important package for Lloyd, who was, it was thought, staying at this very same hotel. He got lucky on the fourth try. Yes, said the concierge politely, checking the official manifest, he could leave the package right there, as a matter of fact.

Ron did so. Then he repaired back to his hired limousine, paid the worthy Paco, who had spoken not a word since he had been engaged at the airport curb, took his overnight bag from the trunk without assistance from his devoted Phaëthon, and dragged himself into the lobby and up to the desk. A corporate card was a wonderful thing. Why had they not shut his off yet? Too soon, probably. End of month, certainly. Until then . . . party time.

He looked around. There was a macaw in a cage, and a casino off the main area. He was anxious not to be spotted. In the lobby bathroom, he ducked into a stall and, perching his bag on the toilet, effected his first disguise—loud shorts, a lime green and orange shirt that matched no other article of clothing on the planet, big ragged straw hat that flopped over his eyes and obscured his face, large, perfectly round sunglasses with amber-tinted lenses, and sandals. He emerged from the stall and looked at himself in the mirror. He took off his hat and laughed. It had been a brilliant touch to shave his head. It was a look that worked as well with a business suit as it did in this getup. Nobody questioned a man in his twenties without hair.

Ron went up to the desk and checked in. It was hard finding a room at first, but a hundred-dollar bill to the guy at the computer and a willingness to pay for the very best suite in the establishment eventually got the job done.

After he filled his nose, Ron sat on the veranda of his splendid suite. He had changed to his smallest, darkest Ray·Bans, a plump hotel bathrobe, and a tiny gray fedora with a red feather in the band. He had also strategically placed a pillow beneath the waistband of the bathrobe, to appear fatter if anyone in a helicopter came by to observe him. It didn't pay to be careless.

Possibly the best thing about this hotel had to be the quality of the mini-bar. At his elbow, on the low table provided for that purpose, were a Heineken and about sixty dollars' worth of pistachio nuts—that is, one bottle. Crunch and sip, thought Ron, sip and crunch. He raised the Nikon binoculars he had purchased at the airport Hoffritz and scanned the pool area. There they were. Lloyd was sleeping. His wife, Donna, was reading. The kids were somewhere else, but he didn't need the kids to do what needed to be done. He required nothing more than to get Lloyd alone and have a chat with him. In this set-ting, far from the pressures and distortions of the real world, he would be able to talk some sense into Lloyd.

Lloyd was moving! Ron watched, standing now, his pillow slipping lower and lower onto his abdomen until it poked out of the bottom of his bathrobe like an egg he was laying. Lloyd was looking up at him! It took all of Ron's concentration not to bolt and run. He held his position, and, after a nervous look upstairs again, Lloyd moved off. Ron put down the field glasses; now that Lloyd was out of sight, he felt nervous.

Ron went into the room to change his outfit, donning his next clever dis-guise for phase two of his brilliant plan. On the way out of the room, he grabbed several of those individual-sized bottles of Bacardi.

In the River Pool

Lloyd leaned back in the tire and floated down the swiftly moving stream. Ah, he thought. How relaxing. His children were coming up hard behind him, laughing hysterically. They had just come through the waterfall, which had vio-lently doused them with very cold water. This they found uncontestably funny. What was funny about getting wet? That was the big laugh riot? No. It was not the getting wet that made them weak with mirth. It was the joy of knowing that the family was together, that soon there would be lunch, and then dinner, and after that a movie on the hotel television, and possibly even later than that a trip to the minibar, where they could eat forbidden candy and stay up later than anyone would wish. Nora and Bob had Super Soaker water cannons with them, big weapons that could nail a parent at fifty yards. As quietly as they could, they maneuvered their tubes to the left and right of their father.

"Now!" screamed Nora.

"Eat this!" yelled Bob.

They shot Lloyd ferociously until their guns were empty. Lloyd endured it. He found himself slightly annoyed that he didn't have a water gun himself, but what the hell. The water was cool, and it stung a little. He found himself feeling somewhat strange as the protracted attack went on. After the pique had passed, he detected an inexplicable feeling of jolliness rising in his stomach. It began as a low, knowing chuckle, an adult laugh born of the understanding that he was destined to be the butt of this particular exercise and should probably be a good sport about it. After this low-level laughter was unleashed, however, there came bubbling after it a genuine burbling guffaw, as one emits when tickled gently by expert hands, and after that what could only be called a torrent of giggles emerged from Lloyd, who was then seized with a bona fide spasm of outright tee-heeing that he could control no better than a child could control a flood of tears. Lloyd laughed and laughed, and his kids laughed with him.

As they passed underneath the walking bridge that separated the hotel gardens from the beach, Lloyd peered up, his eyes misted over and squinting with glee, and fastened on a most bizarre sight. On the wooden walkway that spanned the river, looking down, not particularly at him, but at all voyagers floating by, was what looked to be a young man with ice white skin in a revoltingly tiny thong bikini, clogs, wraparound shades, and a towel around his head like a turban. As Lloyd looked up at the fellow, the man seemed to remember something extremely important to him, threw up his hands in the air as if in a parody of surprised dismay, and bolted off in the direction of the ocean. Since just a moment before Lloyd had surveyed approximately four hundred pounds of flesh in a bathing suit that would have challenged the physique of a supermodel, Lloyd simply chalked the incident up to the fact that weird people got even weirder when not constrained by the vicissitudes of everyday life.

They had reached the bottom of the river pool, which emptied out into a large expanse of chlorinated tropical water. On the far side of this expanse was an area where people could play water volleyball, and beyond that, there was a tremendous winding slide that towered over all. In the middle of the swimming area was a small island that was inhabited by flocks of twittering, yawping bird life. Nora and her brother immediately disassociated themselves from Lloyd (who continued to float somnolently in his rubber tire), hopped out of the water, and headed for the long flight of steps that led to the top of the slide.

Donna slipped into the pool, swam over to Lloyd underwater, and surfaced directly under his butt, which succeeded in dumping him out of the tube and into the drink. Lloyd didn't mind. Donna's hair was slicked back like an otter's pelt and her eyes were alive with fun.

"Hi," she said.

"Want to go for a ride in the river?" said Lloyd. "It's pretty great."

"Can we leave our stuff?" Donna scanned the area for miscreants.

"What about that guy with the toupee on his chest over there?" said Lloyd.

"He's with his wife."

"Which?"

"The one with the ridiculous implants and the nose that looks like it was mashed with a chisel."

"How do you know that's his wife?"

Donna lowered her voice and leaned into Lloyd's ear conspiratorially. "I've been watching them," she said.

"And based on this, you don't believe they're a danger to our homestead?" said Lloyd.

"No. She's just done her nails and he's completely plastered."

"Okay," said Lloyd. "Let's go."

As they reached the launching area and were slipping into their tubes, Lloyd noticed the guy in the turban again. He was at some distance, regarding the flamingos in a small fenced-in area hard by the entrance to the luncheon buffet. There was something familiar about him, although that was impossible, wasn't it? He was talking to himself, and while Lloyd watched, the man took off his turban and turned his back. His head was completely shaved.

"Look at that guy, Donna," Lloyd said. "Isn't he weird?"

"Come on, Mr. Fleener!" Donna yelled, hurling herself into the torrent. Only at the last minute, as Lloyd's head plunged beneath the foaming deluge, did he glimpse, in the periphery of sight, the image of the turbaned one, streaking across the patio like a madman, heading for nowhere.

Oh well, thought Lloyd. Lunatics need vacations, too.

Dead Night

"Let's take a walk," said Donna. Bob and Nora were watching a film called *Happy Gilmore,* with Adam Sandler in the title role as the demented golfer. It was the only choice that would work for them both on the hotel's Spectravision.

Donna was up, trolling the room, for what, exactly, she didn't know. She had been pacing the rather modest enclosure like a bird looking for an exit from its cage. Then she decided to take a shower, and she had accomplished that task with decisiveness and efficiency. After her shower, she dressed again, which was strange, and was now standing in the middle of the entryway to their room in white tennis shorts and a tank top that revealed her belly button. Lloyd had always loved her belly button, and not just hers, either. A clean belly button, not the eyes, was the window to Lloyd's soul.

"Let's take a walk," she said more emphatically. There was an odd look on her face.

Although he happened to feel quite sedentary at that particular moment, Lloyd knew better than to refuse. This was not a walk they were talking about. This was a . . . walk. A walk to someplace. He wasn't sure it was a destination he had any desire to reach. Still, why put off the inevitable? A strong, solid finger of anticipation reached deep within him and touched the central location that connected with all others. After all this time, Donna could still achieve this result simply by saying a simple declarative sentence. "Let's take a walk." Not why. Not where. Marriage is the only true test of fortitude, thought Lloyd. The rest is patty-cake.

He sat down and put his arm around Nora, who was watching the film as if it were the key to the understanding of life's important secrets.

"When the movie is over, you guys go to your room and go to sleep," he said to them both. Neither gave any indication that sound molecules had been disturbed in the area. "Hel-lloo!" said Lloyd.

"Dad," said Nora. She was munching on a macadamia nut and regarding the screen with that same paranormal intensity. Bob gave Lloyd a look of slack-jawed incredulity. "Walla Walla!" he said.

"Ouagadouga," said Lloyd.

"Come on, Lloyd," said Donna. He did not want to go.

"I'm coming," said Lloyd.

They walked down the corridor in silence and waited at the elevator bank without saying a word. This was unusual in itself. Lloyd thought of a number of small things he could say, like "Where are we going?" which was stupid, since they were simply going for a walk, right? Or "Why are we going?" which was insulting, since why shouldn't a romantic, relatively young couple on a vacation not take a stroll in the Puerto Rican moonlight? Or even "Hey, baby, whassup?" which seemed quite inappropriate under the circumstances. She showed no inclination to speak, so they just stood there and waited for the elevator.

"Fucking elevator!" yelled Lloyd. He hit the doors of the elevator with an open palm; then he kicked them, once, with all his might.

"Jesus, Lloyd," said Donna. She put a soft little hand on his elbow.

Donna watched the floor indicator closely as it moved from L to 1 to 2. They were on four. She seemed content to watch the progress of the lift. It appeared as if she was trying to piece together a statement of some sort but couldn't quite mount it.

Lloyd looked around. At the other end of the area was a small room that housed the ice machine. In the room, he now saw, was an extremely fat man in a colorful caftan. He had a big garish bath towel wrapped around his head, his back turned to them. Lloyd looked at the guy, who was shoveling ice into one of the hotel-supplied buckets rather frenetically. As Lloyd watched, the fellow reached the top of the bucket, regarded the contents, and, as if surprised by the result of his labors, peered around furtively, then quietly and rather sadly dumped his trove into the ice bin and begin filling it again. He did this twice before the elevator dinged. Donna stepped on.

"Lloyd," said Donna.

"Uh-huh," said Lloyd. He got onto the elevator.

As the doors closed, Lloyd was treated to the sight of this adipose individual, with his finally full ice bucket in tow, twirling to watch them go, crouching like a sprinter on the blocks, then streaking down the hallway to a room at the other end, or—could it be?—to the opposite stairwell, his bathrobe flying behind him like the cape of the headless horseman. Christ! thought Lloyd. What a bunch of weirdos are here!

"Wow," said Donna as the elevator began its slow descent to the ground-floor patio. "We've been having some kind of beautiful weather." Lloyd said nothing. It had been exceptionally nice weather, of course, but he didn't feel like saying so. "I remember when we were in Mexico and it rained the whole first two days of the trip. I was so upset. We kept going to the concierge desk and saying, 'When will it stop raining?' and they'd say, 'It doesn't rain here,' and we'd say, 'But it's raining right now!' and they'd look out at the rain and say, 'No, no, it doesn't rain here in the wintertime. It rains in the summer.' Remember?"

"Yeah," said Lloyd.

"Thank God it stopped raining after a while," said Donna. "We didn't have any money back then and we were spending a fortune. We tried to get out of there, go to Cancún or something, but there was no way to get through to Aeroméxico on the phone. We kept dialing and dialing, and each time we got connected with somebody, it was the wrong number. That was weird. This place is different. This place sort of has its act together completely. But it doesn't change the fact that it would still be a nightmare if it was raining all the time here at a thousand dollars a day, huh?"

The elevator doors had opened. They stepped out into the flagstoned area at the far end of the enormous lobby space. There were bars to the left of them, bars to the right of them, and quite a few revelers in full cry, drinking and pretending to be talking to one another.

"Let's have a drink," said Donna.

"You're reading my mind," said Lloyd.

Come Together

They took a seat at a nook with a low table between two gigantic wicker chairs in an area so noisy that conversation was virtually impossible. She ordered a gin and tonic and looked around. Over in the corner was a couple in their middle fifties, healthy, full of swank, the man in excellent physical condition, tall and ample but by no means fat, hair slicked back, black shirt, open collar, white linen sports jacket, shades, lots of gold on his hands. His wife was by his side, faux blond, that awful copper shade, ornate tortoise and gold barrette holding it up, gold lamé sheath showing tons of bosom, ostentatious ring on the appropriate finger. She laughed at something he said, still capable of mirth together after many years of marriage, marriage building both into something more than the sum of them. She and Lloyd, too, still a lot of laughs when you got right down to it. Maybe that was more important than any other single thing. After the romance and the sex and the acquisition and the kids and the toys and the house and the fights and the talking, all that talking . . . maybe it was all about the laughs.

Lloyd was sitting quietly in the roomy rattan chair opposite her, slugging back his silly tropical drink, eyes doing a quick 180 on the room. They put the drinks in gaudy glasses and decked them out with ridiculous umbrellas, all to disguise the lethal blow they delivered. They didn't call it punch for nothing.

"I just thought it would be a shame if we got away to a beautiful place like this and didn't have a few minutes alone together," she said, twizzling her drink, not looking at him. She couldn't stand to look at him, all of a sudden. She loved him so much, her stomach hurt.

"Yeah. I mean, no," said Lloyd. "I mean, this is nice." He averted his eyes from her, too. "Crazy people here," he said.

"Everybody's crazy, when you get right down to it," said Donna. She drank for a while. So did he.

It was a good drink. Very tasty, and huge. A party drink. That's what this was, after all, wasn't it? One big party. Puerto Rico. Sun. Drinks. A little gambling. Later, maybe, he would play some blackjack, a few slots. He didn't enjoy the casino as much as he used to. As he got older, he couldn't stand to lose, that was it.

"God, it's a beautiful night," said Donna. She slipped out of the chair and stood in front of him. He gazed up at her from the comfort of his seat. "Let's go out and see some of it, Lloyd. Let's get out of here."

There were a few couples strolling in the moonlit garden, watching the flamingos cutely sleeping on their lone, spindly legs. The river pool burped and chuckled in the background. Across a stone sidewalk, they arrived at a wooden platform that held a bench and an outdoor showerhead. Without speaking, they both removed their shoes and placed them neatly on the boards beneath the bench. Lloyd rose from this simple action and felt the dirt and wet of the little platform beneath his feet, the wind between his toes. Donna wasn't talking anymore, he noticed. He wished she were.

On the beach, an occasional runner huffed by. One of them was doing more than jogging, Lloyd noticed. It was a young fellow in sweats from neck to ankle, a baseball cap on his head. He was running flat out, as if in a race for his life, and not in a straight line, either, but hauling his butt at top speed in a wild zigzag, this way and that, running erect, with his chest and stomach jutting out, his chin tucked in, galumphing in the direction away from the spill of boulders that lay to the southeast, toward the lights of the adjacent hotel, more than two miles away.

"Let's stay away from that guy," said Lloyd.

"Sure," said Donna. "Let's head for the rocks."

All Kidding Aside

They walked down to the water's edge and watched the moon and stars play on the surface of the ocean. Most talks have a predetermined path and a relatively predictable ending, beginning inconsequentially, proceeding in a neligible fashion, even if the topic is ostensibly quite important, then ending the same way, with no one the worse for wear. A very few, throughout the course of a life, do not. What happens in those conversations counts, changes everything, not just for a day but forever. Lloyd had spent his life avoiding such discourses, but some things cannot be avoided, even by an expert.

It was terrible, this silence. Lloyd longed to break it but could not. For the first time in years, he could think of absolutely nothing to say. No bullshit would do. No facile schmooze. The horror of this sunk in slowly.

"It's nice here," said Donna at last.

"Yeah," he said. "Why can't we live here?"

They walked down the beach a bit, and before long, Lloyd reached out and took Donna's hand, and she let him take it. There were no more runners now; the crowd had thinned out entirely. There was nothing but the roar and whoosh of the sea against the shore, and the occasional cry of the airborne predator, and the sound of their feet against the wet, cool sand. After about twenty minutes, they reached the rockfall that marked the end of the hotel property. On the other side of this barrier was desolate beach that led up to private homes that were by no means luxurious. Several, at a very great reach, seemed to be trailers. Little lights winked within. Lloyd wondered what their lives were like, these people. Clearly, they were poor. But were they happy?

Just as money didn't always destroy happiness, poverty didn't, either. The site upon which their mobile homes stood would be worth millions if someone with means chose to build there. These structures were nothing much, but the location—wasn't that what really counted? Location, location, location, right? Did they appreciate that? What were they doing right now? Watching TV? How terrible. Get out in the luxuriant Puerto Rican night! Hell, he would probably be inside with a beer and a sitcom if he lived here. Living anywhere, you don't see after a while.

Lloyd turned away from the wilderness on the other side of the property line. On their beach, all was pristine and suitable for framing.

"So I guess you've sort of noticed I've been kind of preoccupied lately," said Donna.

"Naw," said Lloyd. "We've both got a lot on our plates." This seemed to throw Donna for a fifteen-yard loss. She fell quiet, then bent over from the waist and began a desultory hunt for the shells she liked to collect. Lloyd picked up a handful of rocks and began to skim them over the surface of the ocean. Because he hadn't taken the time to select appropriate projectiles, few of these missiles actually skimmed, however. Most arced over the water, emitted a concise plop, then sank.

"I dunno," he said. "Anyhow, what I mean to say is, yes, now that you mention it. Please continue is what I'm saying." He shot Donna a sidelong glance to see if she had pulled this portion of her act together, but she didn't look one bit together. She looked on the verge of tears. What was there to be crying about? Here in paradise, what could be the source of such grief? Nothing local. Something imported, then, carried with them from their native shore.

"You're killing me here, Donna," he added finally.

This seemed to do the trick. Donna shook her head in slight annoyance, as if to clear it from the babble that was going on within. "The thing is, Lloyd," she said, "I was sort of in love with Chuck there for a little while last summer and we kind of had a thing that went on. I don't feel good not telling you about it anymore because I need to tell you about it. So that's what I'm doing. Telling you about it."

Lloyd's legs felt awfully weak. He just stood there in the shallow water at the brink of the ocean. Three thousand miles from there was Europe. But it would be tough to swim.

"Uh-huh," said Lloyd.

"So anyway, that's what I wanted to tell you." Donna sat on a large boulder and stared out into the black of the ocean. She began to cry. Lloyd wanted to comfort her, except that he had a sense that it was he who was supposed to be in need of comfort, and he didn't want to give up that advantage.

"Okay, you told me," he said, and all the rage in the world rose up inside him. Where did he get off being angry, anyway? His mind was drifting, and he suddenly felt very analytical and, yes, smart for the first time in ages. Intelligence! He still had it. So why had he not seen this coming? Sure, for a while, he had suspected something, particularly around the time she was getting suspiciously creative during sex, but that wasn't a bad thing, was it? He had felt quite stupid resenting this new inventiveness. What kind of a lump was he? Was not marriage always supposed to change and grow? He had dismissed his fears.

At the same time, he'd had a few things on his docket, as well. Would this not be a good time to make a clean breast of his improprieties?

Possibly not.

"Oh, man, Donna," he said. The wind was warm at his back. He sat down and buried his face in his hands and tried to collect the strands of his personality, which now felt as if they were flapping in the breeze, with several coming completely undone and wafting off into the ocean. "Oh, man," he said again. Then he was silent. The only sound, other than the whoosh and thump of the water and the occasional sigh of the wind in the trees, was the soft noise of Donna snuffling into a tiny balled-up Kleenex as she sat on one of the big boulders at the lip of the sea.

"I'm so sorry, Lloyd," she said. "You get into a rhythm of things and then something comes along to break that rhythm and you spend so much time skimming along . . . on the top. When a person comes along, not just a person, could be anything, anybody, who makes you feel something very deeply, Lloyd . . . feelings are their own justification, and you sort of feel liberated in a weird way to do whatever you want to do because so much of what you want to do you never get to do, if you know what I mean, that when a thing comes along who just feels so right, even though it's wrong, you feel sort of exempt from the rules, at least for a while, because the way you feel makes its own rules. I don't think I'm explaining myself very well."

A giant embolism of grief was rising inside Lloyd. He could feel it surfacing but could do nothing to estimate its size, or its time of arrival. He simply sat on the sand and waited for it to break.

"I mean, I don't want to say it was essentially innocent, because in a way, that's the most terrible part of it," said Donna in a voice so remarkably disembodied that Lloyd had to hear it with some portion of his inner ear rarely utilized in daily service.

"I'm not sure I want a full blow-by-blow," he said.

"Let me talk, Lloyd," she said, not without tenderness. "Don't try to manage this one."

"Okay," said Lloyd.

"Chuck is a good guy. You know he is. He came over during the day quite a bit when he was doing the kitchen. He never came on to me. You know I wouldn't have been hospitable to that kind of thing. We just talked. I guess that was the insidious part of it. We spent a lot of time chatting, and after a while, I found I was really looking forward to him coming over, and then after the kitchen was done, he found little excuses to come over to fix up tiny things and I could tell he was looking forward to coming over also. I don't mean this to sound like any kind of an accusation, because, God knows, I'm in no position to accuse anybody of anything, and I'm not trying to mitigate my . . . sin . . . but this was a time when you were very distant for some reason, Lloyd, very distant, and then you were away for a good part of the summer, and I realized at the time there were a lot of things on your mind. I didn't want to bother you, but the truth is, I guess, that I didn't want you to bother me, either, and I suppose I thought I could manage the situation. But some situations, you can't manage. Some situations manage you."

"Uh-huh," said Lloyd. He sat on the sand and thought about himself and Donna and Mona and Ron and Walt and Doug and Bob and Nora and Darling and Sweet and Fitz and all that remained to be done before he could lie down and rest. "Some situations, you can't manage," his wife had said. "Some situations manage you."

"So how many times did you do it?" he said.

"Oh, Lloyd," said Donna, and gazed off in the direction of Spain.

"I have to know whether this essentially innocent friendship blossomed into a brief but torrid dalliance or exploded into a rutting paroxysm of blind lust," said Lloyd.

"Sort of the former," said Donna. "There was a week or so there when we kind of lost it."

"Mmm," said Lloyd.

"And then it was over, at least the physical part, I swear to you, Lloyd, I swear. I mean, Chuck is married. So am I. I don't think either of us wanted to . . . I know this sounds strange, but I don't think either of us wanted to cheapen what was a pretty good friendship by declining into a caricature of ourselves, skulking around, screwing all over the place. I've seen people involved in that kind of thing, and the whole experience turns them stupid. Anyhow, I thought that once the other stuff ended, I could put a nail in the entire incident and keep it to myself, and that you need never know, but I couldn't stand walking around with the knowledge inside me all the time, Lloyd. It didn't get lighter; it got heavier. And finally, I guess I had to get rid of it, I had to, Lloyd, because I love you and I can't love you the way I should until this horrible mass is moved out of the space between us."

"I think I get you," said Lloyd. Christ, he thought to himself. Let it go. What was he holding it in for? Let it out! But . . . what would emerge, and what would follow after? The anger, first. But what was under the anger? Something colder, then. Yes. The knowledge that he could hurt her just as badly—no, worse, because he could slice open his dark secret and show her months and months of humping and even, God, a proposal of marriage that had yet to be formally taken off the table. Ha! How would she chew on that? What had begun as a cleansing exercise in truth would certainly end up in an apocalyptic conflagration that would leave their marriage looking like Main Street Nagasaki after game day. Sure. Tell her all about it. Mona. Watch her face move from the grief and contrition she now felt into shock, into rage, into alienation, evaluation, detachment, determination, and, ultimately, calm. The information about Mona, while devastating in a certain kind of way, was data that Donna could eventually manage. It would let her off the hook, and that was bad, but that was not the worst thing. It would undermine everything she was right now fighting for. And she was fighting for them, wasn't she? Why should he sabotage that? To make himself feel better? To get his own guilt off his chest? To strike back at her? He raised his head from the sand and looked at his wife. She was sitting on the rock, her head lowered, her sleek hair combed straight back, her hands dangling between her knees, spent, drained of force. He could knock her over with the load he was carrying right now. But what would come after that? Something unknown. Right now, he had control of the situation. He could manage it. In an environment where an excess of free, unfettered truth was flying around, could he say the same?

And beyond all this cogitation, there was something else. That pocket of pure feeling that was rising within him, screaming toward the surface. He took a breath and opened himself to it. Come on, he thought. Come on, baby. Let's see what you've got.

"How about you, Lloyd?" said Donna. She rose, walked over to the patch of beach right next to him, sat down, and began to dig in the sand with a stick. She looked somewhat perkier than she had in a great long while. And vulnerable, too. Stripped of something sticky and heavy that had been encrusting her personality as varnish obscures wood.

"Hm?"

"We've been married for more than a decade. You're on the road a lot. How about you? Have you ever? I want to know. I want us to leave this beach in full possession of all the facts so we can move on, Lloyd, move on together."

"No," said Lloyd.

There was a silence.

"Is that no, you never, or no, you don't want to move on together?" Donna said.

"I do. I do want to move on together," said Lloyd.

"So that would be a definitive no kind of answer, then," said Donna.

"That's right," said Lloyd. He let it sit there for a while. If she wanted to pursue it, fine. If not, all the better.

"I don't believe you, Lloyd," she said after a while.

"Well," said Lloyd, and his chosen path reached up and embraced him fully, and forever, "that would be up to you."

Lloyd sat on the beach and thought things over. Then he closed his eyes and sat some more. After a while, a strange moan rose from his chest and escaped into the night.

"Lloyd," said Donna. She sounded concerned. "What?" she said. "Tell me." The crease of doubt and mistrust on her brow had almost disappeared.

"Nothing," said Lloyd.

"Don't tell me nothing. It's not nothing."

"No," said Lloyd. He rooted around in the sand with his finger and watched water bubble up from underneath. Where they were sitting then was basically built on water: a layer of hard surface, then underneath . . . water.

"What, Lloyd?" Donna reached out and touched his arm. "What?" she said.

"No, no," said Lloyd. "It's nothing, really." Something was happening in the region of his chest. It was a heavy sensation, like swirling clouds coalescing around a central point of darkness. He wasn't lying to Donna, either. He didn't know what to say. There were no words for what he was feeling. It was an enormous pain, a constriction in the core of his self that was squeezing all the coherent thought out of his body. He could barely breathe. His face felt hot. The corners of his mouth were pulling downward, too, inexorably, turning his aspect into the quintessential, almost-comic mask of tragedy. His goddamned lower lip was trembling. Christ! This had to stop!

"I'm just hurt is all," he said. His chest caved in and his gut contracted as if it had been socked with a club, and his mouth, which had been struggling to stay shut with some propriety, broke open, and his eyes squeezed shut as two big, plump, salty tears erupted from their corners. "Ugh," said Lloyd. His entire system began to rock up and down and from his throat came a terrible choking noise that sounded something like *whuff whuff whuff*. And he could not see, because his entire visual apparatus was fully engaged in producing a steady stream of hot fluid.

"Oh boo hoo hoo," said Lloyd.

"Lloyd," said Donna. She fell against him on the sand and kissed his face lightly. She did not make him turn his head or look at her. Her face, too, had turned down in all directions, tears quietly meandering down her cheeks, into her mouth, falling now and then, *plop plop,* on the sand as she leaned downward to comfort Lloyd. But she made no noise in her crying; possibly, she was unaware that she was even engaged in it.

Lloyd could not stop. When was the last time he had cried like this? More than ten years ago, when he had received the phone call telling him that his father would never truly recover from the stroke that had laid him low the day before. Lloyd had received that news with great maturity, then closed his office door, put his head down on his desk, and sobbed until he came back to himself and it seemed stupid and futile to go on weeping, because it wouldn't change anything. Then he had gone to a meeting about the wisdom of divesting several small-market plants in order to boost short-term earnings. He had been against it but had not prevailed.

"I'm all right," he said to Donna. But he could not stop crying, and as he cried, he realized he didn't want to stop crying, that crying felt very good, that as he cried, he was getting lighter, and that what he was shedding in this pointless exercise was nothing less imposing than the awesome burden of being a grown-up. And Christ, didn't it feel good. As a way to live, for a grown-up, it was second to none! Why did he even try to be a grown-up? Had it ever helped him? Most of the successful people he knew acted like petulant, insane children with fully adult malevolence and power. The hell with the burden. He was done with it.

Lloyd wiped his nose on his sleeve and took a deep breath.

"Ungh," he said.

"Lloyd," said Donna. She pushed him down on the sand and climbed on top of him. They were way out by the boulders, half a mile from the nearest life. "Lloyd," she said again. "Are you sure you have nothing to tell me?"

"I love you, Donna," said Lloyd, pulling her down to him.

After a while, they walked down the shore to the hotel. About halfway there, Lloyd began to run, which was no pretty sight, but that was all right, because he wasn't thinking about how he looked. He didn't run very fast, but he kept at it for quite some time. Before he tired out, he was back at the little platform that housed their shoes. Donna arrived sometime thereafter. Then, together, they walked back into the hotel, took the elevator up to their rooms in silence, kissed the children, who were asleep in their room, and went to bed without saying one single word more.

Except, of course, it didn't work out that way.

Ron Gets Serious

Ron sat in the palm tree and hung his head. It's over, he thought. He felt relief, and also a crushing sadness. Worse, he was sober.

The cocaine had given out long ago, and it was just as well, seeing as how his nose was a complete mess, clogged and tender to the point of bursting. About an hour ago, he had climbed the tree and settled in with his twelve-power Nikon binoculars. This gave him an exquisite view of the happenings at the far end of the beach, but not so powerful as to be intrusive. Lloyd had a right to his privacy.

The ensuing scene between Donna and Lloyd had stirred him deeply, both as a stalker and as a man, particularly when, as they reached the beach outside the hotel, Lloyd broke into a leaden trot down the shoreline. Lloyd's gait was not graceful, and the action was conducted at such a phenomenally tedious pace as to appear in slow motion. Ron watched Lloyd run, and he was assaulted with a painfully acute sense of Lloyd's humanity. It made his heart hurt.

What was he doing here? He had come for a purpose. What was it? To affect Lloyd in some dramatic way, to show Lloyd . . . something. Now it all seemed so arbitrary and vague. What was his life all about, really? Nothing. Why? Because he was nothing. In a very real sense, he did not exist.

Inside his chest was a vast emptiness. Inside his head was a vast emptiness. In whatever muscle of the spirit the will is contained, the same. He took out the small plastic gun that he had been carrying in his waistband. It was tiny and very, very light. He put it to his head.

"Click," he said. He did not pull the trigger. But he liked the feeling that he could do so anytime he wanted. Ron climbed down from the tree and headed back to the lobby of the hotel, where he intended to go into the casino and lose as much of his money as he could before closing time. Then he would see. He was a completely empty vessel—no purpose, no context, no clue. He would wait for a sign. It would come. Then he would flow into it like steel into an empty mold.

"Try me, God," he said to himself as he silently took his place at one of the fifteen-dollar gaming tables.

And God said, *Ron, baby! I was wondering when you'd get in touch!*

Lloyd Gets the Message

Lloyd stood in the vestibule of their sumptuous vacation suite and inhaled down to the tops of his sandals. On the plastic telephone on the table by the side of their ridiculously enormous bed, an amber light was blinking.

Lloyd knew what this meant. They had a message. It could be a message from the hotel management, inviting them to a cocktail party the next night. But it was awful late for one of those, and, in any event, they had been in the manager's office for a small, select gathering of about eighty disassociated oddballs, including themselves, just the night before.

The message could be a wrong number. That happened. Several years ago, Lloyd had been in a hotel in Des Moines, Iowa, where quite naturally he did not know a soul. Exactly just such a message light had greeted him in his room when he came back from a tough-steak dinner with key suppliers. A message was on the voice mail: "Call home immediately. Something terrible has happened." He had called home. There was no answer. Lloyd went nuts, climbed on a small rented charter Cessna, flew to Chicago, called home from O'Hare. Still no answer. In those days before cellular penetration, mobile telephones were few and far between, and there had been none on the flight on which he sat that night, consumed with dread. When he landed at La Guardia, he fled to a pay telephone near the luggage-claim area. It took him a while to find one that wasn't trashed, this being the middle 1980s, when everything was falling apart. He finally located a working implement and dialed.

"Hello?" said a groggy voice. It was Donna. She had been sleeping. Of course she was! It was dawn.

"Donna?" Lloyd felt tears spring from the corners of his eyes. From a space over by the electric doors, a limo driver held a card with Lloyd's name on it. Joy flooded through him. "Donna! I got your message!"

"What message? Where are you?" He told her. "Could you pick up some chive cream cheese on the way home?" she added after some thought.

Who would call him on vacation like this? A foolish subordinate whipped into a snit about an issue he didn't feel empowered to resolve? Some moron seeking his faxed signature on something?

"You have sixteen unplayed messages," said the metallic voice of the system. The voice was vaguely female, and friendly without being warm. "Press seven to retrieve your messages, nine for other options."

Lloyd pressed seven. There were no other options.

"Lloyd," said a voice he knew only too well. "This is Doug. I'm sorry to bother you on vacation, but something has come up that you should know about. Tomorrow morning, we're going to issue a statement from Arthur's office, informing the New York headquarters that it is being phased out, effective immediately, and its operational duties shifted to corporate headquarters in Chicago."

"Whuff," said Lloyd.

"Of course, this has several implications for you personally. First, all four hundred people who work in New York—including Walt, I'm sorry to say—must be transitioned almost immediately if we're going to contain the severance implications in the first quarter."

"Whoo," said Lloyd. He sat down on the bed and dangled his head between his knees, the phone still on his ear.

"You and, I believe, young Mona are invited to relocate your respective acts to Chicago as soon as possible."

"I see," said Lloyd.

"The good thing is that, if the boys in Finance are correct, we may be able to eliminate more than ten thousand jobs worldwide and concentrate all serious compensation within a very small circle located at the corporate center in Chicago. Do you have any idea what that will do to the value of any stock options you may now possess? Lloyd, this is going to be even more impressive than we had first believed. It will be . . . our legacy. Call me as soon as you can." There was a click.

"Press five to discard your message. Press eight to save it in your mailbox," the machine said. Lloyd discarded the message. He felt sick. His entire home base—destroyed! This was . . . too much!

"Message two," said the machine. "Lloyd. Walt," it added. "I'm sorry to bother you on vacation, but there's something happening here and I don't know what it is. What I'm hearing seems unbelievable, Lloyd. What I want to say is . . ." There was a lengthy, somewhat liquid pause on the other end of the line. Lloyd could hear Walt pinching his lower lip with autonomic intensity. "What's goin' on? That's basically what I'd like you to find out, and then give me a call about it." There was a click. "Press five to discard your message," said the machine. "Press eight to save it in your mailbox." Lloyd pressed eight. There was a beep.

"Lloyd? This is Mona," said the machine. Lloyd held the receiver so close to his ear, he could almost feel it pressing into his central nervous system. Mona was whispering. "Lloyd. You have to call me. I'm hearing the most amazing things." There was a strange hiatus. What was Mona doing in that void? He imagined her sitting at her desk, the most terrible news of her career bouncing off the sterilized enclosure, her forehead cupped in her delicate, perfectly manicured hand, her sweet, slightly minty breath fogging up the silver letter opener she kept on her blotter. "Lloyd," she said at last. "It's possible, I guess, that we're just plain fucked. After all the fucking that's gone on, maybe we're just plain . . . fucked. Call me, Lloyd. I don't know what support you could possibly provide. When a boat goes over a waterfall, does it need a competent captain?" It occurred to Lloyd that Mona had been drinking. He almost sniffed the receiver. "Lloydnik," she said after a while. Click.

"Press five to discard your message. Press eight to save it in your mailbox," the machine said. Lloyd discarded the message. What would Donna think if she heard it? Would she intimate some nonbusiness context? Lloyd looked over at his wife. She was sitting on the edge of the bed in an aquamarine T-shirt that said PUERTO RICO! on it in gigantic red letters. Above the words, there was a picture of a fish. It was a very colorful fish. Below the T-shirt, Lloyd glimpsed a tiny patch of frilly lace.

"I have sixteen messages," said Lloyd. "None of them are any good."

"I can see that," Donna said. She leaned over to the edge of her night table and snagged a big plastic hairbrush and brushed her hair.

Message four was from Darling, who was sorry to bother him on vacation but had heard something. Message five was in Japanese. Message six was three minutes in length. It seemed to come from an empty room, and it had a strange echo to it. In the background, there was a robotic clanking, and, very faint, the sound of a dog barking. Then a burst of rather hostile Spanish, clearly directed to a listener huddled up very close, then a click. Message seven? In German. Lloyd picked out the word *Anschluss,* which almost cleared his memory barrier, but not quite. Messages eight through fifteen were clicks. Each one rang in Lloyd's soul like a mallet hitting a bell. Eight clicks. How many bits of information were contained therein? Who would be on the other end of the line when he was finally around to answer it? One very obsessive, possibly angry individual starved for his attention?

During the series of automated phone instructions following the sixth click, Lloyd, cradling the receiver to his ear, scooted over to the minibar that was located in the alcove across from the bathroom. In the door of the refrigerator, he found what he was looking for—minibottles of Bombay Sapphire. He selected three small doses of the world's finest gin and brought them back to the night table. There was a water glass there with perhaps an ounce of liquid in it. He poured it out on the carpet, twisted open the blue dispensers, loaded up a mammoth shot, and downed it by the time message sixteen was spooling in.

"Lloyd," said a deeply relaxed male voice that seemed only doors away. "It's me. I'm down in the casino. It's like I can't lose. I'm up, oh . . ." There was a pause. "I'm up twelve thousand dollars and I've only been playing for twenty minutes. I think it's a sign, man. Come on down, huh? I'll be at the craps table."

There was a click. Who the hell? It sounded like Ron Lemur, but what could Ron be doing here? And the voice . . . the voice sounded different from Ron's somehow. More placid, mature. If it was Ron, it meant that he was here, and therefore that he had popped a gasket and was really and truly, at long last, insane. That was possibly a bad thing, although maybe not.

Lloyd stood up and rubbed his face. He was drunk. Not mad drunk, or sad drunk, but empowered with a healthy buzz that filled his spirit with the sense that nothing could come in his way. Beneath that was an abyss jammed with every rainbow feeling known to man. He had kicked off his sandals when he sat down to listen to his messages. Now he pulled them on again. In the three and a half seconds it took him to do so, several things went through his mind and he came to some decisions.*

"Where are you going, Lloyd?" said Mona. No, no. It wasn't Mona. It was Donna.

"To the casino," said Lloyd. "There's a maniac downstairs I'm going to need if I'm going to make things work out the way I want."

"Are you all right?" she said. It wasn't an expression of anxiety. It was a request for information.

"I will be," said Lloyd. He went.

Ron Puts It All Together

"I'll take it the hard way," said Ron. He made quite a sight as Lloyd finally glommed on to him across the crowded morass of humanity that was the hotel casino. He was dressed in a shiny sateen kaftan, dead white, with gold piping. He had on a pair of wraparound shades that completely concealed his mental aspect. On his head was a New York Yankees baseball cap, backward. He fit right in with the rest of the casino clientele. It was Lloyd, in his shorts and T-shirt, who stuck out.

Ron threw the dice. "Yes!" he shouted, and bent to pick up the chips.

Lloyd slowly crossed the casino, dropping dollar tokens in the slots as he went. At several, there was a brief alarm and several additional coins dropped from the guts of the machine and into the bin. Lloyd collected these and fed

---

*Lloyd's thoughts: Walt is toast, huh? He'll have to be told. I guess that's supposed to be my job. Part of the initiation. Prove you're true senior-management material by killing your father. The whole office, too. Bye-bye. So long. Hundreds of people into the pit. I like those people. Clara and Edna, who make the soup in the cafeteria. Nice ladies. Where are they going to find another job? They'll be bag ladies. Tough. Wall Street will love it. Kill ten thousand jobs and up bump the buy recommendations. And you know what? I don't want to move to Chicago to a corner office way up high, surrounded by a tossed salad of overcologned guys who speak English as a second language. Where do I fit in that scenario? Who's running the show? What's my title gonna be? Will I like it? Will I be at the nexus of the power matrix? How come I'm talking like this? I've become such an incredible asshole. I hate myself.

them into the same machine until they were gone. On several occasions, it took him a bit of time to lose it. But he always succeeded. After a while, he worked himself next to the space in which the individual who appeared to be Ronald Lemur in a kaftan was attracting money.

"Do I know you?" Lloyd said to the bizarre figure who stood next to him, sucking up chips, a placid expression on its countenance.

"Hi, Lloyd," said the creature.

"What are you doing here, Ron?"

"I'm winning."

Lloyd watched Ron play for a while, and it was awe-inspiring. No matter what the boy did, boom, out came the cheers, the oohs and aahs from the women, the click of chips being placed on his stack.

"What's your secret?" Lloyd asked after as much of this as he could stand.

"Divine intervention," said Ron. He abruptly stood and passed the dice to his right. The table gave him a lusty hand and he acknowledged the applause warmly, like a movie star gracious enough to notice the groupies waiting at the gate for his limo to pass. "I want to speak with you, Lloyd. I was just killing time."

"Great, Ron. I mean it."

They went into the lobby, where rattan chairs suitable for the fattest of cats were strategically arrayed into conversation areas. They took two and sat for a while.

"I was seriously pissed off at you, Lloyd, for wrecking my life."

"Uh-huh," said Lloyd. "So what were you doing? Tailing me?"

"Yeah. I'm sorry."

"To what end?"

Ron leaned back and put his hands over his face. It appeared, for a moment, that he was on the verge of offering something interesting. "Oh, wow," he said instead. "Do you have a tissue?" He raised his head, and Lloyd was surprised to see that his nose was bleeding, and quite a lot, too.

"Hey, man," said Lloyd. He saw a stack of bar napkins on a small side table near his elbow, and he handed them over to Ron.

"Dagoo," said Ron. He applied the paper to his nose for a while. Lloyd watched him carefully and waited. "De thig id," Ron said after he had twirled two tissues and gently placed one in each nostril. "I kide of flibbed by lid. I'b dot zure if I wadded do hurt oo or scare oo or just throw bysef od your bercy. Bud id dud't batter. I'b buch better dow. I habb't had a drik or . . . anythig . . . all dight."

"I'm glad to hear it," said Lloyd. "Because we're going to need each other, Ron, and I'd like to think I can count on you."

"Bleeze, Lloyd. I cad't lib outside de corporashud. Let be cub hobe. I'll do adythig."

"Then listen carefully," said Lloyd. "What I want to do, Ron, and I can explain more about this to you later, but this is the crux of it . . . what I want to do, Ron, is to kill the deal."

"Doh!"

"Yep. And I want to do it today."

"Dooday!"

"So go and clean yourself up, and put on a suit, and meet me in the lobby at five A.M. We're going to be on the first plane out of here tomorrow morning."

"Oo dote wadt de deal adybore?"

"No. It's not working out well for the folks I care about, not the least of whom is me. I haven't really figured out what that's going to take yet. But it's not going to be easy, and we may have to do some pretty horrible things that don't, on the surface, seem quite right. I don't see how I can get that part of it done without you."

"Oh, Lloyd, ban. Adythig. I bean dat."

Ron impulsively thrust out his hand to seal the deal. Lloyd took it.

On the Airplane

Lloyd sat in the first-class compartment and sipped at his vodka and tonic. To his left, seated in the roomy window seat, sat Ron, an empty husk waiting to be filled by the next compelling order. Lloyd was pretty sure that if he timed that order right, it could work to his advantage. That was all one could ask of any subordinate.

Ron was sitting in relative quiescence and munching on the hot nuts. He had also requested a portion of the celery sticks and ranch dressing, and he was at that moment thoughtfully dipping a large pecan into the creamy mixture. "Mmmm," he said, but not too loudly.

Lloyd felt tired, but knew he could not sleep.

"You lean back and catch some z's, Lloyd, man," said Ron.

It's strange, thought Lloyd as he slipped on a pair of headphones and settled back into a seat the size of a small hospital bed. Here was this person, who had only recently been a source of anxiety and, apparently, some form of danger to him, and now he was an ally, if not a friend. Who knew what was going on inside that head? Anything? Lloyd sneaked a look. Ron was still ruminating over that same nut.

"Swallow it, Ron," he said.

Ron swallowed it.

What was the situation as they sat on the plane, headed for New York? Lloyd closed his eyes and forced himself to think about it. Walt had dreamed a dream more than two years ago. He had articulated it to Lloyd first, and Lloyd had thought it was absurd. To acquire so much market share that the entire business universe could not function without purchasing a product or service from their corporation? Madness. It would take capital, but was capital ever the issue? It would take an exercise of vision and power, but that could be supplied, too. It would take, above all, what were known in the corporate world as "auspices"—the framework of associations, funding, or sheer potential energy that gave a person or group the right to proceed. Lloyd enjoyed having operated under some of the best auspices ever. Some of those auspices were, of course, provided by Doug, but Doug's auspices came from Arthur. But who was Arthur? What did Arthur do? What kind of guy was he? Was he a guy at all? Did he care what happened to anyone as a result of his actions? Did he take actions? Would he respond if spoken to? Could one speak to him in order to generate a desired response? Could he change his mind?

Somewhere along the line, he and his pals had lost control. They had thought they could ride the wave. But they could not. It got too big. Others fell in love with the deal, its size, complexity, and beauty. Now it wasn't theirs anymore. Whom did the deal belong to now? The shareholders, who viewed their world as nothing but an investment? The lawyers and bankers? The employees who would suffer for it? For that was certain. Any transaction was a revolution of one form or another, and revolutions invariably hurt people. Some people, true, they also helped, but not as many as Lloyd and his generation had once thought. People died. Stuff changed. The winners wrote the annual report. Was he even one of the winners anymore?

A colossal olive of remorse and shame lodged in Lloyd's throat, and suddenly he felt like crying. He looked over at Ron to see if this eruption of human feeling was noticed. Ron was sleeping, his chair tilted back so far, it functioned as a bed. His mouth was open and he was snoring very lightly. A driblet of spittle had collected in the corner of his mouth. Was he dreaming? Do uncontemplative people dream?

Now they were well and truly screwed, all of them. Fitz was fifty years old, just short of retirement. He had a kid in college and a mother who needed constant dialysis. Darling? Fifty-eight and a fat, obsessive slob who would never get another gig like this one. Sweet and Burbage and Flom. Rosa, the cleaning woman. Megan, the lady who sold Fig Newtons at the cafeteria. The drivers and accountants and window washers and salespeople and mouse exterminators and Human Resources administrators and strategic planners and all of them, including, quite arguably, he, Lloyd himself, who was

382

expected to transplant his act into a new and infinitely more threatening venue. The whole building. Up in flames. Why? Because the deal was beautiful and they had to have the deal.

Well, the deal was like anything else. It could be killed. There were no rule books on this kind of thing. Best, perhaps, simply to start where one could and begin destroying stuff as one went along.

"Ron," said Lloyd. "Are you awake?"

Drooling Ron was silent for a very long time. Then he said, in a weird, commanding voice, "You worry too much, Lloyd. You'd be better off if you stopped worrying so much and just, like, did . . . whatever."

Lloyd considered Ron's suggestion, aware that he was getting the very best advice anyone born in the 1970s could provide.

"Yeah," said Lloyd. "I'll do that."

Over Atlanta

"Ladies and gentlemen, this is the captain speaking. Those of you on the left side of the plane can get a pretty good view of the city of Atlanta, Georgia," said a Chuck Yeager voice from the control desk of the 767. "The weather in New York is twenty-four degrees and it's snowing pretty hard. I'll get back to you when we're making our final approach in about . . . about an hour and a half or so." There was a click. The cabin went silent.

Lloyd realized that he had been sleeping, but he was awake now. Ron, too, was sentient, staring straight ahead of him, a vacant expression on his already-inexpressivce countenance. His lower lip stuck out a bit, and it trembled, for the voice of the Lord had chosen that very moment to have a word with Ron.

Ron, man. Are you doing everything you can to support Lloyd here? You seem to be doing a lot of eating and sleeping.

"I'm doing my best," said Ron. "It's not clear yet what he wants of me."

"Did you say something?" said Lloyd.

The thing is, Ron, I want to remind you that you have a problem completing things. You're smart. You're determined. But are you a winner? The jury is out.

Ron sat, fuming. He didn't feel it necessary to dignify this nonsense with a reply of any sort.

I mean, for instance, you came to Puerto Rico to impact Lloyd, and all you did was wreck your nose. I'm not saying things haven't worked out sort of all right. But you certainly didn't stay on mission.

"The mission changed! I'm flexible! That's a mark of maturity."

Hey. Come to think of it . . . Where's the gun? You didn't lose it, did you?

A bolt of terror tore through Ron. What indeed? He had not thought about the little developmental weapon since he had shoved it into his pocket out there on the beach. When was that? The night before. Where, if he had been thinking afterward, would he have put it? And then he saw it, in his inner eye, glowing in the depths of his flight bag, inside of a shaving kit sitting in the bottom, just beneath the personal CD player.

"It's in my bag, for God's sake," he said.

"Ron, are you speaking to me, man?" said Lloyd.

"No, I'm not."

Do you really still need it? I mean, you've been lucky so far, but do you really think you can hide it forever?

"I don't see why not. It's plastic. The bullets are plastic. You let me worry about that."

You could be putting the whole project in jeopardy, you moron!

"There's no need to shout at me!"

You don't even know what's going on! You haven't even asked!

"Ron, man," said Lloyd. "Are you in some kind of psychic arrest or what?"

Ron turned his full gaze on Lloyd, and Lloyd saw in those milky, dislocated orbs all the possibilities in an arbitrary universe.

"Lloyd?" Ron said. "Could you tell me what's going on?"

"Okay. Now listen. What's happening is that Doug has decided to eradicate the entire New York office and move a couple of guys to Chicago. The rest of the organization is out of here. Everything's over, Ron, unless we do something about it."

Wow! What a kick in the chops!

"Well," said Ron. "Then let's do something about it."

"We will, buddy." And for the first time, Lloyd felt that this was true, and, quite unexpectedly, a bubbling wellspring of gratitude, empathy, and affection for Ron rose within him like sap through a maple tree in springtime. He went with the feeling. "Somehow, in some way, man, we'll work it out. I have no idea how, but we'll do it if we all hang together." He stopped, unable to continue.

Boy. I'm thirsty. Get me a drink.

"Do you have any reaction to what I've been saying to you, Ron?"

"I do," said Ron. "I do have a reaction."

"Well, what is it?"

Ron was motioning for the flight attendant to come over. What could he possibly want in the middle of this delicate discussion?

"Could I please have a double vodka on the rocks with a twist?" said Ron to the flight attendant. She went.

"Well, what is your reaction, Ron, man?" said Lloyd.

"My reaction, Lloyd, is that maybe we ought to explore the option of beating the shit out of the motherfuckers."

"Uh-huh," said Lloyd, and sat back, facing front. He was pleased. At least Ron was thinking clearly.

Lloyd kept speaking, but Ron did not hear him. He was attempting cognition. This was incredible news for everybody, but where did it leave him? He certainly didn't want his old job back. What a stupid job it had been, too, meaningless crap that would float away on the jet stream of history like ashes after a campfire. Idiotic. But something awaited. He was on this portion of the trek for a purpose. He felt quite strongly that he belonged on this plane, not anywhere else in the world. He belonged here alongside Lloyd, nowhere else. He looked at Lloyd, who had stopped speaking and had taken out the telephone that resided in his armrest. He was looking at it curiously.

Lloyd passed his corporate card through the handpiece of the telephone, which was completely rectangular and about the size of a bread stick. A green light winked on the implement beneath the word *Wait*. Lloyd waited.

"Nice weather we've been having," said Ron.

"Please, Ron," said Lloyd. He waited some more, then pushed End and swiped his card again. "Friggin' things," he said.

"I like the fact that you can choose your own personal movie," Ron observed. What a catalog they had offered! If he had wanted, he could have asked for one of a series of business videos that offered professors from august business institutions discussing the rational works of Drucker, Porter, Peters, and other twentieth-century philosophers dedicated to the science of business. Instead, he had selected Three Stooges, which had been on the "For Kids Only" menu. Ron punched Play.

"What's the point of having these things if they don't work!" yelled Lloyd. He slammed the implement on the armrest and swiped his card again.

Right off the bat, it seemed that Moe had grown angry with Larry and Curly for not following his instructions, which had been quite foolish in their own right, Moe, being a stooge as well, in fact, the head stooge, and what kind of job description was that? As a boss, Moe was always angry. When enraged, he assaulted his subordinates repeatedly, shoving them in the midsection, hitting them on their heads with a frying pan, and more than once thrusting his index and middle finger into the the tender flesh of their eyeballs. Terrorized, they immediately sprang into action, newly determined to get the job done, which they did not, because they were stooges. And so it went. Violence and rage on one side, resentment and incompetence on the other. And it would never get any better for any of them. Each movie was the same as the next. Why? Because they were and always would be . . . stooges. This thought struck Ron as incredibly hilarious. He turned to Lloyd to share his good humor, chortling like mad.

"Be quiet, man," said Lloyd. Then he sat some more, his head cradled in one gently massaging hand, hanging in limbo as he listened for a distant synapse somewhere in space to fire.

Ron cringed. Was Lloyd mad at him? He was alive with paranoia.

"Hello, Lyle?" said Lloyd. Incredible, but this was the guy himself, not his voice mail. "This is Lloyd. I'm on a plane, so let me skip the schmoozing, okay?"

Ron gawked at Lloyd, jaw slightly ajar. What a dude. What a player! And then, miraculously, Lloyd caught his eye and shot him a wink. Could it be? It was! Lloyd had winked at him. You didn't wink at a guy you were mad at!

"What I'm going to tell you is off the record," Lloyd continued in a voice substantial enough to be heard via fiber optics, but so soft, it didn't carry six inches from his lips. "And bear with me, Lyle, what I mean is that this is not to be sourced at all, it's just information, and it came to you from nowhere. I'm not someone close to the company. I'm not a person with knowledge of the situation. I'm not speaking to you. Absolutely no fingerprints on this one. Deal? I'm trusting you here, man."

Lloyd took a small pad from his shirt pocket, flipped it open, and, producing a slender silver pen from somewhere in the briefcase that lay at his feet, began to take notes as he spoke.

"Well, what we have going on here, Lyle, is the first hundred-billion-dollar deal in the history of the human race. It destroys the concept of the nation-state, forever. Yeah. Sure I'll hold."

Lloyd leaned back in his recliner, his phone at his ear. His game face had descended like a cloud. "Essentially a gigantic acquisition designed to corner the entire world market in associated industries. Bundeskrieg, which, as you know, represents about thirty percent of the pie globally. Niente and Niente, based in Rome and Florence. Right. Another twenty-two percent, since their acquisition of Hebridox U.K., which is now its subsidiary, right? And then there's our chunk. Uh-huh. Sure I'll hold." Lloyd once again leaned back far into his flying couch.

"You rule, Lloyd, man," said Ron.

"The part of it that's interesting," said Lloyd into the phone, "is that a very big blob of capital—in the neighborhood of thirty billion, or slightly less than half the initial up-front load—is coming from the folks who are bringing you the new Hong Kong. Yep. I was there last month. Got to be careful over there. They eat dog."

Ron looked at the tabletop before him. In the middle, there sat an almost full glass of vodka, a shred of lime in its crystal depths. Ron grasped it with joy in his heart and downed it in a draft.

"I'm cutting off the guy in Eight C," said one flight attendant to the other. "He's acting rather strangely."

"Do you think there's anything wrong with him?" said the other. "Is he in any discomfort of any kind?"

"I doubt it." The first looked over at Ron carefully from the safety of her service station. "He's had seven Stolis."

"Yeah, sure, financing was interesting," said Lloyd to the reporter from the *Wall Street Journal*. "We're talking in the neighborhood of eighty billion dollars, so I believe if someone was to look into it, they might find that every single bank in the world had a piece of it. Uh-huh. Every single one, dude."

The reporter said something Lloyd couldn't quite catch. All that came through was the phrase "significant regulatory hurdles." An icicle of pure excitement pierced Lloyd's chest. "Good thinking, Lyle," he said.

"Fx mrtx luffernut," said the reporter.

"You're breaking up on me. I'll call you back in an hour or so, when we're landed in New York. And remember. No trace of this, man. Fuck up and I'll kill you. And I can do it, too." Then Lloyd laughed as if he had been joking, and pressed End.

"Ron," he said to the semicomatose individual in the next seat. "Are you going to be able to hang in there and perform as required?"

"I'll do more than what's required, Lloyd," said Ron, turning to face him, his eyes brimming with emotion. "I know I've been a high-maintenance reportee. But I'm your guy, Lloyd."

"I know that, man." Lloyd put a gentle hand on Ron's trembling elbow. "You're gonna be okay. I can't quite give you a complete job description yet, but it's definitely gonna be some kind of VP thing, reporting to the chief operating officer, who will be in New York, goddamn it."

"As long as that's you, Lloyd. I wanna report to you."

"And Ron, tell me something, and be truthful." Lloyd honed in on Ron, whose eyeballs popped open, showing a lot of white. "Are you crazy? I mean, not just crazy like everybody's crazy, but really and truly insane in a way that renders you dysfunctional in a business sense? I need to know, for strategic planning purposes."

Ron turned this important nugget over in his mind. He knew how he replied would have an effect on things later, so he wanted to make his answer count. "I think I might be," he said at last. "As the situation changes, so do I, until I don't quite understand where I'm coming from or who I might be at any given point in time. Does that make me crazy?"

"Not so far," said Lloyd. He put out his arm and squeezed Ron's right shoulder, once, then twice. Ron sat very still, his head down, gulping air a tiny bit.

Lloyd pressed a button marked New Call and dialed.

"Hi," he said to Mona, so softly that even Ron could not hear. "I don't believe I've ever said this to you before, but . . . get dressed. Call Walt and the boys. Tell them to be in the conference room at"—Lloyd looked at his watch—"at ten or so." He listened for a moment. "You're breaking up on me. Listen. What you heard was true. Tell everyone to bring something they think will help kill the deal as it's currently constituted. . . . Because if we don't, we're all fired, that's why. Yep. Call you when I get to a secure line. . . . I already started. Leaked it to the *Journal*. I know. See ya."

He pressed New Call and dialed again. He did not finish dialing and talking, obsessively talking, until he had almost reached his home in the beautiful stretch limousine the company hired to meet him whenever and wherever he landed, in any part of the world. Once there, he showered, shaved, put on his best camel's hair slacks, a new dark brown alligator shirt, knee-length silk socks, and a pair of $245 cordovan slippers he had picked up in Italy, topping it all off with a lush tweedy Armani blazer that always made him feel slender. At 9:00 A.M., Lloyd vaulted a snowdrift and slid into a Town Car he had called as a luxurious indulgence designed in some slight way to defray the indignity of being forced to work on one of the most indolent days of the year. He took his place in the backseat and opened his weekend briefcase. The car pulled away from the curb. Lloyd looked up at his empty house. The next time he returned to it, everything would be different.

"Make time," he said to the driver. Then he picked up the phone and got back to work.

Family Reunion

The building loomed above Lloyd, empty in the dim light of the winter morning. In the lobby, one sleepy, disgruntled guard dozed on holiday duty.

"Earnest, my man," said Lloyd as he ran his magnetic key card through the security system at the front desk.

"Happy New Year," said Earnest without expression. He was reading a large volume. Lloyd could just make out the name on the spine: *Moby-Dick*.

"They all die in the end," he said to Earnest.

"Nah," said the guard. "You're shitting me."

"No, man," Lloyd said. "I was just kidding."

"Good . . . Wow." The guard, who had been sitting up in alarm, eased back in his seat. "That would be some bad ending."

"I hear you," said Lloyd.

"Especially when you work through, like, four hundred pages to get there."

"Yeah," said Lloyd. "That would be whack."

Lloyd went all the way to the top floor. The space was dead empty, empty the way only an office building in the middle of a long weekend can be. The heat was turned way down low, and if he tried, Lloyd could almost see his breath. He walked over to the double glass doors and placed his key card on a small brass medallion that carried the company logo, and the doors hissed open on a magnetic track. Lloyd stepped through into the reception area, which was dark and silent. How many times had he strode manfully through this zone without seeing, immersed in one agenda or other? The receptionist's phone bank was covered with a plastic sheet to eliminate dust from its workings. Lloyd walked over to the towering plate-glass windows and looked out at the frozen city. It was a killer view. By that very window, Walt had given him his first promotion, from associate to manager. Walt had put his arm on Lloyd's shoulder and delivered the news with great pomp and paternal warmth. It was the first time that Walt had established any physical contact with him, short of an occasional pat on the back, and the tactile message was far more powerful than even the promotion itself.

Lloyd turned from the window and felt the silence around him. There was a very faint underscent of something he couldn't quite place, a faint mix of odors left over from the rush and flow of executives, secretaries, deliverymen, food, flowers, cardboard, the leather of briefcases, the slightly moldy scent of wet wool, the rubber of galoshes. Even now, the smells were fading, after only two or three days of inactivity, and underneath it, nothing but dust, slightly dirty carpet, and drywall. If Doug had his way and the deal as written went down, that smell of death would be the only one that remained.

In the distance, Lloyd heard a noise, clear but unmistakable—the sound of a modem connecting to a distant source. He meandered down the hallway until he came to the source of the sound. Walt stood at his assistant's desk, in the alcove outside his vast, magnificent office, looking in desultory fashion at her computer monitor. He was massaging his upper lip, and he did not look up when Lloyd entered.

"Checking the Asian wires," he said.

Lloyd said nothing. He simply entered the antechamber where Walt was and allowed Walt's glow to envelop him. Walt was in casuals also, khaki pants and a sumptuous plaid shirt, a thin alligator belt and shoes to match. His hair was neatly combed, as always, but incredibly, Lloyd noticed a thin dew of very blond and white stubble coated the lower portion of his face. Walt had not shaved.

"There's an item on the Dow Jones news wire outlining pretty much the entire guts of our deal," said Walt noncommittally. "Quite inopportune, given the antitrust and other regulatory issues, not to mention the delicacy of the financing situation and the potential upheaval premature disclosure to the European Union could cause."

"Those guys could really blow things up," said Lloyd with equal sangfroid.

"Hm," said Walt brusquely. "Too bad."

"Anything else there?" Lloyd approached Walt from behind as the older man stood over the monitor, reading, and put his arm gently around Walt's shoulder in order to get a better look at the words as they paraded across the screen.

"Interesting. The writer speculates that—aside from the antitrust and global policy implications—the deal is predicated on the expertise of existing line management in New York, Berlin, and Rome, and that any disruption in the essential infrastructure of these entities might upset the delicate confidence in the global and banking communities that made this whole thing conceivable. He also calls this kind of dealmongering 'impossibly retro.' Ha."

"I don't know that I disagree with him."

"Nope." Walt minimized the icon for the wire service and straightened up, still not looking directly at Lloyd. "What's your plan?" he said with full military crispness. He strode into his vast office and went to his desk.

Lloyd followed as far as the doorway. "How ya doon?" he said.

"Well, you know," said Walt. "Kind of discouraging after everything and all." He was simply standing behind his gleaming marble desk, fascinated by a small imperfection in its surface. He raised his eyes and looked at Lloyd, established eye contact for the briefest nanosecond, then looked down once again, and in that small peek into Walt's tormented red eyes, Lloyd saw all he needed to see.

"It's not written yet, Walt," said Lloyd. "The end of this thing isn't set is what I'm saying."

"Yes, well," said Walt, continuing to gaze into the crystal ball of his desktop. "I'll shoot straight with you, Lloyd. I've been instrumental in ramping this thing up, but now that it's taken this particular turn . . ." There was a very scary silence then, one Lloyd could not break, filled with feeling between them so deep that if it was disturbed in the slightest, it might uncontrollably warp into the interpersonal dimension. "I think you know what I'm talking about," he said at last.

"Come on down and join us in a couple of minutes," said Lloyd.

"Ten-four," said Walt.

Lloyd went to the big double doors of the boardroom, took a deep breath, and pushed his way inside.

They all looked up as one, eyes wide open, like deer browsing by the side of a highway, transfixed by the high beams of an oncoming truck. Darling was closest to the door, slumped into a chair, his hair jutting up at all angles, inappropriate Top-siders on his feet, no socks. On his lower half was a shockingly ancient pair of yellowish wide-whale corduroy pants. Covering his ample chest and girth was an equally venerable stretched-out turtleneck of a pale yellow hue that bespoke tragic overbleaching. He was leaning forward in his chair, his hands dangling between his knees. His nose was running and his eyes appeared to be quite closed. Here was a man in the final stages of physical collapse, the phase that occurred just before a breakdown due to lack of sleep and an excess of alcohol. New Year's Day. Darling was hungover, fifty-eight years old, adipose, quite unlikable, when you got right down to it, and about to be fired.

"Howzit goin', Bob?" said Lloyd.

"Lloyd!" said Bob, sitting up straight. "Sorry about my personal appearance."

"Really?" said Lloyd. "Since when?"

There was a rumble of laughter; then the group broke apart and came together around Lloyd, who stood in the entryway to the boardroom, where he and this very group of people had endured so much boredom, grief, ambition, wrath, fear, greed, pride. One by one, they went to him, waiting their turn to receive a word, a touch, a sardonic glance. Fitz, in informal dress that probably cost more than a weekend at Disney World, looked grouchy and smelled slightly of last night's cigar and bourbon. Sweet was pale and drawn in his gray flannel suit, as always, neat, clean-shaven, ready for business, perhaps a little more wan than usual. This must be particularly hard on Sweet, thought Lloyd, this irrational tango. And there now, against his side, her hand very lightly resting on his right buttock, below the field of general view, was Mona. How long had it been? Just a week since he had seen her! It seemed like minutes. It seemed like years. Here, nowhere else, was where he wanted to be.

"Let's sit, everybody," said Lloyd. "You smell good," he said to Mona, who sat down next to him.

"Thanks," she said, leaning in toward him. She placed her hand over his for a second or two, then took it away. "And thanks for this. It's amazing how we let it all get so far down the turnpike, without, you know, considering the implications. What were we thinking about?"

"We weren't thinking. We were making a deal." The rest of the guys had cleared off for some serious discourse at the other end of the conference table.

"So," said Mona. "You look rather buff. Got some sun, I see."

"I didn't tell Donna . . . anything," said Lloyd, staring at her elegant midlength fingernails, manicured in a rose-colored shade that matched her lips perfectly. "I had a chance to, and I didn't. I don't think I'm ever going to. It doesn't seem that way, anyhow. So I guess if she ever finds out, it'll be because you decided to boil a rabbit on my stovetop."

"What do you take me for, Lloyd?"

Mona appeared annoyed, and Lloyd was immediately skewered with a sharp needle of regret for almost everything, but not quite. "I'm sorry," he said. And there, at the end of the conference table at which they might be sitting for the very last time, the two leaned their heads together and briefly, very neatly, touched foreheads. Anyone looking might have seen two peers trading a choice financial insight.

"Come on, you guys. Let's start," said Lloyd. The group moved to the end of the table where Lloyd and Mona waited, each sitting back judiciously in their comfy chairs. The door slammed open and Walt marched in and surveyed the troops.

"Hi," he said. He took a chair at the side of the table and immediately descended into his customary prediscussion cone of silence. This time, however, the gap didn't matter. Nobody was waiting for him to speak. This was Lloyd's meeting to screw up. He sat for a while, enjoying the warmth they generated together. He understood now why Walt had always loved this period of accreting potential energy, and he sought to extend it. There was a scratch at the door. Ah yes, thought Lloyd. Somebody was missing. "My arms are full!" said a voice on the other side.

"That would be Ron," said Lloyd. "I think this time we'd best let him in."

Sweet rose and opened the doors.

"I'm packing," said Ron. He laid two enormous Starbucks bags down on the table. Inside one there were many types of designer pastry, none of them healthy. In the other were six Grande Lattes. Lloyd took an apricot Danish and a cup of coffee.

"Well done, Ron. Mission accomplished," Lloyd said, and then, to the group, he said, "I think we've finally gotten to the point where even Ron's skills will be necessary in the hours and days to come."

"Man," said Fitz. "I had no idea things had gotten that desperate."

There was an inappropriately gusty bray of corporate mirth, and the group leaned into its breakfast.

"The way I see it, we have a very small window in which we can kill this puppy," said Lloyd, munching. "Let's look at where we are. Doug has set up the destruction of this and approximately ten other major locations around the globe, the rationale being, as always, the achievement of operating efficiencies. I'm all for operating efficiencies, but only when they are achieved at the expense of people I don't know and don't care about."

Laughter again.

"That's the bad news. The good news, as has been noticed in early newswire stories on our situation, is that the deal, like all gigantic deals that stretch the limits of credulity, is very fragile, and could be destabilized and eventually destroyed if the wrong kind of attention is paid to it. There's the European Union, for instance, which will be very interested in the autonomy and job-loss issues. There're the banks, which have no knowledge how thin the debt load is being stretched, nor the disparity in the fee schedules now under discussion."

"I'm sure Bank Leumi would be interested in the pay structure being offered Citibank," said Sweet.

A softer chuckle.

"Perfect," said Lloyd. "What about the regulatory issues raised by the role played by the People's Republic?"

"I've got a couple of congressmen who might find it objectionable," said Darling, his mouth full of cinnamon bun.

"Anybody else got anything?"

"Labor issues," said Fitz, making a couple of notes.

"Good," said Lloyd. "Walt?"

"Corporate governance," said Walt.

Not long after, they broke up to work the phones. By that time, the ringing was quite incessant, and incoming calls outnumbered outgoing ones by a fair margin.

At 12:37 P.M. precisely, as Lloyd was in the middle of a very satisfying chat with Forbert, a key banker in the Hong Kong loop, the door of the project's mosh pit opened quietly, and there was Doug standing in the doorway. He was dressed in fiercely black slacks, a white silk shirt buttoned to the neck, and a charcoal gray Armani blazer that did not so much crease at the elbows as warp. He watched the group buzz about like overheated beavers for a time, an expression of benign amusement on his dignified features.

"Well, well," he said as the noise level in the room crashed to zero. "Quite a little boiler room."

Lloyd remained seated. He merely watched Doug take in the activities, which, after all, were simply those attending any serious business meeting. Except this one was taking place on New Year's Day, with most of those in attendance now all but officially off the active-players roster.

"Walt? You here, too?"

"Naturally," said Walt.

"Lloyd, could I speak with you for a moment?"

"Gee, Doug," said Lloyd. "I'm pretty sure that whatever you choose to say to me can be said in front of the team."

"All right, then. Mind if I have one of these?" He selected a minicroissant from the paper plate and bit into it. "Thanks. Okay." He flopped into a vacant chair and looked them over. "What you folks are attempting is irresponsible and inconvenient, but all it's achieved so far is to gum up the works a little bit and annoy a great number of very powerful people who used to feel relatively cordial, at least to you, Lloyd. This deal is now bigger than any individual who might seek to shape it, control it, or destroy it. It's engaged the intense interest of the entire multinational community, and it is widely viewed as a prototype for the new transnational mercantile state that will redefine the concept of individuality, of loyalty, of nationalism, now and in the future."

"Hurrah," said Walt without expression.

"This is so disappointing. What was being offered to you, Walt, was an extended future of luxury on the beach of your choice. The civilized thing men in business do with such offers is accept them, no matter how painful the transition to leisure might be. The rest of you were to be provided with very smooth access to the next phase of your lives, except perhaps for you, sir, who may quite easily find a post in which you can provide your next corporation a similar level of service." At this point, he gazed with sarcastic brutality directly at Ronald Lemur, whose eyes grew tiny and red under the pressure of this regard.

"And you, Lloyd. You were given the opportunity to serve at a higher level, and bring with you the staff member who meant the most to your ongoing effectiveness on both a professional and personal level."

"Did it occur to you, Doug, that I might not care to operate under that particular mandate?" said Mona.

"Oh, well, that would be your call, of course. As for the big decision to which you are all now reacting, I admit it is hard. Sometimes what we do is flinty and difficult. There's no doubt about that. But the only thing we have to protect us from the chaos that surrounds us is the truth. And the truth in this situation, my friends, is that this particular outpost of civilization has outlived its purpose. We can get slushy about that, or we can do what is necessary. I choose to do what is necessary."

"Is there anything else, Doug?" said Lloyd.

"Nope," said Doug, rising. "Except to say that I am sorry about the way this worked out. I liked you all, personally. You're good people, and I'm sure you'll do well. Now I'm on my way back to Chicago, to present the final structure of the deal to Arthur. He will approve it, and it will be done. And that will be that." He went to the doors, pulled them open, and turned one more time, scanning the group as if to capture them exactly as they were at that moment, frozen in time, for future recollection when all such battles were over and won.

"Bye-bye, then," said Doug.

"Yeah, sure," said Lloyd. *"Hasta la vista,* Doug."

A small shadow of perplexity passed across Doug's brow. "Don't fool with this anymore, Lloyd," he said. "I'm not going to insult your intelligence by leveling empty threats at you. I'll just say that if you continue to tilt at this windmill, it will only make things harder on all of us."

"Gee, I certainly hope so."

"Okay," said Doug. "Be that way."

He was gone. They heard the infinitely tiny whisper of his three-hundred-dollar Gucci loafers on the hallway carpet, in the distance a door opening and closing, then nothing.

Lloyd let the chill left in Doug's wake dissipate a bit. "I don't know about you," he said, "but I'd like to thank Doug for providing that last little bit of personal motivation I needed to vault my determination into the stratosphere."

"What did he mean by what he said to me?" said Ron. "I didn't really get it. But it wasn't good, was it?"

"No, Ron," said Fitz. "He dissed you very, very badly."

"I thought so," said Ron darkly.

Lunch came in at one o'clock, just about the time that Lloyd made a reservation for two on American for the next flight out to Chicago. For a while, it looked as if it would be Mona who would be going, but at the last minute, Lloyd changed his mind and made a different determination.

"It's all right with you, isn't it?" he asked her.

"This is exactly the kind of access I don't need. I'll run the numbers from here and keep in touch with the guys from the European Union. They need some hand-holding, it seems. For some reason, they're kind of upset."

At which point, Lloyd and Mona indulged in a rather nasty little laugh that left them both feeling a lot better. Things were going swimmingly! All that work, all that planning, the charts, the fantasies of power and profit, of delicate hope, of daring, of brilliance and courage, could be deconstructed in a couple of hours! How much easier it was to destroy than to create! Could it possibly be this easy?

At 1:40, a phone call announced that their Town Car was waiting at the south side of the building. Lloyd started stashing material in his briefcase. Ron, he noticed, had no such accoutrement, just what appeared to be a bulge of minor waddage in the left breast pocket of his pinstriped suit jacket. What kind of paper could that be? Lloyd wondered.

"It's . . . documentation," said Ron, who did not elaborate further. Well, that was fine. They could use all the documentation they could get.

At approximately 5:00 P.M., Lloyd and Ron landed at O'Hare, the busiest and certainly one of the most unpleasant airports in the world. After walking for what seemed like twelve miles and sitting in traffic for an hour or so, they checked into the Four Seasons Hotel. They took adjoining rooms on the top floor, which was for very special mogul types who did not smoke. They immediately lit cigars and began their wait for a return call that would tell them when, or if, Arthur would be available.

By 8:00 P.M., they had endured just about as much suspense as they could stand, and the sense that Doug was closing in was becoming unbearable.

"What if Doug got there first?" said Ron.

"It's unlikely," said Lloyd. I sent the corporate jet to Altoona. Which means he had to fly commercial, and we were the only ones on that flight."

"Yeah," said Ron. "But what if Doug got there first?"

Lloyd jumped to his feet, cut a circle or two on the carpet, and tossed an empty ice bucket across the room, where it landed with a series of clicks and clatters on the hardwood floor abutting the ankle-deep carpeting.

"Let's just go over there now," said Ron.

"Just . . . go over?" Lloyd was fast losing courage. He stopped pacing for a moment and looked over at the younger man, who was sitting in a chair, looking very snug indeed. How was Ron able to operate in such rarefied atmosphere without anxiety? Lloyd wished he had the secret. Could it be that Ron had no real perception of what was taking place? What an asset!

"I hear the old geezer actually lives there," said Ron. "We can get in. Once we're in, he has to see us. It's his fiduciary responsibility, or whatever."

"Uh-huh," said Lloyd.

My, how dynamic Ron was getting. He was eating a club sandwich from room service and looked quite happy. It had come with fries that had congealed, but except for that, the platter was quite delicious. Lloyd had no appetite, though. So Ron ate Lloyd's as well. He had a dollop of ketchup on his chin.

"Ron," he said. "You have ketchup on your chin."

"Thanks, Lloyd, man," said Ron, wiping it away. He seemed deeply moved. "This is tasty. Want one?" He held out a ketchup-besotted french fry to Lloyd.

Lloyd looked at the limp little stick of vegetable matter for a long time, then took it. It was cold and mealy, but he swallowed it anyway.

"Thanks," he said.

The phone rang.

Toward Arthur

Ron answered it by pushing the button marked Conference on the telephone. This had the effect of putting the conversation on the squawk box.

"Hello?" said a minuscule and childlike voice on the other end of the phone. "I would like to speak to someone by the name of Lloyd. I can't quite make out the last name."

"Whom shall I say is calling?" said Ron in an officious but still-polite murmur.

"Um . . . Arthur?"

"Hold, please," said Ron, putting the chief executive officer of his $75 billion conglomerate in electronic limbo.

Lloyd took his time walking to the phone. On the way, he found one of the complimentary chocolates on the night table, carefully unwrapped it, and popped it in his mouth before picking up the receiver.

"Hello, sir" was the first thing Lloyd said.

"Well, hello!"

Lloyd was amazed and disarmed immediately. This was like talking to his son, Bob. A voice with no artifice whatsoever. How could one do harm to such a person? How could one not try to please him?

LLOYD

I'm very sorry we had to meet under such complicated circumstances.

ARTHUR

Not at all! This is . . . great! I mean it!

LLOYD

Well . . . Hm!

ARTHUR

So . . . I hope this doesn't sound insulting, but . . . who the hell are you? I mean, I know who you are, but who the hell are you?

LLOYD

Just a loyal employee in your New York office.

ARTHUR

Well, shit! That's not what I hear!

LLOYD

Really. What do you hear?

ARTHUR

I hear you're outta here! I mean . . . unless there's something more I need to get out of the situation.

LLOYD

I guess there might be.

ARTHUR

Why doesn't that surprise me? So listen. I was just kinda getting ready for bed. I go to bed very early lately. And I wake up early, too. So that works out okay.

LLOYD

On the other hand . . .

ARTHUR

Sure! Come to the side door of the building. Speak to Otto. Tell him, "Arthur never sleeps until noon." He'll give you a ride in my personal elevator. Go to the eighty-second floor. Will you have anyone with you?

LLOYD

My assistant.

397

What does he look like?

Hm?

He's not too tall, is he? He's not very tall and thin, with a big Adam's apple, is he?

No.

All right. I suppose I sound somewhat irrational to you. But when you get to my age, you develop certain convictions it doesn't pay to examine too closely after all this time.

I agree. I have this thing about bald guys with tiny ponytails.

Bring me a Snickers!

Lloyd hung up. On the way out of the hotel, he and Ron stopped by the notions shop in the lobby and picked up the requested candy bar, which had always been one of Lloyd's favorites. Things were looking better.

Ron and Lloyd emerged from the Town Car in front of the plaza, which opened up in front of the largest office building Lloyd had ever seen. It was one of those gargantuan towers that covered an entire city block, with mini-spires of varying heights competing for primacy, and one titanic steeple rising out of the center to command them all. Out in front, the company's logo, twice as tall as Lloyd, declared that the entire edifice was dedicated to the operations of one mammoth enterprise. Although it was the dead of night and most civilized human beings were at home with families, dogs, and dinner, the building was fairly lit up, with hundreds of tiny flecks of yellow and white punching a third dimension in what otherwise would have been a flat, unvariegated surface. At the top of the building was a band of yellow, very faint, wrapping around the column, taking up the entire floor and the one above it. Lloyd and Ron looked up at it like two yokels set loose in the big city, their necks craning back to take in the entirety of the structure.

"I guess that must be where we're going," said Lloyd, pointing at the top.

"Fantastic!" said Ron. A feverish glow had popped into his eye, and he was obsessively straightening his jacket. "Look at the size of it! It's as big as the World Trade Center! All right, maybe not that big, but it's big! It's very big!"

"Ron," said Lloyd. "Are you gonna flake out on me here?"

They went in silence to a door around the corner from the main entrance. It was a very strange door, unlike any Lloyd had ever seen, of an unusually minimal height and width, almost like the door to a playhouse, or a service closet. The doorknob was gold, and when Lloyd turned it and pushed, he was amazed to find it very hard going. What was the door made of?

Inside, on a metal folding chair, was a tall, thin, ancient man with stringy yellow-white hair and a gigantic Adam's apple. He had on a security guard's uniform, hat on head, and was bent over a worn copy of the *Reader's Digest*. A long, thin cigarette of a brand usually targeted to young women drooped out of one side of his mouth. It was unlit. There was no ashtray on the metal table to his right, the only other furniture in the room. This, then, must be the aforementioned Otto.

"Yes?" he said without looking up.

"Arthur never sleeps until noon," said Lloyd.

"Oh Christ. Here we go again." He remained seated, squinting up at Lloyd and Ron as if through a veil of smoke, one eye winked shut and tearing slightly.

"I was told to tell you that."

"Uh-huh," said Otto. He did not rise.

"Ron?" said Lloyd. He took one step backward and retired to a corner of the bare little room, inspecting the floor for signs of wear and tear.

"Perhaps you don't understand," said Ron, stepping officiously forward and looking down at Otto. "We spoke with Arthur. He instructed us to enter the building by this door and impart that specific piece of information. At that point, presumably, you would have the data you need to convey us upstairs and into his presence. So please stand up and let's get the show on the road."

"Uh-huh," said Otto. He took the long, ultraslim cigarette from the corner of his mouth and looked at it with disgust. "Do you fellows have any idea how many people Arthur speaks with in any given day?"

"No," said Lloyd.

"Many. He directs a fair number of people to this little office, often giving them some stupid phrase to repeat to me, like this was some kinda James Bond movie. He's a terrific old guy, but there are times I don't believe his elevator runs all the way to the very top floor anymore."

Lloyd and Ron were silent. Was the entire fate of 100,000 people and a trillion dollars in future global revenue to be determined by this wizened geezer?

"Now, you two look extraordinarily serious to me, and you're well enough dressed, I guess."

"Well, thank you," said Lloyd.

"But the drill, boys, is that yes, Arthur got you here. But whether you get upstairs is a hundred percent and completely up to me, and that's the way, at the end of the day, Arthur's got it set up, and the way he wants it. And you know why?"

"No, sir, I don't know why," said Lloyd.

"Because I'm a tall, thin guy with a big Adam's apple."

There was silence in the small gray room. Then Otto began to emit a noise unlike any Lloyd had ever heard, a mix between a file running over a chunk of metal and a toilet flushing. After a second or two of this, Lloyd realized that Otto was laughing.

"Oh my," said Otto. "Well, anyhow, it's late. Why don't you fellows go back to your hotel rooms and grab some shut-eye, and in the morning, you can come right in the front door and wait inside the lobby to see somebody, just like the rest of the folks who want a piece of the old guy."

"I don't think you get it," said Ron. Lloyd didn't like the sound of his voice at all.

"Oh, I get it," said Otto. He got up, very leisurely, and sauntered back behind the steel desk, pulling the steel chair behind him, and sat again. Otto then opened a drawer in the center of the desk, carefully checked its contents, then closed it again, satisfied. Lloyd didn't want to know what was inside of that drawer, but he had some idea.

"Let's go," said Lloyd to Ron.

"I can take this guy," Ron said.

"No, no." Lloyd was horrified.

"Say, by the way," said Otto, as if nothing unpleasant was passing between them, "Arthur didn't tell you to bring anything along with you, did he?"

"Bring?" said Lloyd.

"Yes, as a matter of fact, he did," said Ron, who was eyeing Otto as a snake would regard a tasty egg.

"He did!" said Lloyd, remembering. "He told us to bring this!" And he produced from his briefcase the Snickers bar Arthur had requested.

"Well, damn," said Otto. "Why dint you say so?" He seemed hugely pleased that the situation had taken this tack into more hospitable waters. He had risen, and now he was unlocking a small gray lockbox on the wall by some industrial metal doors. "Sometimes it's a Reese's, sometimes something real hard to find. Last month, he asked some poor bastard to bring along Pez in a motorized dispenser. Ever seen one of them things? I never had. They're pretty amazing. You all have a nice night now, hear?"

The doors whispered open. A small elevator compartment awaited.

"Arthur's office was built in the mid-1970s, when he decided not to go outside anymore," Otto said. "Our founder was in his mid-seventies then, and he told people the direction of modern technology was such that people who could afford it might, if they wished, live their entire lives indoors. He's got a driving and putting range. A two-lane bowling alley. A movie theater. An office suite tucked into a corner overlooking the lake. Apartments for visitors, if he has any. Even a room he can shoot guns in, because Arthur loves guns."

"Cool," said Ron.

"And a little theater for presentations and road shows when he's in the mood."

"And we've been firing secretaries to make annual profit number," Ron muttered.

"There's a rationale for that someplace," said Lloyd, "but I forget what it is."

"Now, this here elevator does go all the way to the top floor," said Otto, putting forth a chuckle that resembled a car backfiring. "You'll be goin' out the same way you come in, so I won't say good-bye. I'll just say see ya later."

"Er . . . thanks," said Lloyd, stepping inside.

"See you later," said Ron. He passed in front of Otto, who was holding the doors open for him, and very deliberately, although not especially violently, planted his foot directly on Otto's instep. "Oh, goodness," he said under his breath. "I hope you'll excuse me."

"Sure I will," said Otto affably as the door slid shut and the elevator started its upward climb.

"Did you see that? Did you see how I tromped down on his stupid old foot?" Ron was exultant.

The elevator stopped and the lights went off.

"Nice job, Ron," said Lloyd. "Excuse me," he murmured into the elevator intercom. "My associate here has something to say to you, sir." All that came from the intercom was a fuzzy, empty buzz, but Lloyd was sure that Otto was listening. Ron's face was a mask of rage, his eyes glimmered white in the overhead emergency light. "Do it, Ron."

"Please accept my apology for stepping on your foot, sir," said Ron. "Believe me, it was an accident."

"Uh-huh," said Otto from the ground level. Their box remained silent and cold. "Can I give you boys a piece of advice?"

"Yes, sir," said Lloyd. "We'd appreciate it."

"How about you, shit stain?"

"Okay," said Ron.

"Whatever you do in this life, wherever you may roam, remember: Don't piss off the guys who run the elevator."

"That's good advice," said Lloyd.

"I will do my best to follow it," said Ron.

"Hope we have a chance to work together again sometime," said Otto. There was a click over the intercom. The elevator light popped on, and the box began once more its slow trek upward. Lloyd and Ron stood in silence. After a while, Lloyd said, "Try to control your insanity from here on in, will you, Ron?"

"Oh sure," said Ron. "You say that now."

The elevator slowed almost to a stop and then, unexpectedly, began moving again, but this time in what felt like a diagonal direction, although they themselves remained upright.

"Strange," said Lloyd.

"Hm," said Ron.

Ron was looking inside his suit jacket. Checking his documentation? Whatever. Lloyd allowed him to rummage without comment.

Now that he had come this far, he had to ask himself, What *was* the plan, anyhow? So far, he had mostly expended his energies in an attempt to gum up the mechanism of their destruction. What did he have to put in its place? The status quo? That was pretty lame. Why was he doing this, anyhow? Because . . . he wanted to. He was on a career track that would lead, relentlessly, to golf, then death. What would he leave behind? A series of double and triple bogeys, a few pars and several triumphant birdies accomplished somewhere remote, in the company of men whose names he would probably, for the most part, fail to remember within a year after they had parted for the last time. Unbidden, the wraith of Rickie Schoendienst rose before him in the tiny elevator, making it very crowded in there indeed. Rickie didn't say much. He simply stood before Lloyd, smoking a cigar. Lloyd looked him over for a while. There wasn't much to say. After a few moments of this—although it seemed much longer—Rickie began to look slightly bored, then annoyed. He looked at his watch, which had no face at all, then leaned in toward Lloyd and whispered something. Lloyd smelled the Macanudo on his breath. Then he was gone.

"What did he say?" said Ron, as if at a very great distance.

"What?" said Lloyd, badly frightened.

"Hm? That guy. Otto. Something about pissing people off. It wasn't dumb. I wish I could remember it."

"Yeah," said Lloyd. What Schoendienst had said was, "Don't blow it."

The elevator paused again for a moment, then headed sideways, like an airport people mover.

"Have you ever been in an elevator that did this kind of thing?" said Ron.

"No," said Lloyd. "But then, this is all new to me."

"This girl Alix. You remember I told you about her?"

"No," said Lloyd.

"Maybe I never told you about her."

They were silent for a while. *Well, what about her?* thought Lloyd.

"If I wasn't so crazy, I would be thinking about marrying her," Ron said.

"Hey, man," said Lloyd. "Don't let it pass you by. You don't get that many shots at the real thing."

"You think? But how do I know?"

"You guys sit around for long periods of time just sort of jerking around and not talking?"

"Yeah, actually."

"You make plans for dinner and movies and stuff, and then, like, don't do them because you both get too lazy and decide to do nothing instead?"

"Why? Is that bad?"

"You occasionally tell her stuff you didn't intend to?"

"I can't believe you said that."

"Lie to her when you have no reason to?"

"Wow, Lloyd. You're psychic! But seriously. Not to change the subject, but . . ." He looked around furtively, as if there was somebody else in the elevator with them. "Of course you know I have a gun in the breast pocket of my jacket," he said. "What do you think I should do with it?"

Lloyd stood in the middle of the elevator and all of the infinite space of the universe surrounded him. He was tiny in its vastness, and floating, so high. His head was gigantic, and full of nothing but air. Down below, in the workings of the elevator, his physical persona squelched between the gears.

"You have a gun."

"Shit, Lloyd, man. I was going to kill you with it. But of course you know that. What a nut I must have seemed at the time!"

"No, Ron. Not at all." Lloyd's mind was whirling. He put his arm around Ron and gave him a little pressure. "But Ron, man. Seriously. Do you think you should be the one who is holding it now?"

"Yes, actually," said Ron. "Yes, Lloyd. I really do. But I think I'll keep it."

The elevator stopped. It is impossible to describe the level of physical terror achieved by Lloyd at the moment the doors slid open.

He's a Little Guy, but His Heart's as Big as All Outdoors

"Boy, you guys must be good," said Arthur. "Otto really hated you, but he still let you up here."

"We had to get pretty obnoxious," said Lloyd as he reached forward for the first handshake. The leathery little mitt that came out to grasp his, very gently, was that of a tiny, hairless, shriveled walnut of a man, no more than four feet eight, tops, of grotesque longevity, uncannily clean, dressed in a child's First Communion suit. The voice that emerged from his porcelain form was a lean, whispering reed. His eyes were a translucent blue, including the whites. What could it be like to see through eyes like that?

Except for a couple of blobs of yellow light, the room was dark, and about the size of a cornfield. Over his crisp white shirt, Arthur was wearing a bib with a needlepoint lobster on it. On a plate he was holding was one very soft poached egg with untoasted white bread broken into it. A humidifier chuckled.

"I'm sorry I interrupted your dinner," said Lloyd.

"Yes." Arthur looked at his plate very seriously. "I hate it when somebody interrupts my dinner."

"This is my staff vice president, Ronald Lemur."

"My God," said Arthur. "Lemur. Yes."

"Thank you, sir," said Ron, choosing to take the remark as a compliment.

"I'd ask you to sit down, but that would make it almost impossible to kick both of your asses," said Arthur.

Lloyd felt as if he should sit down. His knees were gummy.

"Did you bring the Snickers?" said Arthur, brightening considerably.

Lloyd produced the object. "I can take orders as well as disobey them, you know," he said, and handed it over.

Shortly thereafter, they sat down. Several moments later, material began to emerge from Lloyd's mouth. Here is the new deal, as it was presented by Lloyd that evening of January first in the year 2000:

> The need for global reach is acknowledged. The deal as structured, however, is despicable, destroying more than it creates. Big, cumbersome acquisitions that blow up perfectly good corporations are passé, anyhow. What we suggest is to keep things basically as they are, and use the deal that never happened as a template for a series of tasteful, creative joint ventures that build local revenues and autonomy and broaden the revenue base for all. In addition to being unworkable, the original deal would also take an enormous amount of time and money to effect, what with litigation and a million leaks bursting every imaginable issue open in the media almost immediately. What we're proposing is a more sensible, fair, and holistic concept.*
>
> [At this point, Arthur nearly springs vertically out of his chair, his thin, luminescent executive white helmet virtually standing on end. "Yes!" he says.]
>
> Existing management in New York—as well as that in the EC, for that matter—should be treated with equal respect. This point

---

*Lloyd's inner mind, churning in the option-rich soup of a dangerous meeting, found a trace memory at the bottom of his available consciousness: *Time* magazine, one summer ten years ago on Fire Island, when Nora and Bob were little, and he was drinking frozen margaritas on the back deck of his friend Dworkin's house in Saltaire. An article on the tiny, wizened, extraordinarily old leader of his parent corporation, who had just returned from Katmandu, where he had attended a conference on holistic philosophy run by Herb Allen.

was made several hours ago to certain legislators in the European Union, who were disturbed to hear of the implications for some of their members.

["Bullshit!" says Arthur. "You sons of bitches!"]

We'll trim expenses. We'll run the company well. We'll maintain a high level of revenue growth for the next three to five years, creating a new, bold corporation that operates more . . . holistically. For your loyal friends. For your people around the world, who depend on you. It will work better. It will make you a hero, rather than a figure of international controversy. And it will make us all a hell of a lot of money . . . holistically.

[Three minutes of silence ensue.]

"All of this takes place without Doug?"

"Oh, absolutely," said Lloyd. "What do you think we need Doug for?" He rose and began to walk around the space a bit. What was that over in the corner? A flat-screen TV the size of a wall. Never seen one of those before. "Who do you think runs the operations that produced the deal? We do. You can't just shove around middle management like that and expect to get away with it anymore."

"Okay, okay, stop getting so emotional." Arthur had grown very tiny and hard. "Lloyd, if you're going to make it to the next level, you can't be so guided by your feelings."

"Okay," said Lloyd.

"It was my understanding that no particular service was provided by corporate management, and that revenue growth could not be sustained without a dramatic move into international conquest. You're now telling me the whole cockeyed thing is one hundred and eighty degrees otherwise. How can I know? Who should I believe? Doug? You? You're a disinterested party? Everybody's in it for number one. Obviously, you are, too."

"You wound me." Lloyd figured a small joke here wouldn't hurt.

"Do I? Do I really? You think this is a joke?" Arthur barked. Really, thought Lloyd. What an extraordinarily bad temper. Perhaps this wasn't going so well.

"No, sir," said Lloyd. "Not a joke."

"I don't know. Fuck." Arthur rose. He was not much taller standing than sitting. "Where's the vision in this whole goddamn situation?" He went to the desk and got his Snickers, squeezed it in his minuscule fist for a moment. Then he spent at least thirty seconds wrestling with the peculiar form of plastic now being used to wrap candy bars, which cannot be torn by hand, and is also quite resistant to teeth, of which Arthur hadn't many.

"Why should I believe anybody?" he said, and kept gnawing.

"Think about it. On what footing are you beginning this new global enterprise? On an open, holistic platform, with a lean, independent, disciplined team of professionals around the world, hands-on, all willing to walk into fire for the joint venture? Or a bunch of superegos huddled together in a top-heavy, centralized, overly vague corporate structure, all jockeying for position around you in an ever-decreasing circle, far from the expertise and passion of middle management, who have always done all the work? Is that holistic?"

"You're really pushing this holistic angle," said Arthur. "Did you read it in *Time* magazine or something?"

"Well, yes," said Lloyd.

"Ha," said Arthur.

Lloyd figured what the hell, and took the plunge. "Besides, who said there was anything wrong with being holistic?"

"Well, you're certainly right about that," said Arthur. "Tell me more about the economics of retaining the status quo, with ancillary contribution from a variety of global joint ventures."

So Lloyd pulled out some kind of bushwah on the subject. He felt that portion of his pitch was relatively unconvincing, certainly less compelling than the organizational crud. He was always weakest on the interstitial economic goo that made business plans look credible to numbers guys. So far, it hadn't hurt him much. But up here, things could get more rigorous. He hoped not.

So far, Ron hadn't said anything. At the very beginning of the evening's discussion, he had draped himself in what looked to be a highly comfortable chair, arranged his suit jacket in what he believed to be an attractive manner, and attempted to look sagacious.

About fifty parsecs into Lloyd's most tedious financial palaver, Ron leaned forward, his hands on his knees, and shook his head once, then twice. "Man," he said. "Could anybody else use a drink around here?"

Lloyd stopped talking, horrified. Arthur's head turned slowly. Lloyd could almost hear it creak.

"Yes!" the old man crowed. "Mr. . . . Lemur! I was beginning to think you were some sort of bodyguard!"

"That's very funny, sir," said Ron. "But seriously. Do you drink at your age?"

Arthur sat for some time without speaking. Lloyd felt the entire delicate confection that he and Arthur had whipped up teetering in the breeze.

"No, Mr. Lemur," said Arthur at last. "I do not drink at my age anymore. I do, however, want a big stiff one each and every day. Now and then, my physicians insist on injecting me with certain muscle relaxants to reduce the pain of being frail and elderly and close to death. That's not bad. Would you like a snort?"

"No, that's all right," said Ron, ridiculously crestfallen. Not long before, in an issue of *Fortune,* he had read it might not be smart to suck down a flagon of bourbon if every other executive in the room was intent on remaining stone-cold sober.

"No," said Arthur. "I insist."

"Well, if you insist." Ron bolted over to a minibar he had been staring at for the last quarter hour or so. It was very well appointed, with a range of juices, fruits, and sodas. On the lower shelf were two glass carafes in silver sheathing. One was full of a clear liquor; the other radiated a sensuous, luminous bronze. Ron chose the brown stuff and poured himself a hefty shot. "You sure you don't want one?" he said to Arthur, the broad-bottomed goblet perched over a second glass.

"You're going to kill me," said Arthur. He seemed both angry and extremely pleased. He stared at Ron, unblinking. "Okay, yeah," he said then. "Not too much, Mr. Lemur. Let's do it slowly."

"You, Lloyd?"

Lloyd thought about the gun now hugging Ron's bosom. How had he gotten it through airports and turnstiles and corporate security? It must be very tiny, and made of some plastic alloy they were working on somewhere, with bullets of very hard plastic. Wasn't there just such a concept now in development in one of Darling's areas, south of Rangoon?

"Nah," said Lloyd. "Go ahead. I'll be the designated driver."

"Nonsense, Lloyd!" Arthur bellowed, but very, very softly. "If I tell you we're getting hammered, we're getting hammered. Right, Mr. Lemur?"

"Sure, Arthur."

"Right, Lloyd?"

"Yes, Arthur."

"Great. And guys? Call me Arthur." He found this remark extremely funny, and nearly threw an embolism in a spasm of hilarity.

Ron poured Arthur a small amount and, for some reason, even less for Lloyd.

"I disagree with Lloyd. Here's how I think the deal should look," said Ron abruptly as Lloyd stood by, aghast.

"Tell me." Arthur gingerly angled himself against the edge of his desk, leaning into the deal and drink. He looked a half a century younger—say fifty.

"Alternate financing for complete global domination in all operational sectors could be provided by the liquidation into cash and debt instruments of the entire portion of Europe that used to be known as East Germany, along with parts of what used to be Yugoslavia, and, of course, some of Italy, in regions where we have people on the ground. This whole big chunk of Europe, not the best part, to be sure, but very worthwhile areas in their own way, turns out to be worth no more than two hundred billion dollars, monetized, if all assets are sold and the citizens of those former nations are immediately turned into employees for a certain term. After that, head-count cuts could be considered and excess personnel banished to, say, Russia. In this way, half of all necessary cash could be derived from the proper management of the acquired properties. Think about it! That's forty-nine percent off list price, right off the bat."

"Uh-huh," said Arthur. He was peering at Ron so fiercely that Lloyd had to look away.

"Taking up the rest of the slack would be an internal public offering of forty-nine percent of the new enterprise. These steps would produce more than three hundred billion dollars in capital and the power to buy, outright, about ten percent of the existing world, including big positions in China. Do you know what ten bucks is worth in China? Man!" He drank the better part of his tumbler as if it were apple juice.

There was silence in the room. Arthur chewed his gums for a great long while. He had left them.

"Okay," he said finally. "Okay."

Before he even saw him coming, Lloyd felt Arthur's hand on his arm, and the old man was standing directly before him. Since Lloyd was seated and Arthur was standing, they were eye-to-eye. "I have the whole picture now. And before we resolve this matter, I want to say . . . I'm proud of you guys. Give me your hand." Arthur took Lloyd's hand in one of his and patted it with the other. After a while, he realized that Arthur was no longer just patting. He was holding, like a lobster claw, a vise, grasping Lloyd's hand, not letting it go. "And of course I am also very, very proud and satisfied with you, Douglas," he said. "Stop skulking around in there and come on out. Doug? Don't pout, son. I had the right to hear them out—wasn't that the deal? Well, I heard them out. And now I'll tell you what I think."

Doug entered the suite and stood opposite the group, smoking quietly. Lloyd was shocked to see that his jacket was off.

Doug Resolves His Personal Issues

"Disregarding the ravings of this lunatic here, I like the joint-venture model you proposed, Lloyd," said Doug, "self-serving, of course, but that's all right. It's counterintuitive in many respects, because it maintains the current structure and adds very little new to the mix, and backs off a brilliant, sexy deal that a lot of people were betting the ranch on. On the other hand, it's simple, it gets high scores on the humanity factor, and has the benefit of a flatter, more decentralized model, which the business publications and other observers will look kindly upon." He walked up behind Arthur and rested two elegant hands on the ancient craggy back of his superior of the last thirty years. "It does, however, have two critical—I want to say fatal—flaws. First, it is not the will of the senior structure of the corporation, which has already spoken on the subject."

"Er, Doug, on that matter," said Arthur.

"And two," Doug went on, somewhat more grimly. His hands had tightened around the upper back and neck of his elderly superior officer, who froze under the pressure like a gargoyle. "Your scenario will lock the entire corporation into mortal squabbling and internecine battle for, perhaps, years, and I know I speak for my side when I say that you may win a battle here and there, but we are older, and we are stronger, and we will win the war; it may completely wipe this company from the face of the earth before it's over, but we will do it. I will do it." Doug's face was red. "I'm sorry," he said. "I clearly got more angry than I intended."

"You want to bet you'll do it?" said Ron. He had risen to his feet and was regarding Doug with naked loathing.

"Ron," said Lloyd.

"No, Lloyd," said Doug. "Don't worry about me. I can take care of myself." He took a step toward Ron. The two men stared at each other.

"This is . . . excellent!" said Arthur. He was breathing very heavily, with a slight whistle. "Years of rampant destructive speculation fueled by partisan manipulation of the business itself! The stock will zoom! I have two million shares at eight and half! Ha! Ha-ha!" Arthur laughed uncontrollably for more than a minute. Then he stopped. "On the other hand," he said thoughtfully. "While it might be a hoot and a half, this kind of scenario rarely works out in the long run for any portion of the existing management structure. The press comes in, then the banks. A new board is mandated. New senior officers come along to fill in the picture. Corporate governance is tipped all to hell. Succession gets muddled. Control is lost."

Arthur drifted off. His chin touched his chest. Was he sleeping? Lloyd sunk down on an available chair and buried his face in his hands. He was tired, so tired. It looked as if the infighting was just beginning. Arthur, the old creep—he had been stowing Doug in an antechamber all the time. Always have an alternate strategy, that was the rule. But which of them was the main plan, which the alternate?

"Well, it's been real," said Doug. "I've got a number of international flights to catch if I'm going to pull this deal back together again."

"Oh, look," said Ron. "Don't do that." He removed a plastic gun the size of a deck of cards from his jacket pocket. He was standing by the conference table that held the remains of Arthur's meal. "I have this gun, see. It's plastic, and the bullets inside it are made from some kind of polyresin I don't really understand, but Arbuckle in Development tells me they're in use right now in Singapore on people caught chewing gum or talking in movie theaters."

"Really," said Doug. He came close and perused Ron's miniature friend, which was at that moment pointed at his abdomen. "Arbuckle gave you that?"

"Yes," said Ron cordially. "I showed him the letter of clearance issued by you and countersigned by a number of corporate officers. That seemed to satisfy him. Honestly, he didn't even look at it all that closely. I think, secretly, Doug, and I hope I'm not getting the guy in hot water here, but I think he was very excited at showing his little thing to me, letting me take it for a while. I also showed him my license to carry in Connecticut, which of course is pretty easy to get."

"It gets through airport security and the like, as we suspected?"

"Yep."

"Should be a very good seller out of our Taipei subsidiary."

"Factory seconds could also be marketed to less affluent nations under a joint-venture arrangement."

"Could it kill anybody?"

"At this distance, yes."

Lloyd was pleased the meeting had turned so affable all of a sudden. "Can't we just all sit down and talk about this situation like grown-ups? Doug, there's no reason you can't stay in Chicago, with a magnificent title and great solid-line reporting relationships with all key management. You like it here."

"I don't know," said Doug. He moved across the enormous room, where his jacket had been draped across the back of a chair set up to accommodate a small person who wished to partake in a sixty-four-bit video game setup.

"Don't move much farther away than that," said Ron quite pleasantly.

"But the thing is," Doug continued, once again drawing close to Arthur's desk, where they clustered around the old man, who was snoring lightly, "there was a serious breach in corporate ethics here. And trust. What about all the work we did together, the work you two destroyed?"

"That work destroyed us!" Lloyd couldn't believe what he was hearing. Were they actually supposed to feel guilty about some putative betrayal they had visited on these poor unsuspecting pillars of corporate leadership? What . . . mung! Lloyd was inundated by a wave of pure spleen. This obnoxious turd was the cause of everything! A black curtain descended over his field of vision. But Doug was still talking.

"Ultimately, all of us should do what's best for the business, no matter how that shakes out for us personally," he was nattering. "Or at least that's the way it's supposed to be. You guys broke that code. That's the way I feel about it, and I know if it wasn't past Arthur's bedtime, he'd feel that way, too."

"Shut up!" screamed Lloyd. "Shut up, goddamn it! Shut up!" Lloyd realized he was very upset and saying things that could be considered impolitic in a purely businesslike setting, but he felt unable to control himself. Perhaps that was what Arthur was talking about. Perhaps he *was* too emotional.

"Calm down, Lloyd," said Ron. "I don't believe Doug can speak for Arthur like that. Can he, Arthur?"

"No," said Arthur. "I hate it when you speak for me, Doug." Arthur was awake, as sparkly and chipper as a sparrow after a bath.

"Arthur," said Doug, "don't get all quixotic on me now."

"Oh, I'm not. I'm thinking quite clearly."

"Well, I'm glad to hear it."

"What's that? A gun?"

"Yep!" said Ron proudly.

"I can't believe it!" said Arthur. "A gun! Wow! I haven't packed a gun since the 1950s, when I was a young attorney in Boston, attempting to acquire that plastic-extrusion business from Flatley and Brustein! Remember that, Doug?"

"No . . . I believe that was even before my time, Arthur."

"No? Really? Then whom am I thinking of?"

"I have no idea." Doug looked disgusted.

"Let me see it!" said Arthur. Ron looked at Lloyd. Lloyd looked at Ron. Ron handed it over.

"Wow!" said Arthur, hefting the tiny plastic machine. "This is an impressive little gewgaw!"

For the first time, Doug appeared nervous. "Yes, it is," he said. "Do you mind if I look at it for a minute?"

"Yes!" said Arthur. "Yes, I do mind. I like it!"

"Well, frankly, Arthur, I just don't care," said Doug quietly. He leaned across the expanse of the desk and attempted to wrest the pistol from Arthur's grasp.

Lloyd didn't feel at that moment that it would be advisable for Doug to get the gun. Ron obviously had the same feeling, because he leapt forward, over Arthur's desk, and, without touching Arthur, grabbed Doug by both shoulders and pulled him backward. Doug went over, wrapped in Ron's embrace. Arthur and Lloyd watched them. Ron was stronger, but it seemed that Doug had attained mastery of some form of Asian martial art or other. He attempted to insert his long, perfect fingers in Ron's windpipe. Ron, for his part, seemed content to contain Doug's throat in a traditional half nelson.

"This is ridiculous," said Arthur to Lloyd. Lloyd found it impossible to disagree.

"Have you ever seen two grown business executives fight like this?" said Lloyd.

"No. But physical altercations are not altogether rare. I saw a man threaten another with a golf club on the sixteenth fairway of Baldusrol one time. He got his way, too. I saw another intoxicate a business associate to a level where the poor man had to be taken to the hospital. Turned out he was a diabetic and could have been killed by that level of abuse. Of course, it's quite common for the Japanese to use food as a weapon in business discourse. I once saw a fellow cede a two-hundred-million-dollar advantage just so he could get away from a table teeming with live crustacea intended for his consumption."

Doug and Ron had fallen apart, and they were now lying in separate corners of the work area, each puffing for air. Doug was on his hands and knees, his head hanging low. Ron was coughing quite horribly, and laughing at the same time.

"You . . . barbarian," said Doug.

"Can we work together, Doug?" Ron yelled. "Wanna talk about the economic implications of varying merger scenarios?"

"Arthur!" If Doug was calling for some form of assistance, none was forthcoming. Arthur glanced over at Lloyd, and then, on what appeared to be an impulse, he handed over the neat little gun.

"Shoot him," he said.

"Huh?"

"Shoot him, I said."

"Which one?" said Lloyd, wanting to see if he had guessed right.

Both Ron and Doug had grown very still and were gazing at Arthur with genuine curiosity.

"Look," said Arthur with sudden gravity. "Doug, I don't want to make Lloyd shoot you. We've got a lot of mileage on our relationship. But you're being a big pain in the keister. I'm sure if you were thinking clearly, you could see that. You tried to pull a major-league power play along with what looked to be a very good deal, but your guys were too tough, too smart, and, frankly, too crazy to take the deal you offered them. I've always felt that the entire structure of American business would be different if middle management got some sense of their power. Well, these guys have, and I think it might be time for us to get behind it just a little bit. What do you say?"

"Well," said Doug. "I've got a lot of things to consider, and I'll get back to you," he said.

"Shoot him," said Arthur.

"I will not! Are you kidding?" said Lloyd.

"Well, I will!" It was Ron. He moved dynamically over to Lloyd and went for the gun. There was no question that he intended to have it. Lloyd, after one of those periods of thought that seem to take hours but actually involve only the firing of three or four key synapses, decided that he should not. So Lloyd kept ahold of it and Ron wrapped his hand around Lloyd's and they pushed the little plastic object back and forth between themselves until

Lloyd's index finger and Ron's pinkie got jammed in the tiny trigger guard. Ron squeezed his hand quite stupidly.

Whuff, said the gun finally. This surprised Lloyd. He thought it would say, *Bang.*

"Ai!" said Lloyd, whose hand stung as if someone had stepped on it with a metal cleat. "I've been shot!"

"I don't think so, goddamn it," said Doug. Standing well across the room, observing the scuffle, he sat down heavily in one of the large straight-backed chairs reserved for those in direct discourse with Arthur. "Ow, that really hurts."

Arthur leaned forward in his seat, "Are you shot, Douglas?"

"Yes, but I can't find any hole," said Doug. He rubbed his rib cage, and looked for a point in his vest where a bullet might have penetrated. "Good gravy," he said. He got up and walked with great delicacy over to the couch, where he lay down. "I certainly don't feel very good right now. Give me a minute." He leaned back and closed his eyes. "My goodness," he said.

"This has been a long evening," said Arthur. "I believe Doug will be tractable now, after having absorbed what I think is a rather clear message about his positioning in the current organizational framework."

"Yes, Arthur," said Doug in a voice full of disppointment, misery, and personal loss, the voice not of a fully grown man at all, but of a young, uncertain boy on the brink of a new experience for which he is not yet completely ready. He was perched on the edge of something. Nobody wanted to follow him there.

"I've always wanted a boat," he said, his eyes still closed.

"Well," said Arthur. "We'll get you one."

"Look at this thing," said Ron. He had picked up a plastic bauble the size of a pea, completely misshapen, from the carpeting. "It's hard to believe a little thing like this can hurt somebody."

"I assure you it does," said Doug.

"We're sorry, Doug," said Lloyd.

"Yeah," said Ron somewhat unconvincingly.

"No, no. My fault completely. I lost composure."

Lloyd was glad that it had been an accident. It was an accident, after all. Wasn't it?

"At any rate," said Arthur. "This evening is at an end. Lloyd, please return to New York and complete the intricate lattice of joint ventures you described to me. I'd like to keep them in place until we can complete the insane scheme described to us by Mr. Lemur here."

"What? But . . ."

"I think I'm making myself clear," said Arthur. "Do not push me." There was a terrible hardness behind the wavery falsetto, which Lloyd had no desire to test. "Douglas, be of good cheer. This is the way things end, son, and that's all there is to it. Talk to Whipple about your deal. Don't take us to the cleaners, eh?"

Doug rose and gingerly ambled over to Arthur's desk. He stood there for a moment, regarding Arthur with an unreadable mixture of emotions, but Lloyd did not have to wonder how he felt. It was how they would all feel, sooner or later. It was the end of every corporate career. It was their common destiny.

"Oh, and Lloyd." Arthur was looking straight through Doug. For him, the man was simply no longer there. "There is, as you know, only room for one chief executive in any reporting tree."

"I don't think I get you."

"Sure you do. I've had my conversation with Doug here. You're gonna have to have a similar chat with your guy Walt there."

"Walt?" Lloyd felt the hair at the back of his neck rise. "No," he said.

"Certainly you can't mean that," said Arthur.

"I do mean it. I didn't go through all of this in order to fire Walt. I won't."

"What do you plan to do with him, then?" Arthur said, very testy. He rubbed his eyes with two stubby fists.

"I'll make him chairman. I'll be chief executive. We'll work it out."

"It's up to you," said Arthur, rising and stretching. His meeting was over. "But before long, you'll find he's in your hair, and you'll get rid of him. And take a look at the rest of your reporting structure, too. You're top-heavy, particularly if we're going to accomplish this massive global initiative in a year's time. There's only just so nice a guy you can try to be, Lloyd. After that, it's a dangerous indulgence."

"Doug?" Lloyd inquired. "Would you care to accompany me?"

"Ooh," said Doug, rubbing his side and limping slightly. "That's a good product, that little gun. I had no idea. Sometimes you can't pay attention to every product produced by every subsidiary, you know?"

"Sure. It's tough to keep it all in focus." Lloyd put his arm around the older man, who leaned on him. Now that he'd lost position, he looked smaller somehow.

Ron looked at the gun in his hand as if he had never seen it before. "You want this, Arthur?" he said.

"No, no." Arthur was heading off into a darker portion of the enormous suite. "You keep it, son."

"Come on, Ron." Lloyd had never wanted an alcoholic beverage more in his entire life. Ron did not move. He seemed to be waiting for something.

"Oh, no." Arthur had stopped his tortoise creep to his sleep chamber. Lloyd could barely see his face in the dim expanse of the cavern. "Mr. Lemur stays with me," he said. "I want him."

"You want him?" Lloyd searched his heart for some feeling of surprise but found none.

"Of course, he's raw," Arthur was saying, as if Ron was not still in the room and he was conducting an employee review with a fellow superior, "and he probably has personal encumbrances that we'll have to burn away in the near future. But as fine an operating officer as you will be, Lloyd, you will never represent the kind of business material embodied by your screwy friend here. He has none of the baggage toted around by normal men and women. He will one day be big enough"—in the darkness, Lloyd heard Arthur smile, although he could not see it—"or small enough, to fill my chair. When I'm ready. In about ten or twenty years. Otto?"

The elevator doors in the corner of the room silently slid open. Had Otto been listening the whole time?

"What do you mean?" said Ron, still standing in the center of the room. "I can't leave? I'm trapped here?"

"Yep," said Arthur, so far away, he had almost disappeared. "Find the room next to the giant saltwater fish tank over there. I believe you'll find it comfortable."

Ron was silent. He seemed to be listening to a voice only he could hear, as, in fact, he was.

"Bye, Ron," said Lloyd.

"That used to be my room," said Doug. They stepped into the elevator, Doug still leaning heavily on Lloyd's arm. "You know," he said, "I don't want to retire. I'm only sixty-two. I have no interests outside of business. I guess I could sail. When I was a boy, my father wanted me to be a sailor, not professionally, of course, but a good weekend sailor, but as time went by, it became clear I would never be very good at it. I was always more comfortable in an office, talking to intelligent people about things one could effect with one's mind and energy. Sailing, it's all about wind. If the wind is with you, you can do well. If it's not, you will do badly no matter how gifted a sailor you might be. What kind of business is that, to be so completely reliant on something not under one's control?"

"Doug," said Lloyd. "Try not talking for a while."

"I will," said Doug. "I will try that. Soon."

"I'm sure we could work out an aspect of your package involving an international consultancy of some kind, if that appeals to you."

"Really, Lloyd?" Doug's dignified features settled into a mask of pain and gratitude that made Lloyd feel kind of sick. "You would do that for me?"

"Yeah, Doug. We corporate types, we gotta stick together, right?"

The elevator continued downward.

As the clock struck midnight at the end of the first day of the next millennium, Lloyd entered his hotel suite and lay down on the bed. He missed Ron for a couple of minutes, but then it passed. He grabbed the phone.

First, he called New York and set up a comprehensive business review for the next afternoon. He knew this would force a large number of people to work all night, but that did not concern him.

He called Mona, who would now be his number two. Whatever personal aspects might have been mutually detected in their conversation remained unspoken, as they would be, for the most part, in the future.

Then he called his house.

"You guys get home okay?"

"It's a long trip," said Donna. "Everything go all right?"

"Yeah. I guess you'd have to say it went great. Doug's out. I'm in. And one day, we're all going to be working for Ron."

"Well, that will be weird, won't it? Isn't he a psycho?"

"Yes," said Lloyd. "But he's our psycho."

"You're in?" Nora said on the extension. She had no idea what it meant, really, being in, just that it was a whole lot better than being out, which, as she had seen in every available medium since the day of her birth, was a very bad thing.

"Yes, dear," said Lloyd.

"We're gonna be rich?" That was Bob. He was very excited. He had no idea what it meant, really, being rich, just that, as he had seen in every available medium since the day of his birth, it was a very good thing.

"Yes, honey," said Lloyd.

"Congratulations, Lloyd," said Donna, and after the kids had gotten off, they talked for a while longer. They rarely spoke on the phone much anymore, but this time they made an exception, because they felt like it. And if there was an odd chill to her tone, Lloyd put it down to the effects of stress and long distance. Afterward, Lloyd ordered a big steak and a ridiculously pricey bottle of Château Margaux because it tasted good, and because, at last, money was no object.